ACCA

PAPER P6

ADVANCED TAXATION (UK)
FA 2014

P
R
A
C
T
I
C
E

&

R
E
V
I
S
I
O
N

K
I
T

BPP Learning Media is an **ACCA Approved Content Provider** for the ACCA qualification. This means we work closely with ACCA to ensure our products fully prepare you for your ACCA exams.

In this Practice and Revision Kit, which has been reviewed by the **ACCA examination team**, we:

- Discuss the **best strategies** for revising and taking your ACCA exams

- Ensure you are **well prepared** for your exam

- Provide you with **lots of great guidance** on tackling questions

- Provide you with **three** mock exams including the **December 2014 exam**

- Provide **ACCA exam answers** as well as our own for selected questions

Our **Passcards** and **i-Pass** products also support this paper.

FOR EXAMS FROM 1 APRIL 2015 TO 31 JUNE 2016

BPP
LEARNING MEDIA

First edition 2007
Ninth edition January 2015

ISBN 9781 4727 2242 3
(previous ISBN 9781 4727 5305 2)

e-ISBN 9781 4727 2563 9

British Library Cataloguing-in-Publication Data
A catalogue record for this book
is available from the British Library

Published by

BPP Learning Media Ltd
BPP House, Aldine Place
London W12 8AA

www.bpp.com/learningmedia

Printed in the United Kingdom by Martins of Berwick

Sea View Works
Spittal
Berwick-Upon-Tweed
TD15 1RS

We are grateful to the Association of Chartered Certified
Accountants for permission to reproduce past
examination questions. The suggested solutions in the
practice answer bank have been prepared by BPP
Learning Media Ltd, except where otherwise stated.

Contents

A note about copyright

Dear Customer

What does the little © mean and why does it matter?

Your market-leading BPP books, course materials and e-learning materials do not write and update themselves. People write them: on their own behalf or as employees of an organisation that invests in this activity. Copyright law protects their livelihoods. It does so by creating rights over the use of the content.

Breach of copyright is a form of theft – as well as being a criminal offence in some jurisdictions, it is potentially a serious breach of professional ethics.

With current technology, things might seem a bit hazy but, basically, without the express permission of BPP Learning Media:

- Photocopying our materials is a breach of copyright

- Scanning, ripcasting or conversion of our digital materials into different file formats, uploading them to Facebook or emailing them to your friends is a breach of copyright

You can, of course, sell your books, in the form in which you have bought them – once you have finished with them. (Is this fair to your fellow students? We update for a reason.) Please note the e-products are sold on a single user licence basis: we do not supply 'unlock' codes to people who have bought them second-hand.

And what about outside the UK? BPP Learning Media strives to make our materials available at prices students can afford by local printing arrangements, pricing policies and partnerships which are clearly listed on our website. A tiny minority ignore this and indulge in criminal activity by illegally photocopying our material or supporting organisations that do. If they act illegally and unethically in one area, can you really trust them?

Question index

The headings in this checklist/index indicate the main topics of questions, but questions are expected to cover several different topics.

BPP
LEARNING MEDIA

Topic index

Listed below are the key Paper P6 syllabus topics and the numbers of the questions in this Kit covering those topics. If you need to concentrate your practice and revision on certain topics you will find this index useful.

Syllabus topic	Question numbers
Administration of tax – individuals	12, 16, 21, ME2 Qu 4, ME2 Qu 5, ME3 Qu 1
Administration of tax – companies	24, 26, 37, ME3 Qu 5
Capital allowances	3, 4, 5, 8, 10, 26, 31, 32, 41, ME2 Qu 1, ME3 Qu 2
Chargeable gains – reliefs	3, 4, 6, 13, 16, 17, 18, 19, 20, 22, 41, ME1 Qu 1, ME1 Qu 4, ME2 Qu 2, ME2 Qu 4
Chargeable gains – companies	23, 24, 27, 28, 31, 32, 33, ME1 Qu 2, ME2 Qu 1, ME2 Qu 3, ME3 Qu 2
Chargeable gains – individuals	2, 3, 4, 6, 12, 13, 14, 16, 17, 19, 20, 21, 38, 41 ME1 Qu 1, ME1 Qu 4, ME2 Qu 2, ME2 Qu 4, ME3 Qu 1, ME3 Qu 3
Companies – calculation of tax	10, 23, 24, 25, 26, 28, 29, 33, 34, ME1 Qu 2, ME2 Qu 1, ME3 Qu 2
Companies – close/investment	10, 23, 28, 30, 31, ME2 Qu 3
Companies – groups and consortia	10, 23, 24, 25, 26, 27, 28, 29, 32, ME2 Qu 1, ME3 Qu 2
Companies – losses	10, 23, 24, 25, 27, 29, 36, ME2 Qu 3, ME3 Qu 2
Companies – overseas aspects	25, 35, ME1 Qu 5, ME2 Qu 3, ME3 Qu 5
Companies – personal service	6, 39
Companies – repurchase of shares	29, 30
Ethics	10, 16, 17, 23, 27, 29, 41, ME1 Qu 2, ME2 Qu 1, ME3 Qu 1
Income tax computation	1, 4, 5, 6, 11, 14, 18, 20, 31, 40, ME1 Qu 1, ME1 Qu 3, ME1 Qu 4
Individuals – employment income	2, 3, 5, 7, 9, 10, 11, 22, 34, 35, 37, 38, 39, 40, ME1 Qu 3, ME2 Qu 1, ME2 Qu 2, ME3 Qu 5
Individuals – property income	6, 18, ME1 Qu 1
Individuals – trading income	2, 4, 5, 8, 10, 17, 20, 36, ME1 Qu 3, ME2 Qu 2, ME3 Qu 4
Individuals – losses	2, 8, 10, 20, 36, ME1 Qu 3, ME2 Qu 2, ME3 Qu 1
Individuals – overseas aspects	11, 13, 14, 17, 20, ME3 Qu 4
Inheritance tax	4, 12, 13, 14, 15, 16, 17, 18, 19, 20, 21, 37, 38, ME1 Qu 1, ME1 Qu 4, ME2 Qu 2, ME2 Qu 5, ME3 Qu 1, ME3 Qu 3
National insurance contributions	1, 9, 31, 34, 39, 40, ME1 Qu 2, ME1 Qu 3
Partnerships	8, 40, ME1 Qu 3
Stamp taxes	13, 16, ME1 Qu 1
Tax efficient investments	1, 11, 19, 38, 40, ME1 Qu 4
Tax planning and impact of taxes	1, 6, 16, 36, 37, 38, 39, 40, 41
Trusts	15, 37
Value added tax	4, 5, 8, 20, 23, 24, 25, 28, 29, 31, 32, 34, 35, 36, 39, ME1 Qu 2, ME2 Qu 1, ME2 Qu 4, ME3 Qu 1, ME3 Qu 2

ME1 is Mock Exam 1, ME2 is Mock Exam 2 and ME3 is Mock Exam 3.

Helping you with your revision

As ACCA's **Approved Content Provider**, BPP Learning Media gives you the **opportunity** to use **exam team reviewed** revision materials for the exams from 1 April 2015 to 31 June 2016. By incorporating the examination team's comments and suggestions regarding syllabus coverage, the BPP Learning Media Practice and Revision Kit provides excellent, **ACCA-approved** support for your revision.

Tackling revision and the exam

Using feedback obtained from the ACCA exam team review:

- We look at the dos and don'ts of revising for, and taking, ACCA exams
- We focus on Paper P6; we discuss revising the syllabus, what to do (and what not to do) in the exam, how to approach different types of question and ways of obtaining easy marks

Selecting questions

We provide signposts to help you plan your revision.

- A full **question index**
- A **topic index** listing all the questions that cover key topics, so that you can locate the questions that provide practice on these topics, and see the different ways in which they might be examined

Making the most of question practice

At BPP Learning Media we realise that you need more than just questions and model answers to get the most from your question practice.

- Our **Top tips** included for certain questions provide essential advice on tackling questions, presenting answers and the key points that answers need to include
- We show you how you can pick up **Easy marks** on some questions, as we know that picking up all readily available marks often can make the difference between passing and failing
- We include **marking guides** to show you what the examiner rewards
- We include **comments from the examiners** to show you where students struggled or performed well in the actual exam
- We refer to the **Finance Act 2014 BPP Study Text** (for exams between 1 April 2015 to 31 June 2016) for detailed coverage of the topics covered in questions

Attempting mock exams

There are three mock exams that provide practice at coping with the pressures of the exam day. We strongly recommend that you attempt them under exam conditions. **Mock exams 1 and 2** reflect the question styles and syllabus coverage of the exam; **Mock exam 3** is the December 2014 Paper.

Revising P6

Firstly we must emphasise that you will need a good knowledge of the **whole syllabus**. This means **learning/memorising the rules** in order to be able to answer questions. The examiner has commented that it is a **lack of precise knowledge** that causes many candidates problems in the exam.

Any part of the syllabus could be tested within compulsory Section A. Having to choose two out of three optional questions in Section B does not really represent much choice if there are areas of the syllabus you are keen to avoid. That said, there are certain topics which are **particularly important**:

- The **calculation of income tax payable**, including the **restriction of the personal allowance** and **income tax credits**

- **Personal pension schemes**, in particular the **annual allowance** and the **annual allowance charge**

- The **basis of assessment for unincorporated businesses**, including rules on commencement and cessation. Don't neglect the **impact of losses** in these situations

- The **calculation of benefits from employment** so that you can make sensible comparisons between **remuneration packages**. Make sure you can advise on **tax free benefits** too. The rules for **share schemes** and on **termination payments** should be known very well

- The **structure and mechanics** of **inheritance tax** (eg types of transfer, nil rate band, seven year cumulation)

- The **exemptions** and **reliefs available for the different taxes**, in particular **for capital gains tax** (eg entrepreneurs' relief, gift relief, rollover relief) and **inheritance tax** (eg spouse exemption, business property relief). **Exemptions and reliefs** are the **foundation of any tax planning**

- The **computation of corporation tax**, including dealing with **loan relationships**, **intangible assets**, and **research and development expenditure**

- **Close companies** including the position of **participators**

- All aspects of **corporation tax groups** including the impact of associated companies on corporation tax liabilities, loss relief, chargeable gains groups, the effect of group VAT registration and stamp taxes groups. You should pay particular attention to the impact on **corporate restructuring**

- For **value added tax**, the **rules on land and buildings**, the **capital goods scheme**, **special VAT schemes** available for small businesses so that you can advise if and when they might be appropriate, and the **partial exemption rules**

- **Overseas aspects** of income tax, CGT, IHT, corporation tax and VAT

- **Tax administration**, including filing dates, penalties and interest for all taxes

- **Ethical considerations** when acting for clients

You should use the Passcards and any brief notes you have to revise these topics, but you mustn't spend all your revision time passively reading. **Question practice is vital**; doing as many questions as you can in full will help develop your ability to analyse scenarios and produce relevant discussion and recommendations.

You should make sure you leave yourself enough time during your revision to practise Section A questions as you cannot avoid them, and the scenarios and requirements of Section A questions are more complex than Section B questions. You should also leave yourself enough time to do the three mock exams.

Passing the P6 exam

Displaying the right qualities

The examiner expects students to display the following qualities.

Qualities required	
Knowledge development	Basic knowledge of the core taxes from Paper F6 is key, extended to encompass further overseas aspects of taxation, additional aspects of CGT and IHT, trusts, stamp taxes and additional exemptions and reliefs.
Knowledge application	You must be able to apply your knowledge to the issues commonly encountered by individuals and businesses. You will be expected to consider more than one tax at any one time and to identify planning issues and areas of interaction of the taxes.
Skill development	Paper P6 seeks to develop the skills of analysis and interpretation. You must be able to interpret and analyse the information provided in the question, keeping your answers focused and as accurate as possible, while avoiding waffle.
Communication skills	Paper P6 also seeks to develop the skill of communication. It is no good having the knowledge but not being able to communicate it effectively, so ensure you keep your communication appropriate to the intended audience. Practise using the appropriate terminology in your answers: you will need to be more technical when communicating with a tax manager (eg using technical terms for loss relief) and less so when speaking to a client (who may not understand 'early years loss relief'!)
Keeping current	The examiner expects you to advise using established tax planning methods in the exam. Fortunately he does not expect you to invent new ones. However, you must be aware of current issues in taxation.
Computation skills	Computations are not the focus of the P6 exam. However they may be required in support of explanations. It is therefore essential that you can complete calculations of tax liabilities speedily and without difficulty to provide numerical evidence for your tax advice.

You will not always produce the exact same solution as we have in our answer section. This does not necessarily mean that you have failed the question, as marks are often available for any other relevant key points you make.

Avoiding weaknesses

We give details of the examiner's comments and criticisms at various points throughout this Kit. His reports always emphasise the need to demonstrate a fairly wide syllabus knowledge, but also to identify and justify the availability (or non-availability) of particular reliefs and exemptions. There are various things you can do on the day of the exam to enhance your chances. Although these all sound basic, the examiner has commented that scripts show:

- A failure to read the question and requirements properly and answer the question set, instead churning out irrelevant 'set pieces'

- Clear evidence of poor time management

- Tendency to confuse CGT and IHT and even personal and corporation tax issues

Make sure you attempt only four questions (as only four will be marked) and start each question on a new page, clearly labelled.

Finally, never ever cross your workings out. These may be correct and you will not be given credit if you have crossed the working out.

Using the reading time

We recommend that you spend the first part of the 15 minutes reading time choosing the Section B questions you will do, on the basis of your knowledge of the syllabus areas being tested and whether you can fulfil all the question requirements. Remember that Section B questions can cover different parts of the syllabus, and you should be happy with all the areas that the questions you choose cover. We suggest that you should note on the paper any ideas that come to you about these questions.

However don't spend all the reading time going through and analysing the Section B question requirements in detail; leave that until the three hours' writing time. Instead you should be looking to spend as much of the reading time as possible looking at the Section A compulsory questions, as these will be longer and more complex than the Section B questions and cover more of the syllabus. You should highlight and annotate the key points of the questions on the question paper.

Choosing which questions to answer first

You will need to answer the two compulsory questions in Section A and two out of the three optional questions in Section B, with a larger number of marks awarded for the first two questions (60 marks in total).

- The optional questions will be for 20 marks each. Answer the question on your most comfortable topic but be strict with timing. It is all too tempting to tell the examiner everything you know about your favourite topic. Don't!

- The reason for attempting the optional questions first is, in the examiner's own words:

  'The majority of…candidates appeared to attempt the compulsory questions first, and overrun the time allocation, which they may have regretted later when they reached some relatively straightforward areas in the Section B questions, but didn't have time to have a reasonable attempt at them.'

- Doing the optional questions first should mean that you can manage your time more effectively and not run out of time answering the longer compulsory questions. Attempting the easier question first means that you will have been generating ideas and remembering facts for the more difficult question.

- In Section A there will be 35 marks for question 1 (including 4 professional marks) and 25 marks for question 2. Many students prefer to answer question 1 with the larger number of allocated marks first. Others again prefer to answer a question on their most comfortable topic. Usually one question will be a personal tax question and one question a business tax question.

- Whatever the order, make sure you leave yourself **sufficient time** to tackle all the questions. Don't get bogged down in the more difficult areas, or re-write your answer two or three times. Instead move on and try the rest of the question as there may be an easier part. You do not want to be in a position where you have to rush the rest of the paper.

- Allocate your time carefully between different question parts. If a question is split into a number of requirements, use the number of marks available for each to allocate your time effectively.

Tackling questions

You'll improve your chances by following a step-by-step approach along the following lines.

Step 1   Identify the requirements of the question

Identify the knowledge areas being tested and see precisely what the examiner wants you to do. This will help you focus on what's important in the question.

In Section B questions, this means reading the requirement of the question. However, in Section A questions, you will usually need to look also at the more detailed instructions within the body of the question to find out exactly what is required. Look for key phrases in the question such as 'I need the following ....' or 'Please prepare the following for me...'.

Step 2   Check the mark allocation

This helps you allocate time.

Step 3   Read the question actively

You will already know which knowledge area(s) are being tested from having identified the requirements so whilst you read through the question underline or highlight key words and figures as you read. This will mean you are thinking about the question rather than just looking at the words blankly, and will allow you to identify relevant information for use in your advice and supporting calculations.

Step 4   Plan your answer

You may only spend five minutes planning your answer but it will be five minutes well spent. Identify the supporting calculations (and appropriate proformas) you will need to do, if any. Plan the structure of your written answer, even if it is only a series of bullet points, or maybe a spider diagram, using suitable headings and sub headings. Determine whether you can you use bullet points in your answer or if you need a more formal format.

Step 5   Write your answer

Stick carefully to the time allocation for each question, and for each part of each question.

Gaining the easy marks

There are two main ways to obtain easy marks in the P6 exam.

Providing supporting computations

Although computations will not normally be required in isolation in Paper P6 as the focus is on written explanations and advice, there will always be marks available for calculating figures which will support your recommendations. Often you cannot provide any sensible advice until you know the tax cost of a course of action so make sure you can readily set out proformas and fill in the numbers from the question. Make it easy for yourself to pick up the easy marks.

Answering the question

If you need to consider alternative planning strategies in a question and provide advice on which is the most suitable, do exactly that. If you do not advise on the most suitable plan you'll be losing easy marks. Similarly, if you are asked to consider CGT and IHT in a requirement, don't think that by including some income tax considerations you will pick up extra marks – you won't. Show the examiner you have read the question and requirements carefully and have attempted to answer them as expected – not how you would like to.

Exam information

Format of the exam

Time allowed: 3 hours (with 15 minutes of reading time)

Tax rates and allowances and information on certain reliefs will be provided in the examination paper.

Paper P6 is split into sections A and B each comprising scenario based questions which will usually involve consideration of more than one tax, together with some elements of planning and the interaction of taxes. The focus is on explanations and advice rather than computations.

Section A contains two compulsory questions. Question 1 has 35 marks (including 4 professional marks) and question 2 has 25 marks.

Section B consists of three questions, two of which must be answered. Each Section B question has 20 marks.

The exams set before 2013 had a slightly different allocation of marks. Section A questions varied in length between 25 and 37 marks and Section B questions varied between 16 and 20 marks. The time allocation for each mark was 1.8 minutes – the same as for the current exam format. We have therefore retained the original marking structure for questions in the main part of this Kit. The marks for Mock Exams 1 and 2 have been adjusted for the fixed mark structure and these exams have been reviewed by the examiner.

Examiner's general comments

If you are preparing to sit Paper P6 you should pay particular attention to the following in order to maximise your chances of success.

1   *Know your stuff*

- Successful candidates are able to demonstrate sufficient, precise knowledge of the UK tax system. This knowledge must be up to date. Candidates sitting the exam in the period 1 April 2015 to 30 June 2016 must familiarise themselves with changes introduced by Finance Act 2014 as summarised in the Finance Act article published in Student Accountant magazine on the website.

2   *Question practice*

- Practise questions from past exams with the aim of adopting the style of the model answers.

3   *Address the requirement*

- Read the requirement carefully – in the Section A questions the detailed tasks that you are to perform may be set out in one of the documents. It may be helpful to tick off the tasks as you address them. Marks are awarded for satisfying the requirements and not for other information even if it is technically correct.

- The requirement of each question is carefully worded in order to provide you with guidance as regards the style and content of your answers. You should note the command words within the requirement (calculate, explain etc), any matters which are not to be covered and the precise issues you have been asked to address.

- You should also note any guidance given in the question or in any notes following the requirement regarding the approach you should take when answering the question.

- Pay attention to the number of marks available – this provides you with a clear indication of the amount of time you should spend on each question part.

4   *Don't provide general explanations or long introductions*

- If you are asked to calculate, there is no need to explain what you are going to do before you do it; just get on with it – only provide explanations when you are asked to.

- Think before you write. Then write whatever is necessary to satisfy the requirement.

- Apply your knowledge to the facts by reference to the requirement.

5   *Think before you start and manage your time*

- Ensure that you allow the correct amount of time for each question.

- Before you start writing, think about the issues and identify all of the points you intend to address and/or any strategy you intend to adopt to solve the problem set.

Resitting P6

If you are preparing to resit the exam, think about the number of additional marks you need and identify a strategy to earn them. For example:

- Identify those areas of the syllabus where you are weakest and work to improve your knowledge in those areas.

- Ask yourself whether you could improve the way you manage your time in the exam and whether you address all of the parts of all four questions or whether you waste time addressing issues which have not been asked for.

- Make sure that you earn the professional skills marks and that you are prepared to address the ethical issues that may be examined.

Marks available in respect of professional skills

In order to earn marks for professional skills such as report writing, candidates first have to satisfy the requirement in relation to the format of the document requested. Further marks are then available for the clarity of the answer, including the ease with which it can be marked and the degree to which the conclusions reached follow logically from the explanations and calculations provided. These latter marks are more likely to be earned by those candidates who think about the manner in which they intend to satisfy the requirement such that there is a sense of purpose and a coherency to their answers.

Analysis of past papers

The table below provides details of when each element of the syllabus has been examined and the question number and section in which each element appeared.

Covered in Text chapter		Dec 2014	June 2014	Dec 2013	June 2013	Dec 2012	June 2012	Dec 2011	June 2011	Dec 2010	June 2010	Dec 2009	June 2009
	INCOME TAX AND NICs				3(a)								
1	Principles of income tax	1(b)	1(a), 4(a), 5(c)	5(a)	3(a)	2(a)	4(c)	2(a)	1(a)		2	1(a)	
2	Pensions and other tax efficient investment products			3(b)			4(c)		4(b)		4(a)		2
3	Property and other investment income		4(a)	5(a)									
4	Employment income		3(a), 5(c)	4(c), 5(b)	3(a), 5(b)	2(a)	3(b), 3(c)	3(b)	1(a), 2(a)	5	2, 5(c)	1(a), 4	
5	Employment income: additional aspects	5(b)	3(b), 3(c)		5(b)	1(a), 2(a)	4(a)	3(a)		5	4(a)	4(a)	
6	Trade profits	4(a)	1(a)			2(a)	3(b), 4(b)	2(a)	3(a)				
7	Capital allowances	2(a)	1(a), 5(b)	1(b)	4(b)	1(a)	5(c)				5(a)		3(a)
8	Trading losses	1(b)		5(a)		2(a)		2(a)	3(b)		3(a)	3(a)	3(a)
9	Partnerships and limited liability partnerships						4(b)		3(b)				3(a)
10	Overseas aspects of income tax	4(b)			3(b)				2(b)	2		5(b)	
	CAPITAL GAINS TAX												
11	Chargeable gains: an outline	1(a), 3(d)	1(a)	1(b), 3(b), 5(a)	2(b)	4(a)	1(a)	2(a)	1(a)	4	3(b)	3(a)	1
12	Shares and securities			3(b)					4(c)			3(a)	4(a)
13	Chargeable gains: reliefs	3(c)	1(a), 5(b)	1(b), 3(b), 5(a)	2(b)	2(b), 4(a)	1(a)	2(a)	1(a)		5(b)		1, 4(b)
14	Chargeable gains: additional aspects	3(d)	4(b)		2(a)	4(a)		2(a), 2(b)		4		5(a)	
15	Self assessment for individuals and partnerships	1(b)				4(c), 5(a), 5(b)	1(b)			4			
	INHERITANCE TAX												
16	An introduction to inheritance tax	1(a), 3(a)	1(b)	1(b), 3(a)	2(b)	2(b), 5(c)	1(a)	4(b)	1(b), 4(a)	2, 4	2, 3(b)		2, 4(b)
17	Inheritance tax: valuation, reliefs and the death estate	3(b)	1(b)	3(a)	2(b)	5(c)	1(a)	4(b)	1(b)	2	2	3(b)	4(a)

Covered in Text chapter		Dec 2014	June 2014	Dec 2013	June 2013	Dec 2012	June 2012	Dec 2011	June 2011	Dec 2010	June 2010	Dec 2009	Ju 20
18	Inheritance tax: additional aspects	3(c)	4(c)	3(c), 1(b)		5(c)	1(a)	2(b), 4(a), 4(b)	1(b)	2	2	1(b)	
	STAMP TAXES												
19	Stamp taxes				2(b)		1(a)		1(a)	1		1(b)	
	CORPORATION TAX												
20	Computing taxable total profits	2(a), 2(b)		2(a), 2(b)		1(a)	2(b), 5(c)				1	2	1
21	Chargeable gains for companies	2(a)	2(b)	2(a)	4(a)	1(a)	2(b), 2(c)		2(b), 5(c)	1		2	
22	Computing corporation tax payable	2(a), 5(a)		2(a)	1(a)		2(d), 3(b), 5(a), 5(b)	1(a)	2(a)	1	2	2	1
23	Administration, winding up, purchase of own shares				1(c)	3(a)				3			
24	Losses and deficits on non-trading loan relationships	2(a)					2(a)	1(a),5(b)			3(a)		5(a)
25	Close companies and investment companies		5(c)	2(b)		3(a), 3(b)		1(a)		3			
26	Groups and consortia	2(a)	2(a)	2(a)	1(a)	1(a)	2(a), 5(c)	1(a), 5(a)		1	1		5(a)
27	Overseas aspects of corporate tax	5(c)		4(b)		3(b)			5(a), (b)		1		5(
	VALUE ADDED TAX												
28	Value added tax (1)	1(d)			4(c)	4(b)		2(b), 5(c)	2(a), (b)		3(b)		1, 3
29	Value added tax (2)	2(c)	1(a), 5(a)	2(c), 4(a)	1(b)	1(a)	2(b), (c)	1(a), 5(c)	2(a), (b)	1, 5	1	1(a), 2	1
	IMPACT OF TAXES AND TAX PLANNING												
30	Impact of taxes and tax planning	1(c)	1(a), 2(c)	1(a), 5(a)	1(a), 1(c), 1(d), 3(a)	1(b)	1(b), 3(a)	1(b)	2(b)	1	1	1(b)	2

IMPORTANT!

The table above gives a broad idea of how frequently major topics in the syllabus are examined. It should not be used to question spot and predict for example that Topic X will not be examined because it came up two sittings ago. The examiner's reports indicat that the examiner is well aware some students try to question spot. Examiners avoid predictable patterns and may, for example, examine the same topic two sittings in a row.

Useful websites

The websites below provide additional sources of information of relevance to your studies for *P6 Advanced Taxation*.

- www.accaglobal.com

  ACCA's website. The students' section of the website is invaluable for detailed information about the qualification, past issues of Student Accountant (including technical articles) and even interviews with the examiners.

- www.bpp.com

  Our website provides information about BPP products and services, with a link to the ACCA website.

- www.hmrc.gov.uk

  Her Majesty's Revenue and Customs official site. The section for tax agents and advisors is particularly relevant.

Questions

INCOME TAX AND NATIONAL INSURANCE CONTRIBUTIONS

Questions 1 to 11 focus on income tax and national insurance contributions. These are the subject of Chapters 1 to 10 in the BPP Study Text.

1 Styrax

49 mins

You have recently been approached to act as an accountant for Styrax, born in 1982, who is self-employed.

The following information has been extracted from client files and from meetings with Styrax. You should assume that today's date is 15 March 2015.

Styrax:

- Annual trading profits have been fairly constant at approximately £20,000 for the last few years.

- Has building society savings amounting to around £35,000 which generate gross annual interest of approximately £1,000.

- Wife, Salvia, born in 1986, is expecting their first child and has recently given up employed work

- The couple has no other sources of income.

- Disposable income is about £3,000 pa after paying their mortgage and living expenses

Investment strategy:

- Neither Styrax nor his wife have made, and for the present do not wish to start making, any pension provision.

- Risk averse

Stryax's brother, Taxus:

- Single

- Prepared to take medium to high risk in his investments

- Considering investing in the Enterprise Investment Scheme (EIS), the Seed Enterprise Investment Scheme (SEIS), and in Venture Capital Trusts (VCTs). He has not previously made any investments under any of these Schemes.

Required

(a) (i) Prepare notes for a meeting with Styrax setting out any measures that could be undertaken by the couple in order to reduce their income tax and national insurance liabilities following Salvia leaving her employment.

    You should assume that Styrax does not wish to incorporate his business, that Salvia does not wish to join him in partnership and that Styrax already has two employees such that the employment allowance is already utilised against the secondary Class 1 national insurance contributions for these employees.

    Detailed income tax computations are not required in this part of the question.   **(8 marks)**

(ii) Explain the options open to the couple regarding making future pension provision.   **(3 marks)**

    You should assume that the tax rates and allowances for 2014/15 apply throughout.

(b) Write a memorandum to Taxus setting out the income tax consequences of investing in the EIS, the SEIS, and VCTs. You should include details of the risk and taxation implications of each type of investment.

    (16 marks)

    (Total = 27 marks)

2 Spike (ATAX 06/13)

36 mins

Spike requires advice on the loss relief available following the cessation of his business and on the tax implications of share options and a relocation payment provided by his new employer.

Spike:

- Was born in 1980
- Ceased to trade and sold his unincorporated business to an unrelated individual on 30 September 2014
- Sold his house, 'Sea View', on 1 March 2015 for £125,000 more than he had paid for it
- Began working for Set Ltd on 1 May 2015
- Has no income or capital gains other than the amounts referred to in the information below

Spike's unincorporated business:

- There are overlap profits from the commencement of the business of £8,300.
- The sale of the business resulted in net capital gains of £78,000.
- The tax adjusted profits/(loss) of the business have been:

		£
Year ended 31 December 2010	Profit	52,500
Year ended 31 December 2011	Profit	68,000
Year ended 31 December 2012	Profit	54,000
Year ended 31 December 2013	Profit	24,395
Nine months ending 30 September 2014	Loss	(13,500)

Remuneration from Set Ltd:

- Spike is being paid a salary of £65,000 per year.
- On 1 May 2015, Spike was granted an option to purchase ordinary shares in Set Ltd.
- On 1 July 2015, Set Ltd will pay Spike a relocation payment of £33,500.

The option to purchase ordinary shares in Set Ltd:

- Spike paid £3,500 for an option to purchase 7,000 ordinary shares, representing a 3.5% shareholding.

- The option is exercisable on 1 May 2019 at £4.00 per share.

- An ordinary share in Set Ltd was worth £5.00 on 1 May 2015 and is expected to be worth £8.00 on 1 May 2019.

- Set Ltd does not have any tax advantaged share option schemes.

The relocation payment of £33,500:

- Spike sold 'Sea View', and purchased a new house, in order to live near the premises of Set Ltd.
- £22,000 of the payment is to compensate Spike for having to sell his house at short notice at a low price.
- £11,500 of the payment is in respect of the costs incurred by Spike in relation to moving house.

Required

(a) (i) Calculate the trading loss for the tax year 2014/15, and the terminal loss, on the cessation of Spike's unincorporated business. **(4 marks)**

   (ii) Explain the reliefs available in respect of the losses calculated in part (i) and quantify the potential tax savings for each of them. **(10 marks)**

(b) (i) Explain all of the income tax and capital gains tax liabilities arising on Spike in respect of the grant and the exercise of the share options and the eventual sale of the shares in Set Ltd. **(4 marks)**

   (ii) Explain the income tax implications for Spike of the relocation payment. **(2 marks)**

Notes

1 You should assume that the tax rates and allowances for the tax year 2014/15 apply to all tax years.
2 Ignore national insurance contributions throughout this question.

(Total = 20 marks)

3 Vine (ATAX 06/10)   29 mins

Vine requires advice on capital allowances, the incorporation of his business together with a subsequent sale of some of his shares, and the tax implications of measures intended to encourage his employees to become involved in a marketing strategy.

The following information has been obtained from a meeting with Vine.

Vine:

- Was born in 1976
- Purchased a supermarket and began trading on 1 January 2015
- Will make no capital disposals other than those referred to below
- Has capital losses brought forward at 6 April 2015 of £6,500

Vine's plans:

- Vine intends to incorporate the supermarket business, as detailed below, for commercial reasons.

- In June or July 2016 Vine intends to sell 20% of the new company to his store manager for £64,000.

- Vine is developing a marketing strategy called 'the active supermarket'.

- In October 2015 a false ceiling will be installed in the supermarket premises in order to conceal electrical wiring and water pipes.

The incorporation of Vine's business:

- All of the assets and liabilities of the business will be transferred to a new company, Passata Ltd, on 31 July 2015.

- Passata Ltd will be wholly owned by Vine.

- The consideration paid by Passata Ltd will be:

  - The maximum amount of cash that can be paid without giving rise to a capital gains tax liability
  - The issue of 1,200 £1 ordinary shares to Vine in respect of the remainder of the value of the business

- The cash will be left on a loan account payable to Vine.

The assets and liabilities to be transferred to Passata Ltd:

	Cost	Value	Tax written down value on 31 July 2015
	£	£	£
Premises	205,000	260,000	–
Equipment	55,000	35,000	22,000
Trading stock		11,000	–
Liabilities		(10,000)	–
Goodwill	Nil	24,000	–
		320,000	

- All of the equipment qualifies for capital allowances and no item is valued at more than cost.

The active supermarket:

- Passata Ltd will purchase six road bicycles for a total of £2,400 and two stationary exercise bicycles for a total of £720.

- The road bicycles will be made available on loan to all employees for travelling to and from work and for making deliveries to customers.

- Employees will be paid 15 pence per mile if they use their own road bicycles to make deliveries to customers.

- All employees will also be able to use the stationary exercise bicycles in a recreation room in the supermarket.

Required

(a) Explain:

    (i)   The capital allowances implications for Vine of the transfer of the equipment to Passata Ltd

    (ii)   Whether or not the false ceiling to be installed in the supermarket premises will qualify as plant and machinery for the purposes of capital allowances   **(4 marks)**

(b) Calculate the chargeable gain arising on the proposed sale of the shares to the store manager and suggest a minor change in relation to the sale that would reduce the tax payable on the chargeable gain.   **(8 marks)**

(c) Outline the tax implications for Passata Ltd and its employees of the active supermarket marketing strategy.   **(4 marks)**

Note. You should ignore value added tax (VAT) when answering this question.

You may assume that the rates and rules for the tax year 2014/15 will continue to apply for the foreseeable future.

(Total = 16 marks)

4 Ziti (ATAX 06/14)   63 mins

Your manager has received a letter from Ziti. Ziti owns and runs an unincorporated business which was given to him by his father, Ravi. Extracts from the letter and from an email from your manager are set out below.

Extract from the letter from Ziti

I have decided that, due to my father's serious illness, I want to be able to look after him on a full-time basis. Accordingly, I am going to sell my business and use the proceeds to buy a house nearer to where he lives.

My father started the business in 2000 when he purchased the building referred to in the business assets below. He gave the business (consisting of the goodwill, the building and the equipment) to me on 1 July 2011 and we submitted a joint claim for gift relief, such that no capital gains tax was payable. I have no sources of income other than this business.

I have identified two possible methods of disposal.

(i) My preferred approach would be to close the business down. I would do this by selling the building and the equipment on 31 January 2016 at which point I would cease trading.

(ii) My father would like to see the business carry on after I sell it. For this to occur, I would have to continue trading until 30 April 2016 and then sell the business to someone who would continue to operate it.

In each case I would prepare accounts for the year ending 30 April 2015 and then to the date of cessation or disposal.

I attach an appendix setting out the information you requested in relation to the business.

Sadly, I have been told that my father is unlikely to live for more than three years. Please let me know whether his death could result in an inheritance tax liability for me in respect of the gift of the business.

My father's only lifetime gift, apart from the business given to me, was of quoted shares to a discretionary (relevant property) trust on 1 May 2007. The shares had a market value of £190,000 at the date of the gift and did not qualify for business property relief.

Appendix

Business assets (all figures exclude value added tax (VAT))

	Goodwill £	Building £	Equipment £
Original cost of the business assets	Nil	60,000	18,000
Market value at the time of my father's gift on 1 July 2011	40,000	300,000	9,000
Expected market value as at 31 January 2016 and 30 April 2016	40,000	330,000	10,000

Financial position of the business

The tax adjusted trading profits for the year ended 30 April 2014 were £55,000.

From 1 May 2014, it can be assumed that the business generates trading profits of £5,000 per month. The only tax adjustment required to this figure is in respect of capital allowances.

The tax written down value of the main pool as at 30 April 2014 was nil. I purchased business equipment for £6,000 on 1 August 2014. There have been no disposals of equipment since 30 April 2014.

Extract from an email from your manager

Additional background information

- Ziti was born in 1968.
- Ziti and Ravi are both resident and domiciled in the UK.
- Ziti has overlap profits from when he took over the business of £9,000.
- All of the equipment is moveable and no item has a cost or market value of more than £6,000.
- The business is registered for the purposes of VAT.
- No election has been made in respect of the building in relation to VAT.

Please prepare notes, which we can use in a meeting with Ziti, which address the following issues:

(a) **Sale of the business**

    (i)   Calculations to enable Ziti to compare the financial implications of the two possible methods of disposal.

            You will need to calculate:

- Ziti's taxable trading profits from 1 May 2014 onwards and the income tax thereon; and
- Any capital gains tax (CGT) payable.

            You should include:

- Explanations of the availability of any CGT reliefs;
- A summary of the post-tax cash position; and
- Any necessary assumptions.

    (ii)   Explanations of whether or not VAT would need to be charged on either or both of the alternative disposals.

(b) **Inheritance tax**

Calculations of the amount of inheritance tax which would be payable by Ziti for all possible dates of his father's death between 7 June 2015 and 30 June 2018. You should include an explanation of the availability of any inheritance tax reliefs.

When calculating these potential inheritance tax liabilities you should assume that Ziti will sell the business on 30 April 2016.

The best way for you to approach this is to identify the particular dates on which the inheritance tax liability will change.

Tax manager

Required

Prepare the meeting notes requested in the email from your manager. The following marks are available.

(a)   Sale of the business.

    (i)   Comparison of the financial implications of the alternative methods for disposing of the business.
          Note. Ignore national insurance contributions. **(17 marks)**

    (ii)   Value added tax (VAT). **(5 marks)**

(b)   Inheritance tax.   **(9 marks)**

Professional marks will be awarded for adopting a logical approach to problem solving, the clarity of the calculations, the effectiveness with which the information is communicated, and the overall presentation of the notes.   **(4 marks)**

(Total = 35 marks)

5 John and Maureen Robinson (ATAX 06/08)   **67 mins**

You have received the following memorandum from your manager, Irwin Allen.

To:	Tax senior
From:	Irwin Allen
Date:	2 June 2017
Subject:	John and Maureen Robinson

I had a meeting with John Robinson and his wife Maureen yesterday. John was born in 1975 and Maureen in 1978. They have two children; Will, aged seven and Penny, aged nine. John and Maureen have made a number of errors in their income tax returns and Maureen requires advice in connection with her business.

Errors in income tax returns

John inherited a portfolio of quoted shares, an investment property and a large sum of cash in May 2014. Whilst completing his tax return for 2014/15 he decided to 'give' all the income arising from the shares, property and cash deposits to his wife for tax purposes. Accordingly, he omitted the income from his own tax return and included it in that of his wife. He did the same thing in 2015/16.

John has since realised that such a 'gift' has no effect for tax purposes and has decided to notify HM Revenue and Customs (HMRC) of his mistake.

In January 2015 John gave the investment property to Maureen who sold it a week later. The gift to Maureen was the subject of a legitimate legal conveyance but, after the sale, Maureen gave the sales proceeds to John in accordance with an agreement they had made prior to the gift. Maureen declared the capital gain of £13,870 in her 2014/15 income tax return. John used his annual exempt amount for 2014/15 on a disposal in September 2014.

John has asked us to calculate the additional tax payable as a result of his mistaken declaration to HMRC. A schedule prepared by John summarising the family's income for the two years 2014/15 and 2015/16 together with details of the investment property is on your desk. The gain on the sale of the investment property was the couple's only capital gain in the last four years, other than the disposal in September 2014.

Maureen's business

Maureen began trading as Robinson Mapping on 1 November 2014. She registered for value added tax (VAT) immediately and prepared her first accounts to 30 September 2015. A schedule prepared by Maureen summarising the results of the business is also on your desk.

Maureen supplies specialised maps to businesses in the leisure industry. All of her customers are registered for VAT. The business has recoverable input tax of approximately £300 per quarter. Despite accounting for VAT on an annual basis, Maureen is finding the administration of the tax very time consuming and is considering deregistering unless the amount of administration can be reduced.

Please prepare the following for me.

(a)   A calculation of the additional taxes payable by John Robinson in respect of the tax years 2014/15 and 2015/16 as a result of disclosing to HMRC the errors in his tax returns.

        There's quite a bit to do here; please ensure that your calculations are clear and logical so that they are easy to follow. You'll need to work out the extra tax payable by John on the investment income and compare it with the tax paid by Maureen (probably a fairly small amount as most if not all of her income will have fallen into her basic rate band).

        Please **do not** address the issue of interest and penalties for the moment.

(b) Advice for Maureen on her ability to deregister for the purposes of VAT together with the procedure she should follow and implications of deregistration. Include details of any alternative strategy that might solve her problem.

I do not want you to write a letter or to prepare illustrative calculations; just write the necessary paragraphs for me to incorporate in a letter that will cover a number of other issues.

Thank you

Irwin

The schedule summarising all of the family's income, with the exception of that relating to Maureen's business, is set out below.

Robinson Family – Income received in tax years 2014/15 and 2015/16

	Notes	2014/15 £	2015/16 £
Income arising on inherited assets:			
Dividend income received in respect of share portfolio		8,856	9,108
Rental income in respect of investment property		2,550	–
Bank interest income received in respect of cash deposits		2,424	2,576
John – other income:			
Salary		29,838	30,642
Company car	1		
Trust income received	2	660	715
Maureen – other income:			
Unincorporated business	3		
Will – bank deposit interest received	4	Nil	88
Penny – bank deposit interest received	4	Nil	144

Notes

1 I have had use of the car since 1 August 2014 for both business and private use. I also receive free petrol in respect of all of my mileage. The car had a list price when new of £17,400 and has a CO_2 emission rate of 157 grams per kilometre.

2 The trust is a discretionary trust established by my uncle.

3 Maureen will provide you with a summary of the results of her business.

4 I transferred cash from my bank account to two new accounts for the children on 1 June 2015. The interest is credited gross as there is no tax liability on the children's income.

The schedule summarising the result of Maureen's business is set out below.

Maureen Robinson – Robinson Mapping

– Began trading on 1 November 2014

– Purchased a computer and other equipment for £22,917 (excluding value added tax (VAT)) in November 2014 and a car (CO_2 emissions of 120 g/km) for £6,010 (excluding VAT) in December 2014 which is used wholly for business purposes

– Tax adjusted trading profits, before deduction of capital allowances

Period ended 30 September 2015	£53,136
Year ended 30 September 2016	£41,739

Required

(a) Prepare a calculation of the additional taxes payable by John and Maureen Robinson in respect of the tax years 2014/15 and 2015/16 as a result of disclosing to HMRC the errors in their tax returns. **(26 marks)**

Additional marks will be awarded for the clarity with which the information is presented and the extent to which the calculations are structured in a logical manner. **(2 marks)**

(b) Advise Maureen on deregistration for the purposes of value added tax (VAT) and any possible alternative strategy. **(8 marks)**

An additional mark will be awarded for the effectiveness with which the information is communicated. **(1 mark)**

Assume that the tax rates and allowances for 2014/15 apply to subsequent years.

(Total = 37 marks)

6 Monisha and Horner (ATAX 12/13)   36 mins

Your firm has been asked to advise two unrelated clients, Monisha and Horner. The advice relates to furnished holiday accommodation, tax planning for a married couple, and the personal service company (IR 35) rules.

(a) **Monisha:**

- Is married to Asmat
- Earns a salary of £80,000 per year and realises chargeable gains of £6,000 per year
- Owns a UK investment property, which is let to short-term tenants

Asmat:

- Looks after the couple's children and has no income or chargeable gains
- Expects to return to work on 6 April 2021 on an annual salary of £18,000

The UK investment property owned by Monisha:

- The property cost £270,000 and is currently worth £300,000.
- The letting does not qualify as a commercial letting of furnished holiday accommodation.
- Annual income and expenditure:

	£
Rental income	20,000
Repairs and maintenance	1,600
Council tax	1,200
Agent's fees	2,000

- Monisha claims the wear and tear allowance in respect of this property.
- The property will be sold on 5 April 2022 and is expected to create a chargeable gain of £100,000.

Proposals to reduce the couple's total tax liability:

- Monisha will give a 20% interest in the investment property to Asmat on 1 April 2016.

- The couple will ensure that, from 6 April 2016, the letting of the investment property will qualify as a commercial letting of furnished holiday accommodation.

- From the tax year 2016/17 onwards, Monisha will claim annual capital allowances equal to the current annual wear and tear allowance.

Required

(i) State the conditions which must be satisfied in order for the letting of a UK furnished property to qualify as a commercial letting of furnished holiday accommodation. **(3 marks)**

(ii) Calculate the total tax saving in the six tax years 2016/17 to 2021/22 if ALL of the proposals to reduce the couple's tax liabilities are carried out. In respect of the second proposal, you should assume that the letting will qualify as a commercial letting of furnished holiday accommodation for the whole of the period of joint ownership and that all beneficial reliefs are claimed.

Note. You should ignore inheritance tax. **(10 marks)**

(b) **Horner:**

- Horner owns all of the shares of Otmar Ltd.

- Horner is the sole employee of Otmar Ltd.

- All of the income of Otmar Ltd is subject to the personal service company (IR 35) rules.

- Budgeted figures for Otmar Ltd for the year ending 5 April 2016 are set out below. Where applicable, these amounts are stated exclusive of value added tax (VAT).

	£
Income in respect of relevant engagements carried out by Horner	85,000
Costs of administering the company	3,900
Horner's annual salary	50,000
Dividend paid to Horner	15,000
Contributions paid into an occupational pension scheme in respect of Horner	2,000

Required

(i)   Outline the circumstances in which the personal service company (IR 35) rules apply.   **(3 marks)**

(ii) Calculate the deemed employment income of Horner for the year ending 5 April 2016.   **(4 marks)**

(Total = 20 marks)

7 Pita plc (ATAX 06/14)   36 mins

Your firm has been asked to provide advice to Pita plc in respect of providing employees with financial assistance with childcare and encouraging them to work from home, the establishment of an enterprise management incentive scheme, and a redundancy package provided to an employee.

Pita plc:

- Is a UK resident company which trades in the UK and is quoted on the UK Stock Exchange
- Has an issued share capital of 10,000,000 irredeemable £1 ordinary shares
- Has gross assets of £24,000,000 and 180 employees

Issues – Pita plc:

- Intends to provide assistance with childcare to employees and to encourage them to work from home
- Intends to establish an enterprise management incentive (EMI) scheme for nine key employees
- Has provided a redundancy package to Narn, an employee

Financial assistance with childcare and encouraging working from home:

- Pita plc will provide employees with vouchers to purchase £42 of childcare per child per week.
- The vouchers will cost Pita plc 95 pence for each £1 of childcare purchased.
- Pita plc will pay employees an extra £3 per day when they work from home.
- The payments are intended to cover the additional household costs of working from home.

The EMI scheme:

- The scheme would reward seven full-time and two part-time key employees.
- Each key employee will be granted an option to acquire 10,000 shares at £1.75 per share.
- The options will be exercised in six years' time when the shares are expected to be worth £5 each.
- An ordinary share in Pita plc is expected to be worth £2 when the options are granted.

Redundancy package provided to Narn on 31 March 2015:

- Statutory redundancy of £8,100 paid on 31 March 2015
- An additional payment of £26,000 made on 31 March 2015
- Continued use of her company car until 30 September 2015
- Pita plc paid £18,400 for Narn's diesel powered car; it had a list price of £19,500.
- The car has CO_2 emissions of 129 grams per kilometre.

(a)   Explain whether or not the planned financial assistance with childcare and encouragement to work from home will give rise to taxable employment income for the employees.   **(6 marks)**

(b)   (i)   Explain, with reference to the information provided, whether or not Pita plc is a qualifying company for the purpose of the enterprise management incentive (EMI) scheme and if it is able to make the scheme available to just the nine key employees.   **(4 marks)**

(ii)   On the assumption that an EMI scheme is established, explain the income tax and capital gains tax implications for the employees in respect of the grant and exercise of the options and the sale of the shares, including the availability of entrepreneurs' relief.   **(5 marks)**

(c)   Explain, with supporting calculations, the taxable amounts arising in respect of the redundancy package provided to Narn.   **(5 marks)**

(Total = 20 marks)

8 Simone (ATAX 06/09)   32 mins

Simone is a partner in the firm Ellington and Co. She was born in 1965. She is seeking advice on the tax efficient use of her share of the partnership's loss for the year ended 5 April 2015. Simone intends to establish a new business and is considering the need to register for the purposes of value added tax (VAT).

The following information has been obtained from a meeting with Simone.

Simone's income and capital gains:

- Dividends received of £12,600 in the tax year 2013/14, £10,800 in the tax year 2014/15 and £nil in subsequent years. In years prior to this, she had received dividends of £9,000 per annum.

- Share of profits from Ellington and Co for the year ended 5 April 2014 of £48,615.

- Capital gains of £94,000 on the sale of a portfolio of quoted shares on 1 February 2015.

Ellington and Co:

- Has been trading for many years
- Has two partners; Ellington and Simone. A third partner, Basie, retired on 28 February 2015.
- Made a loss in the year ended 5 April 2015
- Is budgeted to make tax adjusted trading profits of no more than £25,000 per year for the next few years
- Is registered for the purposes of VAT

Ellington and Co – results for the year ended 5 April 2015:

- The firm made a tax adjusted trading loss, before deduction of capital allowances, of £90,000.
- The firm purchased office equipment on 1 December 2014 for £21,200 exclusive of VAT.
- The balance on the capital allowances main pool as at 5 April 2014 was £700.

Ellington and Co – profit sharing arrangements:

- From 6 April 2014 until 28 February 2015

	Ellington	Simone	Basie
Annual salaries	£15,000	£11,500	£13,000
Profit sharing ratio	3 :	2 :	2

- From 1 March 2015

	Ellington	Simone
Annual salaries	£14,000	£14,000
Profit sharing ratio	1 :	1

Simone's new business:

- Simone intends to start trading on 1 September 2015.
- Taxable trading profit is budgeted to be approximately £1,500 per month.
- Taxable supplies are expected to be between £80,000 and £100,000 in the first year.
- Simone does not wish to register voluntarily for VAT.

Required

(a) (i) Calculate Simone's share of the tax adjusted trading loss for the year ended 5 April 2015. **(5 marks)**

(ii) State the alternative strategies available to Simone in respect of her share of the taxable trading loss for the year ended 5 April 2015. **(3 marks)**

(iii) Explain, using supporting calculations where necessary, which of the strategies will save the most tax and calculate the total tax saved via the operation of this strategy.

Note. Your calculations should be based on the assumption that the tax rates and allowances for the year 2014/15 apply to all relevant years. **(7 marks)**

(b) Explain when Simone would be required to register and to start charging her customers VAT and, in relation to this, comment on the relevance of Ellington and Co being VAT registered.

Note. You are not required to prepare calculations for part (b) of this question. **(3 marks)**

(Total = 18 marks)

9 Morice (ATAX 12/11)   31 mins

Morice is the finance director of Babeen plc. Babeen plc is a non-close quoted trading company. Morice wants to provide information to the company's employees on a proposed Schedule 3 Save As You Earn (SAYE) share option scheme, a medical care scheme and payments to employees for driving their own cars on business journeys.

The following information has been obtained from a telephone conversation with Morice.

Proposed Schedule 3 SAYE scheme rules:

- Employees will invest in the scheme for five years.

- The scheme will permit monthly investments of between £5 and £750.

- The scheme will be open to all employees and directors who are at least 21 years old and have worked full-time for the company for at least three years.

- The share options granted under the scheme will enable employees to purchase shares for £2.48 each.

Detailed explanations, with supporting calculations, requested by Morice:

- Whether or not **each** of the proposed rules will be acceptable for a Schedule 3 SAYE scheme.

- The tax and national insurance liabilities for the employee in the illustrative example below in respect of the grant and exercise of the share options, the receipt of the bonus and the sale of the shares on the assumption that the scheme referred to meets all of the conditions for approval.

Illustrative example – SAYE scheme compliant with Schedule 3:

- The share options will be granted on 1 January 2016 to purchase shares at £2.48 each.
- The employee will invest £250 each month for five years.
- A bonus equal to 90% of a single monthly payment will be paid at the end of the five-year period.
- The amount invested, together with the bonus, will be used to exercise share options.
- The share options will be exercised on 31 December 2020 and the shares will be sold on the same day.
- The employee's interest in the employing company will be less than 1%.
- A share in the employing company will be worth: £3.00 on 1 January 2016
                                    £4.00 on 31 December 2020

Medical care scheme:

- Babeen plc is to offer free private health insurance to its employees.
- The health insurance will cost the company £470 annually per employee.
- The insurance would cost each employee £590 if they were to purchase it personally.
- Employees who decline the offer will be able to borrow up to £12,500 from Babeen plc to pay for medical treatment.
- The loans will be interest-free and repayable over four years.

Payments to employees for driving their own cars on business journeys:

- For each mile driven – 36 pence
- For each mile driven whilst carrying a passenger – an additional 3 pence

Required

(a) Prepare the DETAILED explanations, with supporting calculations, as requested by Morice in respect of the proposed SAYE scheme. **(10 marks)**

(b) Explain the income tax and national insurance implications for the employees of Babeen plc of:

    (i)   The medical care scheme

    (ii)   The payments for driving their own cars on business journeys

The following mark allocation is provided as guidance for this requirement:

    (i)   3 marks

    (ii)   4 marks   **(7 marks)**

You may assume that the tax rules and rates for 2014/15 will continue to apply for the foreseeable future.

(Total = 17 marks)

10 Banda Ross (ATAX 12/07)   59 mins

You have received the following email from your manager, Kara Weddell.

From: Kara Weddell
Date: 3 December 2015
To: Tax senior
Subject: Banda Ross

I've put a copy of a letter from a potential new client, Banda Ross, on your desk. I've arranged a meeting with Banda for Friday this week to discuss the most appropriate structure for her new business, 'Aral'.

I spoke to Banda yesterday and obtained the following additional information.

- Banda was born in 1976.
- Banda has owned the whole of the ordinary share capital of Flores Ltd since 1 January 2012.
- Flores Ltd pays Banda a salary of £15,225 per annum and pays dividends to her of £20,250 on 31 July each year.
- Banda does not intend to take any income from Aral until the tax year 2018/19 at the earliest.
- Flores Ltd is Banda's only source of income.

Banda also mentioned that Flores Ltd made some sort of 'informal loan' to her in 2012 of £21,000 to pay for improvements to her house. I decided not to press her about this over the phone but I need to discuss with her what she meant by 'informal' and whether or not the loan has been disclosed to HM Revenue and Customs.

Please prepare the following schedules for me to use as a basis for our discussions. I will give Banda copies of schedules (a) and (b) but not schedule (c), as some of its contents may be sensitive.

(a) Calculations of the anticipated tax adjusted trading profit/loss of Aral for its first three trading periods.

(b) Explanations, together with relevant supporting calculations, of the tax relief available in respect of the anticipated trading losses depending on whether the business is run as a sole trader or a limited company. When considering the use of a limited company, don't forget that it could be owned by Banda or by Flores Ltd.

    Please include a recommendation based on your figures but do not address any other issues regarding the differences between trading as a sole trader and as a company; I just want to focus on the losses for the moment.

(c) Explanatory notes of the tax implications of there being a loan from Flores Ltd to Banda and whether or not such a loan might affect our willingness to provide her with tax advice.

Take some time to think about your approach to this before you start; I want you to avoid preparing any unnecessary calculations and to keep the schedules brief.

Thank you

Kara

The letter referred to in Kara's email is set out below.

Dear Kara

Aral business

I am the managing director of Flores Ltd, a company that manufactures waterskiing equipment. I am looking for a tax adviser to help me with my next business venture.

When I began the Flores business in 2010 it was expected to make losses for the first year or so. I was advised not to form a company but to trade as a sole trader and to offset the losses against my income of earlier years. I followed that advice and transferred the business to Flores Ltd on 1 January 2012, once it had become profitable.

Flores Ltd has made taxable trading profits of approximately £120,000 each year since it was formed. It prepares accounts to 30 June each year.

For the past few months I have been researching the windsurfing market. I must have spent at least £6,000 travelling around the UK visiting retailers and windsurfing clubs (half of which was spent on buying people lunch!).

However, it was all worth while as on 1 January 2016 I intend to start a new business, 'Aral', manufacturing windsurfing equipment.

The budgeted results for the first three trading periods of the Aral business are set out below:

		£
6 months ending 30 June 2016	Trading loss	(25,500)
Year ending 30 June 2017	Trading loss	(13,000)
Year ending 30 June 2018	Trading profit	77,000

The figures above have been adjusted for tax purposes but take no account of the tax relief available in respect of the equipment to be acquired in January each year.

The business will purchase equipment (machinery, computers, shelving etc) in January 2016 at a cost of £11,500. Further equipment will be purchased in January 2017 at a cost of £1,500 and in January 2018 at a cost of £1,200.

The next decision I need to make is whether the new business should trade as a company or as an unincorporated entity. It would make more sense commercially to form a company immediately but I would be willing to use the same approach as I used when establishing the Flores business if this maximises the relief obtained in respect of the trading losses. I want to obtain relief for the losses now; I do not want the losses carried forward for relief in the future unless there are no other options available.

Yours sincerely

Banda

Required

Prepare the schedules requested by Kara.

Marks are available for the three schedules as follows:

(a) Tax adjusted trading profit/loss of the new business (Aral) for its first three trading periods. **(4 marks)**

(b) The tax relief available in respect of the anticipated trading losses, together with supporting calculations and a recommended structure for the business. **(16 marks)**

(c) Explanatory notes, together with relevant supporting calculations, in connection with the loan. **(10 marks)**

Additional marks will be awarded for the appropriateness of the format and presentation of the schedules, the effectiveness with which the information is communicated and the extent to which the schedules are structured in a logical manner. **(3 marks)**

Notes

1   You should assume that the rules, rates and allowances for the tax year 2014/15 and for the Financial Year to 31 March 2015 apply throughout the question.

2   You should ignore value added tax (VAT).

(Total = 33 marks)

11 Shuttelle (ATAX 06/13)   36 mins

Your firm has been asked to provide advice to Shuttelle, who was born in 1980, in connection with personal pension contributions and to three non-UK domiciled individuals in connection with the remittance basis of taxation for overseas income and gains.

(a)   **Personal pension contributions:**

- Shuttelle has been the production director of Din Ltd since 1 February 2002.
- Shuttelle joined a registered personal pension scheme on 6 April 2012.

Shuttelle's tax position for the tax year 2014/15:

- Shuttelle's only source of income is her remuneration from Din Ltd.
- Shuttelle's annual salary is £203,390.
- Shuttelle lived in a house owned by Din Ltd for a period of time during the tax year 2014/15.

The house provided by Din Ltd for Shuttelle's use:

- Was purchased by Din Ltd on 1 January 2002 for £595,000 and has an annual value of £7,100.
- Shuttelle lived in the house from 1 February 2002 until 30 June 2014.
- The house had a market value of £870,000 on 6 April 2014.

Contributions to Shuttelle's personal pension scheme:

- Shuttelle has made the following gross contributions.

    6 April 2012 – £19,000
    6 April 2013 – £48,000
    6 April 2014 – £120,000

- Din Ltd contributes £4,000 to the scheme in each tax year.

Required

(i)   Calculate Shuttelle's income tax liability for the tax year 2014/15.   **(8 marks)**

(ii)   Calculate the amount of tax relief obtained by Shuttelle as a consequence of the gross personal pension contributions of £120,000 she made on 6 April 2014.   **(3 marks)**

(b)   The remittance basis of taxation:

- Advice is to be provided to three non-UK domiciled individuals.
- Each of the three individuals is more than 18 years old.

Details of the three individuals:

Name	Lin	Nan	Yu
Tax year in which the individual became UK resident	2004/05	1999/00	2004/05
Tax year in which the individual ceased to be UK resident	Still resident	2013/14	Still resident
Overseas income and gains for the tax year 2014/15	£39,200	£68,300	£130,700
Overseas income and gains remitted to the UK for the tax year 2014/15	£38,500	Nil	£1,400

Required

(i) In respect of each of the three individuals for the tax year 2014/15:

    (1) Explain whether or not the remittance basis is available.

    (2) On the assumption that the remittance basis is available to ALL three individuals, state, with reasons, the remittance basis charge (if any) that they would have to pay in order for their overseas income and gains to be taxed on the remittance basis.

    The following mark allocation is provided as guidance for this requirement:

    (1) 3 marks
    (2) 4 marks   **(7 marks)**

(ii) Give TWO examples of actions that would be regarded as remittances other than simply bringing cash into the UK.   **(2 marks)**

(Total = 20 marks)

Questions 12 to 22 focus on capital gains tax, tax administration for individuals, inheritance tax and stamp taxes. These are the subject of Chapters 11 to 19 in the BPP Study Text.

12 Ava (ATAX 12/09)   36 mins

Ava has not yet submitted her income tax return for the tax year 2014/15. She also requires advice on the capital gains tax and inheritance tax implications of making a gift of a farm to her nephew.

The following information has been obtained from a letter from Ava and from her client file.

Ava's personal circumstances:

- Ava is 84 years old.
- Ava's husband, Burt, died on 1 November 2016 after a long and serious illness.
- Ava has no children.

Ava's income tax reporting:

- Burt had always looked after Ava's tax affairs as well as his own.
- Ava has recently realised that her income tax return for the tax year 2014/15 has not been submitted.
- The notice to file the income tax return for the tax year 2014/15 was sent to Ava on 1 May 2015.

Burt's will and lifetime gifts:

- Burt made no transfers for the purposes of inheritance tax during his lifetime.
- Burt left quoted shares worth £293,000 to his sister.
- Burt left 'Hayworth', a small farm, and the residue of his estate to Ava.
- Consequently, his chargeable death estate was less than his nil rate band.

Ava's lifetime gifts:

- Ava made a gift of quoted company shares (all minority holdings) worth £251,000 to her niece on 1 December 2015.
- Ava intends to gift Hayworth Farm to her nephew on 1 February 2017.
- Capital gains tax gift relief will not be claimed in respect of the intended gift.
- Ava is a higher rate taxpayer.

Hayworth Farm:

- Is situated in the UK
- Was purchased by Burt on 1 January 2007 for £330,000
- Was leased to tenant farmers on 1 January 2008 and was never farmed by Burt
- Will continue to be leased to and farmed by the tenant farmers in the future

Hayworth Farm – Valuations of farm buildings and surrounding land:

	1 November 2016	1 February 2017
	£	£
Market value	494,000	650,000
Agricultural value	300,000	445,000

- It can be assumed that both values will increase by 5% per year from 1 February 2017.

Required

(a) State by when Ava's 2014/15 income tax return should have been submitted and list the consequences of submitting the return, together with Ava's outstanding income tax liability, on 15 December 2016.

   Note. You are not required to prepare calculations for part (a) of this question.   **(4 marks)**

(b) (i) Provide a reasoned explanation for the availability or non-availability of agricultural property relief and business property relief in respect of the intended gift of Hayworth Farm by Ava. **(4 marks)**

(ii) Calculate the capital gains tax and the inheritance tax payable in respect of the gift of Hayworth Farm on the assumption that Ava dies on 1 January 2021. State the due dates for the payment of the tax liabilities (on the assumption that they are not paid in instalments), the date on which any beneficial claim(s) need to be submitted and any assumptions made. **(12 marks)**

(Total = 20 marks)

You should assume that the tax rates and allowances for the tax year 2014/15 will continue to apply for the foreseeable future.

13 Brad (ATAX 06/13) **45 mins**

Your manager has had a meeting with Brad, a client of your firm. Extracts from your manager's meeting notes together with an email from your manager are set out below.

Extracts from meeting notes

Personal details

Brad was born in 1946. He is married to Laura and they have a daughter, Dani, who was born in 1977.

Brad had lived in the UK for the whole of his life until he moved with his wife to the country of Keirinia on 1 January 2012. He returned to live permanently in the UK on 30 April 2015. Therefore, he was non-UK resident for the years 2012/13 to 2014/15 inclusive but otherwise UK resident. The split year treatment did not apply in either 2011/12 or 2015/16. He has always been domiciled in the UK. Brad has significant investment income and has been a higher rate taxpayer for many years.

Capital gains

Whilst living in the country of Keirinia, Brad sold various assets as set out below. He has not made any other disposals since 5 April 2011.

Asset	Date of sale	Proceeds £	Date of purchase	Cost £
Quoted shares	1 February 2012	18,900	1 October 2010	14,000
Painting	1 June 2014	36,400	1 May 2010	15,000
Antique bed	1 March 2015	9,400	1 May 2012	7,300
Motor car	1 April 2015	11,000	1 February 2011	8,500

I explained that, although Brad was non-UK resident for several tax years, these disposals may still be subject to UK capital gains tax because he will be regarded as only temporarily non-UK resident. There is no capital gains tax in the country of Keirinia.

Inheritance tax planning

Brad's estate is worth approximately £5 million. He has not made any lifetime gifts and, in his will, he intends to leave half of his estate to his daughter, Dani, and the other half to his wife, Laura. I pointed out that it may be advantageous to make a lifetime gift to Dani. Brad agreed to consider giving Dani 1,500 of his shares in Omnium Ltd and has asked for a general summary of the inheritance tax advantages of making lifetime gifts to individuals.

Omnium Ltd is an unquoted manufacturing company which also owns a number of investment properties. Brad was given his shares in the company by his wife on 1 January 2011. The ownership of the share capital of Omnium Ltd is set out below.

	Shares
Laura (Brad's wife)	4,500
Brad	3,000
Vic (Laura's brother)	1,500
Christine (friend of Laura)	1,000
	10,000

The current estimated value of a share in Omnium Ltd is set out below.

Shareholding	Value per share
	£
Up to 25%	190
26% to 50%	205
51% to 60%	240
61% to 74%	255
75% to 80%	290
More than 80%	300

Email from your manager

In preparation for my next meeting with Brad, please prepare the following:

(a) **Capital gains tax**

An explanation, with supporting calculations, of the UK capital gains tax liability in respect of the disposals made by Brad whilst living in the country of Keirinia. Your explanation should include the precise reasons for Brad being regarded as only temporarily non-UK resident and a statement of when the tax was/will be payable.

(b) **Inheritance tax**

(i) An explanation of the inheritance tax advantages of making lifetime gifts to individuals, in general.

(ii) In respect of the possible gift of 1,500 shares in Omnium Ltd to Dani:

- A calculation of the fall in value of Brad's estate which will result from the gift

- A detailed explanation of whether or not business property relief would be available in respect of the gift and, on the assumption that it would be available, the manner in which it would be calculated

- A **brief** statement of any other tax issues arising from the gift, which will need to be considered at a later date

Tax manager

Required

Carry out the work required as requested in the email from your manager. The following marks are available.

(a) Capital gains tax **(8 marks)**

(b) Inheritance tax

(i) Explanation of the inheritance tax advantages of making lifetime gifts to individuals **(7 marks)**

(ii) In respect of the possible gift of 1,500 shares in Omnium Ltd to Dani **(10 marks)**

You should assume that the 2014/15 tax rules (including the statutory residence test) and rates apply in all years.

(Total = 25 marks)

BPP note. This question has been rewritten by BPP for the statutory residence test in Finance Act 2013 and reviewed by the P6 examination team.

14 Sushi (ATAX 12/10)   49 mins

An extract from an email from your manager regarding a meeting with a client, Sushi, together with an email from Sushi are set out below.

Email from your manager

I have just had a meeting with Sushi who has been a client of the firm since she moved to the UK from the country of Zakuskia in May 2001. Sushi was born in the country of Zakuskia in 1958. Her father died in 2008 and, as you will see from her email, her mother died in October 2015. Her father and mother were both domiciled and resident in the country of Zakuskia throughout their lives. Zakuskian inheritance tax is charged at the rate of 24% on all land and buildings situated within the country that are owned by an individual at the time of death. There is no capital gains tax in the country of Zakuskia. There is no double tax treaty between the UK and the country of Zakuskia.

Until the death of her mother, Sushi's only assets consisted of her house in the UK, a number of investment properties also situated in the UK, and cash in UK bank accounts. Her total UK assets are worth approximately £3 million. Sushi has taxable income of £34,000 each year and realises taxable capital gains of more than £20,000 each year. She has made significant cash gifts to her son in the past and, therefore, does not require an explanation of the taxation of potentially exempt transfers or the accumulation principle. Sushi is resident in the UK.

I want you to write a letter to Sushi addressing the points below:

(i) **UK inheritance tax and the statue**

   An explanation of:

   - The UK inheritance tax implications of the death of Sushi's mother

   - Which of Sushi's assets will be subject to UK inheritance tax when she dies. This will require some careful and detailed consideration of her domicile position both now and in the future.

   - The manner in which UK inheritance tax would be calculated, if due, on any land and buildings situated in the country of Zakuskia that are owned by Sushi when she dies

   - Why the gift of the statue to her son, as referred to in her email, will be a potentially exempt transfer, and how this treatment could be avoided

   The statue has not increased in value since the death of Sushi's mother. Accordingly, the proposed gift of the statue to Sushi's son will not give rise to a capital gain.

(ii) **The Zakuskian income**

   The Zakuskian income will be subject to tax in the UK because Sushi is UK resident. Accordingly, we need to think about whether or not Sushi should claim the remittance basis. In order to do this I want you to prepare calculations of the increase in her UK tax liability due to the Zakuskian income on the assumption that the remittance basis is not available and then on the assumption that it is available. You should assume that Sushi remits £30,000 (gross) to the UK each year in accordance with her plans.

   In relation to the taxation of the Zakuskian income, the letter should include explanations of the meaning of the terms 'remittance basis' and 'remittance', and whether or not the remittance basis is available to Sushi, together with your conclusions based on your calculations but no other narrative. You should include brief footnotes to your calculations where necessary to aid understanding of the figures.

   There is no need to consider the implication of capital gains on overseas assets as Sushi does not intend to dispose of any of her Zakuskian assets, apart from the statue, for the time being.

Thank you

Tax manager

Required

Prepare the letter to Sushi requested in the email from your manager. The following marks are available.

(a)   UK inheritance tax and the statue   **(12 marks)**
(b)   The Zakuskian income   **(12 marks)**

Professional marks will be awarded in this question for the appropriateness of the format of the letter, the degree to which the calculations are approached in a logical manner, and the effectiveness with which the information is communicated.   **(3 marks)**

(Total = 27 marks)

You should assume that the tax rates and allowances of the tax year 2014/15 will continue to apply for the foreseeable future.

15 Surfe (ATAX 12/11)   31 mins

Surfe has requested advice on the tax implications of the creation of a discretionary trust and a calculation of the estimated inheritance tax liability on her death. The following information was obtained at a meeting with Surfe.

Surfe:

• Is a 63-year-old widow who has two adult nephews
• Intends to create a trust on 1 January 2016

Death of Surfe's husband:

• Surfe's husband, Flud, died on 1 February 2008. He had made no gifts during his lifetime.
• In his will, Flud left £148,000 in cash to his sister and the remainder of his estate to Surfe.

The trust:

• The trust will be a discretionary (relevant property) trust for the benefit of Surfe's nephews.

• Surfe will give 200 of her ordinary shares in Leat Ltd and £100,000 in cash to the trustees of the trust on 1 January 2016.

• The inheritance tax due on the gift will be paid by Surfe.

• The trustees will invest the cash in quoted shares.

Leat Ltd:

• Leat Ltd has an issued share capital of 1,000 ordinary shares.
• Surfe owns 650 of the company's ordinary shares.
• The remaining 350 of its ordinary shares are owned by 'Kanal', a UK registered charity.
• Leat Ltd is a property investment company such that business property relief is not available.

Leat Ltd – value of an ordinary share:

- As at

	1 January 2016	*1 July 2018*
	£	£
As part of a holding of 75% or more	2,000	2,400
As part of a holding of more than 50% but less than 75%	1,000	1,200
As part of a holding of 50% or less	800	1,000

Surfe – lifetime gifts:

- 1 February 2004 Surfe gave 350 ordinary shares in Leat Ltd to 'Kanal', a UK registered charity.
- 1 October 2015 Surfe gave £85,000 in cash to each of her two nephews.

Surfe's death:

- It should be assumed that Surfe will die on 1 July 2018.
- Her death estate will consist of the house in which she lives, worth £1,400,000, quoted shares worth £600,000 and her remaining shares in Leat Ltd.
- Her will divides her entire estate between her two nephews and their children.

Required

(a)   Outline BRIEFLY:

    (i)   The capital gains tax implications of:

        (1)   The proposed gift of shares to the trustees of the discretionary trust

        (2)   Any future sale of the quoted shares by the trustees

        (3)   The future transfer of trust assets to Surfe's nephews

    (ii) The inheritance tax charges that may be payable in the future by the trustees of the discretionary trust.

    Note. You are not required to prepare calculations for part (a) of this question.

    The following mark allocation is provided as guidance for this requirement:

    (i)   4 marks

    (ii) 2 marks   **(6 marks)**

(b)   Calculate the inheritance tax liabilities arising as a result of Surfe's death on 1 July 2018.   **(11 marks)**

You may assume that the tax rules and rates for 2014/15 will continue to apply for the foreseeable future.

(Total = 17 marks)

16 Una (ATAX 06/12)

Your manager has sent you an email, together with an attachment in respect of a new client called Una. The email and the attachment are set out below.

Email from your manager

I have had a meeting with Una, a new client of the firm. Una was born in 1941 and is a widow. She has a son, Won, who was born in 1966.

Una is resident and domiciled in the UK. Her annual taxable income is approximately £90,000. She makes sufficient capital gains every year to use her annual exempt amount.

Una made a gift of cash of £40,000 to Won in May 2011. This is the only transfer she has made for the purposes of inheritance tax in the last seven years. Una has left the whole of her estate to Won in her will. Her estate is expected to be worth more than £3 million at the time of her death.

For the purposes of this work I want you to assume that Una will die on 31 December 2020.

Gift to son

Una is considering making a gift to Won of either some farmland situated in the UK or a villa situated in the country of Soloria. Una has prepared a schedule setting out the details of the farmland and the villa. The schedule is attached to this email. Una will make the gift to Won on his birthday on 18 November 2015; she is not prepared to delay the gift, even if it would be advantageous to do so.

The tax system in the country of Soloria

Capital gains tax   There is no capital gains tax in Soloria.

Inheritance tax   If Una still owns the villa at her death on 31 December 2020, the inheritance tax liability in Soloria would be £170,000.

If Una gifts the villa to Won on 18 November 2015 and dies on 31 December 2020, the inheritance tax liability in Soloria would be £34,000, all of which would be payable following Una's death.

The Double Taxation Agreement between the UK and the country of Soloria includes an exemption clause whereby assets situated in one of the countries that is party to the agreement are subject to inheritance tax in that country only and not in the other country.

Gift to granddaughter

Una's granddaughter, Alona, will begin a three-year university course in September 2015. Una has agreed to pay Alona's rent of £450 per month while she is at university.

Undeclared income

Una purchased a luxury motor car for her own use in 2011, but found that many of her friends wanted to borrow it for weddings. In June 2012, she began charging £200 per day for the use of the car but is of the opinion that the income received cannot be subject to income tax as she only charges a fee 'to help cover the car's running costs'. However, I have considered the situation and concluded that the hiring out of the car has resulted in taxable profits.

I want you to prepare the following:

(a) **Gifts to son and granddaughter**

A **memorandum** for the client file that addresses the following issues.

    (i)   In respect of the gift to Won

- Calculations of the potential reduction in the inheritance tax payable on Una's death as a result of each of the possible gifts to Won. The farmland will not qualify for business property relief, but you will need to consider the availability of agricultural property relief.

- Calculations of the capital gains tax liability in respect of each of the possible gifts

- Explanations where the calculations are not self-explanatory, particularly in relation to the availability of reliefs, and a note of any assumptions made

- A concise summary of your calculations in relation to these capital taxes in order to assist Una in making her decision as to which asset to give to Won

- Any other tax and financial implications in respect of the gifts of which Una should be aware before she makes her decision

    (ii)   In respect of the payment of Alona's rent

- The conditions that would need to be satisfied in order for the payments to be exempt for the purposes of inheritance tax

(b) **Undeclared income**

A **brief letter** to be sent from me to Una in relation to the luxury motor car.

The letter should explain the implications for Una and our firm of failing to declare the income to HM Revenue and Customs and the implications for Una of not having declared the income sooner.

Tax manager

Attachment – Schedule from Una – Details of the farmland and villa

	Notes	Date acquired	Cost	Estimated value 18 November 2015	Estimated value 31 December 2020
			£	£	£
Farmland	1	September 2012	720,000	900,000	1,100,000
Villa	2	August 2001	510,000	745,000	920,000

Notes

1   The agricultural value of the farmland is approximately 35% of its market value. The farmland has always been rented out to tenant farmers.

2   I inherited the villa when my husband died on 14 January 2005. Its market value at that date was £600,000. The villa has never been my principal private residence. It is situated in the country of Soloria and rented out to long-term tenants. The income is subject to Solorian tax at the rate of 50%. I do not own any other assets situated in Soloria.

3   The whole of my husband's nil rate band was used at the time of his death.

Required

(a)   Prepare the memorandum requested in the email from your manager.

        Note. For guidance, the calculations in part (a) of this question are worth no more than half of the total marks available.   **(21 marks)**

        Professional marks will be awarded in part (a) for the overall presentation of the memorandum and the effectiveness with which the information is communicated.   **(3 marks)**

(b)   Prepare the letter requested in the email from your manager.   **(6 marks)**

        A professional mark will be awarded in part (b) for the overall presentation of the letter.   **(1 mark)**

You should assume that the tax rates and allowances for the tax year 2014/15 will continue to apply for the foreseeable future.

                                                                                                                (Total = 31 marks)

17 Grifter (ATAX 12/09)   63 mins

An extract from an email from your manager detailing two tasks for you to perform is set out below.

(a)   You will find a letter on your desk from a new client, Grifter, who is a self-employed information technology consultant. I need you to write a memorandum for the files addressing the matters regarding Grifter set out below. You should include a brief explanation of any tax liabilities that can be deferred but, other than this, keep any narrative to a minimum unless I have specifically asked for it.

   (i) **Property in the country of Shadowsia**

        Calculate the income tax on the rental income in respect of the property in Shadowsia on the basis that Grifter is a higher rate taxpayer for all of the relevant years. Grifter has asked us to assume that there will be interest and penalties payable equal to 100% of the tax due. There is no double tax treaty between the UK and the country of Shadowsia.

        Unfortunately, Grifter's uncle died in November of this year so you will need to include a calculation of Grifter's inheritance tax liability, after any available reliefs, on the gift of the property. Grifter has informed me that his uncle was domiciled in the UK and that, due to gifts made in February 2010, there is no annual exemption or nil rate band available in respect of the gift. There was no inheritance tax liability in Shadowsia in respect of the property.

        You should also include your assessment of Grifter's view of the tax repayment he has received.

   (ii) **Reduction in mortgage**

        Calculate the amount by which Grifter could reduce his mortgage if he were to sell the cars. This will be the after tax proceeds from the sale of the cars less any amounts due under (i) above.

        Please include a detailed explanation of your tax treatment of the sale of the cars based on our knowledge of Grifter's circumstances. I understand from Grifter that he has not previously sold any cars from his collection.

        Calculate the maximum price that Grifter could pay for a new house if he were to sell his existing house. Assume that his existing house will be sold on 28 February 2016 for £1,200,000 and that there will be professional fees of £6,400.

        In calculating the amount available to buy a new house you should assume that Grifter will reduce his mortgage by the same amount as the figure you have computed in respect of the sale of the cars and that there will be professional fees in respect of the purchase of the new house of £4,000.

        When carrying out these calculations you should assume that Grifter's capital gains tax annual exempt amount is not available and that he is a higher rate taxpayer.

(b)   I want you to write a briefing note on the remittance basis of taxation for individuals in respect of both investment income and capital gains. The note will be sent to all of our staff to provide them with a summary of the basic rules so that they will know when there is a need to consider the matter in more detail. I suggest you use the following headings:

- Who is entitled to be taxed on the remittance basis?
- Is a claim required?
- How does the remittance basis affect an individual's UK tax liability?

Thanks

Bob

The letter from Grifter is set out below.

1 Dark Lane
London

Mr B Mitchum
M & M Co
London

1 December 2015

Dear Mr Mitchum

I shall be grateful if you will advise me on the following matters.

Property in the country of Shadowsia

On 1 April 2010 my uncle gave me a small investment property in the country of Shadowsia. The property is only worth £48,000 now but was worth £94,000 at the time of the gift. Rental income in respect of the property of £484 per month has been paid into my UK bank account since I acquired the property.

My understanding has always been that, because I am not domiciled in the UK, the rental income was not taxable in the UK and so I have not reported it on my income tax returns. However, I now realise from talking to you that I should have paid UK tax on the income (despite 12% Shadowsian tax being deducted from the payments made to me). Accordingly, please let me know how much in total I owe to the tax authorities in respect of this income up to and including the tax year 2014/15.

Hopefully the amount payable in respect of the rental income will be less than the tax refund of £14,600 that I received earlier this year. I'm quite sure that HM Revenue and Customs did not owe me this money but, whilst I'm happy to admit to my mistake over the rental income, I don't see any need to point out their mistakes. I have already spent the tax refund so I will need to use the funds generated by the sale of my cars or my house to pay any liabilities due in respect of the rental income.

Reduction in mortgage

I have not had a particularly successful year in 2015 and I have decided to repay some of my mortgage (current balance of approximately £350,000) in order to reduce my outgoings. I am considering two options.

1   Sell three of my cars and use the net proceeds to reduce my mortgage

2   Sell my house and buy a smaller one with a smaller mortgage. I would want to reduce my mortgage by the same amount as in option 1, so the two options are comparable.

My preference would be option 2 provided I could still afford a house of a sufficient size in a suitable location.

1   My cars

I have a collection of four cars that I drive regularly and race against other collectors. I would be very sad to have to sell any of them although, despite doing most of the repairs and maintenance myself, it is a very expensive hobby.

I set out below the details of the three cars that would be sold. I would have to pay a fee of 8% of the selling price to the auction house.

	Mercedes	Bugatti	Porsche
Date of purchase	1 June 2002	1 March 2004	1 October 2008
Cost	£42,000	£89,000	£77,000
Current valuation	£84,000	£127,000	£68,000

2 My house

I bought the house on 1 March 2005 for £500,000. However, I did not move into it until 1 September 2009 as I'd also bought a boat and I was sailing around the Mediterranean Sea. I've been told that I should be able to sell the house for £1,200,000.

Yours sincerely

Grifter

Required

(a) Prepare the memorandum requested by your manager in his email. Marks are available for the sections of the memorandum as follows:

    (i)   Property in the country of Shadowsia   **(11 marks)**

    (ii)   Reduction in mortgage   **(12 marks)**

Professional marks will be added in part (a) for the appropriateness of the format and presentation of the memorandum and the effectiveness with which the information is communicated. **(4 marks)**

(b) Prepare the briefing note on the remittance basis of taxation for individuals are requested by your manager in his email. **(8 marks)**

(Total = 35 marks)

You should assume that the tax rates and allowances for the tax year 2014/15 will continue to apply for the foreseeable future.

18 Kesme and Soba (ATAX 06/14)   36 mins

Assume today's date is 6 June 2015.

Kesme and Soba, a married couple, require advice on Kesme's taxable income and rent a room relief, the capital gain on a future sale of the family home, and the assets which will be received by Soba under Kesme's will.

Kesme:

- Was born on 1 June 1940
- Is UK resident and UK domiciled
- Is married to Soba
- Has not made any lifetime gifts for the purposes of inheritance tax

Soba:

- Is UK resident but non-UK domiciled
- Has elected to be treated as UK domiciled for the purposes of inheritance tax

Kesme's income for the tax year 2014/15:

- State retirement pension of £7,900 (gross)
- A pension from a former employer of £24,515 (gross)
- Rental income in respect of furnished rooms in the family home
- Interest in respect of 8% loan stock in Ramen plc

Rental income in respect of furnished rooms in the family home:

- Kesme and Soba purchased the family home on 1 July 1991 and have lived there since that date.
- Three furnished rooms have been rented out to an individual tenant since 6 April 2014.
- The tenant does not share Kesme and Soba's living accommodation or take meals with them.
- The three rooms represent 30% of the property.
- The annual rent is £14,400 and there are allowable expenses of £1,600 per year.

8% loan stock in Ramen plc:

- Kesme purchased £18,000 of 8% loan stock on 1 May 2008.
- Interest is payable on 31 May and 30 November annually.
- Kesme sold the 8% loan stock on 30 September 2014 cum interest.

Kesme's estate and his will:

- Kesme's share of the family home, a plot of land and chattels are worth £1,280,000 in total.
- The plot of land is worth £370,000 and is situated in the UK.
- Kesme has left the plot of land to his daughter.
- Kesme has left the residue of his estate to his wife, Soba.

Required

(a) Explain the availability and operation of rent a room relief in relation to Kesme and calculate his taxable income for the tax year 2014/15 on the assumption that the relief is claimed. **(8 marks)**

(b) Explain the effect of renting out the furnished rooms on the amount of the taxable capital gain on a future sale of the family home. **(6 marks)**

(c) Explain the implications of the election made by Soba to be treated as UK domiciled for the purposes of inheritance tax, and calculate the value of the residue of the estate which she would receive under Kesme's will if he were to die today. **(6 marks)**

(Total = 20 marks)

19 Pescara (ATAX 12/13)   36 mins

Pescara requires advice on the inheritance tax payable on death and on the gift of a property, and on the capital gains tax due on a disposal of shares, together with the relief available in respect of the purchase of enterprise investment scheme shares.

Pescara and her parents:

- Pescara is a higher rate taxpayer who is resident and domiciled in the UK.
- Pescara's father, Galvez, died on 1 June 2007.
- Pescara's mother, Marina, died on 1 October 2015.
- Both Galvez and Marina were resident and domiciled in the UK.

Galvez – lifetime gifts and gifts on death:

- Galvez had not made any lifetime gifts.
- In his will, Galvez left cash of £80,000 to Pescara and a further £80,000 to Pescara's brother.
- Galvez left the remainder of his estate to his wife, Marina.

Marina – lifetime gifts:

- On 1 February 2011, Marina gave Pescara 375,000 shares in Sepang plc.
- Marina had made no other lifetime gifts.

Marina – gift of 375,000 shares in Sepang plc to Pescara:

- 1 January 2008 –   Marina purchased 375,000 shares for £420,000.
- 1 February 2011 –   Marina gave all of the shares to Pescara.
                       The shares were quoted at £1.84 – £1.96.
                       The highest and lowest marked bargains were £1.80 and £1.92.
- The shares did not qualify for business property relief or capital gains tax gift relief.

Acquisition of Sepang plc by Zolder plc and subsequent bonus issue:

- 1 January 2013 – Zolder plc acquired the whole of the ordinary share capital of Sepang plc.
  Pescara received 30 pence and two ordinary shares in Zolder plc, worth £1 each, for each share in Sepang plc.
  The takeover was for genuine commercial reasons and not for the avoidance of tax.
- 1 July 2014 – Zolder plc declared a 2 for 1 bonus issue.

Pescara's actual and intended capital transactions in the tax year 2015/16:

			£
15 November 2015	Sale	1,000,000 shares in Zolder plc	445,000
1 April 2016	Purchase	Qualifying enterprise investment scheme (EIS) shares	50,000

Pescara – gift of a UK property:

- Pescara intends to give a UK property to her son on 1 October 2016.
  Pescara intends to continue to use this property, rent-free, such that this gift will be a gift with reservation.

Required

(a) Calculate the inheritance tax payable in respect of Marina's gift of the shares in Sepang plc, as a result of her death. **(7 marks)**

(b) (i) Calculate Pescara's capital gains tax liability for the tax year 2015/16 on the assumption that enterprise investment scheme (EIS) relief is claimed in respect of the shares to be purchased on 1 April 2016 and that entrepreneurs' relief is not available. **(6 marks)**

(ii) State the capital gains tax implications of Pescara selling the EIS shares at some point in the future. **(3 marks)**

(c) Explain how the proposed gift of the UK property will be treated for the purposes of calculating the inheritance tax due on Pescara's death. **(4 marks)**

(Total = 20 marks)

20 Mirtoon (ATAX 12/11) 65 mins

Your manager has sent you an email, together with an attachment, in respect of a client called Mirtoon. The email and the attachment are set out below.

Email from your manager

Mirtoon intends to leave the UK on 15 January 2016 in order to live in the country of Koro. He has entered into a full-time contract of employment for a fixed term of four years starting on that date but he may stay in Koro for as long as ten years. He will buy a house in Koro and will not make any return trips to the UK whilst he is living in Koro.

Mirtoon will sell his house in the UK and cease his business prior to his departure. Details of these proposals, together with information regarding agricultural land owned by Mirtoon, are set out in the attached extract from his email.

Background information

Mirtoon was born in 1963. He is divorced. He has always been resident and domiciled in the UK. He will continue to be UK domiciled whilst living in the country of Koro.

He does not own any buildings other than his home. He receives bank interest in respect of UK bank deposits of £24,128 per year. He will continue to hold these bank deposits whilst living in the country of Koro.

Mirtoon has not made any disposals for the purposes of capital gains tax in the tax year 2015/16. He has capital losses brought forward as at 5 April 2015 of £4,000.

Mirtoon is self employed. He has overlap profits brought forward in respect of his business of £7,600. He is registered for value added tax (VAT) and makes standard rated supplies only. He has never made any claims in respect of entrepreneurs' relief.

I want you to prepare the following:

(a) **Mirtoon's financial position**

Mirtoon wants to know how his plans to dispose of assets and his departure from the UK will affect his financial position. The details of his plans are in the following attachment. He has asked us to prepare a calculation of the total of the following amounts:

- The after tax proceeds from the sale of his home and business assets
- The tax saving in respect of the offset of his trading losses

  The trading losses should be offset against the total income of the tax year 2014/15; there is no need to consider any other loss reliefs.

  In order to accurately determine the tax effect of the relief available, you should prepare calculations of Mirtoon's income tax liability for 2014/15 both before and after the offset of the losses.

- Any other tax liabilities arising as a result of Mirtoon's plans to leave the UK

  You should include explanatory notes where this is necessary to assist Mirtoon's understanding of the calculations. This may be particularly useful in relation to the availability of any reliefs and allowances and the tax relief available in respect of the offset of the trading losses.

(b) **A letter to be sent from me to Mirtoon that addresses the following matters**

(i) VAT: The VAT implications of the cessation of the business and the sale of the business assets.

(ii) Income tax and capital gains tax: Whether or not Mirtoon will be liable to UK income tax and capital gains tax whilst he is living in the country of Koro by reference to his residence and domicile status. You should include specific reference to the capital gains tax implications of the proposed sale of the agricultural land in June 2017. There is no double tax treaty between the UK and the country of Koro.

(iii) Inheritance tax: Mirtoon has asked me to discuss some ideas he has had in relation to reducing the potential inheritance tax liability on his death. To help me with this, please include a summary of the rules relating to associated operations and gifts with reservation in the letter.

Tax manager

Attachment – Extract from an email from Mirtoon

Sale of house

I will sell my house on 31 December 2015 for £850,000. I purchased the house for £540,000 on 1 July 2005 and I have lived there ever since that date. Two rooms, representing 20% of the property, have always been used exclusively for the purposes of my business.

Sale of business assets

My business made a tax adjusted profit in the year ended 30 June 2014 of £90,000. However, in the year ended 30 June 2015 it made a tax adjusted loss of £20,000. I have not been able to find a buyer for the business and will therefore cease trading on 31 December 2015. I will then sell any remaining business assets.

I expect to be able to sell the business assets, consisting of machinery and inventory, for £14,000, with no asset being sold for more than cost. The business will make a tax adjusted loss of £17,000 in the six months ending 31 December 2015 after taking account of the sale of the business assets.

Agricultural land

In May 2011 my father gave me 230 acres of agricultural land situated in the UK. A capital gain of £72,800 arose in respect of this gift and my father and I submitted a joint claim for gift relief. I expect the value of the land to increase considerably in 2016 and I intend to sell it in June 2017.

Required

(a) The calculations showing how Mirtoon's disposal of assets and subsequent departure from the UK will affect his financial position as requested in the email from your manager.

Note. Ignore national insurance contributions. **(17 marks)**

(b) Prepare the letter to Mirtoon requested in the email from your manager. The following marks are available.

(i)	Value added tax (VAT)	**(3 marks)**
(ii)	Income tax and capital gains tax	**(7 marks)**
(iii)	Inheritance tax	**(6 marks)**

Professional marks will be awarded in this question for the extent to which the calculations are approached in a logical manner in part (a) and the effectiveness with which the information is communicated in part (b). **(3 marks)**

You may assume that the tax rules and rates for 2014/15 will continue to apply for the foreseeable future.

(Total = 36 marks)

BPP note. This question has been rewritten by BPP for the statutory residence test in Finance Act 2013 and reviewed by the P6 examination team.

21 Sakura (ATAX 12/10) 31 mins

Sakura requires advice on the receipt of insurance proceeds, the sale of a painting in exchange for a boat and the implications of making an error when preparing his tax return.

The following information has been obtained from a telephone conversation with Sakura.

Sakura:

- Is a higher rate taxpayer who is resident and domiciled in the UK
- Is finalising his tax return for the tax year 2014/15
- Has not previously made any gifts or disposals for the purposes of capital gains tax or inheritance tax other than those set out below
- Does not expect to make any gifts or disposals for the purposes of capital gains tax or inheritance tax in the tax years 2015/16 or 2016/17 other than those set out below
- Has received insurance proceeds of £67,000
- Intends to sell a painting to his son, Cashel, in exchange for a boat

The insurance proceeds of £67,000:

- The insurance proceeds were paid to Sakura on 1 June 2015.
- The insurance proceeds relate to the destruction of an antique china figurine on 1 March 2015.
- Sakura paid £28,000 for the figurine on 1 April 2011.
- The figurine had a market value of £80,000 on 1 March 2015.
- Sakura intends to use the money to purchase a modern glass figurine for £57,000.

Exchange of painting for boat:

- Sakura intends to sell a painting with a market value of £48,000 to his son, Cashel.
- The consideration for the sale will be a boat owned by Cashel that has a market value of £25,000.
- The painting and the boat cost £22,000 and £37,000 respectively.

Sakura's tax return:

- Sakura always prepares his tax returns in an honest manner.
- However, he is aware that he could still make an honest mistake.

Required

(a) • Explain, with supporting calculations where necessary, the capital gains tax and inheritance tax implications for Sakura of the receipt of the insurance proceeds and the sale of the painting in exchange for the boat.

    • Advise Sakura of the actions he should take in relation to his plans in order to minimise his capital gains tax liability and point out any matter(s) that would need to be resolved with HM Revenue and Customs.

Note. You should clearly identify the tax years relevant to the disposals and the due date of payment of any minimised capital gains tax liability. **(11 marks)**

(b) State, with reasons, whether there will be any capital gains tax and/or inheritance tax implications for Cashel from the disposal of the boat. **(2 marks)**

(c) Explain the manner in which a penalty would be calculated if Sakura were to make an honest mistake when completing his tax return. **(4 marks)**

You should assume that the tax rates and allowances of the tax year 2014/15 will continue to apply for the foreseeable future.

(Total = 17 marks)

22 Claudia   29 mins

Claudia requires advice on employee shareholder shares and the tax implications of investing through the Seed Enterprise Investment Scheme (SEIS).

The following information has been obtained from discussions with Claudia.

Claudia:

• Is married to Nigel and has one adult daughter, Joanne
• Has been offered employment by Noble plc
• Has been offered 'employee shareholder' shares by Noble plc as part of a remuneration package
• Has never owned any shares in Noble plc and will not acquire any further shares in Noble plc
• Made a gain of £42,000 on the sale of a plot of land in June 2014
• Will have an income tax liability (before any SEIS relief) of £50,000 in the tax year 2014/15

Noble plc:

• Does not have a parent company
• Is listed on the London Stock Exchange

Investment by Claudia in Petite Ltd:

• Subscribed for £60,000 £1 ordinary shares at par value in January 2015
• Investment qualifies for SEIS income tax relief
• Claudia intends to dispose of her shares in Petite Ltd in December 2016

Required

(a) (i) Explain what is meant by the term 'employee shareholder' and outline the conditions that must be satisfied for Claudia to be an employee shareholder. **(4 marks)**

    (ii) Assuming that Claudia takes up employment with Noble plc and is issued with employee shareholder shares worth £5,000, explain the income tax and national insurance consequences for Claudia of the issue of the shares. **(2 marks)**

    (iii) State the capital gains tax consequence of a disposal by Claudia of the employee shareholder shares in Noble plc in the following circumstances:

        1   Sale to an unconnected buyer

        2   Sale to Nigel

        3   Takeover of Noble plc by Token plc and Claudia receives shares in Token plc in exchange for her shares in Noble plc **(4 marks)**

(b)   (i)   State the tax reducer to which Claudia is entitled for the tax year 2014/15 in respect of her investment in Petite Ltd.   **(1 mark)**

       (ii)   State the maximum amount of SEIS reinvestment relief that Claudia can claim for the tax year 2014/15 and state how the relief operates.   **(2 marks)**

       (iii) Explain the income tax and capital gains tax implications of the proposed disposal of Petite Ltd shares by Claudia in December 2016 if she:

              1   Gives the shares to Joanne
              2   Sells them to an unconnected buyer for their market value of £45,000   **(3 marks)**

                                                                                                            (Total = 16 marks)

CORPORATION TAX

Questions 23 to 33 cover the taxation of companies. This is the subject of Chapters 20 to 27 of the BPP Study Text.

23 Hail Ltd (ATAX 12/11)   54 mins

Your manager has sent you a schedule of information received from a client, named Drench, who is the managing director of Hail Ltd. Hail Ltd is a UK resident trading company with a year end of 30 June and Drench owns the whole of the company's ordinary share capital. The schedule is set out below together with an email from your manager.

Schedule of information from Drench

Acquisition of Rain Ltd

I intend to buy 100% of the ordinary share capital of Rain Ltd, a UK resident trading company, on 1 January 2016. I will either purchase the shares personally or Hail Ltd will acquire Rain Ltd as a 100% subsidiary.

Rain Ltd is one of two companies currently wholly-owned by Flake Ltd. All three of the companies in the Flake Ltd group are trading companies. Following its acquisition Rain Ltd will change its year end from 30 September to 30 June such that it will prepare accounts for the nine months ending 30 June 2016.

Budgeted results of Rain Ltd

The budgeted financial results of Rain Ltd for the nine months ending 30 June 2016 are set out below. The results depend on whether or not the company acquires new contracts in 2016. All of the company's sales are standard rated for the purposes of value added tax (VAT). The chargeable gain is in respect of the disposal of a 0.3% shareholding in a quoted company.

	Nine months ending 30 June 2016	
	Without the new contracts	With the new contracts
	£	£
Sales revenue (exclusive of VAT)	380,000	1,425,000
Tax adjusted (loss)/profit	(75,000)	285,000
Chargeable gain	50,750	50,750

Other relevant information

In the year ended 30 September 2015 Rain Ltd realised a tax adjusted trading loss of £27,000 and had no other income or chargeable gains. The trading loss was surrendered as group relief to companies within the Flake Ltd group.

Rain Ltd's main asset is a building which is currently worth £340,000. The building was purchased from Mist Ltd, the other 100% subsidiary of Flake Ltd, on 1 July 2012 for its book value of £248,000. The market value of the building at that time was £260,000. Mist Ltd had purchased the building on 1 January 2003 for £170,000.

Hail Ltd is budgeted to realise taxable total profits in the year ending 30 June 2016 of £240,000.

No elections will be entered into with any company in the Flake Ltd group.

Email from your manager

I want you to prepare the following:

(a)   **A memorandum for the client file that explains the following matters, providing supporting calculations where relevant:**

    (i)   **Acquisition of Rain Ltd**

        A comparison of the tax implications of:

        •   Drench acquiring Rain Ltd personally; and

        •   Hail Ltd acquiring Rain Ltd.

Drench is aware of the general implications of forming a group. Accordingly, your comparison should focus on the following specific issues.

On the assumption that Rain Ltd DOES NOT obtain the new contracts:

- The manner in which the loss for the nine months ending 30 June 2016 should be relieved in order to maximise the tax relief obtained; the tax relief should be quantified where possible. Take care when identifying the rates of corporation tax payable by Rain Ltd and Hail Ltd as I suspect that the situation is not totally straightforward.

  Drench wants the loss to be used as soon as possible and only to be carried forward as a last resort.

- The tax implications of Hail Ltd making a payment to Rain Ltd in respect of any group relief losses surrendered.

On the assumption that Rain Ltd DOES obtain the new contracts:

- The corporation tax liability of Rain Ltd for the nine months ending 30 June 2016.

- The date by when Rain Ltd will need to pay its corporation tax liability for the period in order to avoid interest charges.

(ii) **Degrouping charge**

An explanation of the degrouping charge that will arise in respect of the building owned by Rain Ltd and an identification of any exemptions that might apply in respect of this charge.

(iii) **Loan from Hail Ltd to Drench and VAT cash accounting scheme**

- The tax implications for Hail Ltd of Drench borrowing £18,000 from the company on 1 February 2016. The loan will be interest free and will be repaid by Drench on 1 February 2022.

- The advantages of the VAT cash accounting scheme and whether it will be possible for Rain Ltd to operate the scheme.

(b) **A briefing note to me**

Our firm will be assisting Rain Ltd to obtain the new contracts. We have experience in this area as we used to have a client that successfully applied for government building contracts. The client moved to a rival firm at the end of 2013.

To what extent is it acceptable for us to use the knowledge we gained in respect of our ex-client to assist Rain Ltd?

Tax manager

Required

(a) Prepare the memorandum including supporting calculations requested in the email from your manager. The following marks are available.

(i)	Acquisition of Rain Ltd	**(12 marks)**
(ii)	Degrouping charge	**(3 marks)**
(iii)	Loan from Hail Ltd to Drench and VAT cash accounting scheme	**(8 marks)**

Professional marks will be awarded in part (a) for the extent to which the calculations are approached in a logical manner and the effectiveness with which the information is communicated. **(2 marks)**

Note. The following figures from the Retail Prices Index should be used where necessary.

January 2003   178.4
July 2012   242.1
January 2016   266.4 (assumed)

You may assume that the tax rules and rates for the Financial Year to 31 March 2015 will continue to apply for the foreseeable future.

(b) Prepare the briefing note requested in the email from your manager. **(5 marks)**

(Total = 30 marks)

24 Janus plc group (ATAX 06/12)   59 mins

Your manager has had a meeting with Mrs Pairz, the Group Finance Director of the Janus plc group of companies. The memorandum recording the matters discussed at the meeting is set out below.

Memorandum recording matters discussed at the meeting with Mrs Pairz

To   The files
From   Tax manager
Date   15 June 2015
Subject   Janus plc group

Mrs Pairz has recently been appointed the Group Finance Director of the Janus plc group. She has asked for advice on the use of the trading loss of Janus plc for the year ended 31 March 2015 and on a number of other matters.

The Janus plc group of companies

The group structure indicating the trading loss of Janus plc and the taxable total profits of each of the other group companies for the year ended 31 March 2015 is set out below. All of the companies are UK resident trading companies.

Janus plc purchased Seb Ltd, together with its subsidiary, Viola Ltd, on 1 December 2014 from Mr Twinn. Mr Twinn has never owned any other companies. There have not been any other changes to the group structure in recent years.

The minority holdings in Castor Ltd and Pollux Ltd are owned by UK resident individuals. The minority holding in Duet Ltd is owned by Bi plc, a UK resident company, such that Duet Ltd is a consortium company.

The group policy is for an amount equal to the corporation tax saved to be paid for any losses transferred between group companies.

Each of the companies is separately registered for the purposes of value added tax (VAT).

Additional information in respect of Janus plc

- Janus plc made a chargeable gain of £44,500 in the year ended 31 March 2015.

- Janus plc had taxable total profits in the year ended 31 March 2014 of £95,000 and did not make any charitable donations in the year.

Assets to be sold

(i)   Pollux Ltd is to sell its administrative premises, 'P HQ', to Janus plc on 1 July 2015 for their market value of £285,000. Pollux Ltd acquired these premises from Castor Ltd on 1 March 2012 for their market value of £240,000.

(ii)   Viola Ltd is to sell a warehouse to an unrelated company on 1 August 2015 for £350,000 plus VAT of £70,000. Viola Ltd acquired this warehouse on 1 February 2014 for £320,000 plus VAT of £64,000.

Mrs Pairz understands that the input tax relating to the warehouse should be recovered in accordance with the capital goods scheme because Viola Ltd is a partially exempt company, but suspects that the calculations may not have been done correctly.

The relevant VAT recovery percentages for Viola Ltd are:

Year ended 31 March 2014	70%
Year ended 31 March 2015	55%
Period from 1 April 2015 to 1 August 2015	50%

(iii)   Castor Ltd is to sell patent rights to an unrelated company on 1 September 2015 for £41,000. Castor Ltd acquired these patent rights for use in its trade on 1 September 2011 for £45,000. The patent rights are being written off in Castor Ltd's accounts on a straight-line basis over a ten-year period. Castor Ltd is not eligible to make a patent box election in respect of these patent rights.

Investment in Kupple Inc

Janus plc intends to purchase 15% of the ordinary share capital of Kupple Inc on 1 October 2015. Kupple Inc is a profitable trading company, resident in the country of Halven. Kupple Inc will provide consultancy services to Janus plc. This is intended to be a short-term commercial investment; Janus plc will sell the shares at some point in the next two years.

Required

(a)   Use of the trading loss of Janus plc:

(i)   Explain the alternative ways in which the loss can be relieved, on the assumption that it is not to be carried forward.

(ii)   Advise how the loss should be relieved in order to maximise the corporation tax saved. You should include a summary showing the rates(s) of tax at which relief for the loss will be obtained.

(11 marks)

(b)   Assets to be sold:

(i)   Explain how the chargeable gain on the disposal of P HQ will be calculated and state any further information required form Mrs Pairz to enable us to carry out this calculation.   **(5 marks)**

(ii)   Calculate the input tax recoverable from/repayable to HM Revenue and Customs in respect of the warehouse for each of the three years ending 31 March 2016, on the assumption that the sale of the warehouse goes ahead as planned.   **(4 marks)**

(iii)   Explain, with supporting calculations, the corporation tax implications of the sale of the patent rights.

(3 marks)

(c)   Investment in Kupple Inc:

(i)   Explain the VAT implications for Janus plc of purchasing the consultancy services from Kupple Inc.

(2 marks)

(ii)   Explain the corporation tax treatment of any profit or loss arising on the eventual sale of the shares in Kupple Inc.   **(4 marks)**

(d)   Janus plc group senior accounting officer:

Explain, briefly, whether or not Mrs Pairz will be the senior accounting officer of the Janus plc group, the circumstances in which the rules relating to the group's tax accounting systems will apply to the Janus plc group, and the statutory responsibilities of a senior accounting officer when the rules apply.   **(4 marks)**

You should assume that the tax rates and allowances for the financial year to 31 March 2015 will continue to apply for the foreseeable future.

(Total = 33 marks)

25 Sperry Ltd group (ATAX 12/11)   31 mins

The management of the Sperry Ltd group require advice on minimising the corporation tax liability in respect of a chargeable gain, the tax relief available in respect of loan interest payable and group registration for the purposes of value added tax (VAT).

The following information has been obtained from the management of the Sperry Ltd group.

The Sperry Ltd group:

*   The structure of the group, which has not changed for many years is:

*   All of the companies, with the exception of Teton Inc, are UK resident manufacturing companies.
*   Teton Inc is resident and trades in the country of Glaciera.

The budgeted results of each of the group companies for the year ended 31 March 2016 are:

	Sperry Ltd £	Wahl Ltd £	Neny Ltd £	Teton Inc £	Byrd Ltd £
Taxable trading profit	540,000	20,000	35,000	480,000	180,000
Chargeable gain	–	–	–	–	50,000

*   None of the companies has any other source of income.
*   There are no trading losses or capital losses brought forward as at 1 April 2015.
*   Byrd Ltd's gain arose on the disposal of a building; rollover relief is not available.

Proposed acquisition of a building:

*   Sperry Ltd intends to purchase a building.
*   The building will not be used in Sperry Ltd's trade but will be rented to a third party for £8,000 per month.
*   Sperry Ltd intends to borrow £1,300,000 from a UK bank in order to purchase the building.
*   Sperry Ltd will opt to tax the building for the purposes of VAT.

Proposed group registration for the purposes of VAT:

*   It is intended that Sperry Ltd and Byrd Ltd will register as a group for VAT purposes.
*   Sperry Ltd makes only standard rated supplies.
*   Byrd Ltd makes only exempt supplies.
*   Byrd Ltd's supplies will represent 30% of the value of the total supplies of the proposed VAT group.
*   Sperry Ltd levies a monthly management charge on Byrd Ltd.

Required

(a) Explain IN DETAIL the strategy that should be adopted by the Sperry Ltd group in order to minimise the corporation tax charge in respect of the chargeable gain of Byrd Ltd and state the date by which the necessary election(s) should be submitted.   **(7 marks)**

(b) Explain how tax relief may be obtained for the interest charged to Sperry Ltd on the loan to acquire the building.   **(4 marks)**

(c)   Explain BRIEFLY the possible effects of registering Sperry Ltd and Byrd Ltd as a value added tax (VAT) group in relation to both the total input recovered by the Sperry Ltd group and the monthly management charge. **(6 marks)**

You may assume that the tax rules and rates for the Financial Year to 31 March 2015 will continue to apply for the foreseeable future.

(Total = 17 marks)

26 Sank Ltd and Kurt Ltd (ATAX 06/12)   32 mins

Sank Ltd and Kurt Ltd are two unrelated clients of your firm. Sank Ltd requires advice in connection with the payment of its corporation tax liability and the validity of a compliance check enquiry it has received from HM Revenue and Customs. Kurt Ltd requires advice in connection with the purchase of machinery and expenditure on research and development.

(a)   **Sank Ltd:**

- Has paid corporation tax at the main rate for many years
- Has a large number of associated companies
- Will prepared its next accounts for the 11 months ending 30 September 2015
- Has received a compliance check notice from HM Revenue and Customs

Taxable total profits for the 11 months ending 30 September 2015:

- Figures prepared on 31 March 2015 indicated taxable total profits for this 11-month period of £640,000.
- As at 1 June 2015, taxable total profits for this 11-month period are expected to be £750,000.

The compliance check notice from HM Revenue and Customs:

- HM Revenue and Customs gave notice of the compliance check on 31 May 2015.
- It relates to Sank Ltd's corporation tax return for the year ended 31 October 2012.
- No amendments have been made to the corporation tax return since it was submitted.

Required

In relation to Sank Ltd:

(i)   Explain, with supporting calculations, the payment(s) required in respect of the company's corporation tax liability for the 11 months ended 30 September 2015 and the implications of the increase in the expected taxable total profits. **(7 marks)**

(ii)   In relation to the date on which the compliance check into the corporation tax computation for the year ended 31 October 2012 was notified, explain the circumstances necessary for the notice to be regarded as valid. You should assume that Sank Ltd has not been fraudulent or negligent. **(3 marks)**

(b)   **Kurt Ltd:**

- Was incorporated and began to trade on 1 August 2014
- Is owned by Mr Quinn, who also owns three other trading companies
- Has made a tax adjusted trading loss in the eight months ending 31 March 2015
- Has no other income or chargeable gains in the eight months ending 31 March 2015
- Is expected to be profitable in future years
- Is a small enterprise for the purposes of research and development

Expenditure in the period ending 31 March 2015:

- Machinery for use in its manufacturing activities – £510,000
- The cost of staff carrying out qualifying scientific research in connection with its business – £28,000

Required

In relation to Kurt Ltd, explain the tax deductions and/or credits available in the period ending 31 March 2015 in respect of the expenditure on machinery and scientific research and comment on any choices available to the company.

(8 marks)

(Total = 18 marks)

27 Opus Ltd group (ATAX 06/14)   45 mins

Your manager is due to attend a meeting with the finance director of Opus Ltd. A schedule of information obtained from the client files and an email from your manager in connection with the Opus Ltd group are set out below.

Schedule of information

Opus Ltd – holdings in other companies as at 31 March 2015

Results for the period ended 31 March 2015

	Opus Ltd £	Akia Ltd £	Ribe Ltd £	Lido Ltd £	Venere Ltd £	Binni Ltd £
Trading profit/(loss)	10,000	(93,000)	41,000	75,000	160,000	78,000
Property income	8,000	–	–	–	–	–
Chargeable gain	Note 3	6,000	–	21,000	–	–

Notes

Holdings in other companies

1   All of the companies are UK resident trading companies.

2   All of the companies, including Binni Ltd, have always paid corporation tax at the main rate due to a large number of overseas associated companies.

3   Opus Ltd – acquisition of the holdings in other companies

    •   Opus Ltd acquired Akia Ltd and the shareholding in Ribe Ltd (together with its subsidiary Lido Ltd) on 1 January 2000.

    •   Venere Ltd has an issued share capital of 1,000,000 ordinary shares. Opus Ltd acquired 170,000 ordinary shares in Venere Ltd on 1 July 2005 for £65,000. It sold 120,000 of these shares on 1 October 2014 for £150,000. Assume the indexation factor from July 2005 to October 2014 is 0.346.

    •   Opus Ltd acquired Binni Ltd on 1 December 2014.

4   The minority interests in Ribe Ltd and Lido Ltd are owned by individuals.

5   Venere Ltd is a 75% subsidiary of Jarrah Ltd, a company with no connections to the Opus Ltd group.

Results for the period ended 31 March 2015

6   All of the companies, with the exception of Binni Ltd, have prepared accounts for the year ended 31 March 2015. Binni Ltd has prepared accounts for the ten months ended 31 March 2015.

7   Where necessary, the results shown above have been adjusted for tax purposes.

8   Akia Ltd's trading loss includes writing down allowances in the main pool of £35,000.

9   Akia Ltd is not expected to return to profitability for a number of years.

10   Ribe Ltd has trading losses brought forward of £68,000 as at 1 April 2014.

Email from your manager

Please carry out the following work in preparation for the Opus Ltd meeting.

(a)   Relieving the trading losses of Akia Ltd and Ribe Ltd

The objective of the group is to relieve all losses as soon as possible.

Prepare calculations, together with supporting explanations, to show how the group's objective can best be achieved, clearly identifying any losses to be carried forward as at 31 March 2015 and any further information which may need to be obtained.

There may be some interesting planning possibilities here; you should think carefully about the tax position of each company.

(b)   Sale of the shares in Venere Ltd

Opus Ltd has received an offer of £80,000 for its remaining 50,000 ordinary shares in Venere Ltd. If the sale were to go ahead, it would take place on 30 June 2015. However, the management of Opus Ltd are of the opinion that the results of Venere Ltd for the year ending 31 March 2016 will be such that the shares could be worth as much as £100,000 if the sale were to be delayed until 30 April 2016.

Set out the matters which the management of Opus Ltd should consider in order to decide on which of the two dates it would be more financially advantageous to sell the shares in Venere Ltd. When calculating the indexation allowance, use an approximate indexation factor of 0.400 for the period from 1 July 2005 until the date of sale.

(c)   Error in the corporation tax return of Binni Ltd

A detailed review of the results of Binni Ltd for the year ended 31 May 2013 has revealed that no adjustment was made in respect of an amount of disallowable expenditure. As a result of this, the company's corporation tax liability for the year was understated by £8,660. I have told the company that there may be interest and penalties in respect of this error.

Explain how the interest on the underpaid tax will be calculated and state the matters which would need to be considered if the company were unwilling to disclose the error to HM Revenue and Customs.

Tax manager

Required

Carry out the work required as set out in the email from your manager. The following marks are available.

(a)   Relieving the trading losses of Akia Ltd and Ribe Ltd.   **(14 marks)**

(b)   Sale of the shares in Venere Ltd.   **(5 marks)**

(c)   Error in the corporation tax return of Binni Ltd.

Note. You are not required to calculate the amount of interest payable or to consider any penalty which may be charged.   **(6 marks)**

(Total = 25 marks)

28 Forti Ltd group (ATAX 12/13)

You have received an email from your manager with an attached schedule in connection with the Forti Ltd group of companies. The schedule and the email are set out below.

Email from your manager

Forti Ltd group

Forti Ltd has an issued share capital of 120,000 ordinary shares. It is owned by 12 shareholders, each of whom owns 10,000 ordinary shares.

All six of the companies are trading companies. Gordini Co is resident in and trades in the country of Arrowsia; it does not carry out any activities in the UK. The other five companies are all resident in the UK. There is no double tax treaty between Arrowsia and the UK.

The only changes to the group structure in recent years relate to the purchase and subsequent sale of Marussia Ltd as set out in note 2 to the attached schedule.

Ligier Ltd has no links to the Forti Ltd group other than its shareholding in Eagle Ltd.

The work I require you to do is set out below.

(a) **Brawn Ltd – Review of the corporation tax computation**

   I attach a schedule detailing the corporation tax computation for Brawn Ltd for the year ended 31 March 2015. This schedule has been prepared by an inexperienced tax assistant. I can confirm that the substantial shareholding exemption is not available and that the figures given for the indexed cost of Marussia Ltd in the schedule, the degrouping charge in note 2, and the tax adjusted trading losses referred to in notes 3 and 4 have all been calculated correctly.

   Please review the computation and related notes in order to identify any errors and prepare a revised schedule showing calculations of the correct taxable total profits and the corporation tax liability. You should include notes explaining the errors you have identified and the changes you have made.

(b) **Other corporate matters**

   (i) Brawn Ltd will only be a close company if Forti Ltd is a close company.

      Set out the matters which need to be considered in order to determine whether or not Forti Ltd is a close company.

   (ii) Set out the matters which need to be considered in connection with the sale of components to Gordini Co referred to in note 6 to the schedule.

(c) **Value added tax (VAT) annual accounting scheme**

   The management of the Forti Ltd group have asked for advice on the VAT annual accounting scheme.

   State the conditions which must be satisfied by any company wishing to operate the annual accounting scheme and explain the operation of the scheme.

Tax manager

Schedule prepared by a tax assistant

Brawn Ltd – Corporation tax computation for the year ended 31 March 2015

	Notes	£	£
Tax adjusted trading income	1		250,500
Sale of Marussia Ltd – Proceeds	2	484,000	
Less: indexed cost		(390,000)	
annual exempt amount		(11,000)	
			83,000
			333,500
Less: losses transferred from:			
Marussia Ltd (£60,000 × 5/12)	3		(25,000)
Eagle Ltd (£52,500 × 20%)	4		(10,500)
Taxable total profits			298,000
Corporation tax @ 21%	5		62,580

Notes

1   The treatment of the following items of expenditure needs to be checked.

	£	
The cost of establishing a company share option plan	6,000	Disallowed
The cost of entertaining overseas customers	4,000	Disallowed
Accrued management bonuses to be paid on 1 February 2016	7,000	Allowed

2   Marussia Ltd was purchased on 1 August 2014. On 1 November 2014, Brawn Ltd signed a contract to sell Marussia Ltd for £484,000, and the sale took place on 31 December 2014. Accordingly, the substantial shareholding exemption was not available. The sale of Marussia Ltd resulted in a degrouping charge of £21,600. This has been included as a chargeable gain in the corporation tax computation of Marussia Ltd.

3   Marussia Ltd made a tax adjusted trading loss of £60,000 in the year ended 31 March 2015.

4   Eagle Ltd made a tax adjusted trading loss of £52,500 in the year ended 31 March 2015 and did not pay a dividend.

5   Although there are five companies in the group, I have calculated corporation tax at the main rate because I think that Brawn Ltd is a close company.

6   During the year ended 31 March 2015, Brawn Ltd began selling components to Gordini Co. Are there any issues which need to be considered in respect of these sales in relation to Brawn Ltd's corporation tax liability?

Required

Carry out the work required as set out in the email from your manager. The following marks are available.

(a)   Brawn Ltd – Review of the corporation tax computation

       Note. Ignore value added tax (VAT). **(12 marks)**

(b)   Other corporate matters:

       (i)   Close companies **(5 marks)**

       (ii)   Note 6 to the schedule **(3 marks)**

(c)   Value added tax (VAT) annual accounting scheme **(5 marks)**

       (Total = 25 marks)

29 Epon Ltd group (ATAX 06/13)

Your manager has had a telephone conversation with Burt, the Group Finance Director of the Epon Ltd group of companies. Extracts from both a memorandum and an email from your manager are set out below.

Extract from a memorandum from your manager

On 5 June 2015 I spoke to Burt, the Group Finance Director of Epon Ltd. He is coming to the office on Monday to appoint us as tax advisers to the group, and possibly to the individual directors, and to discuss the group's affairs.

Epon Ltd group

Epon Ltd is owned by a large number of unrelated individuals. Epon Ltd owns 100% of the ordinary share capital of Wahzah Ltd, Yoko Ltd and NewCo Ltd. All four companies are UK resident and prepare accounts to 30 June each year. It is the policy of the group to maximise the tax saved when relieving losses and only to carry losses forward if there is no alternative relief available.

	Epon Ltd	Wahzah Ltd	Yoko Ltd	NewCo Ltd
Business activity	Manufacture of exercise equipment	Ownership and management of fitness clubs	Servicing of swimming pools	None
	£	£	£	£
Budgeted results				
Year ending 30 June 2016				
Tax adjusted trading profit/(loss)	740,000	90,000	(80,000)	Nil
Chargeable gains	18,000	Nil	12,000	Nil
Capital loss	Nil	(20,000)	Nil	Nil
Budgeted trading losses carried forward as at 30 June 2015	Nil	Nil	(65,000)	Nil

The purchase of the Aquapower business

NewCo Ltd is currently dormant. It was incorporated on 1 May 2015 in order to purchase the assets of the Aquapower business (Aquapower) from an unincorporated trader. It was intended that NewCo Ltd would purchase Aquapower on 1 July 2015. However, Burt has now decided that he would prefer the business to be purchased by Yoko Ltd, provided that this is not more expensive from a tax point of view. Under this option, Yoko Ltd would then be carrying on two separate trades.

Aquapower's business is the distribution of bottled drinks. The budgeted trading profit of Aquapower for the year ending 30 June 2016 is £60,000. None of the assets of the Aquapower business qualifies for rollover relief.

The purchase of equipment from the country of Candara

A new supplier of equipment for the fitness clubs has been identified in Candara. Wahzah Ltd intends to purchase equipment from this supplier in July 2015. The country of Candara is not a member of the European Union.

The purchase of Kari's shares

The planned changes to the Epon Ltd group have resulted in a dispute with Kari, the Group Sales Director. In order to resolve this, it has been proposed that Epon Ltd will carry out a purchase of its own shares on 31 July 2015 and acquire the whole of Kari's shareholding.

Kari subscribed £10,000 for 10,000 £1 ordinary shares in Epon Ltd on 1 December 2010. It has been agreed that Epon Ltd will purchase all of these shares on 31 July 2015 for £90,000. Kari has been advised that the money she will receive will be treated as a dividend. Kari's annual taxable employment income (before deducting her personal allowance) is £72,000. In the tax year 2015/16, she will not receive any other income or make any disposals for the purposes of capital gains tax. Kari was born in 1978.

Extract from an email from your manager

Please prepare a memorandum for the client file that addresses the following issues:

(a) **The purchase of the Aquapower business – corporation tax liabilities**

Calculations of the corporation tax liabilities of the four companies for the year ending 30 June 2016 on the assumption that Aquapower is purchased by:

(i) NewCo Ltd

(ii) Yoko Ltd

You should assume that any claim(s) for loss relief will be made in accordance with group policy, as described in the memorandum. The **only** explanatory notes I need are in respect of the use of any losses.

(b) **The purchase of equipment from the country of Candara**

Explain the value added tax (VAT) implications for Wahzah Ltd of the purchase of the equipment from the country of Candara.

(c) **The purchase of Kari's shares**

I want you to:

(i) Review each of the conditions for capital gains tax treatment in order to determine the reason(s) why the amount received will be treated as a dividend. I can confirm that Epon Ltd satisfies the condition of being an unquoted trading company.

(ii) Calculate the increase in tax cost for Kari as a result of the sale of the shares being subject to income tax as opposed to capital gains tax. You should assume that entrepreneurs' relief would be available and would be claimed.

(d) **Appointment as tax advisers**

An explanation of whether or not it is acceptable for the firm to be appointed tax advisers to the companies' directors as well as to the Epon Ltd group of companies. On the assumption that it is acceptable, outline any safeguards that the firm should consider in relation to this joint appointment.

Tax manager

Required

Prepare the memorandum requested in the email from your manager. The following marks are available.

(a) The purchase of the Aquapower business – corporation tax liabilities

Note. For guidance, approximately 60% of the marks available in part (a) are for the calculations.

(13 marks)

(b) The purchase of equipment from the country of Candara **(2 marks)**

(c) The purchase of Kari's shares:

(i) Review of each of the conditions for capital gains tax treatment **(5 marks)**

(ii) Calculation of the increase in tax cost for Kari **(6 marks)**

(d) Appointment as tax advisers **(5 marks)**

Professional marks will be awarded in this question for adopting a logical approach to problem solving, the clarity of the calculations, effectiveness with which the information is communicated, and the overall presentation of the memorandum. **(4 marks)**

You should assume that the tax rates and allowances of the tax year 2014/15 and for the Financial Year to 31 March 2015 will continue to apply for the foreseeable future.

(Total = 35 marks)

30 Trifles Ltd (ATAX 12/10)

31 mins

Trifles Ltd intends to carry out a purchase of its own shares. The shareholders from whom the shares are to be purchased require advice on their tax position. Trifles Ltd also intends to loan a motorcycle to one of the shareholders.

The following information has been obtained from the shareholders in Trifles Ltd.

Trifles Ltd:

- Is an unquoted company specialising in the delivery of small, high value items
- Was incorporated and began trading on 1 February 2008
- Has an issued share capital of 10,000 ordinary shares subscribed for at £2 per share
- Has four unrelated shareholders: Torte, Baklava, Victoria and Melba
- Intends to purchase some of its own shares from Victoria and Melba
- Victoria and Melba have been directors of the company since they acquired their shares but will resign immediately after the purchase of their shares

The purchase by Trifles Ltd of its own shares:

- Will take place on 28 February 2016 for Victoria's shares, and on 31 March 2016 for Melba's shares at an agreed price of £30 per share
- Will consist of the purchase of all of Victoria's shares and 450 shares from Melba

Victoria:

- Is resident in the UK
- Has taxable income of £40,000 in 2015/16
- Will make no other capital disposals in the tax year 2015/16
- Has a capital loss carried forward as at 5 April 2015 of £3,400
- Will have no link with Trifles Ltd following the purchase of her shares
- Inherited her holding of 1,500 ordinary shares on the death of her husband, Brownie, on 1 February 2014
- Brownie paid £16,500 for the shares on 1 February 2012
- The probate value of the 1,500 ordinary shares was £16,000 on 1 February 2014

Melba:

- Is resident in the UK
- Has taxable income of £40,000 in 2015/16 and 2016/17
- Acquired her holding of 1,700 ordinary shares when Trifles Ltd was incorporated
- Following the purchase of her shares Melba's only link with Trifles Ltd will be her remaining ordinary shareholding and the use of a motorcycle belonging to the company

The motorcycle:

- Will be purchased by Trifles Ltd for £9,000 on 1 April 2016
- Will be made available on loan to Melba for the whole of the tax year 2016/17
- Melba will pay Trifles Ltd £30 per month for the use of the motorcycle

Required

(a) Explain whether or not Victoria and/or Melba satisfy the conditions relating to period of ownership and reduction in level of shareholding such that the amount received from Trifles Ltd on the purchase of own shares may be treated as capital. **(6 marks)**

(b) Calculate Victoria's after tax proceeds from the purchase of her shares:

- If the amount received is treated as capital
- If the amount received is treated as income **(6 marks)**

(c)   Explain, with supporting calculations where necessary, the tax implications of the purchase and loan of the motorcycle for both Melba and Trifles Ltd.   **(5 marks)**

Note. Ignore value added tax (VAT).

You should assume that the tax rates and allowances of the tax year 2014/15 and for the financial year to 31 March 2015 will continue to apply for the foreseeable future.

(Total = 17 marks)

31 Bamburg Ltd (ATAX 06/14)   36 mins

Charlotte is the owner of Bamburg Ltd. She requires advice on the value added tax (VAT) flat rate scheme, the sale of a substantial item of machinery, and the alternative methods by which she can extract additional funds from the company.

Charlotte:

- Is UK resident and UK domiciled
- Owns 100% of the ordinary share capital of Bamburg Ltd
- Earns an annual salary from Bamburg Ltd of £46,000 and has no other income
- Has two ideas to generate additional cash in Bamburg Ltd
- Wants to receive an additional £14,000 (after the payment of all personal taxes) from Bamburg Ltd on 30 June 2015

Bamburg Ltd:

- Is a UK resident trading company which pays corporation tax at the small profits rate
- Is registered for VAT
- Has budgeted sales revenue for the year ending 31 March 2016 of £120,000 excluding VAT
- Makes wholly standard rated supplies apart from £6,000 of exempt supplies
- Has a nil tax written down value on its main pool as at 31 March 2015
- Will not purchase any plant and machinery in the year ending 31 March 2016

Charlotte's ideas to generate additional cash in Bamburg Ltd:

- 'Bamburg Ltd should join the VAT flat rate scheme in order to save money.'
- 'Bamburg Ltd should sell the 'Cara' machine and offset the resulting loss against its profits.'

The 'Cara' machine:

- Was purchased on 1 January 2013 for £94,000
- Rollover relief was claimed in respect of this purchase to defer a chargeable gain of £13,000
- The 'Cara' machine is currently worth £80,000
- Following the sale of the 'Cara' machine, Bamburg Ltd will rent a replacement machine

Alternative methods of extracting an additional £14,000 from Bamburg Ltd:

- Bamburg Ltd to pay Charlotte a bonus
- Bamburg Ltd to pay Charlotte a dividend
- Bamburg Ltd to make an interest-free loan of £14,000 to Charlotte

Required

(a)   Explain, with reference to the information provided, whether or not Bamburg Ltd would be permitted to join the value added tax (VAT) flat rate scheme and set out the matters which would need to be considered in order to determine whether or not it would be financially beneficial for the company to do so.   **(5 marks)**

(b)   Explain the tax and financial implications of Bamburg Ltd selling the 'Cara' machine during the year ending 31 March 2016.   **(5 marks)**

(c)   (i)   Prepare calculations to determine whether it would be cheaper for Bamburg Ltd to pay Charlotte a bonus or a dividend, such that she would receive £14,000 after the payment of all personal taxes.   **(5 marks)**

(ii) Explain the immediate tax implications for Bamburg Ltd and Charlotte of Bamburg Ltd making an interest-free loan of £14,000 to Charlotte. **(5 marks)**

(Total = 20 marks)

32 Liza (ATAX 06/13) 36 mins

Liza requires detailed advice on rollover relief, capital allowances and group registration for the purposes of value added tax (VAT).

Liza's business interests:

*   Liza's business interests, which have not changed for many years, are set out below.

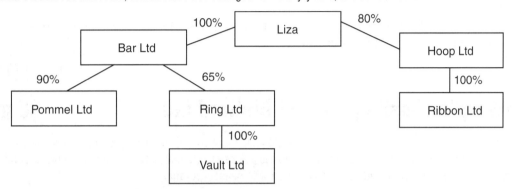

*   All six companies are UK resident trading companies with a 31 March year end.
*   All of the minority holdings are owned by individuals, none of whom is connected with Liza or with each other.

A building ('Building I') sold by Bar Ltd:

*   Bar Ltd sold Building I on 31 May 2015 for £860,000.
*   Bar Ltd had purchased the building on 1 June 2009 for £315,000 plus legal fees of £9,000.
*   On 5 June 2009, Bar Ltd had carried out work on the building's roof at a cost of £38,000 in order to make the building fit for use.
*   On 1 July 2014, Bar Ltd spent £14,000 repainting the building.
*   Bar Ltd used Building I for trading purposes apart from the period from 1 January 2011 to 30 June 2012.
*   It is intended that the chargeable gain on the sale will be rolled over to the extent that this is possible.

A replacement building ('Building II') purchased by Bar Ltd:

*   Bar Ltd purchased Building II, new and unused, for £720,000 on 1 May 2015.
*   Bar Ltd uses two thirds of this building for trading purposes; the remaining one-third is rented out.

The trading activities of the Bar Ltd and Hoop Ltd groups of companies:

*   The number of transactions between the Bar Ltd group and the Hoop Ltd group is increasing.
*   Vault Ltd makes zero rated supplies; all of the other five companies make standard rated supplies.

Required

(a) (i) Calculate the chargeable gain on the sale of Building I, ignoring any potential claim for rollover relief.
(3 marks)

(ii) In relation to claiming rollover relief in respect of the disposal of Building I, explain which of the companies in the Bar Ltd and Hoop Ltd groups are, and are not, able to purchase qualifying replacement assets, and state the period within which such assets must be acquired. **(4 marks)**

(iii) Explain, with the aid of supporting calculations, the additional amount that would need to be spent on qualifying assets in order for the maximum amount of the gain on Building I to be relieved by rollover relief. **(4 marks)**

Notes

1   You should ignore value added tax (VAT) when answering part (a) of this question.
2   The following figures from the Retail Prices Index should be used, where necessary.

         June 2009   213.4
         July 2014   256.4 (assumed)
         May 2015   263.7 (assumed)

(b)   Explain the capital allowances that are available in respect of the electrical, water and heating systems that were acquired as part of Building II.   **(2 marks)**

(c)   Explain which of the companies in the Bar Ltd and Hoop Ltd groups would be able to register as a single group for the purposes of value added tax (VAT) and discuss the potential advantages and disadvantages of registering them as a single VAT group.   **(7 marks)**

You should assume that the tax rates and allowances of the tax year 2014/15 and for the Financial Year to 31 March 2015 will continue to apply for the foreseeable future.

(Total = 20 marks)

33 Swan plc, Gosling plc and Mallard Ltd   36 mins

Swan plc, Gosling plc and Mallard Ltd are three unrelated clients of your firm. Swan plc requires advice in connection with profits from patents. Gosling plc requires advice in connection with expenditure on research and development. Mallard Ltd requires advice in connection with disincorporation.

(a)   **Swan plc:**

- In the year to 31 March 2015, has total taxable profits of £2,000,000 (before any adjustment relating to patents), of which the net patent profit is £500,000

- Carries on qualifying development in relation to patents

- Has no associated companies

The patent box percentage for the year to 31 March 2015 is 70%.

Required

In relation to Swan plc, compute the tax saving in the year to 31 March 2015 that will be made if the company makes a patent box election.   **(4 marks)**

(b)   **Gosling plc:**

- Is a large company for the purposes of research and development (R&D)
- In the year to 31 March 2015 spent £500,000 on qualifying R&D
- Has taxable total profits, before taking into account R&D expenditure, of £4,500,000

Required

In relation to Gosling plc, calculate the corporation tax payable for the year ended 31 March 2015 if the company claims:

(i)   R&D deduction relief   **(2 marks)**
(ii)   Above the Line tax credit for R&D expenditure   **(3 marks)**

(c)   **Mallard Ltd:**

- Carries on a trade of computer repairs
- Owns a freehold shop and a motor car
- Has goodwill built up since incorporation in 2006
- Has inventory of computer spare parts

Nathan Drake:

- Is the sole shareholder of Mallard Ltd, acquiring his shares on incorporation

- Wishes to disincorporate Mallard Ltd in 2015, acquiring ownership of all its assets, and thereafter will carry on the computer repair business as a sole trade

Required

In relation to Mallard Ltd:

(i) Explain the conditions for an election for disincorporation relief to be made, identifying any further information required. **(4 marks)**

(ii) State who must enter into the election for disincorporation relief and the date by which it must be submitted to Her Majesty's Revenue and Customs. **(2 marks)**

(iii) Outline the effect of disincorporation relief. **(3 marks)**

(iv) Explain the effect of any other reliefs which may be relevant on the disincorporation of Mallard Ltd. **(2 marks)**

(Total = 20 marks)

VALUE ADDED TAX

Questions 34 and 35 cover value added tax (VAT). This is the subject of Chapters 28 and 29 in the BPP Study Text.

34 Jerome (ATAX 06/12)   32 mins

Jerome, who was born in 1976, is an unincorporated sole trader who is about to sell his business to a company. He requires advice on the value added tax (VAT) implications of the sale of the business, whether a new lease in respect of a motor car for use by him should be entered into by him or by the company and the payment of travel expenses in respect of the family of an employee working overseas.

Jerome's business:

- Has annual taxable profits of £75,000 and is growing

- Is registered for the purposes of VAT

- Jerome leases a motor car in which he drives 20,000 miles per year of which 14,000 miles are on business. He anticipates that this level and pattern of mileage will continue in the future.

- The assets of the business include a building that was completed in 2013 and purchased by Jerome in April 2013 for £320,000.

The sale of Jerome's business to Tricycle Ltd:

- The business will be sold to Tricycle Ltd on 1 August 2015.

- Jerome will own the whole of the share capital of Tricycle Ltd.

- Tricycle Ltd will not change the nature of the business but will look to expand it by exporting its products to Italy.

The lease of the motor car:

- The existing lease will end on 31 July 2015.
- A new lease will be entered into on 1 August 2015 by either Jerome or Tricycle Ltd.
- The annual leasing costs of the new car will be £4,400.

The motor car to be leased on 1 August 2015:

- Will be diesel powered and have a list price when new of £31,000
- Will have CO_2 emissions of 157 grams per kilometre
- Will have annual running costs, including fuel, of £5,000 in addition to the leasing costs

Remuneration to be paid by Tricycle Ltd to Jerome:

- A salary of £4,000 per month

- If Tricycle Ltd leases the motor car, Jerome will use it for business and private purposes and will be provided with fuel for all his motoring.

- If Jerome leases the motor car, he will be paid 50 pence per mile for driving it on business journeys.

Expansion into Europe:

- An employee of Tricycle Ltd will work for up to three months in Italy between April and July 2016.

- The employee will continue to be resident and domiciled in the UK.

- Tricycle Ltd will pay the travel costs of the employee's wife and three-year-old child when they visit him in June 2016.

- The travel costs will be taxable in the hands of the employee as employment income.

Required

(a) Explain the value added tax (VAT) implications of the sale of Jerome's business to Tricycle Ltd. **(6 marks)**

(b) Prepare calculations for the 12-month period to show the total tax cost, for Tricycle Ltd and Jerome, of the car being leased by:

   (i)   Tricycle Ltd
   (ii) Jerome

   Note. Ignore VAT for part (b) of this question. **(10 marks)**

(c) State the conditions that must be satisfied for a deduction for the travel costs paid by Tricycle Ltd to be given against the employee's total employment income. **(2 marks)**

You should assume that the tax rates and allowances for the tax year 2014/15 and for the Financial Year to 31 March 2015 will continue to apply for the foreseeable future.

(Total = 18 marks)

35 Spetz Ltd group (ATAX 12/13) 36 mins

The management of the Spetz Ltd group requires advice on the value added tax (VAT) annual adjustment for a partially exempt company, the tax position of a company incorporated and trading overseas, and the income tax treatment of the costs relating to an employee working abroad.

Spetz Ltd group of companies:

*   Spetz Ltd has a large number of subsidiaries, such that they all pay corporation tax at the main rate.
*   Novak Ltd and Kraus Co are two of the 100% subsidiaries of Spetz Ltd.
*   Novak Ltd has a VAT year end of 30 September.
*   Spetz Ltd acquired Kraus Co on 1 October 2014.
*   Meyer, an employee of Spetz Ltd, has been seconded to work for Kraus Co.

Novak Ltd – Figures for the year ended 30 September 2015:

		£
Taxable supplies (excluding VAT)		1,190,000
Exempt supplies		430,000
Input tax:	attributed to taxable supplies	12,200
	attributed to exempt supplies	4,900
	unattributed	16,100
	recovered on the four quarterly returns prior to the annual adjustment	23,200

Kraus Co:

*   Is incorporated in, and trades through, a permanent establishment in the country of Mersano

*   Has no taxable income or chargeable gains apart from trading profits

*   Has taxable trading profits for the year ended 30 September 2015 of £520,000, all of which arose in Mersano

*   Is not a controlled foreign company

*   Has not made an election to exempt its overseas trading profits from UK tax

The tax system in the country of Mersano:

*   It can be assumed that the tax system in the country of Mersano is the same as that in the UK.
*   However, the rate of corporation tax is 18%.
*   There is no double tax treaty between the UK and Mersano.

Meyer:

*   Will work for Kraus Co in the country of Mersano from 15 December 2015 to 31 March 2016
*   Will continue to be employed by Spetz Ltd
*   Will continue to be resident and domiciled in the UK

The costs relating to Meyer's secondment to Kraus Co:

- Meyer will be reimbursed for the cost of the flights at the start and end of the contract.

- Meyer will return to the UK for a holiday in February 2016, and will pay his own transport costs.

- Meyer will be reimbursed for the cost of laundry and telephone calls home.

- Spetz Ltd does not have a Form P11D dispensation (PAYE dispensation) in place with HM Revenue and Customs.

Required

(a) Calculate the value added tax (VAT) partial exemption annual adjustment for Novak Ltd for the year ended 30 September 2015 and state when it must be reported to HM Revenue and Customs. You should state, with reasons, whether or not each of the three *de minimis* tests is satisfied. **(7 marks)**

(b) (i) Explain how to determine whether or not Kraus Co is resident in the UK. **(3 marks)**

    (ii) Explain, with supporting calculations, the UK corporation tax liability of Kraus Co for the year ended 30 September 2015 on the assumption that it is resident in the UK, and discuss the advantages and disadvantages of making an election to exempt its overseas profits from UK tax. **(5 marks)**

(c) Explain the UK income tax implications for Meyer of the costs relating to his secondment to Kraus Co.

(5 marks)

(Total = 20 marks)

Questions 36 to 41 cover impact of taxes and tax planning. These are the subject of Chapter 30 in the BPP Study Text.

36 Desiree (ATAX 06/10)   29 mins

Desiree requires advice on whether she should run her new business as an unincorporated sole trader or via a company together with the financial implications of registering voluntarily for value added tax (VAT).

The following information has been obtained from a meeting with Desiree.

Desiree:

- Was born in 1976
- Resigned from her job with Chip plc on 31 May 2015
- Had been employed by Chip plc on an annual salary of £72,000 since January 2012
- Has no other income apart from bank interest received of less than £1,000 per year
- Intends to start a new business, to be called Duchess, on 1 September 2015

The Duchess business:

- The business will sell kitchen equipment and utensils.
- Market research consultants have estimated that 80% of its sales will be to commercial customers.
- The consultants were paid fees in November 2014 and March 2015.

Budgeted results of the Duchess business:

- The budgeted tax-adjusted trading profit/(loss) for the first three trading periods are:

	£
Ten months ending 30 June 2016	(46,000)
Year ending 30 June 2017	22,000
Year ending 30 June 2018	64,000

- The fees paid to the market research consultants have been deducted in arriving at the loss of the first period.

Desiree's financial position:

- Desiree has not yet decided whether to run the business as an unincorporated sole trader or via a company.

- Her primary objective when deciding whether or not to operate the business via a company is the most beneficial use of the loss.

Registration for VAT:

- The turnover of the business is expected to exceed the VAT registration limit in January 2016.
- Desiree would consider registering for VAT earlier if it were financially advantageous to do so.

Required

(a) (i)   Calculate the taxable trading profit or allowable trading loss of the business for each of the first three taxable periods for the following alternative structures:

   –   The business is unincorporated
   –   The business is operated via a company   **(4 marks)**

   (ii)   Provide Desiree with a thorough and detailed explanation of the manner in which the budgeted trading loss could be used depending on whether she runs the business as an unincorporated sole trader or via a company and state which business structure would best satisfy her primary objective.

   Note. You are not required to prepare detailed calculations for part (ii) of this part of this question or to consider non-taxation issues.   **(8 marks)**

(b)   Explain in detail the financial advantages and disadvantages of Desiree registering voluntarily for VAT on 1 September 2015.   **(4 marks)**

You may assume that the tax rules and rates for 2014/15 will continue to apply for the foreseeable future.

(Total = 16 marks)

37 Poblano (ATAX 06/10)   **67 mins**

Your manager has had a meeting with Poblano. Poblano is the Finance Director of Capsicum Ltd, a subsidiary of Scoville plc. He is a higher rate taxpayer earning £60,000 per year with no other income. Scoville plc together with its subsidiaries and its directors have been clients of your firm for many years. The memorandum recording the matters discussed at the meeting and an extract from an email from your manager detailing the tasks for you to perform are set out below.

Memorandum recording matters discussed at meeting with Poblano

To	The files
From	Tax manager
Date	4 June 2015
Subject	Poblano

I had a meeting with Poblano on 3 June 2015.

(i)   **Working in Manchester**

Poblano was born in 1968. He currently lives and works in Birmingham. However, Capsicum Ltd has recently acquired the Manchester operations of the group from a fellow subsidiary of Scoville plc. As a result of this, Poblano is going to be based in Manchester from 1 August 2015 for a period of at least five years. He will be paid an additional £15,000 per year during this period.

Poblano does not want to relocate his family to Manchester for personal reasons. He has been offered the use of a furnished flat in Manchester belonging to Capsicum Ltd to live in during the week. He will drive home each weekend. Details of the company's flat are set out below.

	£
Current market value	555,000
Purchase price (1 June 2012)	415,000
Annual value	8,450
Monthly contribution required from Poblano	200

Alternatively, if he does not live in the flat, Capsicum Ltd will pay him a mileage allowance of 50 pence per mile to cover the cost of travelling to Manchester every Monday and returning home every Friday. During the week, whilst he is in Manchester, Poblano will stay with his aunt, paying her rent of £325 per month

Poblano estimates that he will drive 9,200 miles per year travelling to Manchester each week and that he will spend £1,400 per year on petrol. There would also be additional depreciation in respect of his car of approximately £1,500 per year. Capsicum Ltd has a policy of not providing its employees with company cars.

Poblano expects to be better off due to the increase in his salary. He wants to know how much better off he will be depending on whether he lives in the company flat or receives the mileage allowance and stays with his aunt.

(ii)   **Financial accounting problems in Manchester**

Poblano is aware that there are rules relating to the responsibility of senior accounting officers for taxation matters of a company. He asked me for a brief summary of the rules and whether or not they could apply to him in the future.

Poblano's interest in the new rules has been prompted by the review he has performed on the results of the Manchester operation for the year ended 30 September 2014. During that review Poblano identified a number of expenditure classification errors including capital expenditure in respect of improvements to the factory roof that had been classified as plant and machinery in the corporation tax return submitted to HM Revenue and Customs.

(iii) **Father's property in the country of Chilaca**

Paprikash (Poblano's father) owns a property in the country of Chilaca that he uses for holidays. It has always been intended that the property would be left to Poblano in his father's will. However, Paprikash has recently agreed to give the property to Poblano now, if to do so would make sense from a tax point of view. Paprikash may still wish to use the property occasionally in the future.

The property is currently worth £600,000. However, due to the economic situation in the country of Chilaca, it is possible that this figure could either rise or fall over the next few years.

Paprikash is domiciled in the UK and is a higher rate taxpayer. He is in poor health and is not expected to live for more than a further five years. His total assets, including the property in the country of Chilaca, are worth £2 million. Paprikash makes gifts on 1 May each year in order to use his annual exemption. His only other gift in the last seven years was to a trust on 1 June 2014. The gift consisted of a number of minority holdings of quoted shares valued at £290,000 in total. The trust is for the benefit of Poblano's daughter, Piri. It can be assumed that Paprikash will not make any further lifetime gifts.

There is no capital gains tax or inheritance tax in the country of Chilaca.

(iv) **Trust created for the benefit of Poblano's daughter**

The trust was created on 1 June 2014 as noted above. Poblano's daughter, Piri, received income from the trust for the first time in March 2015. Poblano did not have any further information on the trust and agreed to bring the relevant documentation to our next meeting. Piri's only other income is an annual salary of approximately £35,000.

Tax manager

Email from your manager

I want you to prepare notes for a meeting that we will both attend with Poblano. You will be leading the meeting. Set out the information so that it is easy for you to find what you need as we go through the various issues. Include the briefest possible notes where the numbers are not self-explanatory. The meeting notes need to include:

(i) **Working in Manchester**

- Calculations showing how much better (or worse) off Poblano will be under each of the alternatives as compared to his current position. If he is worse off under either of the alternatives, include a calculation of the amount of salary he would have to be paid, in addition to the £15,000, so that he is not out of pocket.

- An explanation of the tax treatment for the recipients of the mileage allowance to be paid to Poblano and the rent to be paid to his aunt

- Any further information required and the effect it could have on the calculations you have prepared

(ii) **Financial accounting problems in Manchester**

- The information requested by Poblano

- The further action required by the company and, potentially, ourselves in respect of the classification errors

(iii) **Father's property in the country of Chilaca**

- Calculations of the inheritance tax liability that will become due in respect of the property in the country of Chilaca depending on whether the property is gifted to Poblano on 1 August 2015 or via his father's will. You should assume the following:

  - His father, Paprikash, will die on either 31 December 2017 or 31 December 2019.

  - The property will be worth £600,000 on 1 August 2015.

  - Three possible values of the property at the date of Paprikash's death: £450,000, £600,000 and £900,000.

You should calculate the inheritance tax for each of the 12 possible situations on the property only assuming that Paprikash does not use the property after the date of the gift. You should start by calculating the tax on a lifetime gift with Paprikash's death on 31 December 2017. If you then think about the relationships between the different situations you should find that the calculations do not take too long. In order for the calculations to be comparable, when calculating the tax on the gift via Paprikash's will, you should assume that any available nil band is deductible from the property.

- Conclusions drawn from the calculations.

- Any other issues that we should draw to Poblano's attention.

(iv)   **Trust created for the benefit of Poblano's daughter**

- A summary of the tax treatment of the income received by Poblano's daughter Piri, as beneficiary, depending on the nature of the trust. I understand from Poblano that the only income of the trust is dividend income.

Required

Prepare the meeting notes requested in the email from your manager. The following marks are available.

(a)	Working in Manchester	**(10 marks)**
(b)	Financial accounting problems in Manchester	**(7 marks)**
(c)	Father's property in the country of Chilaca	**(12 marks)**
(d)	Trust created for the benefit of Poblano's daughter	**(6 marks)**

Professional marks will be awarded in this question for the appropriateness of the format and presentation of the notes and the effectiveness with which the information is communicated.   **(2 marks)**

You may assume that the tax rules and rates for 2014/15 will continue to apply for the foreseeable future.

(Total = 37 marks)

38 Dokham (ATAX 06/10)   29 mins

Dokham requires advice on his pension position at retirement, the rules relating to enterprise management incentive (EMI) schemes and the tax implications of his mother helping to pay his children's school fees.

The following information has been obtained from a telephone conversation with Dokham.

Dokham:

- Was born in 1975 and is married with two children
- Is domiciled and resident in the UK
- Has been offered a job by Criollo plc
- His mother, Virginia, has offered to contribute towards Dokham's children's school fees

The job offer from Criollo plc:

- Dokham's salary will be £70,000 per year.
- Criollo plc will make annual contributions of £8,000 into Dokham's personal pension scheme.
- Criollo plc will invite Dokham to join the company's EMI scheme.

Dokham's pension arrangements:

- Dokham has not made any pension contributions to date and has not been a member of a pension scheme.
- Dokham intends to make gross annual contributions of £11,000 into a registered personal pension scheme.

The EMI scheme:

- The scheme will have five members including Dokham.

- Criollo plc will grant Dokham an option to purchase 26,185 shares at a price of £9.00 per share. This will represent a holding of less than 1% of the company.

- The option can be exercised at any time until 31 December 2020.

- Criollo plc's current share price is £9.53.

Dokham has requested explanations of the following in respect of the job offer from Criollo plc:

- What would be the difference for me, from a tax point of view, if Criollo plc increased my salary by £8,000 instead of contributing into my personal pension scheme and I made additional gross annual pension contributions of £8,000?

- What benefits will I receive from the pension scheme, how will they be taxed and when can I receive them?

- Why might Criollo plc have told me that it is 'not possible' to increase the number of shares I can purchase within the EMI scheme?

- What are the tax implications for me when I exercise my EMI share option and when I sell the shares? I hope to continue to work for Criollo plc even after selling my shares.

Virginia:

- Was born in 1946
- Is domiciled and resident in the UK
- Has taxable income of more than £120,000 per year
- Owns a portfolio of quoted shares that is worth more than £500,000
- Uses her capital gains tax annual exempt amount and inheritance tax annual exemption every year
- Is considering three alternative ways of contributing towards Dokham's children's school fees

The three alternative ways of contributing towards the children's school fees:

- Make a one-off gift to Dokham of £54,000 in cash

- Make a one-off gift to Dokham of 9,800 shares (a holding of less than 1%) in Panatella plc, a quoted company, worth £54,000

- Make a gift to Dokham of £8,000 in cash every year for the next seven years

Required

(a) Provide the information requested by Dokham in respect of the job offer from Criollo plc as set out above.

(9 marks)

(b) Explain in detail the possible tax liabilities that could result from the three alternative ways proposed by Virginia to contribute towards the children's school fees.

(7 marks)

You may assume that the tax rules and rates for 2014/15 will continue to apply for the foreseeable future.

(Total = 16 marks)

39 Robusto Ltd (ATAX 12/10)

31 mins

Robusto Ltd, a partially exempt company for the purposes of value added tax (VAT), requires advice on the cost of purchasing services from various suppliers and an explanation of the implications if the relationship between the company and the person providing the services is one of employer and employee.

The following information was obtained during a meeting with the managing director of Robusto Ltd.

Robusto Ltd – Budgeted results for the year ending 31 March 2016:

•	Turnover (exclusive of VAT):	£
	Standard rated	850,000
	Exempt	330,000
	Zero rated	120,000

- The irrecoverable VAT for the year will exceed the *de minimis* limits.
- Robusto Ltd is growing quickly and intends to purchase market analysis services relating to all aspects of its business.

Potential providers of market analysis services:

- There are three potential service providers: Cognac Ltd, Fonseca Inc and Pisco.
- Robusto Ltd will use the provider that results in the lowest cost to the company.
- Alternatively, Robusto Ltd will take on a new employee to carry out the market analysis.

Cognac Ltd:

- Cognac Ltd is a UK resident company wholly owned by Offley, a UK resident individual.
- Offley is the company's only employee.
- Offley would be contractually obliged to perform all of the market analysis services provided by Cognac Ltd.
- Cognac Ltd would charge a fixed fee of £28,500 plus VAT.

Fonseca Inc:

- Fonseca Inc is a company resident in the country of Parejo.
- The country of Parejo is not a member of the European Union.
- Fonseca Inc would charge a fixed fee of £29,000.

Pisco:

- Pisco is a UK resident unincorporated sole trader who is not registered for VAT.
- Pisco would charge a fixed fee of £29,500.

Required

(a) In respect of the market analysis services:

- Explain, with the aid of supporting calculations, which service provider would result in the lowest cost to Robusto Ltd.

- Calculate the maximum salary that could be paid by Robusto Ltd to an employee such that the total cost would be no more than that of the cheapest service provider. You should assume that Robusto Ltd has other employees such that the employment allowance is already utilised against the secondary Class 1 national insurance contributions for these employees. **(9 marks)**

(b) On the assumption that the services are purchased from Pisco, give **three** examples of specific contractual arrangements that would assist HM Revenue and Customs in arguing that the relationship between Robusto Ltd and Pisco is that of employer and employee. **(3 marks)**

(c) On the assumption that HM Revenue and Customs could successfully argue that the relationship between Robusto Ltd and the individual carrying out the market analysis services, Offley or Pisco, is one of employer and employee:

- Explain the tax implications for Robusto Ltd and Cognac Ltd if the services are purchased from Cognac Ltd.

- Explain why Robusto Ltd might prefer to offer the contract to Cognac Ltd rather than to Pisco.

Note. You are not required to prepare any calculations for part (c) of this question or to describe in detail how any deemed salary payment would be calculated. **(5 marks)**

You should assume that the tax rates and allowances of the tax year 2014/15 and for the Financial Year to 31 March 2015 will continue to apply for the foreseeable future.

(Total = 17 marks)

40 Tetra (ATAX 06/12)   32 mins

Tetra has recently been made redundant and joined a trading partnership. He requires advice on the redundancy payments he has received, a potential investment in a venture capital trust and on making pension contributions. He has also asked for a calculation of his class 4 national insurance contributions in respect of his income from the partnership.

Tetra:

- Was born in 1970
- Was made redundant by Ivy Ltd on 31 March 2015
- Became a partner in the Winston partnership on 1 June 2015
- Is considering two alternatives investments

Redundancy payments made by Ivy Ltd to Tetra:

- Statutory redundancy of £4,200
- A non-contractual payment of £46,000 as compensation for loss of office
- £7,000 in consideration of Tetra agreeing not to work for any competitor of Ivy Ltd for 12 months

The Winston Partnership:

- Prior to 1 June 2015, there were two partners in the partnership: Zia and Fore.
- Budgeted tax adjusted trading profits of the partnership:

  - Year ending 31 December 2015 – £300,000
  - Year ending 31 December 2016 – £380,000

- Profit sharing arrangements

		Zia	Fore	Tetra
Up to 31 May 2015	– Profit share	60%	40%	N/A
From 1 June 2015	– Annual salary	–	£24,000	£18,000
	– Profit share	40%	30%	30%

Two alternative investments:

- In the tax year 2015/16 Tetra will either:
  subscribe £28,000 for shares in a venture capital trust; or
  make a payment of £28,000 to a registered personal pension fund.

Required

(a)   Explain briefly whether or not the redundancy payments made by Ivy Ltd to Tetra are subject to income tax.
(3 marks)

(b)   Calculate the class 4 national insurance contributions payable by Tetra for the tax year 2015/16.   **(7 marks)**

(c)   Compare the effect of the two alternative investments on Tetra's income tax liability for the tax year 2015/16 and identify any non-tax matters relevant to the investment decision of which he should be aware.

   Note. For part (c) of this question it should be assumed that Tetra's net income in the tax year 2015/16 (before deduction of the personal allowance) will be £125,000, none of which is savings income or dividend income.   **(8 marks)**

You should assume that the tax rates and allowances for the tax year 2014/15 will continue to apply for the foreseeable future.

(Total = 18 marks)

41 FL Partnership (ATAX 12/13)   63 mins

Your manager has had a meeting with Farina and Lauda, potential new clients, who are partners in the FL Partnership. The memorandum recording the matters discussed, together with an email from your manager, is set out below.

Memorandum

To: The Files
From: Tax manager
Date: 5 December 2015
Subject: FL Partnership

Background

Farina and Lauda began trading as the FL Partnership on 1 May 2010. Accounts have always been prepared to 31 March each year. They are each entitled to 50% of the revenue profits and capital profits of the business.

On 1 March 2016, the whole of the FL Partnership business will be sold as a going concern to JH plc, a quoted trading company. The consideration for the sale will be a mixture of cash and shares. Capital gains tax relief on the transfer of a business to a company (incorporation relief) will be available in respect of the sale.

Farina and Lauda will both pay income tax at the additional rate in the tax year 2015/16 and anticipate continuing to do so in future years. They are very wealthy individuals, who use their capital gains tax annual exempt amounts every year. Both of them are resident and domiciled in the UK.

The sale of the business on 1 March 2016

The assets of the FL Partnership business have been valued as set out below. All of the equipment qualified for capital allowances.

	Value £	Cost £
Goodwill	1,300,000	Nil
Inventory and receivables	30,000	30,000
Equipment (no item to be sold for more than cost)	150,000	200,000
Total	1,480,000	

The total value of the consideration will be equal to the value of the assets sold. Farina and Lauda will each receive consideration of £740,000; £140,000 in cash and 200,000 shares in JH plc. Following the purchase of the FL Partnership, JH plc will have an issued share capital of 8,400,000 shares.

Future transactions

Farina:

On 1 August 2016, Farina will make a gift of 15,000 of her shares in JH plc to the trustees of a discretionary (relevant property) trust for the benefit of her nieces and nephews. Farina will pay any inheritance tax liability in respect of this gift. The trustees will transfer the shares to the beneficiaries over the life of the trust.

Lauda:

On 1 June 2017, Lauda will give 40,000 of her shares in JH plc to her son.

For the purposes of giving our advice, the value of a share in JH plc can be assumed to be:

	£
On 1 March 2016	3
On 1 August 2016	4
On 1 June 2017	5

Email from your manager

I want you to prepare a memorandum for the client file in respect of the following:

(i) **Capital allowances**

A DETAILED explanation of the calculation of the capital allowances of the FL Partnership for its final trading period ending with the sale of its equipment to JH plc for £150,000 on 1 March 2016.

(ii) **Farina**

BRIEF explanations of:

(1) The manner in which any inheritance tax payable by Farina in her lifetime in respect of the gift of the shares to the trustees of the discretionary (relevant property) trust will be calculated and the date on which the tax would be payable.

(2) The availability of capital gains tax gift relief in respect of the transfer of the shares to the trustees of the discretionary (relevant property) trust and the subsequent transfers of shares from the trustees to the beneficiaries.

(iii) **Lauda**

A review of whether or not Lauda should disclaim incorporation relief.

The review should encompass the sale of the FL Partnership business, the gift of the shares to Lauda's son and the effect of incorporation relief on the base cost of the remaining shares owned by Lauda, as she intends to sell all of her shares in JH plc in the next few years.

It is important that you include a summary of your calculations and a statement of the key issues for me to discuss with Lauda. You should also include BRIEF explanations of the amount of incorporation relief available, the availability of any additional or alternative reliefs, and the date(s) on which any capital gains tax will be payable.

Tax manager

Required

(a) It is anticipated that Farina and Lauda will require some highly sophisticated and specialised tax planning work in the future.

Prepare a summary of the information which would be required, together with any action(s) which should be taken by the firm before it agrees to become the tax advisers to Farina and Lauda. **(5 marks)**

(b) Prepare the memorandum requested in the email from your manager. The following marks are available:

(i) Capital allowances **(5 marks)**
(ii) Farina **(7 marks)**
(iii) Lauda **(14 marks)**

Note. Ignore value added tax (VAT).

Professional marks will be awarded in part (b) for the overall presentation of the memorandum, the provision of relevant advice and the effectiveness with which the information is communicated. **(4 marks)**

(Total = 35 marks)

Answers

1 Styrax

Marking scheme

				Marks
(a)	(i)	Salvia's PA wasted	1	
		Styrax needs to transfer income	1	
		Employment of Salvia	1	
		Tax savings	2	
		Use of NISAs	2	
		Tax savings	1	
				8
	(ii)	Personal pension provision	1	
		Maximum contributions	1	
		Occupational scheme	1	
		Suitability	1	
		Max		3
(b)		*Enterprise Investment Scheme*		
		Aim of scheme	1	
		Income tax reducer	2	
		Carry back	1	
		Withdrawal of relief	1	
		Risk	1	
		Seed Enterprise Investment Scheme		
		Aim of scheme	1	
		Income tax reducer	2	
		Withdrawal of relief	1	
		Risk	1	
		Venture Capital Scheme		
		Aim of scheme	1	
		Income tax reducer	1	
		Dividends	1	
		Withdrawal of relief	1	
		Risk	1	
				16
				27

(a) (i) **Notes for meeting with Styrax**

Use of Salvia's personal allowance

Now that Salvia has given up employed work, she does not have any source of income. This means that her personal allowance (£10,000) is being wasted. It is not possible to transfer the benefit of this to Styrax. Therefore, Styrax needs to transfer some of his income to Salvia. Styrax could do this by employing Salvia in his business (the question states that she does not want to be a partner so this is not considered).

Salvia's salary must be commercially justifiable for the work that she will do. Styrax will then be able to deduct the salary from his trading profits. This will save income tax at 20% and also reduce his Class 4 NICs at 9%.

A salary up to the income tax personal allowance of £10,000 will be free of income tax and a salary up to the national insurance contributions thresholds of £7,956 will also be free of Class 1 NICs for both Salvia as employee and Styrax as employer. A salary of up to £7,956 will therefore save tax and NICs of 29%.

If Styrax were to pay anything above the level of the personal allowance to Salvia, this would be subject to 20% income tax and 12% employee Class 1 NICs in the hands of Salvia. Styrax will also have to pay 13.8% employer Class 1 NICs. Therefore the overall tax rate is 45.8%. However, Styrax would also save income tax and NICs at approximately the rate of 33% (income tax of 20%, Class 4 NICs at 9%, and income tax and Class 4 NICs on the employer's Class 1 contributions which would be 13.8% × (20% + 9%) = 4%). Therefore, it would not be advantageous to pay this additional amount as the overall additional tax is more than the tax saving.

Therefore if the salary exceeded the personal allowance for Salvia, this would not be tax efficient as both Styrax and Salvia would be basic rate tax payers and the Class 1 NIC costs would outweigh the tax saving for Styrax.

Savings income

The couple should take advantage of New Individual Savings Accounts.

Each of them can invest up to £15,000 per tax year in cash, stocks and shares, or a combination of each. The income generated by the accounts is tax free as are any gains on shares.

Since the couple are risk adverse, shares are not a suitable investment for them. Each of them should open an NISA and invest the maximum amount allowable in cash. (Styrax would need to transfer £15,000 to Salvia.) This would save income tax on their interest income of £30,000/35,000 × £1,000 × 20% = £171.

(ii) **Future pension provision**

Styrax and Salvia could both start personal pensions.

The maximum tax relievable contributions that Styrax could make would be the higher of:

(1) £3,600
(2) The amount of his earnings

Salvia could make contributions up to £3,600 even though she has no earnings (unless she becomes employed by Styrax).

Alternatively, if Salvia becomes an employee of Styrax, he could set up an occupational pension scheme for her.

Since the couple only have disposable income of £3,000 per year, they would probably not wish to spend all of it on pension provision! Possibly both of them could try to invest a small amount per month (say £50).

(b)   **Memorandum**

Enterprise Investment Scheme

The Enterprise Investment Scheme (EIS) is designed to promote enterprise and investment. It helps such high-risk, unlisted trading companies raise finance by issuing new shares (usually ordinary shares) to unconnected individuals.

If you subscribe for EIS shares you can claim a tax reduction of the lower of:

(i)   30% of the amount subscribed for qualifying investments (maximum qualifying investments are £1,000,000 in 2014/15)

(ii)   Your tax liability for the year after deducting VCT relief (described below)

For example, if you subscribed the maximum of £1,000,000, you could claim a tax reduction of £1,000,000 × 30% = £300,000. However, if your tax liability is less than £300,000, you can only bring that liability down to nil.

You can also claim to treat all or any of the shares as being issued in 2013/14, instead of 2014/15 and thus claim a tax reducer in 2013/14 instead of 2014/15.

You must hold the shares for at least three years if the income tax relief is not to be withdrawn or reduced. The main reason for the withdrawal of relief will be the sale of the shares by you within the three year period mentioned above.

EIS investments are high risk because there is total exposure to unquoted companies engaged in risky trades.

Seed Enterprise Investment Scheme (SEIS)

This is similar to the EIS but is designed to encourage investment into small early stage companies.

If you subscribe for SEIS shares you can claim a tax reduction of the lower of:

(i)   50% of the amount subscribed for qualifying investments (maximum qualifying investments are £100,000 in 2014/15)

(ii)   Your tax liability for the year after deducting VCT relief and EIS relief

The maximum tax reducer under the SEIS is therefore £100,000 × 50% = £50,000.

You can also claim to treat all or any of the shares as being issued in 2013/14, instead of 2014/15 and thus claim a tax reducer in 2013/14 instead of 2014/15.

The same rules apply to SEIS as for EIS concerning the three year holding period to avoid withdrawal or reduction of the relief.

SEIS investments are even more high risk than EIS investments as the companies in which investments are made are small, start up companies.

Venture capital trusts (VCTs)

Venture capital trusts (VCTs) are listed companies which invest in unquoted trading companies and meet certain conditions.

If you invest in a VCT, you will obtain the following income tax benefits on a maximum qualifying investment of £200,000 in 2014/15:

(i)   A tax reduction of 30% of the amount invested

(ii)   Dividends received are tax-free income

You must hold the shares for at least five years if the income tax relief is not to be withdrawn or reduced. The main reason for the withdrawal of relief will be the sale of the shares by you within five years of acquisition.

The VCT scheme differs from EIS or SEIS in that you can spread your risk over a number of higher-risk, unquoted companies. However, it is still a moderately high risk investment.

2 Spike (ATAX 06/13)

Text references. Loss relief is covered in Chapter 8. Chargeable gains, including the rates of CGT, are to be found in Chapter 11. Share options are dealt with in Chapter 5. Employment income is the subject of Chapter 4.

Top tips. It is important to realise that the trading loss which can be relieved against general income (and gains) is computed differently from the terminal loss.

Easy marks. There were some easy marks in part (b)(i) for explaining the gain on the disposal of the shares and also in part (b)(ii) in respect of the relocation expenses.

Examiner's comments. Part (a) concerned losses realised on a cessation of trade and was in two parts. Part (a)(i) was short and direct; it was intended to ensure that all candidates attempting this question addressed the two possibilities that needed to be considered when they went on to part (a)(ii) and had to explain the reliefs available in respect of the loss. In part (a)(i) candidates were required to calculate the trading loss in the year of cessation and the terminal loss of the last 12 months. Very few candidates made a reasonable job of this; the majority of candidates simply did not know the rules. Accordingly, many candidates simply did not appreciate the difference between the loss of the tax year and the terminal loss. Of those candidates who were aware that the terminal loss is calculated in its own particular way, very few knew how to do it. In addition, many candidates deducted the overlap profits from the loss rather than using them to increase the loss. In part (a)(ii) things did not really improve. Although many candidates were aware that there was the possibility of carrying back a loss on cessation to the three years prior to the loss, there was a general lack of precision as regards the rules and a confused approach to the figures. When dealing with losses, there are only really two things that need to be known: the years in which the losses can be offset and the type of income or gains that the losses can be offset against. Marks were available in part (a)(ii) for knowing these fundamental rules but they were not awarded as frequently as one might have expected. The approach of most candidates to part (a)(ii) was not as measured or considered as was necessary. Candidates would have benefited from clearly defining the possibilities in their minds and then writing brief, precise points that addressed each of the possibilities. Instead, most candidates wrote too much that was confused and often contradictory. In addition, because they did not give themselves sufficient time to consider the possibilities, many candidates did not consider the possibility of relieving the capital gains. Those that did often did so in general terms as opposed to addressing the particular gains in the question.

Part (b) was in two parts and concerned share options and a relocation payment. It was done reasonably well. Part (b)(i) concerned the tax implications of the grant and exercise of a non-tax advantaged option to purchase shares and the eventual sale of the shares. The question made it clear that the option was not part of a tax advantaged scheme and it was important that candidates identified this point. There were many satisfactory answers to this question but also many unsatisfactory ones. The candidates who did well tended to be those who were better organised and were methodical in their approach. In particular, the requirement listed the three matters to address: the grant, exercise and sale of the shares. Some candidates did not address all three of these matters, making it much more difficult to pass this part of the question. Part (b)(ii) concerned the £8,000 exemption available in respect of relocation costs and was answered well.

					Marks
(a)	(i)	Loss for the tax year 2014/15		1	
		Terminal loss		3	
					4
	(ii)	Relief of the loss for the tax year 2014/15			
		The reliefs available		2	
		Tax savings 2014/15			
		Business assets		1½	
		House		2	
		Tax savings 2013/14		1	
		Relief of the terminal loss			
		The reliefs available		3	
		Tax savings – terminal loss		1	
		Tax savings – excess of trading loss over terminal loss		1½	
			Max		10
(b)	(i)	Grant		1	
		Exercise		2	
		Sale of shares		2	
			Max		4
	(ii)	Relocation payment			2
					20

(a) (i) **Loss relief available on the cessation of the trade**

Trading loss for the tax year 2014/15

	£
Loss for the period from 1 January 2014 to 30 September 2014	13,500
Add: overlap profits	8,300
Trading loss 2014/15	21,800

Tutorial note

The basis period for the tax year 2014/15 runs from 1 January 2014 (the end of the basis period for the previous year) until 30 September 2014 (the cessation of trade).

Terminal loss

	£	£
6 April 2014 to 30 September 2014		
Loss £13,500 × 6/9		9,000
Add: overlap profits		8,300
		17,300
1 October 2013 to 5 April 2014		
1 October 2013 to 31 December 2013		
Profit £24,395 × 3/12	6,099	
1 January 2014 to 5 April 2014		
Loss £13,500 × 3/9	(4,500)	
Net profit ignored for the purposes of terminal loss	1,599	
		0
Terminal loss		17,300

(ii)   **The reliefs available in respect of the trading loss and the terminal loss**

Relief of the loss for the tax year 2014/15

The loss for the tax year 2014/15 can be offset against Spike's general income of 2014/15 and/or 2013/14.

Once the loss has been offset against the general income of a particular tax year, it can also be offset against the capital gains of that same year.

Spike has no general income in the tax year 2014/15. But, a claim can be made for the whole of the loss to be relieved against his 2014/15 capital gains. Relieving the loss against the gains on the sale of the business assets would save capital gains tax at the rate of 10% due to the availability of entrepreneurs' relief. The tax saved would be £21,800 × 10% = £2,180.

Spike's sale of his house will be an exempt disposal of his principal private residence if he has always occupied it, or is deemed to have always occupied it. If part of the gain on the house is taxable, capital gains tax will be payable at 28% because the gains on the business assets will have used the basic rate band. Accordingly, if this is the case, the loss should be offset against any gain on the house in priority to the gain on the business assets.

In the tax year 2013/14, the loss would be offset against the general income of £24,395. The claim cannot be restricted in order to obtain relief for the personal allowance of that year. The tax saved would be (£(24,395 − 10,000) = £14,395) × 20% = £2,879.

Relief of the terminal loss

The terminal loss can be offset against the trading profit of the business for 2014/15 and the three preceding tax years, starting with the latest year.

The trading profit in the tax year 2014/15 is nil, such that the terminal loss will be relieved in the tax year 2013/14. This would save tax of (£(24,395 − 10,000) = £14,395) × 20% = £2,879.

The excess of the trading loss of 2014/15 over the terminal loss is £(21,800 − 17,300) = £4,500. This amount can be offset against general income and capital gains in 2014/15 and 2013/14 as set out above. However, once the terminal loss has been relieved in the tax year 2013/14, Spike's remaining general income of £(24,395 − 17,300) = £7,095 is less than the personal allowance, thus there is no taxable income and, therefore, no further tax saving to be achieved in either of the two relevant years. Accordingly, the remaining loss should be relieved against the capital gains of 2014/15. This would save tax of £4,500 × 10% = £450 if the loss is relieved against the gains on the sale of the business, or £4,500 × 28% = £1,260 if it is relieved against a non-exempt gain arising on the sale of the house.

(b)   (i)   **The option to purchase ordinary shares in Set Ltd**

There will be no tax liability in respect of the grant of the option.

When Spike exercises the option and acquires the shares, he will be subject to income tax on the excess of the market value of the shares at that time over the price paid for the option and the shares, ie £(8.00 − 0.50 − 4.00) = £3.50 per share. Accordingly, there will be an income tax liability of 7,000 × £3.50 × 40% = £9,800 when the option is exercised on the assumption that Spike continues to be a higher rate taxpayer.

On the sale of the shares, the excess of the sales proceeds per share over £8.00 (the market value of the shares when the option was exercised) will be taxed as a capital gain. The capital gain, less the annual exempt amount, will be subject to capital gains tax at 28% on the assumption that Spike continues to be a higher rate taxpayer. Entrepreneurs' relief will not be available unless Spike has acquired more shares, such that he owns at least 5% of the company's share capital.

(ii)   **The relocation payment**

The compensation in respect of the sale of the house at short notice at a low price will be regarded as having been derived from employment, such that it will be taxable in full. £8,000 of the payment in respect of the costs of moving house will be exempt; the remaining £(11,500 − 8,000) = £3,500 of the payment will be taxable.

3 Vine (ATAX 06/10)

Text references. Capital allowances are covered in Chapter 7. Reliefs for chargeable gains are dealt with in Chapter 13. Employment income is covered in Chapter 4.

Top tips. Although P6 is primarily a tax exam, you also need to think through the practicalities of any suggestions which you make to reduce or defer tax liabilities. The questions are scenarios which show situations which might arise in the real world and you must demonstrate an awareness of commercial and personal factors as well as technical tax knowledge.

Easy marks. The calculation of the gain in part (b) and incorporation relief should have been well-known and provided easy marks.

Examiner's comments. Part (a) was not done particularly well. Many candidates thought that on incorporation the assets would be transferred to the company at tax written down value whereas the correct position is that a balancing charge would arise unless a succession election were entered into. A number of candidates wrote that a balancing charge or a balancing allowance would arise when it was clear from the facts that it would be a balancing charge.

Common errors in part (b) included calculating a capital loss on the equipment (not available due to the availability of capital allowances). The quality of the answers to this part of the question depended on the clarity of the candidates' knowledge. There were many candidates who knew how to perform the necessary calculations and whose only common error was the failure to deduct the gain relieved on incorporation from the base cost of the shares. There was then another group of candidates who had no clear knowledge of the rules and consequently did not score well. Candidates were asked to suggest a minor change in relation to the sale of shares that would reduce the chargeable gain. Suggestions needed to be sensible and commercial and not, as put forward by a number of candidates, 'reduce the selling price of the shares'.

In the final part of the question, candidates were asked to outline the tax implications for the company and its employees of the various benefits. There were three benefits, so all answers should have consisted of six brief elements. Unfortunately, most answers were not that well organised with candidates addressing the issues in what was often a haphazard manner such that they did not score as well as they could have done.

Marking scheme

			Marks
(a)	Transfer of equipment	2½	
	False ceiling	2	
	Max		4
(b)	Incorporation		
	Gains arising	2	
	Calculation of the loan amount	3	
	Gain on sale of the shares	2	
	Entrepreneurs' relief	2	
	Max		8
(c)	Passata Ltd	1	
	Employees		
	Road bicycles	1	
	Mileage allowance for own bicycles	1½	
	Stationary bicycles	1	
	Max		4
			16

(a) **Capital allowances**

The transfer of the equipment to Passata Ltd

The market value of the equipment exceeds its tax written down value such that a sale would normally result in additional taxable income for Vine in the form of a balancing charge. However, because Vine and Passata Ltd will be connected persons (Vine will control Passata Ltd), an election is available to transfer the equipment at tax written down value such that no balancing charge will arise.

The false ceiling to be installed in the supermarket premises

For the purposes of capital allowances, the meaning of the term machinery is taken to be its ordinary, everyday meaning. The meaning of the term plant has been considered in many cases and certain items are dealt with by statute.

Case law tends to draw a distinction between items that perform a function in the operation of the business, and may therefore be plant, and those which comprise the setting in which the business is carried on, which are not plant. It has been held that a false ceiling does not perform a function but is merely part of the setting in which the business is carried on. Accordingly, the false ceiling will not qualify as plant and machinery.

(b) **The proposed sale of the shares to the store manager**

Chargeable gain on sale of shares to store manager

	£
Proceeds	64,000
Less cost (W1) £187,614 × 20%	(37,523)
Chargeable gain	26,477

Entrepreneurs' relief

Entrepreneurs' relief would reduce the rate of tax on the gain from 18% or 28% to 10%. However, it is only available if the shares have been owned for at least a year which does not apply in this case since Vine will only acquire the shares on 31 July 2015. Accordingly, Vine should delay the sale until August 2016 in order to qualify for the relief.

Workings

1 Base cost of the shares

	£
Value of the business transferred	320,000
Less amount left on loan account (W2)	(70,886)
Market value of shares received on incorporation	249,114
Less gain deferred 249,114/320,000 × £79,000 (W3)	(61,500)
Base cost of shares for future disposals	187,614

2 Amount left on loan account

	£
Value of the business transferred	320,000
Less required to be in the form of shares	
61,500/79,000 (W3) × £320,000	(249,114)
Amount left on loan account	70,886

3 Gain deferred under incorporation relief

	£
Gains on assets transferred	
Premises £(260,000 – 205,000)	55,000
Goodwill	24,000
Total gains	79,000
Less capital loss available	(6,500)
Less annual exempt amount	(11,000)
Gain to be deferred	61,500

(c)   **The tax implications of the active supermarket marketing strategy**

Passata Ltd

The cost of all of the bicycles will qualify for capital allowances.

The mileage allowance paid to employees will be a tax allowable expense.

Employees

The loan of the road bicycles will not give rise to a taxable benefit provided they are used mainly for travel to and from work and for business purposes.

A tax-free mileage allowance of up to 20 pence per mile can be paid to employees who use their own bicycles for business purposes. The employees of Passata Ltd will be entitled to a tax deduction from their employment income if the company pays them less than this amount. Accordingly, with the mileage rate set at 15 pence per mile, they will be entitled to a tax deduction of five pence per business mile cycled.

The provision of sport or recreational facilities to employees (not available to the public), such as the stationary bicycles, does not give rise to a taxable benefit.

4 Ziti (ATAX 06/14)

Text references. Trade profits are covered in Chapter 6 and capital allowances in Chapter 7. The income tax computation is dealt with in Chapter 1. Capital gains tax computations are covered in Chapter 11 and reliefs in Chapter 13. Value added tax on land and buildings is dealt with in Chapter 29 and the conditions for transfer of a going concern in Chapter 30. Inheritance tax on lifetime transfers is covered in Chapter 16 and business property relief in Chapter 17.

Top tips. It is important to adopt a methodical approach to questions where there are alternative dates for actions. First, work out the income tax position for a cessation on 31 January 2016 and, second, the position for a cessation on 30 April 2016. Then repeat for the capital gains tax disposals. As required in the question, finally bring the computations together in a summary.

Easy marks. There were some easy marks for basic income tax computations in part (a)(i) and inheritance tax computations in part (b).

Examiner's comments. Part (a)(i) was quite substantial and was worth 17 marks. Stronger candidates structured their answers in such a way that it was very clear which of the possible methods of disposal they were addressing and then dealt with the two methods one at a time. Weaker candidates did not spend sufficient time thinking about the facts of the question and simply dealt with a disposal without making it clear which of the possibilities they were considering. The income tax aspects of the disposal revolved around the closing year rules for the unincorporated trader. It was important to be able to identify the tax years of the proposed disposal and the basis of assessment for each of the relevant years. Many candidates did not have a clear understanding of these basic rules, such that they were not able to identify the relevant tax years or to accurately calculate the taxable profits for each of the relevant tax years. The trader had purchased equipment, which was then to be sold on the cessation of the business. Most candidates identified the annual investment allowance (AIA) but many then omitted to follow the story through to the disposal, such that the balancing charge was left out. In addition, weaker candidates prepared comprehensive (and time-consuming) calculations of capital allowances in order to arrive at an AIA of £6,000. The treatment of overlap profits, the personal allowance and the calculation of income tax was done well by the vast majority of candidates. The capital gains tax implications of the sale of the business were straightforward and were handled reasonably well. However, one common error was to treat the sale of the business as if it were a sale of a single asset as opposed to a sale of the individual assets of the business. Many candidates concluded that the capital gains tax implications were the same regardless of which of the methods of disposal took place. However, this was not the case because there was a disposal of goodwill only where the business was sold as a going concern. Finally, candidates were required to prepare a summary. In order to score the maximum three marks available, candidates had to include the trading income and the proceeds from the sale of the assets together with both the income tax and the capital gains tax. It was also important to exclude any non-cash items. Very few candidates managed to score all three marks; and many candidates failed to produce any sort of summary.

Part (a)(ii) concerned the VAT implications of the disposal. This was handled well by the majority of candidates with many candidates demonstrating a good knowledge of the various conditions necessary for a sale to be regarded as a transfer of a going concern.

Part (b) concerned the basic mechanics of inheritance tax; it was done well by many candidates. Almost all candidates identified the gift of the business as a potentially exempt transfer that would become chargeable following the death of the donor within seven years. They were also competent at dealing with the annual exemptions, the nil rate band (with one exception – see below), the tax rate and taper relief. The one area where a lot of candidates did not perform as well was when it came to business property relief (BPR). To begin with, many candidates omitted BPR altogether. Those candidates who did include BPR in their answers often failed to realise that if the business was sold by Ziti (the donee) before the death of his father (the donor), BPR would not be available because the rules require the donee to own the assets gifted at the date of the donor's death. The point referred to above regarding the nil rate band relates to the relevance of the chargeable lifetime transfer (CLT) made by the donor of the business on 1 May 2007. It was thought by some candidates that this gift would have no effect on the nil rate band available as it was more than seven years prior to the death of the donor. However, because the CLT was made within seven years of the gift of the business on 1 July 2011, the nil rate band available when calculating the tax due in respect of the gift of the business has to be reduced by the amount of the CLT.

Marking scheme

				Marks
(a)	(i)	Income tax position		
		Cessation on 31 January 2016		
		Trading income	1	
		Capital allowances	1½	
		Overlap profits	½	
		Basis period	1	
		Income tax payable	1	
		Cessation on 30 April 2016		
		Basis period	1	
		Trading income	½	
		Capital allowances	1½	
		Overlap profits	½	
		Income tax payable	1	
		Capital gains tax position		
		Cessation on 31 January 2016		
		Capital gains	2	
		Capital gains tax	1	
		Availability of entrepreneurs' relief	1	
		Cessation on 30 April 2016		
		Capital gains	½	
		Capital gains tax	½	
		Availability of entrepreneurs' relief	1	
		Summary	3	
		Assumption	1	
		Max		17
	(ii)	Sale on 31 January 2016	1½	
		Sale on 30 April 2015		
		Charge VAT unless TOGC	1	
		TOGC conditions	3	
		Max		5

			Marks
(b)	Death prior to disposal of business	2	
	Death post disposal of business		
	Value of transfer	1½	
	Annual exemptions	1	
	Business property relief not available	1½	
	Taper relief	1	
	Nil rate band available	1½	
	Inheritance tax liabilities	2	
	Max		9
Approach to problem solving		1	
Clarity of calculations		1	
Effectiveness of communication		1	
Overall presentation		1	
			4
			35

Notes for meeting

Prepared by: Tax senior
Date: 6 June 2015
Subject: Ziti – sale of business and inheritance tax

(a) **Sale of business**

    (i) **Post-tax income and sales proceeds**

        Income tax position

        Business cessation on 31 January 2016

        Taxable trading profits

        Y/e 30.4.15

	£
Profits 12 × £5,000	60,000
Less: annual investment allowance on equipment 1.8.14	(6,000)
Taxable trading profits	54,000

        P/e 31.1.16

	£
Profits 9 × £5,000	45,000
Add: balancing charge on equipment £(0 – 10,000)	10,000
Less: overlap profit on commencement	(9,000)
Taxable trading profits	46,000

        Income tax 2015/16

        Final year of trading: basis period 1 May 2014 to 31 January 2016.

	£
Trading income £(54,000 + 46,000)/Net income	100,000
Less: personal allowance	(10,000)
Taxable income	90,000

		£
Income tax:		
£31,865 @ 20%		6,373
£58,135 @ 40%		23,254
Income tax liability		29,627

Business cessation on 30 April 2016

Taxable trading profits

Y/e 30.4.15

	£
As above	54,000

Y/e 30.4.16

	£
Profits 12 × £5,000	60,000
Add: balancing charge on equipment £(0 – 10,000)	10,000
Less: overlap profit on commencement	(9,000)
Taxable trading profits	61,000

Income tax 2015/16

Current year basis: basis period 1 May 2014 to 30 April 2015.

	£
Trading income/Net income	54,000
Less: personal allowance	(10,000)
Taxable income	44,000

	£
Income tax:	
£31,865 @ 20%	6,373
£12,135 @ 40%	4,854
Income tax liability	11,227

Income tax 2016/17

Final year of trading: basis period 1 May 2015 to 30 April 2016.

	£
Trading income/Net income	61,000
Less: personal allowance	(10,000)
Taxable income	51,000

	£
Income tax:	
£31,865 @ 20%	6,373
£19,135 @ 40%	7,654
Income tax liability	14,027

Capital gains tax position

Sale of assets on 31 January 2016

Capital gains tax 2015/16

	£
Building £(330,000 – 60,000(N1))	270,000
Equipment (N2)	0
Chargeable gains	270,000
Less: annual exempt amount	(11,000)
Taxable gains	259,000

	£
Capital gains tax:	
£259,000 @ 10% (N3)	25,900

Notes

1   The base cost of the building for Ziti is the original cost for Ravi as gift relief was claimed on the disposal of the business assets from Ravi to Ziti.

2   All of the equipment has a market value and cost of £6,000 or less and so is exempt from capital gains tax.

3   Entrepreneurs' relief is available on the disposal of the assets because the business has been owned by Ziti throughout the period of one year ending with the date on which the business ceased to be carried on and the date of cessation is within three years before the date of the disposal.

Sale of business on 30 April 2016

Capital gains tax 2016/17

	£
Capital gains tax:	
On gains as above (N)	25,900
Goodwill £40,000 @ 10% (N)	4,000
Capital gains tax	29,900

Note

Entrepreneurs' relief is available as this is the disposal of whole or part of a business by Ziti who has owned the business throughout the period of one year ending with the date of the disposal. As with the building, the base cost of the goodwill for Ziti is the original cost to Ravi ie nil, because of gift relief on the disposal from Ravi to Ziti.

Summary of post-tax cash position

	Sale on 31.1.16 £	Sale on 30.4.16 £
Trading income £(60,000 + 45,000)	105,000	
Trading income £(60,000 + 60,000)		120,000
Equipment purchase 1 August 2014	(6,000)	(6,000)
Proceeds of sale:		
Goodwill	0	40,000
Building	330,000	330,000
Equipment	10,000	10,000
Less: income tax 2015/16	(29,627)	(11,227)
income tax 2016/17	0	(14,027)
capital gains tax 2015/16	(25,900)	0
capital gains tax 2016/17	0	(29,900)
	383,473	438,846

Conclusion

Delaying the sale until 30 April 2016 would be financially beneficial.

It would also delay the payment of some of the income tax and all of the capital gains tax by one year.

Assumptions

Ziti has not used his annual exempt amount for 2015/16 (for a sale on 31 January 2016) or 2016/17 (for a sale on 30 April 2016).

(ii)   **Value added tax (VAT)**

Sale of assets on 31 January 2016

VAT @ 20% will need to be charged on the sale of the equipment.

The sale of the building will be exempt since it is more than three years old and the option to tax has not been exercised.

Sale of assets on 30 April 2016

VAT @ 20% will need to be charged on the sale of the equipment and the goodwill unless the sale qualifies as the transfer of a going concern.

The conditions for the transfer of assets not to be treated as a supply for VAT purposes and to be treated as a transfer of a going concern are:

- The assets are to be used purchaser in the same kind of business (whether or not as part of an existing business) as that carried on by Ziti, the business being transferred as a going concern.
- The purchaser is a taxable person when the transfer takes place or immediately becomes one as a result of the transfer.
- There is no significant break in the normal trading pattern before or immediately after the transfer.

As above, the sale of the building is exempt.

(b) **Inheritance tax**

Date of death	Notes	IHT liability £
7 June 2015 to 30 April 2016	1	0
1 May 2016 to 30 June 2016	2	48,480
1 July 2016 to 30 June 2017	3(i)	32,320
1 July 2017 to 30 June 2018	3(ii)	16,160

Notes

1 If Ravi dies whilst Ziti still owns the business, business property relief at 100% will apply on the value of the transfer. This is because the transfer was of an unincorporated trading business owned by Ravi for at least two years.

2 Business property relief will not apply as Ziti does not own the business when Ravi dies and he has not reinvested the whole of the proceeds in replacement business assets.

Taper relief applies as there are at least three years between the transfer and the death of Ravi.

The inheritance on the transfer is computed as follows:

	£	£	£
Transfer of value			
£(40,000 + 300,000 + 9,000)			349,000
Less: annual exemptions			
2011/12 and 2010/11 b/f			(6,000)
Chargeable transfer			343,000
Nil rate band at death of Ravi		325,000	
Transfer of value 1 May 2007	190,000		
Less: annual exemptions			
2007/08 and 2006/07 b/f	(6,000)		
		(184,000)	
Available nil rate band		141,000	
Inheritance tax:			
£141,000 @ 0%			0
£202,000 @ 40%			80,800
			80,800
Less: taper relief (4 to 5 years)			
£80,800 @ 40%			(32,320)
Inheritance tax liability			48,480

3   IHT liability after additional taper relief

(i)	Taper relief of 60% (5 to 6 years) £(80,800 – 48,480)	32,320
(ii)	Taper relief of 80% (6 to 7 years) £(80,800 – 64,640)	16,160

5 John and Maureen Robinson (ATAX 12/13)

Text references. Income tax and employment income is covered in Chapter 1 to 5. Trade profits are in Chapter 6. Capital allowances are in Chapter 7. Basic chargeable gains is in Chapter 11. VAT deregistration is covered in Chapter 28 and the flat rate scheme in Chapter 29.

Top tips. Be methodical. You needed to consider the tax liability of each person for both years assuming that the income had been both correctly and incorrectly treated in order to compute the error. Whilst there are a lot of calculations to do they were quick once you got started. A lot of marks could be scored quickly.

Easy marks. Listing out the income tax computations for each year for each person should have been straightforward.

Examiner's comments. Part (a) of this question required candidates to carry out a series of calculations to determine the income tax underpaid where the income of one spouse was incorrectly declared on the tax return of the other. This is an example of a question that tests fundamental tax knowledge (brought forward from Paper F6) in a Paper P6 context.

There was a large number of marks here for dealing with basic aspects of investment income, employment income and trading income and the calculation of income tax liabilities. Most of these matters were handled well by the majority of candidates although knowledge of the trading income opening years rules and capital allowances was noticeably weaker than that relating to other matters.

Further marks were then available for determining the additional tax due on the income declared in the incorrect tax return. This could be handled most efficiently by working at the margin; calculating the tax on the additional income only and comparing it with the tax already paid on that income. However, this approach was not taken by the majority of students who wasted time preparing full income tax computations both with and without the incorrectly declared income.

Part (b) required candidates to explain the implications of deregistration for the purposes of VAT and to identify an alternative strategy that would assist in reducing the administration of VAT. Although the rules regarding deregistration were known by many candidates, a considerable amount of time was wasted by some who went on to describe the advantages and disadvantages of being registered in detail. The identification of an alternative strategy was not done particularly well, with many candidates providing a comprehensive list of VAT schemes rather than identifying the flat rate scheme as the one which would genuinely help the client.

Marks

(a) The additional income:

	Interest – ½ mark for each year	1
	Dividends – ½ mark for each year	1
	Property income	½
	Children's interest – identification of issue	1
	De minimis	1
John's income tax:		
2014/15		
	Car benefit	1
	Fuel benefit	½
	Trust income	1
	Personal allowance	½
	Remainder of basic rate band	½
	Additional tax liability	2
	Tax credits	1
	Comparison with the tax paid by Maureen	½
2015/16		
	Car	½
	Fuel benefit	½
	Trust income	½
	Personal allowance	½
	Remainder of basic rate band	½
	Additional tax liability	2
	Tax credits	1
	Comparison with the tax paid by Maureen	½
Maureen's income tax:		
	Trading income:	
	Capital allowances	2
	2014/15 assessment	1
	2015/16 assessment	1½
Tax on investment income:		
	2014/15	2½
	2015/16	2½
Additional capital gains tax due:		
	Annual exempt amount	½
	Additional tax	1½
Total additional tax due		½

Max   26

Clarity of presentation and use of headings		1
Logical structure		1

2

(b)

Conditions for voluntary deregistration		1
Effective date		½
Deemed supply		1
De minimis limit		1
Stop charging VAT		½
Cannot recover input tax		½
Deductible for income tax		½
Need to monitor turnover		1
Suggestion of flat rate scheme		1
Operation of the scheme		2
Possible financial advantage		½

Max   8

Effectiveness of communication		1

37

(a) **John and Maureen Robinson – Additional tax payable**

Additional income tax payable – 2014/15

£		£
2,550 × 20% (property income (W1))		510
<u>2,021</u> × 20% (interest income (W1))		404
<u>4,571</u> (reminder of basic rate band)		
1,009 × 40% (interest income (£3,030 – £2,021))		404
9,840 × 32.5% (dividend income (W1))		<u>3,198</u>
		4,516
Less: Tax credits		
£3,030 × 20%		(606)
£9,840 × 10%		<u>(984)</u>
		2,926
Tax paid by Maureen (W3)		<u>(510)</u>
Additional income tax payable		<u>2,416</u>

Additional capital gains tax payable – 2014/15

Additional capital gains tax payable £11,000 × 28% + £(13,870 – 11,000) × 10% (Note)	<u>3,367</u>

Note. The gift of the property to Maureen would not be effective for capital gains tax purposes due to the prior agreement whereby Maureen gave the sales proceeds to John. Therefore an amount equal to Maureen's unused annual exempt amount becomes taxable. The rate of tax is 28% because John is now a higher rate taxpayer. Furthermore Maureen would have paid CGT on her taxable gain of £(13,870 – 11,000) = £2,870 at 18% whereas John's rate of CGT is 28%.

Additional income tax payable – 2015/16

		£
<u>539</u> × 20% (interest income (W1))		108
<u>539</u> (remainder of basic rate band(W2))		
2,681 × 40% (interest income (£3,220 – £539))		1,072
144 × 40% (interest income – Penny (W1))		58
10,120 × 32.5% (dividend income (W1))		<u>3,289</u>
		4,527
Less: Tax credits		
£3,220 × 20%		(644)
£10,120 × 10%		<u>(1,012)</u>
		2,871
Tax paid by Maureen (W4)		<u>(923)</u>
Additional income tax payable		<u>1,948</u>
Total additional tax payable (£2,416 + £3,367 + £1,948)		<u>7,731</u>

Workings

1 John – Additional taxable income

	2014/15	2015/16
	£	£
Arising on inherited assets:		
Property income	2,550	–
Interest income (£2,424/£2,576 × 100/80)	3,030	3,220
Dividend income (£8,856/£9,108 × 100/90)	9,840	10,120
Children's bank accounts:		
Will – below *de minimis* limit of £100	–	–
Penny	–	144

2   John – Reminder of basic rate band

	2014/15 £	2015/16 £
Salary	29,838	30,642
Car benefit:		
12 + (155 – 95)/5 = 24%		
£17,400 × 24% × 8/12	2,784	
£17,400 × 24%		4,176
Fuel benefit:		
£21,700 × 24% × 8/12	3,472	
£21,700 × 24%		5,208
Trust income (£660/£715 × 100/55)	1,200	1,300
Less: Personal allowance	(10,000)	(10,000)
Taxable income	27,294	31,326
Basic rate band	(31,865)	(31,865)
Remainder of basic rate band	4,571	539

3   Maureen – Tax paid on investment income 2014/15

	£
Trading income (W5)	13,285
Property income	2,550
Interest income (W1)	3,030
Dividend income (W1)	9,840
	28,705
Less: Personal allowance	(10,000)
Taxable income	18,705
Tax on property income (Note)	
£2,550 × 20%	510

Note. All of the investment income fell into the basic rate band. The tax liability in respect of the interest and dividend income was covered by the related tax credits. Accordingly, in respect of the income arising on the inherited assets, only the property income gave rise to income tax payable.

4   Maureen – Tax paid on investment income 2015/16

	£
Trading income (W5)	32,630
Interest income (W1)	3,220
Dividend income (W1)	10,120
	45,970
Less: Personal allowance	(10,000)
Taxable income	35,970
Tax on dividend income in higher rate band (Note)	
£4,105 × 32.5%	1,334
Less: Tax credit	
£4,105 × 10%	(411)
	923

Note. The tax liability in respect of the investment income that fell into the basic rate band was covered by the related tax credits. Accordingly, income tax was payable in respect of the dividend income that fell into the higher rate band only, ie £4,105 (£35,970 – £31,865).

5   Maureen – Trading income

	Period ended 30 September 2015 £	Year ended 30 September 2016 £
Adjusted trading profit	53,136	41,739
Less: capital allowances (W6)	(23,909)	(903)
Taxable trading income	29,227	40,836

2014/15
1 November 2014 – 5 April 2015
£29,227 × 5/11   13,285

2015/16
1 November 2014 – 31 October 2015
1 November 2014 – 30 September 2015   29,227
1 October 2015 – 31 October 2015
£40,836 × 1/12   3,403
                                                                          32,630

6   Capital allowances

	AIA £	Main pool £	Allowances £
p/e 30.9.15			
Additions qualifying for AIA			
11.14 Equipment	22,917		
AIA	(22,917)		22,917
Additions not qualifying for AIA			
12.14 Car		6,010	
WDA @ 18% x 11/12		(992)	992
TWDV c/f		5,018	
Allowances			23,909
y/e 30.9.16			
WDA @ 18%		(903)	903
TWDV c/f		4,115	
Allowances			903

(b) **Advice on Maureen's VAT position**

Deregistration

In order to voluntarily deregister for VAT you must satisfy HMRC that the value of your taxable supplies in the next 12 months will not exceed £79,000. You will then be deregistered with effect from the date of your request or a later date as agreed with HMRC.

On deregistering you are regarded as making a supply of all stocks and equipment in respect of which input tax has been claimed. However, the VAT on this deemed supply need only be paid to HMRC if it exceeds £1,000.

Once you have deregistered, you must no longer charge VAT on your sales. You will also be unable to recover the input tax on the costs incurred by your business. Instead, the VAT you pay on your costs will be allowable when computing your taxable profits.

You should monitor your sales on a monthly basis; if your sales in a 12-month period exceed £81,000 you must notify HMRC within the 30 days following the end of the 12-month period. You will be registered from the end of the month following the end of the 12-month period.

Flat rate scheme

Rather than deregistering you may wish to consider operating the flat rate scheme. This would reduce the amount of administration as you would no longer need to record and claim input tax in respect of the costs incurred by your business.

Under the flat rate scheme you would continue to charge your customers VAT in the way that you do at the moment. You would then pay HMRC a fixed percentage of your VAT inclusive turnover each quarter rather than calculating output tax less input tax. This may be financially advantageous as compared with deregistering; I would be happy to prepare calculations for you if you wish.

6 Monisha and Horner (ATAX 12/13)

Text references. The principles of income tax, including jointly held property, will be found in Chapter 1. Property income is covered in Chapter 3. The basics of chargeable gains are dealt with in Chapter 11 and reliefs in Chapter 13. Personal service companies are covered in Chapter 4.

Top tips. You might want to start with part (b) of this question as it was self-contained and would have taken less time to achieve the available marks than part (a) which needed a bit more thought.

Easy marks. The conditions for FHLs in part (a)(i) should have been known from your F6 studies. The computation of the deemed employment income in part (b) was relatively straightforward.

Examiner's comments. Part (a)(i) required a statement of the conditions that must be satisfied for the letting of a UK furnished property to qualify as furnished holiday accommodation. This was answered very well by the majority of candidates. The only difficulty related to confusion over the meaning of 'longer term accommodation' and the maximum number of days of such occupation permitted in a tax year.

Part (a)(ii) was the more difficult part of the question. It required a calculation of the total tax saving on the transfer of a 20% interest in a rental property from one spouse (Monisha) to the other (Asmat) together with the property being let as furnished holiday accommodation in the future. This was done poorly by many candidates who either did not have a thorough attempt at it or worked very hard but did not pause to think about how to approach the problem. The key was to first calculate the taxable property income in order to identify the amount of taxable income that would be taxed in the hands of Asmat rather than Monisha. It was then necessary to recognise that for the first five years under consideration, Monisha would be a higher rate taxpayer whereas Asmat's income would be covered by his personal allowance, such that no tax would be payable. Accordingly, by working at the margin, it was easy to see that for the first five years the saving would be 40% of the income transferred. In the sixth year, Asmat was expected to be employed, such that the income transferred would be taxed at 20% and the saving would therefore be 20% (40% – 20%) of the income transferred. The problem was that very few candidates chose to work at the margin. Instead, many chose to prepare income tax computations for the two individuals before and after the transfer of the interest in the property in order to quantify the difference in the total liability. This was very time consuming. Some candidates even prepared calculations for each of the five years despite the fact that the figures were the same in each year. Calculating tax liabilities can be very time consuming. Candidates should always stop and think about the most efficient way of approaching a set of calculations before they start writing. The capital gains tax element of this part of the question was not handled particularly well. This was perhaps due to a shortage of time. It required candidates to recognise that an additional annual exempt amount would be available and that tax would be charged at 10%, due to the availability of entrepreneurs' relief, rather than at 28%. Only a minority of candidates were able to quantify the effect of these points.

Part (b)(i) required an outline of the circumstances in which the personal service company rules (IR35) apply. The majority of candidates struggled to satisfy this requirement despite a reasonable knowledge of the rules. It was generally recognised that the rules were in place in order to prevent the avoidance of tax but there was some confusion as to exactly where tax was being avoided. Very few candidates were able to state the commercial relationship between the taxpayer, the personal service company and the client in a clear manner.

Part (ii) required a calculation of the deemed employment income under the rules. This was done well or very well by the majority of candidates. The only common error was a failure to calculate employer's national insurance contributions in respect of the salary paid.

				Marks
(a)	(i)	Conditions for FHL – 1 mark each	3	
		Longer term occupation	1	
		Max		3
	(ii)	Income tax		
		Property business income	2	
		Allocated equally	1	
		First five tax years	1½	
		Final tax year	1	
		Capital gains tax		
		No gain, no loss disposal	1	
		CGT if proposals not carried out	1½	
		CGT if proposals are carried out	2½	
		Total tax saving	½	
		Max		10
(b)	(i)	Conditions for IR35 – 1 mark each	4	
		Employment/self employment test reference	1	
		Max		3
	(ii)	95% of income	1½	
		Deductions:		
		Salary and pension contributions	1	
		Employer's NIC on actual salary	1½	
		Employer's NIC on deemed employment income	1	
		Max		4
				20

(a) **Monisha**

(i) **Furnished holiday accommodation in the UK – conditions**

- Availability – during the relevant period (usually a tax year), the accommodation is available for commercial letting as holiday accommodation to the public generally for at least 210 days.

- Letting – during the relevant period, the accommodation is commercially let as holiday accommodation to members of the public for at least 105 days (the days let exclude any days that are longer term occupation – below).

- Pattern of occupation – during the relevant period, not more that 155 days fall during periods of longer term occupation. Longer term occupation is defined as a continuous period of more than 31 days during which the accommodation is in the same occupation unless there are abnormal circumstances.

(ii) **Total tax saving for six years ending 5 April 2022**

Income tax

	£
Income tax saved in first five tax years £6,660 (W) × 40% × 5	13,320
Income tax saved in final tax year £6,660 (W) × 20%	1,332
Total income tax saved	14,652

For the first five tax years, Asmat will not have any other income so that his share of the property income will be covered by his personal allowance thus saving tax at 40%. In the final tax year, Asmat will have employment income so that the property income will be taxed at 20%, saving tax at (40% − 20%) = 20%.

Working – Property business income taxable on Asmat

	£
Rental income	20,000
Less: allowable expenses £(1,600 + £1,200 + £2,000)	(4,800)
capital allowances equal to wear and tear allowance £(20,000 – 1,200) × 10%	(1,880)
Property business income	13,320
Property business income taxable on Asmat £13,320 × ½	6,660

Tutorial note

The income of a jointly held asset is automatically split equally between a married couple, regardless of their actual interests in the property. (Monisha and Asmat could elect to split the income between them in the ratio 80:20, but to do so would not be beneficial in their particular circumstances.) Accordingly, property income of £6,660 will be subject to income tax on Asmat.

Capital gains tax

The gift of the 20% interest in the property will take place on a no gain, no loss basis because Monisha and Asmat are a married couple. The gain on the sale of the property will therefore be allocated between Monisha and Asmat in the ratio 80:20. A gain on the sale of furnished holiday accommodation qualifies for entrepreneurs' relief.

	£
Capital gains tax on sale of property if proposals *not* carried out	
Monisha: £(100,000 – £[11,000 – 6,000]) × 28%	26,600
Capital gains tax on sale of property if proposals *are* carried out	
Monisha: £(80,000 – £[11,000 – 6,000]) × 10% (entrepreneurs' relief)	7,500
Asmat: £(20,000 – 11,000) × 10% (entrepreneurs' relief)	900
Total capital gains tax on sale	8,400
Capital gains tax saved £(26,600 – 8,400)	18,200

Total tax saving

	£
Income tax saving	14,652
Capital gains tax saving	18,200
Total tax saving	32,852

(b) **Horner**

(i) **Circumstances in which personal service company (IR 35) rules apply**

- An individual ('the worker') performs, or has an obligation to perform, services for 'a client'.

- The performance of those services is referable to arrangements involving a third party (eg the personal service company), rather than referable to a contract between the client and the worker.

- If the services were to be performed by the worker under a contract between himself and the client, the worker would be regarded as employed by the client (using the usual tests which distinguish between employment and self-employment).

- The worker (alone or with associates) control more than 5% of the ordinary share capital of the company, or are entitled to receive more than 5% of any dividends from the company, or the worker receives, or could receive, payments or benefits from the company which are not salary, but could reasonably be taken to represent payment for the services he provides to clients.

(ii)   **Deemed employment income for the year ending 5 April 2016**

	£	£
Otmar Ltd – 95% of income from relevant engagements		
£85,000 × 95%		80,750
Less: salary paid to Horner		(50,000)
pension contributions		(2,000)
employer's NIC on actual salary		
£(50,000 – 7,956) = £42,044 × 13.8%	5,802	
Less: employment allowance (sole employee)	(2,000)	
		(3,802)
		24,948
Less: employer's NIC on deemed payment		
£24,948 × 13.8/113.8		(3,025)
Deemed employment income		21,923

Tutorial note

The dividend paid to Horner will be treated as exempt to avoid a double charge to tax on the same income.

7 Pita plc (ATAX 06/14)

Text references. Taxable and exempt benefits are covered in Chapter 4. Share schemes and lump sum payments are covered in Chapter 5.

Top tips. Make sure that you attempt all parts of a multi-part question such as this. Use the allocated marks to guide your answer. For example, you should not have spent more than 11 minutes answering part (a).

Easy marks. There were some easy marks for describing the benefits in part (a) and the rules on lump sum payment in part (c) should have been well-known.

Examiner's comments. Part (a) tested the provision of vouchers to purchase childcare and payments made to employees when they work from home. The taxation of vouchers to be used for the purchase of childcare was tackled well by the majority of candidates. The majority of candidates were aware that an exemption was available in respect of the provision of such vouchers, with many knowing that the amounts of the exemption depend on the employee's marginal rate of tax. The rules regarding the ability of an employer to make tax-free payments to employees who work from home were not as well known, such that very few candidates scored well on this aspect of the question.

Part (b) tested various aspects of the enterprise management incentive (EMI) scheme and was split into two sub-requirements. The first part concerned the ability of the company concerned to establish such a scheme and to make it available to nine key employees. This part of the question was done reasonably well. The majority of candidates knew that there were conditions relating to the number of employees and the gross assets of the company, although not all knew the precise detail of the conditions. Most candidates were also aware that it is acceptable for an EMI scheme to be provided to key employees (rather than to all of a company's employees) but many did not realise that part-time employees are not permitted to be members of such a scheme. The second part related to the tax implications of the grant and exercise of the share options and the sale of the shares. This was arguably a more difficult requirement and was not done particularly well. As always, those candidates who adopted a methodical approach and dealt with the grant, exercise and sale as three separate issues did better than those who tried to address everything at once. Candidates will almost always benefit from starting a new paragraph for each new issue that needs to be addressed.

The final part of the question concerned a redundancy package to be received by an employee of the company. The package consisted of a payment of statutory redundancy, an additional payment and the provision of a company car after the employment ceased. All three matters were handled well by many candidates with most candidates demonstrating awareness of the £30,000 exemption. The one area where almost all candidates could have improved their performance was the additional payment. The question was deliberately silent as to the reason for and the nature of the payment. It was up to candidates to raise the matter as to whether or not the payment was for work carried out or a restriction to be placed on the employee's future working activities, such that it would be taxable in full.

Marks

(a)	Vouchers to purchase childcare			
		Taxable employment income	1	
		Availability of exemption	1	
		Amount of exemption	2	
	Payments for working from home		2½	
			Max	6
(b)	(i)	Qualifying company	3	
		Qualifying employees	2	
			Max	4
	(ii)	Grant of options	1	
		Exercise of options	1½	
		Sale of shares	3	
			Max	5
(c)	Statutory redundancy		1	
	Additional payment		3	
	Continued use of car		2	
			Max	5
				20

(a) **Financial assistance with childcare and encouraging working from home**

Vouchers to purchase childcare

The general rule is that the employee is taxed on the cost to the employer of providing the voucher rather than the childcare that is purchased by the voucher.

However, a certain amount of childcare is tax free if the employer provides childcare vouchers to pay an approved childcarer. The childcare vouchers must usually be available to all employees.

A £55 per week limit applies to basic rate employees who receive childcare vouchers giving tax relief of £11 per week. Higher and additional rate employees can receive vouchers tax-free up to £28 per week and £25 per week respectively, giving them the same amount of tax relief. Whether an employee is considered basic rate, higher rate or additional rate for these purposes is determined by the level of the employee's employment income only (and not other income).

Payments for working from home

Employer contributions towards additional household costs incurred by an employee who works wholly or partly at home may be exempt.

Payments up to £4 per week (or £18 per month for monthly paid employees) may be made without supporting evidence. Payments in excess of that amount require supporting evidence that the payment is wholly in respect of additional household expenses.

Tutorial note

Credit was available for identifying the exemption limits in respect of the vouchers and home working payments but it was possible to score full marks without this knowledge.

(b) (i) **Ability to establish an enterprise management incentive (EMI) scheme**

Pita plc is a qualifying company for the purposes of the EMI scheme because it has:

- Gross assets of no more than £30 million, and
- Fewer than 250 full-time employees, and
- A permanent establishment in the UK.

Under the EMI scheme rules, Pita plc is allowed to make the scheme available to just its nine key employees. However, the two part-time key employees cannot join the scheme unless they work for Pita plc for at least 25 hours per week or, if lower, 75% of their working time.

Tutorial notes

1   The following conditions would also be relevant but the information necessary to address them was not provided in the question.

- An employee owning 30% or more of the company's ordinary shares would not be permitted to join the scheme.

- Pita plc must carry on a qualifying trade and must not be controlled by another company.

2   The answer does not include the need for the shares to be fully paid up irredeemable ordinary shares as the requirement refers to the conditions relating to the company and the employees, and not to the shares.

(ii)   **Income tax and capital gains tax implications for the employees**

There will be no income tax on the grant of the share options.

The options are to be exercised within ten years of the date on which they were granted. Therefore income tax will only be charged on the excess of the market value of the shares at the time the options were granted over the price paid on exercise which is
£(2.00 – 1.75) = £0.25 per share.

When the shares are sold, there will be a capital gain per share equal to the excess of the sales proceeds over the market value at the time the options were granted, which is
£(5.00 – 2.00) = £3.00 per share.

On a disposal of EMI shares in Pita plc, entrepreneurs' relief will be available if:

- Pita plc was a trading company throughout the year prior to the disposal, and
- The shareholder was employed by the company throughout the year prior to disposal, and
- The options were granted at least one year prior to the date of the disposal of the shares.

Tutorial note

There is no requirement for the individual to own at least 5% of the shares in the company where the shares are EMI shares.

(c)   **Redundancy package for Narn**

The statutory redundancy payment is covered by the £30,000 exemption which is available in respect of termination payments which are not in respect of services provided by the employee.

The additional amount of £26,000 will be taxable in full if:

- Narn was contractually entitled to receive it, for example a terminal bonus in respect of work done by Narn or a payment in lieu of notice, or

- Narn's agreed to limit his future conduct or activities in return for the payment (a restrictive covenant).

If the payment is not taxable in full, £(30,000 – 8,100) = £21,900 will be exempt and the balance of £4,100 will be taxable.

The continued use of the company car will result in a taxable benefit in the tax year 2015/16 after Narn has left the company. The benefit will be (6/12 × £19,500 × 21% (12% + ((125 – 95)/5)% + 3%)) = £2,047.

8 Simone ATAX 06/09)

Text references. Capital allowances are covered in Chapter 7, trading losses in Chapter 8 and partnerships in Chapter 9. VAT registration is covered in Chapter 28.

Top tips. Use a proforma to calculate the share of the loss for each partner.

Easy marks. The calculation of capital allowances should have been an easy marks.

Examiner's comments. In part (a) the calculation of the capital allowances was done well. However, the allocation of the loss between the partners was done poorly with the majority of candidates treating the salaries as employment income rather than as a share of the trading loss. The use of the loss was also problematic. Weaker candidates were confused as to corporate and personal loss offset rules.

Even many stronger candidates lacked the precise knowledge required to score well; a statement of how losses can be used must describe precisely the income against which the loss can be offset, for example, 'against future profits of the same trade' in order to earn all of the marks available. Many candidates ignored the requirement to calculate the total tax saved and simply prepared various income tax computations.

In part (b) weaker candidates wasted time describing the future test in detail despite it not being relevant to this particular question. In addition, many candidates lacked precise knowledge (for example in relation to the date registration comes into effect) such that they did not score as well as would have been expected.

Marking scheme

					Marks
(a)	(i)	Capital allowances	1½		
		6 April 2014 to 28 February 2015	2		
		1 March 2015 to 5 April 2015	2		
			Max	5
	(ii)	Against general income of 2014/15 and/or 2013/14	1		
		Against capital gain in 2014/15	1		
		Against future profits of the same trade	1		
				3
	(iii)	Evaluation of offset against future profits of the same trade	2		
		Evaluation of offset against general income and gains in 2014/15	2		
		Evaluation of offset against general income in 2013/14	3		
		Calculation of maximum tax saving	½		
			Max	7
(b)		Taxable supplies exceed limit in the previous 12 months	1		
		Exclude capital assets	½		
		Notify within 30 days	½		
		Date of effective registration	1		
		Relevance of Ellington and Co being VAT registered	1		
			Max	3
				18

(a) (i) **Share of the taxable trading loss for the year ended 5 April 2015**

	Total £	Ellington £	Simone £	Basie £
Tax adjusted trading loss	(90,000)			
Capital allowances				
Additions in the year within AIA limit	(21,200)			
Writing down allowance (N)	(700)			
Loss available for relief	(111,900)			
6 April 2014 – 28 February 2015				
Loss £(111,900) × 11/12	(102,575)			
Salaries				
£15,000/£11,500/£13,000 × 11/12	(36,209)	13,750	10,542	11,917
Balance 3:2:2	(138,784)	(59,478)	(39,653)	(39,653)
1 March 2015 – 5 April 2015				
£(111,900) × 1/12	(9,325)			
Salaries £14,000 × 1/12	(2,334)	1,167	1,167	0
Balance 1:1	(11,659)	(5,830)	(5,829)	(0)
	(111,900)	(50,391)	(33,773)	(27,736)

Note

As the unrelieved expenditure on the main pool is less than £1,000, a WDA can be claimed equal to this amount.

(ii) **Alternative strategies**

The following alternative strategies are available to Simone in respect of her share of the taxable trading loss.

Offset against her general income for the current year (2014/15) and/or the previous year (2013/14).

Following a claim against her general income in 2014/15, the remaining loss could be offset against her capital gains of that year.

Any losses not used as set out above will be carried forward for offset against her share of the taxable trading profits of Ellington & Co in the future.

(iii) **Advice**

Offset against future profits of the same trade

Assuming an annual taxable trading profit of £25,000, Simone's share of the budgeted profit of Ellington and Co in 2015/16 and future years will be £12,500 (£25,000 × 1/2). The profit from her new business is budgeted to be £10,500 (£1,500 × 7) in 2015/16 and £18,000 (£1,500 × 12) in future years. Accordingly, Simone will be a basic rate taxpayer and the total tax saved via the offset of the loss will be £6,755 (£33,773 @ 20%). The tax saved in 2015/16 and in 2016/17 will be £2,500 (£12,500 @ 20%) and the balance of £1,755 (£6,755 – (2 × £2,500)) will be saved in 2017/18.

Offset against general income and capital gains in 2014/15

Simone's only income in 2014/15 is dividend income of £10,800. Offsetting her loss against this income will not save any tax as the dividend tax credit is not repayable.

However, having offset the loss against her general income in 2014/15, Simone would then be able to offset the remaining loss of £21,773 (£33,773 – (£10,800 × 100/90)) against her capital gain. The capital gains tax saved would be £6,096 (£21,773 @ 28% – this is Simone's highest marginal rate on her gains). However, this is not as beneficial as using the loss in 2013/14 (see below) both considering the rate at which tax is saved and the time at which is it saved.

Offset against general income in 2013/14

Simone's original income tax liability in 2013/14 is set out below.

	Non-savings income £	Dividend income £	Total £
Trading income	48,615		
Dividend income £12,600 × 100/90		14,000	
Net income	48,615	14,000	62,615
Less: personal allowance	(10,000)		
Taxable income	38,615	14,000	52,615

	£
Tax on non-savings income	
£	
31,865 @ 20%	6,373
6,750 @ 40%	2,700
38,615	
Tax on dividend income	
£14,000 × 32.5%	4,550
Tax liability	13,623
Less dividend tax credit £14,000 @ 10%	(1,400)
Tax payable	12,223

Simone's liability in 2013/14 following the offset of the trading loss is:

	Non-savings income £	Dividend income £	Total £
Trading income	48,615		
Dividend income £12,600 × 100/90		14,000	
Total income	48,615	14,000	62,615
Less: trading loss	(33,773)		
Net income	14,842		28,842
Less: personal allowance	(10,000)		
Taxable income	4,842	14,000	18,842

	£
Tax on trading income	
£4,842 @ 20%	968
Tax on dividend income	
£14,000 @ 10%	1,400
Tax liability	2,368
Less dividend tax credit £14,000 @ 10%	(1,400)
Tax payable	968

The tax saved via the offset of the trading loss would be £11,255 (£12,223 – 968).

Conclusion

Simone will save the most tax by offsetting the loss against her general income in 2013/14. This claim saves some tax at the higher rate and saves tax at the basic rate at the earliest time.

Note

The use of the loss would also have resulted in a saving of Class 4 NICs which could also have been mentioned.

(b) **VAT registration**

Simone is required to register for VAT when her cumulative taxable supplies (standard and zero rated), excluding supplies of capital assets, exceed £81,000 in the previous 12 months.

Simone must notify HMRC within 30 days of the end of the month in which the limit is exceeded.

Simone will be registered and must charge VAT from the end of the month following the month in which the limit is exceeded, or from an earlier date if she and HMRC agree.

As Simone and Ellington and Co are separate taxable persons, the fact that Ellington and Co is VAT registered is irrelevant when considering Simone's position.

9 Morice (ATAX 12/11)

Text references. SAYE schemes are covered in Chapter 5. Employment income in general is dealt with in Chapter 4.

Top tips. In part (a), it was vital that you provided *detailed* explanations relating to the proposed SAYE scheme. In part (b), you were only required to discuss the implications for the *employees* of the proposed benefits.

Easy marks. There were some easy marks in part (a) for basic details concerning the capital gains tax computation. In part (b), the rates for cars are in the Tax Tables.

Examiner's comments. Part (a) required a detailed knowledge of Save As You Earn share option schemes in order to comment on the acceptability or otherwise of a proposed set of rules and to calculate the income tax and national insurance liabilities in respect of shares acquired. In order to score well it was important for candidates to address each of the detailed rules in the question as opposed to writing generally about share option schemes.

Many candidates who attempted this question were knowledgeable about Save As You Earn schemes but only a minority took a sufficiently disciplined approach to score well. The explanation of the tax liabilities in respect of the shares acquired under the scheme was not done particularly well. Many candidates lacked precise knowledge of this area such that they did not know that no tax would be charged until the shares were sold. In addition, it needed to be recognised that the position of each employee would vary depending on whether or not they had made any other capital gains and on the level of their taxable income; very few candidates considered these matters.

Part (b) concerned the medical care scheme and the payments to employees for driving their own cars on business journeys. The medical care scheme was not handled particularly well in that many candidates incorrectly stated that the provision of health insurance would be an exempt benefit for the employees. However, this was not too important as it was only a minor part of the answer. The provision of an interest free loan was also not dealt with as well as might have been expected. The question stated that the loan would be 'up to £12,500' so it was necessary to point out that loans of no more than £10,000 would be exempt. The explanation of the implications of the payments to employees for driving their own cars was handled well. The only common error was the failure to recognise that there would be no national insurance implications. The question asked for the tax implications 'for the employees' as opposed to the tax implications generally. Accordingly, it was necessary to consider the national insurance issues for the employees (but not the employer) and there was no need to address the ability of the employer to obtain tax relief for the costs incurred.

			Marks
(a)	Scheme rules		
	Investment period and investment limits	1½	
	Eligible employees	1½	
	Share price	1½	
	Illustrative example		
	Grant and exercise of option, receipt of bonus	1½	
	Gain	1½	
	Capital gains tax	3	
	National insurance contributions	1	
	Max		10

			Marks
(b)	(i)	Health insurance	½
		Interest-free loan	2½
		National insurance contributions	½
	(ii)	Driving on company business	
		Income tax	2
		National insurance contributions	1
		Carrying passengers	1½
		Max	7
			17

(a) **Schedule 3 SAYE scheme**

Whether or not the proposed rules will be compliant with Schedule 3

The investment period of five years and the minimum monthly investment limit of £5 are acceptable. The maximum monthly investment limit for a Schedule 3 SAYE scheme is £500.

It is not acceptable to have a minimum age requirement.

It is not acceptable to exclude part-time employees (although it is possible to exclude part-time directors).

It is acceptable to exclude employees who have worked for the company for less than a qualifying period, provided that the period chosen does not exceed five years.

The price at which shares are offered under the scheme must be at least 80% of the market value of the shares at the time the option is granted. Accordingly, the price proposed of £2.48 will only be acceptable if the value of a share on 1 January 2016 is no more than £3.10 (£2.48/80%).

Illustrative example – Schedule 3 compliant SAYE scheme

Grant and exercise of share options

There is no tax liability in respect of the grant and exercise of the share options.

Receipt of the bonus

There is no tax liability in respect of the receipt of the bonus.

Sale of shares

The total amount invested will be £15,225 ((12 x £250 × 5) + (0.9 × £250)). The number of shares purchased will be 6,139 (£15,225/£2.48).

Therefore, there will be a capital gain on the sale of the shares as set out below.

	£
Proceeds 6,139 × £4.00	24,556
Less cost 6,139 × £2.48	(15,225)
Gain	9,331

Entrepreneurs' relief will not be available as the employee will not own 5% of the company's ordinary share capital. The gain will be reduced by the annual exempt amount (currently £11,000). Accordingly, there will be no tax liability where an employee has at least £9,331 of their annual exempt amount available for the tax year 2020/21.

Where the employee has other gains in the tax year such that the total gains exceed the employee's available annual exempt amount, the excess will be subject to capital gains tax. The rate of tax depends on the employee's level of taxable income.

Capital gains tax will be charged at 28% if the individual's taxable income exceeds the income tax basic rate band of £31,865. Where the individual's taxable income is less than £31,865, the amount of the gain that falls within the basic rate band will be taxed at 18% with the balance being taxed at 28%.

National insurance contributions

There are no national insurance implications in respect of a Schedule 3 SAYE scheme.

(b) **Income tax and national insurance implications for the employees of Babeen plc**

(i) *Medical care scheme*

The cost to the company of providing the health insurance of £470 will be a taxable benefit for each P11D employee.

There is no taxable benefit where the total low-interest loans to an employee do not exceed £10,000. Where an employee's total low-interest loans exceed £10,000, there will be a taxable benefit equal to interest at the official rate of 3.25% on the amount outstanding. The benefit is calculated by reference to the average balance for the tax year but either HM Revenue and Customs or the taxpayer can choose to calculate the benefit by reference to the balance outstanding on a daily basis.

There are no national insurance implications for the employees in respect of the taxable benefits relating to either the health insurance or the loans.

(ii) *Payments to employees for driving their own cars*

The total amount paid to each employee in a tax year for driving on company business will need to be compared to the statutory mileage allowances of 45 pence per mile for the first 10,000 miles and 25 pence per mile thereafter.

- Where the amount paid is more than the statutory amount, the excess is subject to income tax.

- Where the amount paid is less than the statutory amount, the shortfall is an allowable deduction when computing an employee's taxable employment income.

There will be no national insurance implications regardless of the mileage driven as the amount per mile is less than 45 pence.

The amount paid for carrying a passenger will not be subject to income tax or national insurance contributions as it is less than the statutory maximum of 5 pence per mile. The shortfall of 2 pence per mile is not an allowable deduction when computing an employee's taxable employment income.

10 Banda Ross (ATAX 12/07)

Text references. Chapters 6 and 7 deal with computation of trading profits and capital allowances. Losses for a sole trader are covered in Chapter 8. Corporation tax losses are dealt with in Chapter 24 and group relief in Chapter 26. Close companies are covered in Chapter 25 and taxable employment benefits in Chapter 4. Ethics are covered in Chapter 30.

Top tips. It was very important to follow the order of the schedules set out in the question. You needed to calculate the losses available for relief in part (a) first and then apply loss relief in part (b).

Easy marks. The calculation of the losses and profits and the application of basis periods to tax years was knowledge that you should have been familiar with from the F6 syllabus. You should also have been able to state some basic rules on loss relief.

Examiner's comments. Part (b), representing almost half of the question, required candidates to determine the tax relief available in respect of the anticipated trading losses depending on the legal structure of the venture. This necessitated some clear thinking, ideally communicated to the examiner via the use of subheadings, such that a distinction was drawn between operating as an unincorporated trader and operating as a company. In many cases there was little evidence of such thinking taking place.

The majority of candidates either ignored the opening year rules for the unincorporated trader or failed to apply them to the situation. To be fair this was a relatively tricky situation due to the presence of the losses but it did seem as though many candidates had forgotten the basic rules governing the taxation of an unincorporated trader.

In order to calculate the potential tax relief it was necessary to determine the taxpayer's income tax liability for the years in which loss relief was available. Candidates had no problems calculating the income but were unsure how to proceed from there. In particular there was a lack of thought with many candidates performing calculations for all years rather than recognising that the income was the same in each year such that only one calculation was necessary.

Answers improved when considering the position of a company but there was a lack of precision when describing the loss reliefs available. There was also some confusion as to whether group relief would be available if the two companies were owned personally by the individual taxpayer (it wouldn't). Finally, there was a general unwillingness to satisfy the requirement and calculate the 'tax relief available'.

The final part of the question concerned a loan from a close company to a participator. Candidates did well in identifying the tax implications of the loan but many ignored the ethical considerations inherent within the question.

Marking scheme

			Marks
(a)	Pre-trading expenditure	1	
	Capital allowances on plant and machinery	1½	
	Tax adjusted profit/(losses)	1½	
			4
(b)	*Business run as sole trader*		
	Basis periods	1½	
	Losses	2½	
	Available loss reliefs	2	
	Set against general income	1	
	Dividend tax credit not repayable	1	
	Tax saving each year	2	
	Overall tax relief	1	
	Business run as company		
	Allowable losses	1½	
	Loss relief if Aral Ltd owned by Banda	1½	
	Loss relief if Aral Ltd owned by Flores Ltd	2	
	Recommendation	1	
	Max		16
(c)	*Tax implications of loan*		
	Tax payable to HMRC on close company loan	1	
	Due date	½	
	Reason for tax being due	1½	
	Repayment of tax by HMRC if loan ceases	1	
	Taxable employment benefit	½	
	Report on P11D	1	
	Income tax due	1	
	Interest and penalties	1	
	Willingness to act for Banda		
	Threat to fundamental principles	1	
	Requirement for full disclosure	1	
	Deliberate concealment	1	
	Max		10
Appropriate style and presentation		1	
Effectiveness of communication		1	
Logical structure		1	
			3
			33

(a)   Tax adjusted profit/(loss) of the Aral business

	Period ending 30 June 2016 £	Year ending 30 June 2017 £	Year ending 30 June 2018 £
Budgeted profit/(loss)	(25,500)	(13,000)	77,000
Less: pre trading expenditure			
(£6,000 × 1/2) (note)	(3,000)		
capital allowances (less than max. AIA)	(11,500)	(1,500)	(1,200)
Tax adjusted profit/(loss)	(40,000)	(14,500)	75,800

Note

Expenditure incurred in the seven years prior to the start of trading is treated as if incurred on the first day of trading. Entertaining expenditure is not allowable.

(b)   Banda Ross

Tax relief available in respect of the anticipated trading losses

(i)   *Business run as a sole trader*

The anticipated allowable losses for the business are set out below.

	Trading income £	Allowable loss £
2015/16 (1 January 2016 to 5 April 2016)		
Allowable loss £40,000 × 3/6	0	(20,000)
2016/17 (1 January 2016 to 31 December 2016)		
Allowable loss £40,000 – £20,000 + (£14,500 × 6/12)	0	(27,250)
2017/18 (Year ending 30 June 2017)		
Allowable loss £14,500 – (£14,500 × 6/12)	0	(7,250)

Banda can use the losses by deducting the losses:

- From her general income in the year of loss and/or the previous year; or
- From her general income in the three years preceding the year of loss, starting with the earliest year, under early years trading loss relief.

All of the losses can be used in this way and therefore the possibility of carrying the losses forward has not been considered.

Banda's income throughout the years in which the losses can be relieved (2012/13 to 2017/18) consists of her salary and dividends from Flores Ltd. In any year in which she claims loss relief, she will save the income tax on her employment income only. There will be no saving in respect of her dividend income because Banda is a basic rate taxpayer and the 10% tax credit is not repayable.

The income tax position of Banda before taking account of loss relief is as follows:

	Non-savings income £	Dividend income £	Total £
Salary	15,225		
Dividend income (£20,250 × 100/90)		22,500	
Total/Net income	15,225	22,500	37,725
Less: personal allowance	(10,000)		
Taxable income	5,225	22,500	27,725

Tax	£
£5,225 × 20%	1,045
£22,500 × 10%	2,250
Tax liability	3,295
Less: tax credit on dividend	(2,250)
Tax payable	1,045

The total tax saved would be £1,045 × 3 = £3,135 as the losses would be set off against non-savings income in preference to dividend income.

The best use of relief would be to use the losses under early years trading loss relief as this would give the earliest tax relief (in 2012/13, 2013/14 and 2014/15).

Tutorial note

The examiner did not expect you to provide any more detailed computations than those shown above, but you might find it easier to understand why the loss relief applies in this way if you look at the following computations.

Banda could use the loss of 2015/16 against general income in 2012/13 as follows:

	Non savings income £	Dividend income £	Total £
Salary	15,225		
Dividend income (£20,250 × 100/90)		22,500	
Total income	15,225	22,500	37,725
Less: early years loss relief	(15,225)	(4,775)	(20,000)
Net income	0	17,725	17,725
Less: personal allowance	(0)	(10,000)	(10,000)
Taxable income	0	7,725	7,725

Tax	£
£7,725 × 10%	772
Less: tax credit on dividend	(772)
Tax payable	0

Tax saved £(1,045 − 0)	£1,045

Banda could use the loss of 2016/17 against general income in 2013/14 as follows:

	Non savings income £	Dividend income £	Total £
Salary	15,225		
Dividend income (£20,250 × 100/90)		22,500	
Total income	15,225	22,500	37,725
Less: early years loss relief	(15,225)	(12,025)	(27,250)
Net income	0	10,475	10,475
Less: personal allowance	(0)	(10,000)	(10,000)
Taxable income	0	475	475

Tax	£
£475 × 10%	47
Less: tax credit on dividend	(47)
Tax payable	0

Tax saved £(1,045 − 0)	£1,045

Banda could use the loss of 2017/18 against general income in 2014/15 as follows:

	Non savings income £	Dividend income £	Total £
Salary	15,225		
Dividend income (£20,250 × 100/90)		22,500	
Total income	15,225	22,500	37,725
Less: early years loss relief	(7,250)	(0)	(7,250)
Net income	7,975	22,500	30,475
Less: personal allowance	(7,975)	(2,025)	(10,000)
Taxable income	0	20,475	20,475

Tax	£
£20,475 × 10%	2,047
Less: tax credit on dividend	(2,047)
Tax payable	0

Tax saved £(1,045 – 0)	£1,045

(ii) **Business run as a company – Aral Ltd**

The anticipated allowable losses for Aral Ltd are as follows:

	Trading income £	Allowable Loss £
6 months ending 30 June 2016	0	(40,000)
Year ending 30 June 2017	0	(14,500)

Aral Ltd owned by Banda

The losses would have to be carried forward and deducted from the trading profits of the year ending 30 June 2018.

Aral Ltd cannot offset the loss in the current period or carry it back as it has no other income or gains.

Aral Ltd owned by Flores Ltd

The two companies will form a group relief group if Flores Ltd owns at least 75% of the ordinary share capital of Aral Ltd. The trading losses could be surrendered to Flores Ltd in the year ending 30 June 2016 (note) and the year ending 30 June 2017.

The total tax saved would be £(40,000 + 14,500) × 20%   £10,900

Note

The whole of the loss for the period ending 30 June 2016 can be surrendered to Flores Ltd as it is less than that company's profit for the corresponding period, ie £60,000 (£120,000 × 6/12).

Recommended structure

The Aral business should be established in a company owned by Flores Ltd.

This will maximise the relief available in respect of the trading losses and enable relief to be obtained in the period in which the losses are incurred.

(c) **Tax implications of there being a loan from Flores Ltd to Banda**

Flores Ltd should have paid tax to HMRC equal to 25% of the loan, ie £5,250. The tax should have been paid on the company's normal due date for corporation tax in respect of the accounting period in which the loan was made, which was 1 April following the end of the accounting period.

The tax is due because Flores Ltd is a close company that has made a loan to a participator and that loan is not in the ordinary course of the company's business.

HMRC will repay the tax when the loan is either repaid or written off.

Flores Ltd should also have included the loan on Banda's Form P11D in order to report it to HMRC because it is a taxable benefit as the loan is interest-free.

Banda should have paid income tax on an annual benefit equal to 3.25% of the amount of loan outstanding during each tax year as follows:

£21,000 × 3.25% × 20% £136

Interest and penalties may be charged in respect of the tax underpaid by both Flores Ltd and Banda and in respect of the incorrect returns made to HMRC.

Tutorial note

If the Aral business is carried on as a sole trade, these annual benefits will be covered by early years trading loss relief in part (b)(i) above.

Willingness to act for Banda

We would not wish to be associated with a client who has engaged in deliberate tax evasion as this poses a threat to the fundamental principles of integrity and professional behaviour.

Accordingly, we should refuse to act for Banda unless she is willing to disclose the details regarding the loan to HMRC and pay the ensuing tax liabilities.

Even if full disclosure is made, we should consider whether the loan was deliberately hidden from HMRC or Banda's previous tax adviser and, if so, should refuse to act for her.

11 Shuttelle (ATAX 06/13)

Text references. Employment income is covered in Chapter 4 and pensions in Chapter 2. The income tax computation is dealt with in Chapter 1. Overseas aspects of income tax are the subject of Chapter 10.

Top tips. Although there are no specific marks for presentation in this question, it would be advisable to set out the computations in part (a) neatly to make sure that relevant marks were awarded.

Easy marks. There were some easy marks in part (a) for basic income tax computations. In part (b), the remittance basis charge should have been well known.

Examiner's comments. Part (a) was in two closely related parts. It required candidates to calculate the benefit in respect of accommodation provided by an employer and to appreciate the effect on an individual's income tax liability of making pension contributions in excess of the annual allowance, where contributions of less than the annual allowance had been made in earlier years. Candidates also had to recognise that the pension contributions would affect the personal allowance available and the tax bands. This was a tricky question to get absolutely correct, and very few candidates did so, but there were plenty of marks available to candidates who knew how to put an income tax computation together and were aware of the rules relating to the determination of the annual allowance for a particular year. On the whole candidates scored reasonably well. In particular, most candidates handled the accommodation benefit well and knew that the tax bands needed to be extended. Many candidates were also aware that there was a three-year rule in respect of the annual allowance, although many were not absolutely clear as to how the rule worked. Many candidates missed the fact that the personal allowance would be available in full possibly because they did not pause and think at that stage of the calculation. Tax calculations should be done as a series of small steps with thought at each step in order to ensure that important matters are not missed.

Part (b) concerned the remittance basis and was not done particularly well. The problem here was that candidates did not have a clear set of rules. Instead, they had an awareness of a series of technical terms and time periods that were all confused. This made it very difficult to score well. The first thing candidates had to do was to explain whether or not the remittance basis was available to each of three individuals. This required a statement of the availability of the remittance basis together with a reason. For those who did not know the rules there was a 50:50 chance as regards the availability of the remittance basis. However, the reason for its availability or non-availability caused a lot more problems. Candidates must learn the rules and be able to apply them and state them clearly. In addition, the marks available for giving a reason are only awarded where the whole of the reason given is correct.

For example, the remittance basis was available to Lin because he was UK resident but not UK domiciled. Candidates who stated this together with various time periods of residency could not score the mark for the reason as it was not clear from their answer whether it was his residence and domicile status that was relevant or the time periods. The second thing candidates had to do was to state, with reasons, the remittance basis charge applicable to each of the individuals on the assumption that the remittance basis was available to all of them. Again, this was not done particularly well due to many candidates having a very confused knowledge of the rules. One particular area of confusion related to the automatic applicability of the remittance basis where **unremitted** income and gains are less than £2,000; many candidates thought the rule related to the level of **remitted** income and gains.

Marking scheme

					Marks
(a)	(i)		Benefit in respect of accommodation	2	
			Personal allowance	1	
			Tax bands	1½	
			Relevance of employer's pension contribution	1	
			Annual allowance	2	
			Tax on excess pension contributions	1½	
			Max		8
	(ii)		Comparison with original liability	2½	
			Tax relief at source on pension contributions	1	
			Max		3
(b)	(i)	(1)	Availability of remittance basis		
			General rule	1½	
			Application of the rule to the individuals	1½	
		(2)	The remittance basis charge		
			Lin	1	
			Nan	1½	
			Yu	1½	
					7
	(ii)		Example of remittances – one mark each		2
					20

(a) Shuttelle

(i) Income tax liability for the tax year 2014/15

	£
Salary	203,390
Accommodation (W1)	6,000
Net income	209,390
Less: personal allowance (W2)	(10,000)
Taxable income	199,390

Income tax liability

£(31,865 + £120,000) = £151,865 × 20%	30,373
£(199,390 – 151,865) = 47,525 × 40%	19,010
Excess pension contributions £59,000 (W3) × 40%	23,600
Income tax liability	72,983

Tutorial notes

1 The higher rate limit has been increased to £270,000 (£150,000 + £120,000), due to the pension contributions. Accordingly, the excess pension contributions will be taxed at 40%.

2 In the exam, equal credit was given to candidates who included the excess pension contributions within taxable income.

Workings

1   *Benefit in respect of accommodation*

	£
Basic benefit: annual value	7,100
Additional benefit £(595,000 – 75,000) = £520,000 × 3.25%	16,900
Total benefits for full tax year	24,000
Benefits in 2014/15: £24,000 × 3/12 (available 6.4 to 30.6)	6,000

2   *Personal allowance*

The adjusted net income is as follows:

	£
Net income	209,930
Less: gross personal pension contributions	(120,000)
Adjusted net income	89,930

Since the adjusted net income does not exceed the limit of £100,000, the personal allowance is available in full.

3   *Excess pension contributions*

	£
Gross contributions by Shuttelle	120,000
Gross contributions by Din Ltd	4,000
Annual allowance available in 2014/15 (W4)	(65,000)
Excess pension contributions	59,000

4   *Annual allowance available in 2014/15*

	£	£
Annual allowance for 2014/15		40,000
Brought forward from 2012/13		
£(50,000 – 19,000 – 4,000)	27,000	
Less: used in 2013/14		
£(50,000 – 48,000 – 4,000)	(2,000)	
		25,000
Annual allowance available in 2014/15		65,000

(ii)   **Total tax relief in respect of the gross personal pension contributions of £120,000**

	£
Income tax on taxable income of £209,390	
(ie ignoring the pension contributions)	
£31,865 × 20%	6,373
£(150,000 – 31,865) = £118,135 × 40%	47,254
£(209,390 – 150,000) = £59,390 × 45%	26,725
Income tax liability, ignoring the pension contributions	80,352
Less: Income tax liability, after pension contributions (part (i))	(72,983)
Add: Tax relief on pension contributions at source £120,000 × 20%	24,000
Total tax relief in respect of pension contributions	31,369

Tutorial notes

1   When calculating the liability ignoring the pension contributions, there would be no personal allowance due to the level of the net income.

2   By charging tax on the excess pension contributions, relief is effectively only given for the balance of the contributions, £61,000 (£120,000 – £59,000), as set out below:

	£
Tax saved in respect of pension contribution of £61,000	
£59,390 × 45%	26,725
£1,610 × 40%	644
Tax saved in respect of PA becoming available	
£10,000 × 40%	4,000
	31,369

(b) **The three non-UK domiciled individuals**

(i) *The availability of the remittance basis and the remittance basis charge*

(1) The availability of the remittance basis

The remittance basis is available to UK resident individuals who are not domiciled in the UK. Accordingly:

– The remittance basis is available to Lin and Yu.

– The remittance basis is not available to Nan as he is not UK resident (and so his overseas income is not liable to UK income tax and so remittance is irrelevant).

(2) The remittance basis charge

Lin has unremitted overseas income and gains of less than £2,000. Accordingly, the remittance basis will apply automatically, such that there will not be a remittance basis charge.

Nan has unremitted overseas income and gains of more than £2,000. If Nan were able to make a claim for the remittance basis, he would be liable for the remittance basis charge of £50,000 because Nan has been resident in the UK for 12 of the 14 tax years prior to 2014/15.

Yu has unremitted overseas income and gains of more than £2,000. If Yu made a claim for the remittance basis, he would be liable for the remittance basis charge of £30,000 because Yu has been resident in the UK for seven of the nine tax years prior to 2014/15.

(ii) *Actions that would be regarded as remittances*

Bringing property into the UK which was purchased out of overseas income/gains.

Paying for services received in the UK out of overseas income/gains.

The use of overseas income/gains to pay the interest/capital on a debt where the funds borrowed have been brought into the UK or used to acquire property or services in the UK.

Tutorial note. Only two examples were required.

12 Ava (ATAX 12/09)

Text references. Income tax administration is covered in Chapter 15. The inheritance tax aspects of this question are dealt with in Chapters 16 and 17.

Top tips. Where you are told that two spouses or civil partners have died, always check to see if the first spouse had a nil rate band which was not fully utilised.

Easy marks. Part (a) covered basic income tax administration and should have produced easy marks.

Examiner's comments. Part (a) required a list of the consequences of the late submission of an income tax return and the late payment of the individual's income tax liability. This was a relatively straightforward requirement and the majority of candidates earned marks for the points they made. However, the list should have included four separate consequences whereas most candidates only included two.

Part (b) concerned the inheritance tax and capital gains tax implications of the gift of a farm and was in two parts.

Part (i) required a reasoned explanation of the availability of both agricultural property relief and business property relief in respect of the gift. This part was answered well with many candidates scoring full marks.

Part (ii) required calculations of the capital gains tax and inheritance tax payable in respect of the gift together with the due dates of payment. Answers to this part varied considerably. Stronger candidates were able to score well with accurate calculations and correct dates. Weaker candidates confused the two taxes and the reliefs and exemptions available by, for example, including agricultural property relief in the capital gains tax computation. They also failed to include the dates asked for. The majority of students missed the fact that a proportion of the husband's nil rate band could be transferred to the widow.

Marking scheme

				Marks
(a)	Submission date for return		1	
	Penalty for late submission		1	
	Penalty on overdue tax		1	
	Interest on overdue tax		1	
				4
(b)	(i)	*Agricultural property relief*		
		Location in EEA	½	
		Amount of relief	1	
		Qualifying period	2	
		Business property relief	1	
		Max		4
	(ii)	*Capital gains tax*		
		Amount payable	2	
		Due date	1	
		Inheritance tax		
		Amount chargeable to IHT	2	
		Nil rate band	3	
		IHT due	1½	
		Due date	1	
		Date of claim to transfer unused nil rate band	1	
		Assumption	1	
		Max		12
				20

(a)   **Late submission of 2014/15 income tax return**

The latest date for submission of the 2014/15 income tax return was 31 January 2016. The penalty date is the day after the due date.

An immediate penalty of £100 will have arisen because the return was late. As the return was over three months late, HMRC could charge a daily penalty of £10 per day for a maximum of 90 days. A further penalty for submission of the return more than six months but less than twelve months following the penalty date applies being the greater of 5% of the tax liability and £300.

A penalty also arises on the late payment of the balancing payment. The penalty date in this case is 30 days after the due date of 31 January 2016.

A penalty equal to 10% of the outstanding income tax will be levied because the tax will be paid between five months but not more than 11 months after the penalty date.

Interest will be charged on the outstanding income tax from 31 January 2016 until 14 December 2016 at an annual rate of 3%.

BPP
LEARNING MEDIA

(b) (i) **Availability of agricultural property relief and business property relief**

Hayworth Farm is agricultural property situated in the EEA (which includes the UK) and therefore qualifies for agricultural property relief. The relief is given on the agricultural value of the property rather than its market value. 100% relief is available.

Because the farm is farmed by tenants, it must have been owned by Ava and farmed by someone (in this case the tenants) for at least seven years prior to the transfer. Ava is able to satisfy this condition because she inherited the farm from her husband and therefore his period of ownership can be added to hers.

Business property relief is not available in respect of the gift of the farm as it has always been held as an investment and not as a business asset.

(ii) **Tax payable on gift of Hayworth Farm**

Capital gains tax

	£
Market value (February 2017)	650,000
Less: cost (probate value November 2016)	(494,000)
Gain	156,000
Less: annual exempt amount (assumed available)	(11,000)
Taxable gain	145,000

	£
Capital gains tax @ 28% (due 31 January 2018)	40,600

Inheritance tax

	£	£
Potentially exempt transfer		
Market value (February 2017)		650,000
Less: APR £445,000 @ 100%		(445,000)
Transfer of value		205,000
Less: annual exemption 2016/17		(3,000)
Potentially exempt transfer now chargeable		202,000
Nil rate bands available		
Ava's nil rate band	325,000	
Less: gift on 1.12.15 £(251,000 – 6,000)	(245,000)	
		(80,000)
Burt's nil rate band	325,000	
Less: legacy to sister	(293,000)	
		(32,000)
Amount chargeable to inheritance tax		90,000
Inheritance tax @ 40%		36,000
Less: taper relief (3 to 4 years @ 20%)		(7,200)
Inheritance tax payable on PET		28,800

The inheritance tax will be payable on 31 July 2021 (six months after the end of the month of Ava's death).

The claim to transfer Burt's unused nil rate band to Ava must be made by 31 January 2023 (two years from the end of the month of Ava's death).

Assumption: Ava's nephew still owns the farm on 1 January 2021, or has died prior to that date whilst owning it, and so APR is available on the farm when the PET comes into charge on Ava's death.

13 Brad (ATAX 06/13)

Text references. Overseas aspects of capital gains tax are covered in Chapter 14. The basics of inheritance tax are dealt with in Chapter 16. Related property valuation and business property relief are covered in Chapter 17. The basics of chargeable gains are in Chapter 11 and stamp taxes in Chapter 19.

Top tips. It is important to read the question very carefully and produce an answer which covers all of the requirements. For example, in part (a), you were given a very specific brief about what to include in your answer.

Easy marks. There were some easy marks in part (b)(i) for a basic description of inheritance tax advantages of making lifetime gifts to individuals.

Examiner's comments. This question was done well by many candidates. Part (a) required candidates to explain Brad's UK capital gains tax liability and the reasons for him being only temporarily non-UK resident and to state the payment date for the tax due. The majority of candidates had some knowledge of the temporary non-UK resident rules and quite a reasonable knowledge of capital gains tax generally, such that they scored reasonably well. Most candidates knew the five-year rule although a much smaller number stated the four years out of seven rule. A minority of candidates stated a rule correctly in general terms but failed to apply it to the facts of the question. For example, some candidates stated that assets bought and sold during the period of non-residence were not subject to UK capital gains tax but then went on to calculate a gain in respect of the antique bed. Other candidates failed to apply the basics. For example, a minority of candidates omitted the annual exempt amount whilst others either provided an incorrect payment date or failed to provide one at all. When providing a payment date it is important to make it clear which tax year is being addressed. There were three possible relevant tax years in this question so stating a date without a year could not score unless the candidate explained in general terms how the date is determined, ie 31 January after the end of the tax year.

Part (b)(i) was an invitation to candidates to be general rather than specific as it required an explanation of the advantages of lifetime giving. Many candidates did very well but the performance of the majority was unsatisfactory. The advantages of lifetime giving are scattered throughout the inheritance tax system with certain exemptions only being available in respect of lifetime gifts, potentially exempt transfers being exempt once the donor has lived for seven years, taper relief once the donor has lived for at least three years, and the value of a gift being frozen at the time of the gift together with the availability of relief for any fall in value of the assets gifted. Most candidates would have known all of these rules but many did not include them all in their answers. Instead they wrote at length about some of them whilst omitting others. In particular, many candidates did not address the exemptions available in respect of lifetime giving. This is likely to be because candidates simply started writing and kept writing until they felt they had written enough. These candidates would have benefited from thinking their way through the inheritance tax system and noting each of the advantages of lifetime giving before they started writing. Part (b)(ii) concerned a particular gift of shares and required knowledge of the valuation rules and business property relief. The valuation, which involved fall in value together with related property, was done well with many candidates scoring full marks. A minority of candidates were not aware that it is only the spouse's property that is related whilst others failed to appreciate that it is only the donor's property that is valued (the related property is only relevant when determining the valuation). The business property relief was done well with the majority of candidates identifying the two year rule and the relevance of the investments. Fewer candidates stated the need for the donee to continue owning the shares until the death of the donor.

Candidates did not do so well when it came to identifying other tax issues. Most candidates simply repeated the basics of the inheritance tax rules in relation to potentially exempt transfers when what was required here was consideration of capital gains tax and stamp duty.

			Marks
(a)	Conditions	2	
	Antique bed and motor car	1½	
	Quoted shares	3	
	Tax liabilities	3½	
	Max		8
(b) (i)	Seven year rule	1	
	Valuation	2	
	Exemptions	3	
	Taper relief	2	
	Max		7
(ii)	Fall in value	3½	
	Availability of business property relief		
	Business of Omnium Ltd	1½	
	Brad's ownership of the shares	1	
	Circumstances on Brad's death	1	
	Calculation of business property relief		
	Rate of relief	1	
	Excepted assets	2	
	Other tax matters	2½	
	Max		10
			25

(a) Capital gains tax

Brad will be regarded as only temporarily non-UK resident whilst living in Keirinia because:

- He was non-UK resident for less than five years; and

- Having always lived in the UK prior to moving to Keirinia, he was UK resident for at least four of the seven tax years immediately prior to the tax year of departure.

As a temporary non-UK resident, Brad will be subject to UK capital gains tax on the assets sold whilst he was non-UK resident, which he owned at the date of his departure from the UK. Accordingly, the antique bed is excluded from these rules as it was both bought and sold during the period of temporary non-UK residence. The profit on the sale of the motor car is ignored as motor cars are exempt assets for the purposes of capital gains tax.

The shares were sold in 2011/12, the tax year of departure, so the gain on these shares was subject to tax in that year under general principles, as Brad was UK resident in that year. However, there will have been no tax to pay as the capital gain of £4,900 (£18,900 – £14,000) was covered by the annual exempt amount for 2011/12.

The capital gains tax due on the sale of the painting is calculated as follows:

	£
Capital gain £(36,400 – 15,000)	21,400
Less: annual exempt amount	(11,000)
	10,400
Capital gains tax @ 28%	2,912

The gain on the sale of the painting is subject to tax in 2015/16, the tax year in which Brad became UK resident again, and not in the year of sale. Accordingly, the tax is due on 31 January 2017.

(b) **Inheritance tax**

(i) **The inheritance tax advantages of making lifetime gifts to individuals**

A lifetime gift to an individual is a potentially exempt transfer. It will be exempt from inheritance tax if the donor survives the gift by seven years.

If the donor dies within seven years of making the gift, such that the gift is chargeable to inheritance tax, the value used will be the value at the time of the gift and not the value at the time of death. Any increase in the value of the asset will be ignored, although relief will be available if the asset falls in value following the gift.

Certain exemptions are available only in respect of lifetime gifts. These exemptions are:

- Annual exemption of £3,000 each year
- Gifts in consideration of marriage/civil partnership up to certain limits
- Regular gifts out of income that do not affect the donor's standard of living
- Small gifts exemption of £250 per donee per tax year

Any inheritance tax due on the donor's death will be reduced by taper relief if the donor survives the gift by more than three years. The tax due will be reduced by 20% if the donor survives the gift by more than three but less than four years. The percentage reduction will increase by 20% for each additional year that the donor survives the gift.

(ii) **In respect of the possible gift of 1,500 shares in Omnium Ltd to Dani**

Fall in value of Brad's estate

The fall in value of Brad's estate on a gift of 1,500 shares in Omnium Ltd will be calculated as follows:

	Related property	
	Included	*Ignored*
	£	£
Value of shares held prior to the gift:		
3,000 × £290 (30% + 45% = 75%)	870,000	
3,000 × £205 (30%)		615,000
Value of shares held after the gift:		
1,500 × £240 (15% + 45% = 60%)	(360,000)	
1,500 × £190 (15%)		(285,000)
Transfer of value	510,000	330,000

The higher fall in value of £510,000, produced by reference to related property, will be used.

Tutorial note

The value of Brad's shares is determined by reference to the shares held by him and his wife under the related property rules.

Business property relief

Business property relief will not be available if the business of Omnium Ltd consists wholly or mainly of dealing in securities, stocks or shares or land and buildings or the making or holding of investments. Accordingly, it will be necessary to determine the significance of the investment properties to the activities of Omnium Ltd as a whole.

Brad must have owned the shares for at least two years at the time of the gift. This condition is satisfied.

Business property relief will not be available unless Dani still owns the shares at the time of Brad's death (or had died whilst owning the shares) and the shares continue to qualify for the relief.

If all of the conditions set out above are satisfied, business property relief will be available at the rate of 100%, because Omnium Ltd is an unquoted company.

However, where there are excepted assets, business property relief will be restricted to:

$$100\% \times \text{the fall in value} \times \frac{\text{Omnium Ltd's non-excepted assets}}{\text{Omnium Ltd's total assets}}$$

Excepted assets are assets that have not been used for the purposes of the company's business in the two years prior to the transfer and are not required for such use in the future. Some or all of Omnium Ltd's investment properties may be classified as excepted assets.

Tutorial note

Business property relief will only be relevant if Brad were to die within seven years of making the gift, such that the potentially exempt transfer became a chargeable transfer. Business property relief would also be available if Dani has disposed of the shares prior to Brad's death and acquired qualifying replacement property within three years of the disposal.

Other tax issues

The gift of shares will be a disposal at market value for the purposes of capital gains tax. Gift relief will be available but will be restricted because of the investment properties owned by Omnium Ltd.

Gifts of shares are not subject to stamp duty.

Tutorial note

The question asked for a brief statement only of the other tax issues.

14 Sushi (ATAX 12/10)

Text references. Inheritance tax overseas aspects and variations are covered in Chapter 18. Overseas aspects of income tax are dealt with in Chapter 10.

Top tips. Remember to use a letter format in your answer – there is a specific mark for this aspect.

Easy marks. The remittance basis is a favourite topic of this examiner and there were some easy marks for basic points.

Examiner's comments. Part (i) concerned inheritance tax and, in particular, the relevance of domicile to an individual's tax position. The level of knowledge here was good with some very strong, thorough answers. However, many candidates who scored well for this part of the question often did so in an inefficient manner which may have left them short of time for the remainder of the exam. As always, there was a need to pause; this time in order to determine the best way to say what needed to be said. Weaker candidates simply kept writing, often repeating themselves, until they finally got to where they wanted to be. Stronger candidates wrote short, precise phrases which earned all of the marks despite using very few words. Candidates should practise explaining areas of taxation making sure that their explanations are concise and clear.

There was a need to address the position of both the mother and the daughter but many candidates simply addressed 'inheritance tax' rather than the situation of the individuals. Candidates will be more successful in the exam if they think in terms of providing advice to individuals and companies rather than addressing technical issues as this will help them to stick to the point and to satisfy the questions' requirements.

A somewhat surprising error made by a significant minority of candidates was to state that the inheritance tax position on the death of Sushi's mother depended on the domicile status of Sushi as opposed to that of her mother. It is, of course, the status of the person whose estate has fallen in value that is relevant.

A final thought on this part of the question is that many candidates wasted time calculating inheritance tax, despite not having sufficient information, whilst others provided a considerable amount of detail regarding the taxation implications of making a potentially exempt transfer, despite being specifically told not to in the question.

Part (ii) concerned overseas income and the remittance basis. The performance of candidates for this part was mixed. To begin with there was much confusion regarding the conditions that must be satisfied in order for the remittance basis to be available with candidates mixing up domicile and residence with the remittance basis charge rules (and the rule for inheritance tax deemed domicile). The application of the £2,000 rule was also misunderstood by many.

Candidates were asked to explain the meaning of 'remittance' and the 'remittance basis'. Most candidates attempted to do this, which was very encouraging, but few had much knowledge beyond the absolute basics. Similarly, most candidates were aware of the remittance basis charge but a significant number were confused as to the situation in which the charge would be levied. On the plus side, the vast majority of candidates provided a conclusion (as requested) and many produced neat and reasonably accurate calculations.

Marks were available for professional skills in this question. In order to earn these marks candidates first had to satisfy the requirement in relation to the format of the document requested. Further marks were then available for providing clear explanations and coherent calculations.

On the whole, the performance of candidates in this area was good with the majority of candidates producing correctly formatted documents in a style that was easy to follow. However, many candidates failed to maintain the correct style of a document throughout their answer such that, for example, the letters written in response to this question often referred to the client correctly as 'you' to begin with but then reverted to using the client's name later in the answer.

Marking scheme

			Marks
(a)	Assets subject to inheritance tax	1½	
	Mother's death	1	
	Sushi's death		
	UK assets	½	
	Foreign assets	½	
	Domicile of origin	1	
	Domicile of choice	1	
	Deemed domicile	2½	
	UK IHT on land and buildings in Zakuskia		
	Valuation	1½	
	UK IHT and double tax relief	2	
	The statue	3½	
	Max		12
(b)	Meaning and availability of remittance basis	1½	
	Meaning of remittance	3	
	Calculations		
	Remittance basis not available	2	
	Remittance basis available		
	Remittance basis charge	1	
	Loss of personal allowance and annual exempt amount	2	
	Tax on remitted income	1	
	Explanatory notes (1 mark per sensible point) – maximum	3	
	Conclusion	1	
	Max		12
	Appropriate style and presentation	1	
	Effectiveness of communication	1	
	Approach to problem solving	1	
	Max		3
			27

Sushi's address
6 December 2015

Dear Sushi

Personal taxation

I set out below my advice in connection with the assets you have inherited from your mother.

(a) **UK inheritance tax and the statue**

UK inheritance tax is charged on assets situated in the UK. It is also charged on assets situated overseas where the owner is domiciled or deemed domiciled in the UK. A person's domicile is, broadly speaking, the country in which they have their permanent home.

On the death of your mother

Your mother was domiciled in Zakuskia and did not own any UK assets. Accordingly, there will be no UK inheritance tax liability on her estate.

On your death

You now own both UK and Zakuskian assets. On your death, UK inheritance tax will, inevitably, be charged in respect of the UK assets but the treatment of the assets in Zakuskia will depend on your domicile position. When you were born you would have acquired a domicile of origin in Zakuskia as your father was domiciled there. You will have retained this domicile unless you have acquired a domicile of choice in the UK. You will have acquired a domicile of choice in the UK if it can be seen that you have severed all of your ties with Zakuskia with the intention of making the UK your permanent home. You will continue to be domiciled in Zakuskia if we can show that you have retained ties there with the intention of returning there one day.

However, even if you continue to be domiciled in Zakuskia, you will be deemed domiciled in the UK (for the purposes of inheritance tax only) once you have been resident here for 17 of the 20 tax years ending with the year in which any assets are transferred. At the end of the tax year 2015/16 you will have been resident here for 15 years. Accordingly, 2017/18 will be your seventeenth year of UK residence and you will be deemed domiciled in the UK from that year onwards such that your Zakuskian assets, in addition to your UK assets, will then be subject to inheritance tax. Until 2017/18, provided you have not acquired a domicile of choice in the UK, your Zakuskian assets will not be subject to inheritance tax.

UK inheritance tax on land and buildings situated in Zakuskia

Land and buildings situated in Zakuskia but subject to UK inheritance tax will be included in your death estate at the market value in Zakuskia converted into sterling at the UK buying rate as this gives the lowest sterling equivalent. Expenses incurred in Zakuskia in connection with administering and realising the property will be deductible up to a maximum of 5% of the value of the property.

Any available nil rate band will be deducted from your death estate and the balance will be subject to UK inheritance tax at 40%. The amount payable in respect of the land and buildings in Zakuskia is calculated by determining the percentage, by reference to market values, of your assets held at death represented by the land and buildings and applying that percentage to the total UK inheritance tax due. The inheritance tax due in Zakuskia will be deductible from the UK liability but cannot result in a repayment.

The statue

Once you bring the statue into the UK it will become a UK asset and the gift will be a potentially exempt transfer regardless of your country of domicile. However, the gift of the statue will not be a potentially exempt transfer if we are able to demonstrate that you are currently domiciled in Zakuskia (ie you have not acquired a domicile of choice in the UK), and you give the statue to your son whilst it is in Zakuskia. Such a gift would be outside UK inheritance tax as the asset would be overseas and you, the donor, would not be UK domiciled.

If you have already acquired a UK domicile of choice the gift of the statue will be a potentially exempt transfer regardless of where it is situated.

Alternatively, you could make a variation of your inheritance from your mother as if the statue had been left by your mother to your son. The variation must be made by you within two years of your mother's death, in writing and state that it is to have effect for inheritance tax purposes. The result would be that the transfer would be treated as made to your son by your mother on her death of an asset not situated in the UK. Accordingly, there will be no UK inheritance tax liability on this transfer.

(b) **The Zakuskian income**

If you are domiciled in Zakuskia you can choose to be taxed on the remittance basis such that you will only be taxed on remittances to the UK. If you have acquired a domicile of choice in the UK you will be taxed on all of the Zakuskian income regardless of whether or not it is remitted to the UK.

The most obvious example of a remittance occurs where the overseas income is brought into the UK. However, the definition of remittance is much wider than this. For example, it includes the situation where the overseas income is used to repay an overseas debt where the funds borrowed have been brought into the UK. A remittance would also occur where the overseas income is used to purchase items which are themselves brought into the UK. There are exceptions to this latter rule in respect of: items costing less than £1,000, items for personal use (clothes, watches etc), and items brought into the UK for repair or for no more than 275 days. There are also exceptions where money or property is brought into the UK to acquire shares in or make a loan to a trading company or a member of a trading group or to pay the remittance basis charge.

My calculations are included in the appendix to this letter.

You can see that if you remit £30,000 per annum, it will not be beneficial for you to claim the remittance basis due to the remittance basis charge (at the higher level since you have been resident in the UK for 12 of the 14 tax years preceding 2015/16) and the loss of tax reliefs. The additional UK tax payable in respect of the Zakuskian income will therefore be £16,500 per year on the arising basis.

Please do not hesitate to contact me if I can be of any further assistance.

Yours sincerely

Tax manager

Appendix

Sushi – increase in UK tax liability due to the Zakuskian income

A *Remittance basis not available*

	£
Zakuskian income gross of Zakuskian tax	55,000
UK income tax at 40% (as non-savings (property) and savings income) (N1)	22,000
Less: relief for Zakuskian tax at 10% (lower than UK tax)	(5,500)
Annual increase in UK tax payable	16,500

B *Remittance basis available and claimed – Remit £30,000 (gross) per annum*

	£
Remittance basis charge (N2)	50,000
Loss of income tax personal allowance (£10,000 × 40%) (N3)	4,000
Loss of capital gains tax annual exempt amount (£11,000 × 28%) (N3)	3,080
Cost of claiming remittance basis	57,080

	£
Zakuskian income remitted to the UK, gross of Zakuskian tax	30,000
UK income tax at 40% (N4)	12,000
Less: relief for Zakuskian tax at 10% (lower than UK tax)	(3,000)
UK income tax on remitted income	9,000
Annual increase in UK tax payable £(57,080 + 9,000)	66,080

Notes

1   Your taxable income, before taking into account the Zakuskian income, is £34,000. This amount is after deducting your personal allowance and means that your net income is £(34,000 + 10,000) = £44,000. When the Zakuskian income of £55,000 is added to this, your net income will rise to £99,000 which is below the limit of £100,000 after which the personal allowance is gradually reduced. Therefore the Zakuskian income of £55,000 is taxable at 40% (with no additional tax due to abatement of the personal allowance).

2   The remittance basis will not be available to you automatically because you will have unremitted income of more than £2,000. The remittance basis charge of £50,000 will be payable because you are claiming the remittance basis and you have been resident in the UK for 12 of the 14 preceding tax years.

3   On claiming the remittance basis you will no longer be entitled to the income tax personal allowance and the capital gains tax annual exempt amount.

4   Income taxed under the remittance basis is taxed as non-savings income regardless of its true nature. Accordingly, the amount remitted will be taxed at 40%.

15 Surfe (ATAX 12/11)

Text references. Trusts are covered in Chapter 18. Inheritance tax is dealt with in Chapters 16 to 18.

Top tips. Where there is a gift of unquoted shares, watch out for the loss to donor rules when computing the transfer of value. Also, think about the effect of related property.

Easy marks. There were some easy marks relating to inheritance tax exemptions. The calculation of the death estate was also straightforward.

Examiner's comments. Part (a) required an outline of the capital gains tax implications of various transactions relating to the trust and the inheritance tax charges that may be payable in the future by the trustees. It was important for candidates to be methodical in their approach to this question. There were three transactions to be addressed in relation to capital gains tax whereas the inheritance aspects of the question were more open ended.

The majority of candidates knew some of the capital gains tax implications of the transactions but very few knew all of them. In particular, there was a lack of understanding that capital gains would arise when the trustees transfer trust assets to the beneficiaries of the trust. As always, when dealing with capital gains tax, it is vital to consider the availability of reliefs; gift relief is available when assets are transferred to a discretionary trust and again when they are transferred to the beneficiaries.

The inheritance aspects of part (a) were not handled as well as the capital gains tax aspects. The majority of candidates failed to mention the ten-yearly charges and exit charges payable out of the trust's assets.

Part (b) required a calculation of the inheritance tax liability arising on the death of an individual who had made a number of lifetime gifts. This was a fairly straightforward question, albeit with a couple of tricky points within it, but it was not handled particularly well.

There was a lack of appropriate structure to candidates' answers that indicated that, perhaps, there had been insufficient practice of this area. Inheritance tax computations should all look the same, starting with the tax on any chargeable lifetime transfers, followed by the consideration of gifts within seven years of death and ending with the death estate. However, many candidates began with the death estate and worked their way backwards towards the lifetime gifts; a method that was never going to be successful.

There was confusion as to which gift benefited from the annual exemptions and in respect of the utilisation of the nil rate band. There was also a general lack of knowledge of the impact of related property on the valuation of a gift. Other technical errors, made by a minority of candidates, included the treatment of cash as an exempt asset and business property relief being given in respect of the shares owned by the taxpayer.

On the positive side, the majority of candidates identified the availability of the husband's nil rate band and the death estate was handled well.

Marks

(a)	(i)	Gift of shares	1½	
		Future sale of quoted shares	½	
		Transfer of trust assets to beneficiaries	1½	
		Election details	1	
	(ii)	Inheritance tax	2½	
		Max		6
(b)		Inheritance tax in respect of lifetime gifts		
		Gift to charity	½	
		Gift to nephews	1½	
		Gift to trust		
		Shares – fall in value	2	
		Cash	½	
		Lifetime tax	1½	
		Gross chargeable transfer	½	
		Nil rate band available on death	2½	
		Inheritance tax payable on death	1½	
		Inheritance tax in respect of death estate	1½	
		Max		11
				17

(a) (i) **Capital gains tax**

A capital gain will arise on the gift of the shares to the trustees by reference to the market value of the shares. Gift relief will be available because the gift is a chargeable lifetime transfer for the purposes of inheritance tax. The gift relief election should be signed by Surfe and submitted by 5 April 2020 (within four years of the end of the tax year of the gift).

Capital gains made by the trustees whilst they are managing the assets of the trust will be subject to capital gains tax. The tax will be paid out of the trust assets.

A capital gain will arise on the transfer of trust assets from the trustees to Surfe's nephews by reference to the market value of the trust assets. Gift relief will be available because the transfer is immediately chargeable to inheritance tax. The gift relief election should be signed by the trustees and the recipient nephew and submitted within four years of the end of the tax year in which the transfer occurs.

Tutorial note. The detailed rules in connection with the calculation of capital gains tax payable by the trustees of a trust are not in the P6 syllabus.

(ii) **Inheritance tax**

It is assumed in the question that Surfe will die on 1 July 2018, ie within seven years of the gift of the shares and cash to the trust. Accordingly, the trustees will have to pay inheritance tax on the gift at 40% less the lifetime tax paid.

The trust will be subject to an inheritance tax charge every ten years (the 'principal' charge). The maximum charge will be 6% (30% of the lifetime tax rate of 20%) of the value of the trust assets at the time of the charge.

The transfer of trust assets from the trustees to the beneficiaries will also result in an exit charge to inheritance tax. The maximum charge will be 6% (30% of the lifetime tax rate of 20%) of the value of the assets transferred, times 39 quarters out of 40 quarters.

The principal charges are payable by the trustees, out of the trust assets. The trustees may also pay exit charges out of the trust assets.

(b)   **Inheritance tax payable on Surfe's death on 1 July 2018**

Gifts in the seven years prior to death

The gift on 1 February 2004 to the charity was an exempt transfer.

The gifts on 1 October 2015 to Surfe's nephews were reduced by the annual exemptions for 2015/16 and 2014/15. The potentially exempt transfer of £164,000 ((£85,000 × 2) – (£3,000 × 2)) will be covered by the nil rate band.

The gift of the shares to the trust on 1 January 2016

	£
Gross chargeable transfer (W1)	543,750
Inheritance tax:	
£325,667 (W2) × 0%	0
£218,083 × 40%	87,233
£543,750	87,233
Less: lifetime tax paid (W1)	(43,750)
	43,483

There will be no taper relief as the gift is less than three years prior to death.

Workings

1   *Gift to trust 1 January 2016*

	£
Value of Surfe's holding prior to gift 650 × £2,000 (N)	1,300,000
Less: value of Surfe's holding after gift 450 × £2,000 (N)	(900,000)
	400,000
Cash	100,000
Net transfer of value	500,000
Inheritance tax:	
£325,000 × 0%	0
£175,000 × 20/80 (Surfe is paying tax – grossing up required)	43,750
£500,000	43,750
Gross transfer of value £(500,000 + 43,750)	£543,750

Note.

The value per share of Surfe's holding is determined by reference to the number of shares she owns personally and any related property. Related property includes shares given by Surfe to a charity that the charity still owns. Accordingly, Surfe's holding prior to the gift, including related property, will be 100% (65% + 35%). Her holding after the gift, including related property, will be 80% (45% + 35%).

2   *Nil rate band on death*

	£
Nil rate band as at the date of death	325,000
Add: unused nil rate band of Flud adjusted for increase in nil rate	
band £(300,000 – 148,000) = £152,000 × £325,000/£300,000	164,667
	489,667
Less: amount utilised by gifts on 1 October 2015	(164,000)
Available nil rate band	325,667

The death estate on 1 July 2018

	£
House	1,400,000
Quoted shares	600,000
Shares in Leat Ltd (450 × £2,400) (N)	1,080,000
Chargeable estate	3,080,000

Inheritance tax:

£3,080,000 × 40% (nil rate band utilised by gifts on 1 January 2016 and
1 October 2015)

£

1,232,000

Note.

Surfe's holding, including the related property held by the charity, will be 80% (45% + 35%).

16 Una (ATAX 06/12)

Text references. Inheritance tax is covered in Chapters 16 to 18. Stamp taxes are covered in Chapter 19. Capital gains tax computation is dealt with in Chapter 11 and reliefs in Chapter 13. Income tax administration is in Chapter 15 and ethics in Chapter 30.

Top tips. When you are asked to include 'other tax implications' in your answer as in part (a) of this question, it is a good idea to jot down the main taxes that might be relevant to an individual and then consider whether any points arise from the scenario you have been given. Don't forget stamp duties!

Easy marks. There were some easy marks for the inheritance tax calculations in part (a). The four professional marks should also have been easy to obtain.

Examiner's comments. Part (a) was answered reasonably well. In particular, only a minority of candidates confused the rules of inheritance tax and capital gains tax. Also, many candidates demonstrated strong technical knowledge of the mechanics of inheritance tax and agricultural property relief. Now that inheritance tax has been part of Paper F6 for a while, candidates sitting Paper P6 can expect to see more questions in this style, ie questions which work at the margin rather than requiring complete tax computations.

The one common error in relation to inheritance tax was a failure to realise that the earlier cash gift had no effect on the nil band in respect of the later gift as it was made more than seven years prior to death. Other, less common, errors included deducting taper relief from the value transferred rather than from the inheritance tax liability and deducting the annual exemptions from the death estate.

The capital gains tax elements of the question were not handled as well as inheritance tax. Many candidates did not know the conditions relating to the availability of capital gains tax reliefs and simply assumed, incorrectly, that gift relief would be available. A substantial minority also forgot the fundamental point that there is no capital gains tax on death and calculated liabilities in respect of both lifetime gifts and gifts via Una's will.

However, the main problems experienced by candidates related to exam technique. There were three particular problems; failing to read the question sufficiently carefully, failing to address all of the requirements and running over time.

When reading the question, many candidates failed to identify the relevance of the exemption clause in the Double Taxation Agreement. The effect of the clause was to exempt the overseas villa from UK inheritance tax. This meant that, when dealing with the villa, candidates needed only to consider the tax suffered overseas. Those candidates who failed to appreciate this did not lose many marks but wasted time calculating UK inheritance tax on the villa.

The question required calculations of the 'possible reduction in the inheritance tax payable as a result of Una's death' in respect of each of the possible lifetime gifts. This required candidates to compare the tax arising on a lifetime gift with that arising if the asset passed via Una's will for both of the assets. There was then the need to consider the capital gains tax on the lifetime gift whilst remembering that there would be no capital gains tax if the assets were retained until death. Finally, candidates were asked to provide a concise summary of their calculations 'in order to assist Una in making her decision'. The problem was that many candidates were not sufficiently methodical such that they did not carry out all of the necessary tasks and missed out on easy marks. In particular, many candidates did not provide the final summary.

The final problem in relation to exam technique related to time management: it was evident that some candidates did not have a sufficient sense of urgency when answering this question. This resulted in lengthy explanations of how inheritance tax, and, to a lesser extent, capital gains tax, is calculated together with details of Una's plans.

The question asked for 'explanations where the calculations are not self-explanatory, particularly in relation to the availability of reliefs'. Candidates need to think carefully before providing narrative as writing is very time consuming. They should identify, in advance, the points they are planning to make and should then make each point in as concise a manner as possible. There is likely to be a mark for each relevant point so each one should take no more than two short sentences.

Part (b) was done reasonably well. There were two elements to a good answer: the penalties that could be levied on the taxpayer and the professional issues relating to the firm of accountants. The two elements were indicated clearly in the question which stated that 'the letter should explain the implications for Una and our firm'. Those candidates who failed to address both elements struggled to do well.

Marking scheme

				Marks
(a)	Calculations			
	Farmland – inheritance tax			
		Owned at death	2	
		Lifetime gift	4	
	Farmland – capital gains tax		1	
	Villa – inheritance tax (Soloria)		1	
	Villa – capital gains tax (UK)		1½	
	Notes on availability of relevant reliefs – one mark each		3	
	Other relevant tax and financial requirements – one mark each		5	
	Relevant assumption		1	
	Summary of position re capital taxes		2	
	Payment of rent		3	
		Max		21
	Professional marks for the overall presentation of the memorandum and the effectiveness with which the information is communicated			3
(b)	Determination of taxable profit		1	
	The need to disclose		4	
	Interest and penalties		3	
		Max		6
	Professional mark for overall presentation of the letter			1
				31

(a) To   The files
    From   Tax senior
    Date   15 June 2015
    Subject   Una – Gifts to son and granddaughter

The purpose of this memorandum is to provide advice to Una on the tax implications of a gift to be made to her son, Won, and the payment of rent on behalf of her granddaughter, Alona. For the purposes of this memorandum, it has been assumed that the gift to Won will be made on 18 November 2015 and that Una's death will occur on 31 December 2020.

(i) **Gift to Won**

Inheritance tax

Farmland situated in the UK

If Una owns the farmland at her death it will be included in her death estate. The inheritance tax on the farmland in the death estate will be as follows.

	£
Market value in death estate	1,100,000
Less APR £1,100,000 × 35% (100% of agricultural value)	(385,000)
Value included in death estate	715,000
Inheritance tax @ 40% (nil rate band used by other assets)	286,000

If Una gifts the farmland to Won – it will be a potentially exempt transfer (N1). The death tax in relation to this gift will be as follows:

	£
Market value (N2)	900,000
Less: annual exemptions 2015/16 and 2014/15 b/f	(6,000)
Potentially exempt transfer (PET)	894,000

Inheritance tax on death on 31 December 2020	
£325,000 (N3) @ 0%	0
£569,000 @ 40%	227,600
£894,000	227,600
Less: taper relief (death within 5 to 6 years of gift) @ 60%	(136,560)
	91,040
Add: additional tax on death estate due to use of nil rate band	
£325,000 @ 40%	130,000
Total death tax arising as a result of lifetime gift of farmland	221,040
Potential saving £(286,000 – 221,040)	64,960

Notes

1   There will be no UK inheritance tax when the gift is made as it will be a potentially exempt transfer.

2   Agricultural property relief will not be available in respect of a gift on 18 November 2015 as Una will not have owned the farm for the requisite seven years. This is on the assumption that the farmland did not replace other agricultural property which, together with this farmland, had been owned for seven out of the previous ten years.

3   The gift to Won in 2011 was initially partially exempt (2 annual exemptions) and the remaining value was a PET. The PET element became an exempt transfer when Una survived until May 2018. Therefore the full nil rate band is available against the PET of the farmland.

Villa situated in Soloria

There will be no UK inheritance tax due to the exemption clause in the UK–Soloria Double Taxation Agreement. There will be no inheritance tax in Soloria until Una's death.

The gift will save inheritance tax in Soloria as set out below.

	£
Liability if Una owns the villa at her death on 31 December 2020	170,000
Liability if Una gifts the villa to Won on 18 November 2015	(34,000)
Inheritance tax saved	136,000

Capital gains tax

Farmland situated in the UK

A gift of the farmland would result in a liability to capital gains tax as set out below. No gift relief would be available as the farmland is an investment (as opposed to a business asset), does not qualify for agricultural property relief, and the gift does not give rise to an immediate charge to inheritance tax. The farmland is not a qualifying asset for entrepreneurs' relief as it is not a business asset.

	£
Proceeds (market value)	900,000
Less cost	(720,000)
Gain	180,000
Capital gains tax @ 28% (Una is a higher rate taxpayer)	50,400

Villa situated in Soloria

A gift of the villa would result in a liability to UK capital gains tax as set out below. The villa is an investment and not a business asset, so no capital gains tax business reliefs would be available. There is no capital gains tax in Soloria.

	£
Proceeds (market value)	745,000
Less cost (probate value)	(600,000)
Gain	145,000
	£
Capital gains tax @ 28% (Una is a higher rate taxpayer)	40,600

Summary of capital taxes position

	Farmland £	Villa £
Inheritance tax – potential saving	64,960	136,000
Capital gains tax – liability	(50,400)	(40,600)
Net tax saving	14,560	95,400

Other tax implications in respect of the gift to Won

Inheritance tax

If Una were to die after 18 November 2021, there would be an additional 20% taper relief in the UK. If she were to survive the gift by seven years, there would be no UK inheritance tax in respect of the asset gifted and the inheritance tax nil rate band would be available against the death estate.

Stamp duty land tax

There is no charge to stamp duty land tax in the UK on a gift of land. The situation in Soloria would need to be investigated if a gift of the villa is proposed.

Financial implications in respect of the gift to Won

The potential gifts are income generating assets. Accordingly, Una should be aware that the gift will reduce her available income. The income in respect of the villa is subject to income tax in Soloria at the rate of 50%, so no UK income tax is payable due to double tax relief. The income in respect of the farmland is subject to UK income tax at the rate of 40%.

The capital gains tax would be payable on 31 January 2017 (31 January following the end of the tax year in which the gift is made). This is at least four years prior to the eventual inheritance tax saving. Because there is a gift of land but gift relief is not available, it would be possible to pay the capital gains tax in ten equal annual instalments (provided Won continues to own the asset gifted), but interest would be charged on the balance outstanding.

(ii) **Payment of Alona's rent**

The payments will be exempt if they represent normal expenditure out of income. For this exemption to be available, Una would have to show that:

- Each gift is part of her normal expenditure.
- The gifts are made out of income rather than capital.
- Having made the gifts, she still has sufficient income to maintain her usual standard of living.

Una must be able to demonstrate that her annual income exceeds her normal expenditure by the annual rental cost of £450 x 12 = £5,400 (maximum – less if Alona's rent is only payable during university term-time).

Una's address

15 June 2015

Dear Una

Income received in respect of the luxury motor car

I set out below our advice in relation to the income received in respect of the luxury motor car.

I have considered the circumstances surrounding the rental income in respect of the car and concluded that the profits from the hiring of the car are liable to income tax. In determining the taxable profit, the income you have received can be reduced by the expenses relating to the running and maintenance of the car. We can assist you in determining the taxable profit.

The taxable profit must be reported to HM Revenue and Customs; failure to disclose the profit would amount to tax evasion, which is a criminal offence. In addition, you will appreciate that we would not wish to be associated with a client who has engaged in deliberate tax evasion, as this poses a threat to the fundamental principles of integrity and professional behaviour. Accordingly, we cannot continue to act for you unless you are willing to disclose the hiring activity to HM Revenue and Customs and to pay any ensuing tax liabilities. We are required to notify the tax authorities if we cease to act for you, although we would not provide them with any reason for our action.

HM Revenue and Customs will charge interest on any tax liabilities that are overdue. A penalty may also be charged in respect of the non-declaration of the income. The maximum penalty is 70% of the tax liability for a deliberate non-disclosure of income where there is no attempt to conceal it (for example, by submitting false evidence in support). This penalty may be reduced if the income is disclosed to the authorities at a time when there is no reason to believe that the non-disclosure is about to be discovered and full assistance is provided to the authorities to enable them to quantify the error. The minimum penalty in these circumstances is 20% of the tax liability.

Yours sincerely

Tax manager

17 Grifter (ATAX 12/09)

Text references. Income tax administration is covered in Chapter 15. Inheritance tax is covered in Chapters 16 to 18. Overseas income tax is dealt with in Chapter 10 and overseas aspects of capital gains tax in Chapter 14, which also covers principal private residence relief. Badges of trade are covered in Chapter 6. Ethics are covered in Chapter 30.

Top tips. Set out your memorandum neatly with appropriate headings.

Easy marks. The calculation of the income tax on the overseas property should have been easy marks, in particular because you were told to assume that the interest and penalties would amount to 100% of the income tax liability.

Examiner's comments. Part (a) required a memorandum concerning a number of personal tax issues relating to Grifter, a man who was considering two possible strategies to reduce his mortgage. The question included a letter from Grifter setting out various aspects of his financial position and the two options to be considered. There was also an email from the candidate's manager, which set out the steps to be carried out in order to evaluate the two options. It was very pleasing to note that the vast majority of candidates followed the instructions carefully such that many were able to score high marks for this part of the question.

The memorandum was in two parts. Part (i) required calculations of the income tax due in respect of undeclared income relating to an overseas investment property and calculations of the inheritance due in respect of the property following the death of the person who gave it to Grifter. It also required candidates to comment on the client's behaviour in relation to a tax refund that he had received.

This first part of the memorandum was done well by the majority of candidates with many scoring full marks in respect of the income tax and some scoring full marks for both the income tax and the inheritance tax. The most common error was the failure to gross up the income in respect of the tax suffered overseas. Most candidates identified the need for Grifter to determine whether or not the tax refund had been received in error and to refund it to the tax authorities if he was not entitled to it.

The second part of the memorandum concerned the two possible ways of reducing the mortgage; the sale by Grifter of either a number of motor cars or his house. The sale of the motor cars was not handled as well as expected due mainly to a lack of thought and self-belief. Whilst many candidates pointed out, correctly, that motor cars were exempt from capital gains tax, a large number then went on to calculate capital gains tax on the sale of Grifter's cars as if the rules somehow could not apply to this particular situation. There was also a failure by a significant minority of candidates to include the 'detailed explanation' of the tax treatment of the sale of the cars as requested by the manager, which required consideration of the badges of trade. This was not technically difficult and most candidates would probably have made a good job of it if they had taken sufficient care to identify the need to do so.

In questions of this type candidates need to start by identifying all of the tasks they have been asked to carry out by both the client and the manager. They should then ensure that all of these tasks are addressed in the time available. Sufficient time will be available provided candidates do not allow themselves to be sidetracked into discussing irrelevant issues.

The sale of the house was handled quite well by most candidates with the majority recognising the relief available because the property was Grifter's principal private residence. The only common mistake here was to allow three years of the period of absence as deemed residence. This was not available as the period of absence was not preceded by a period of actual occupation.

Despite many candidates scoring well on this question, there are two general criticisms of their performance:

1   Many candidates could save themselves time by not providing explanations unless they are asked for. In his email the manager requested candidates to 'keep any narrative to a minimum unless I have specifically asked for it'. Unfortunately, this guidance was ignored by a large number of candidates who provided very time consuming step-by-step explanations of the calculations they were about to perform. A requirement to calculate means just that: calculate.

2   Candidates must recognise the commercial aspect of the tasks they are performing. In this question there was a need to think in terms of after tax proceeds, i.e. the cash proceeds less any tax liabilities as opposed to, in the case of Grifter's house, the taxable gain less the tax liability (which was a meaningless figure). A failure to do this led to some candidates reaching the conclusion that the Porsche should not be sold because 'it would result in a loss' whereas, of course, the Porsche should be sold because its sale would result in £62,560 (£68,000 × 92%) in the hands of Grifter.

Part (b) required a briefing note on the remittance basis. This is an area of the tax system that has recently been the subject of significant changes and candidates were clearly well prepared for it to be examined. Although there was often a lack of precision over the terminology used, candidates' knowledge of this complicated area was often very good with many scoring very high marks for this part of the question. Again, however, many candidates' exam technique let them down in that they were not satisfied in explaining the rules once but for some reason felt the need to repeat them, thus wasting time. In addition, many candidates wasted further time by explaining the meaning of residence and domicile which was not required.

				Marks
(a)	(i)	*Amount payable in respect of rental income*		
		Taxable rental income	1½	
		Tax, interest and penalties due	2½	
		Inheritance tax on property in Shadowsia	3	
		Instalment option	3	
		Tax refund	3	
		Max		11
	(ii)	*Sell the cars*		
		Net sale proceeds	1	
		Treatment of profit on sale of cars		
		Trading income or capital gain	3	
		Badges of trade	3	
		Other adjustments	1½	
		Sell the house		
		Gain before PPR relief	1	
		PPR relief	2	
		CGT	½	
		Other adjustments	1	
		SDLT	1	
		Max		12
		Appropriate style and presentation	1	
		Effectiveness of communication	2	
		Logical structure	1	
				4
(b)		*Who is entitled to be taxed on remittance basis?*		
		Income tax	2½	
		Capital gains tax	2½	
		Is it necessary to claim remittance basis?	2	
		How does claiming the remittance basis affect an individual's UK tax liability?		
		Unremitted income and gains not taxed	1	
		Taxation of remitted income	1	
		Personal allowance and annual exempt amount	1½	
		Remittance basis charge	2	
		Max		8
				35

(a)

Memorandum

To :   The files
From: Tax assistant
Date: 7 December 2015
Subject Grifter

(i) **Property in Shadowsia**

Income tax and inheritance tax liabilities

The income tax due on the rental income is calculated below.

	£
Annual rent remitted £484 × 12	5,808
Add: Shadowsian tax deducted £5,808 × 12/88	792
Taxable rental income	6,600
UK income tax @ 40%	2,640
Less: DTR – Shadowsia tax (clearly lower than UK)	(792)
Tax due for one year	1,848
Tax 2010/11 to 2014/15 £1,848 × 5	9,240
Add: estimated interest and penalties	9,240
Total amount due	18,480

The death of Grifter's uncle within seven years of giving him the property in Shadowsia results in an inheritance tax liability as set out below.

	£
Value of property	94,000
Less: fall in value £(94,000 – 48,000)	(46,000)
Potentially exempt transfer now chargeable (no AEs available)	48,000
IHT @ 40% (no nil rate band available)	19,200
Less: taper relief (5 to 6 years @ 60%)	(11,520)
Inheritance tax payable on PET	7,680

Grifter can choose to pay the inheritance tax in ten equal annual instalments starting on 31 May 2016 if he wishes because the PET consisted of land and buildings which Grifter retained until his uncle's death. However, interest will be charged from that date on the whole amount outstanding. Any outstanding inheritance tax liability will be payable immediately if Grifter sells the property. In (ii) below, when calculating the amount by which Grifter could reduce his mortgage, I have accounted for the whole of the inheritance tax liability.

The tax refund

If Grifter is certain that the tax refund has been made to him in error, he should repay it immediately. He may be committing a civil and/or a criminal offence if he fails to do so.

If Grifter does not return the refund, we should consider ceasing to act as his advisers. If we do, we must notify the tax authorities that we no longer act for him, but we do not have to provide any reason. Our money laundering reporting officer should also submit a money laundering report to the National Crime Agency as the retention of the refund may amount to a crime.

(ii) **Reduction in mortgage**

Sell the cars

	£
Sale proceeds £(84,000 + 127,000 + 68,000)	279,000
Less: auctioneer's fees	(22,320)
Net proceeds of sale	256,680
Tax on profit on sale of cars (see below)	0
Less: income tax payable as in (i) above	(18,480)
inheritance tax payable as in (i) above	(7,680)
repayment of income tax refund	(14,600)
Available to reduce mortgage	215,920

The tax treatment of the proposed sale of the cars

The tax implications of the proposed sale of the cars depend on whether Grifter is regarded as trading or not. If he is regarded as trading, the profit on each of the cars would be subject to income tax. If he is not regarded as trading, the profit on the sale of each car would be a capital profit. These capital profits would not be subject to tax because cars are exempt from capital gains tax.

It is my view that the profits from the sale of the cars would be treated as capital profits. This conclusion is based on reference to the 'badges of trade' which are used to determine whether or not a trade is being carried on. The particular factors which have led me to this conclusion are:

- Cars are not a category of asset that is purchased solely with the intention of realising a profit. They can also be purchased to be used and enjoyed.
- The cars were purchased to be used (and have been so used) rather than to be resold at a profit.
- The proposed sale of the cars is not one of a series of disposals.
- The cars have been owned for considerable periods of time.

Sell the house

	£
Net proceeds of sale £(1,200,000 − 6,400)	1,193,600
Less: capital gains tax payable (W1)	(79,449)
other amounts as in (i) above £(18,480 + 7,680 + 14,600)	(40,760)
payment to reduce mortgage as above	(215,920)
Available to purchase house	857,471
Less: professional fees in respect of purchase	(4,000)
	853,471
Less: SDLT @ 4% £853,471 × 4/104	(32,826)
Maximum capital cost of house	820,645

Workings

1   *Capital gains tax on sale of house*

	£
Net proceeds of sale £(1,200,000 − 6,400)	1,193,600
Less: cost	(500,000)
Gain before PPR relief	693,600
Less: PPR relief (W2)	
$\dfrac{78}{132} \times £693,600$	(409,855)
Chargeable gain	283,745
CGT payable @ 28%	79,449

2   *PPR relief*

Period	Total months	Exempt months	Chargeable months
1.3.05 – 31.8.09 (absent – no prior occupation)	54	0	54
1.9.09 – 28.2.16 (actual occupation)	78	78	0
	132	78	54

(b)

Briefing note

The remittance basis

Who is entitled to be taxed on the remittance basis?

Income tax

The remittance basis is available in respect of overseas investment income to individuals who are:

- Resident in the UK and thus subject to UK income tax on overseas income,
- But are not domiciled in the UK.

Capital gains tax

The remittance basis is available in respect of gains on overseas assets to individuals who are:

- Resident in the UK and thus subject to UK capital gains tax on overseas gains,
- But not domiciled in the UK.

Is a claim required?

The remittance basis applies automatically to individuals with unremitted overseas income and/or gains of less than £2,000 in a tax year or who have no UK income or gains other than taxed investment income not exceeding £100, do not remit income or gains to the UK in the year and have been UK resident in not more than six out of the nine tax years immediately preceding that year or are under the age of 18 throughout the year.

Other individuals are required to submit a claim for the remittance basis to apply in a tax year.

How does the remittance basis affect an individual's UK tax liability?

The individual will not be subject to tax on:

- Unremitted foreign income
- Unremitted gains on overseas assets

Remitted income is taxed as non-savings income at 20%, 40% or 45%.

An individual who claims the remittance basis will not be entitled to:

- The income tax personal allowance, or
- The capital gains tax annual exempt amount

The remittance basis charge:

- Is a charge of £30,000 on unremitted income and gains for every year in which the individual claims for the remittance basis to apply where the individual has been UK resident for at least seven of the nine years prior to the year of claim
- Is a charge of £50,000 on unremitted income and gains for every year in which the individual claims for the remittance basis to apply where the individual has been UK resident for at least twelve of the fourteen years prior to the year of claim

18 Kesme and Soba (ATAX 06/14)

Text references. Property income and the accrued income scheme is covered in Chapter 3 and taxable income in Chapter 1. Principal private residence relief is dealt with in Chapter 14. Overseas aspects of inheritance tax are covered in Chapter 18.

Top tips. In part (b) it would be useful to structure your answer using bullet points to make sure that you cover all the relevant issues.

Easy marks. There were easy marks in part (a) for a basic computation of taxable income. The rules about PPR relief and letting relief in part (b) should have been well known from F6.

Examiner's comments. Part (a) required an explanation of the availability and operation of rent-a-room relief together with a calculation of an individual's taxable income. The basics of rent-a-room relief were reasonably well-known by many candidates. However, a minority thought that the £4,250 could be deducted in addition to expenses incurred as opposed to instead of those expenses. Also, many candidates neglected to divide the £4,250 between the two owners of the property. Very few candidates mentioned the need to make an election for the relief to apply. The calculation of the individual's taxable income was done well by the majority of candidates in relation to the pension income and the personal allowance, where a restriction was required due to the level of the individual's income. The interest arising in respect of the loan stock was not handled particularly well with the majority of candidates failing to recognise that the accrued income scheme applied, such that ten months of interest needed to be included.

Part (b) was more challenging. It required candidates to consider the effect of renting out part of the family home on the amount of the taxable capital gain on a future sale of the home. Almost all candidates realised that this required them to consider the principal private residence exemption but many were not sufficiently methodical in their approach. The main area of difficulty related to thinking about the whole of the period over which the property will have been owned as opposed to just the period during which the property will have been let. The period of ownership should be split into three parts: the period prior to letting (wholly exempt), the last three years of ownership (wholly exempt) and the period in between (70% exempt). Very few candidates addressed these three periods in a clear manner. There was then the need to consider the letting exemption. Most candidates recognised the need to refer to this exemption and their knowledge of it was satisfactory. However, a minority of candidates did not mention the exemption at all.

The final part of the question concerned inheritance tax and was done reasonably well. It required an explanation of the implications of electing to be treated as UK domiciled for the purposes of inheritance tax and a calculation of the residue of an estate. The explanation of the election required two main points to be made: the effect on the spouse exemption and the fact that overseas assets would become subject to UK inheritance tax. Many candidates identified both of these points, although a minority wrote about the remittance basis, which did not have any relevance here. The calculation aspect of the question was more challenging than the explanations and very few candidates did particularly well. The difficulty was that most candidates wanted to calculate an inheritance tax liability when what was required was a calculation of the residue. The residue was calculated by deducting the legacy to the daughter and the inheritance tax liability from the estate. So a calculation of the inheritance tax liability was a necessary step on the way but was not an end in itself. The calculation of the inheritance tax liability also required the gift to the daughter to be grossed up because the residue of the estate was exempt. Very few candidates identified this point but it was possible to score a very good mark without it.

Marking scheme

			Marks
(a)	Rent a room relief		
	Availability	1	
	Operation	1½	
	Claim	1½	
	Pension income	1	
	Property business income	½	
	8% loan stock	2	
	Personal allowance	1½	
		Max	8
(b)	Situation prior to letting rooms	1	
	Principal private residence exemption	3	
	Letting exemption	3	
		Max	6

		Marks
(c)	Election to be treated as UK domiciled	2½
	Value of assets	
	Calculation of amount received by Soba	1½
	Inheritance tax liability	2
		6
		20

(a) **Income tax**

Availability and operation of rent a room relief

Rent a room relief is relevant because Kesme and Soba are letting furnished rooms in their main residence. The limit for each of them is £4,250/2 = £2,125.

Since gross rents exceed the limit, Kesme and Soba would be taxed under the normal property business income rules unless they elect for the 'alternative basis'. If they so elect, they will each be taxable on gross receipts less £2,125, with no deductions for expenses.

An election for the alternative basis must be made by 31 January 2017 (22 months after the end of the tax year 2014/15). The election will then continue to apply until it is withdrawn.

Tutorial note

The election would also cease to apply in the unlikely event that the gross annual rent fell below £4,250.

Taxable income for the tax year 2014/15

	£
State retirement pension	7,900
Pension from former employer	24,515
Property business income (W1)	5,075
8% loan stock interest (W2)	1,200
Net income	38,690
Less: personal allowance (W3)	(10,000)
Taxable income	28,690

Workings

1 *Property business income*

	£
Income receivable £14,400/2	7,200
Less: rent a room limit	(2,125)
Assessable income	5,075

2 *Loan stock interest*

	£
Interest received 31 May 2014	
£18,000 × 8% × 6/12	720
Accrued interest deemed received 30 September 2014	
£18,000 × 8% × 4/12	480
Interest assessable	1,200

Tutorial note

Kesme has sold the loan stock cum interest. Under the accrued income scheme, Kesme will be treated as having received interest for the period from 1 June 2014 to 30 September 2014.

3   *Personal allowance*

	£	£
Higher personal allowance (born between 6 April 1938 and 5 April 1948)		10,500
Net income	38,690	
Less: limit	(27,000)	
Excess	11,690	
× ½		(5,845)
		4,655

But higher personal allowance cannot be less than standard personal allowance of £10,000.

(b)   **Capital gain on the eventual sale of the family home**

No chargeable gain arises on the sale of a house which has always been occupied by its owner due to the availability of principal private residence (PPR) relief. Therefore if the rooms were not rented out, no chargeable gain would arise on the eventual sale of the family home.

However, following the renting out of the furnished rooms, part of the property (30%) is no longer occupied by Kesme and Soba, so a chargeable gain may arise on the eventual sale. This chargeable gain will be calculated as follows:

- The initial gain is the excess of the sales proceeds over the original cost. This will then be reduced by PPR relief and the letting exemption.

- PPR relief is calculated by assuming that the gain has accrued evenly over the period of ownership from 1 July 1991 until the sale of the property. It exempts the total of the following:

  - 100% of the gain which accrued from 1 July 1991 until 5 April 2014 (ie the period up to the date on which the rooms were first rented out), and

  - 70% (the proportion of the property occupied by Kesme and Soba) of the gain which accrued from 6 April 2014 until the date 18 months before the date of sale, and

  - 100% of the gain which accrued during the last eighteen months of ownership.

- That part of the gain not covered by PPR relief (ie the 30% of the gain which accrued during the period from 6 April 2014 until the date eighteen months prior to the date of sale) is then reduced by letting relief. This is equal to the lowest of:

  - PPR relief as calculated above, and
  - Gain attributable to the letting, and
  - £40,000.

The letting exemption cannot convert a gain into an allowable loss.

(c)   **Soba**

Election to be treated as UK domiciled

This election will remove the limit (equal to the nil band of £325,000) on the spouse exemption which would otherwise apply on transfers from Kesme to Soba.

However, it will also mean that any overseas assets owned by Soba will be subject to UK inheritance tax in the future as they will no longer be excluded property for inheritance tax purposes.

Tutorial note

The limit of £325,000 on the spouse exemption applies where the transferor spouse is UK domiciled and the transferee spouse is non-UK domiciled.

Value of the residue of the estate

Soba will receive the residue of the estate, ie the estate less the gift to the daughter and the inheritance tax on that gift. The inheritance tax is calculated as follows:

	£
£325,000 @ 0%	0
£ 45,000 @ 40/60	30,000
£370,000	30,000

The gross transfer is £(370,000 + 30,000) = £400,000.

The residue available to Soba is £(1,280,000 − 400,000) = £880,000.

Tutorial note

The inheritance tax due on the specific gift to the daughter will be paid out of the residue of the estate, such that it will be borne by Soba. Because the residue of the estate is exempt, due to the spouse exemption, the gift must be grossed up.

19 Pescara (ATAX 12/13)

Text references. Valuation of quoted shares and the transfer of the nil rate band are covered in Chapter 17. Lifetime transfers of value are dealt with in Chapter 16. The basic chargeable gains computation, the annual exempt amount and rates of capital gains tax will be found in Chapter 11. Capital gains tax on disposals of shares, including takeovers, are covered in Chapter 12. EIS relief is covered in Chapter 2 and Chapter 13. Gifts with reservation of benefit are dealt with in Chapter 18.

Top tips. Where the nil rate band from a deceased spouse is transferred, account must be taken of the increase in the amount of the nil rate band between the date of death of the first spouse and the date of death of the second spouse.

Easy marks. There were some easy marks in part (a) for a basic inheritance tax computation on a potentially exempt transfer. The rules about gifts with reservation of benefit in part (c) should have been well known.

Examiner's comments. In part (a) the majority of candidates performed well and scored high marks. Less well-prepared candidates were unable to value the shares in Sepang plc and/or the amount of the nil rate band to be transferred from the donor's deceased husband. This was because they either did not know the rules or were unable to apply them to the facts in the question. Some candidates failed to identify that the husband's nil rate band was available for transfer.

Part (b) concerned capital gains tax and was in two parts; neither part was done particularly well.

Part (b)(i) required a calculation of the tax due on the sale of shares. The shares had been acquired via gift and had then been the subject of a share for share takeover and a bonus issue. Accordingly, the calculation of the base cost required a certain amount of work. It was first necessary to realise that, due to the fact that gift relief was not claimed on the original gift (the question stated that gift relief was not available), the base cost of the original shares was their market value at the time of the gift. Following the takeover, this original cost had to be split between the new shares and cash received by reference to the market value of the consideration. Finally, the bonus issue increased the number of shares but had no effect on the total base cost. A significant number of candidates lost marks here because they side-stepped the first two stages of this calculation by attributing a cost to the new shares equal to their market value at the time of the takeover. The majority of candidates had no problem with the bonus issue. When calculating the amount subject to capital gains tax it was necessary to deduct EIS deferral relief equal to the whole of the £50,000 invested in EIS shares. Many candidates confused this relief with the relief available in respect of income tax when EIS shares are acquired.

Part (b)(ii) required a statement of the capital gains tax implications of the future sale of the EIS shares. The first problem that some candidates had here was that they answered the question by reference to income tax rather than capital gains tax. Many of those who did address capital gains tax did not score as many marks as they might have done because they were not methodical in their approach. It was important to (briefly) consider four possible situations, i.e. sale of the shares at a profit or a loss both within and after the three-year period.

Part (c) was not done particularly well as those candidates who clearly had some knowledge did not pay sufficient attention to the requirement. The question asked how the gift would be treated for the purposes of calculating the inheritance tax due on death. This required consideration of the value to be used, whether or not the reservation was lifted prior to death and the relief available in order to avoid double taxation. Many candidates wrote more broadly about gifts with reservation, explaining the rationale behind the rules and the actions necessary in order for the reservation to be lifted. These generalisations did not score any marks.

Marking scheme

			Marks
(a)	Value of shares		2
	Annual exemptions		1
	Nil rate band		2½
	Inheritance tax liability		1½
			7
(b)	(i)	Proceeds less cost	4
		EIS deferral relief, annual exempt amount and liability	2
			6
	(ii)	Zolder plc	1
		EIS shares	3½
		Max	3
(c)	Initial gift		1
	Reservation lifted within seven years		1½
	Reservation in place at death		1
	Double taxation avoidance		1½
		Max	4
			20

(a) **Marina – Inheritance tax payable in respect of the gift of the shares in Sepang plc**

	£
Value of shares: 375,000 × £1.86 (W1)	697,500
Less: annual exemption 2010/11	(3,000)
annual exemption 2009/10 b/f	(3,000)
Potentially exempt transfer now chargeable	691,500

	£
£476,667 (W2) @ 0%	0
£214,833 @ 40%	85,933
£691,500	85,933
Less: taper relief (4 to 5 years) @ 40%	(34,373)
Death tax payable	51,560

Workings

1 *Value of shares in Sepang plc as at 1 February 2011*

Quarter up £1.84 + ([1.96 – 1.84]/4)	£1.87
Average highest and lowest marked bargains £[1.80 + 1.92]/2)	£1.86
Lower of quarter up and average bargains	£1.86

2   *Nil rate band available*

	£	£
Nil rate band: Marina		325,000
Nil rate band: Galvez 2007/08	300,000	
Less: legacies to Pescara/brother 2 × £80,000	(160,000)	
	140,000	

Increase pro-rata

$$\frac{£325,000}{£300,000} \times £140,000 \qquad\qquad 151,667$$

Total nil rate band available to Marina   476,667

(b)   (i)   **Pescara – Capital gains tax liability for the tax year 2015/16**

	£
Proceeds: sale of 1,000,000 shares in Zolder plc	445,000
Less: cost (W)	(269,565)
Chargeable gain	175,435
Less: EIS deferral relief	(50,000)
annual exempt amount	(11,000)
Taxable gain	114,435
Capital gains tax @ 28%	32,042

Working – Base cost of 1,000,000 shares in Zolder plc

	Number	Cost £
Sepang plc shares – MV of gift (part (a))	375,000	697,500
Zolder plc shares		
Cost of new shares $\frac{£2}{£2+£0.30} \times £697,500$	750,000	606,522
Bonus issue 2 for 1	1,500,000	0
	2,250,000	606,522
	(1,000,000)	(269,565)
Disposal $\frac{1,000,000}{2,250,000} \times £606,522$		
C/f	1,250,000	336,957

(ii)   **Pescara – Capital gains tax implications of selling the EIS shares**

The gain deferred in respect of the sale of the shares in Zolder plc will be chargeable in the year the EIS shares are sold.

If the EIS shares are disposed of within the minimum holding period (usually three years from the date of issue), any gain is computed in the normal way. If the shares are disposed of after the end of the minimum holding period, any gain is exempt from CGT.

If EIS shares are disposed of at a loss at any time, the loss is allowable but the acquisition cost of the shares is reduced by the amount of EIS income tax relief attributable to the shares which has not been withdrawn on sale.

(c)   **Pescara – Gift of a UK property**

The gift of a property will be a potentially exempt transfer (PET). The value of this PET will be the market value of the property at the time of the gift less any available annual exemptions.

The amount which will be subject to inheritance tax in respect of this gift with reservation depends on whether or not the reservation of benefit ceases before Pescara dies, for example if she stops using the property rent-free.

(i)   If the reservation ceases within the seven years before Pescara's death, then the gift is treated as a PET made at the time the reservation ceased. The charge is based on its value at that time. Annual exemptions cannot be used against such a PET.

(ii)   If the reservation still exists at the date of Pescara's death, the asset is included in her death estate at its value at that time (not its value at the date the gift was made).

Where Pescara dies within seven years of the original PET such that the gift is taxable as a PET when made, as well as taxed under (i) or (ii) above, it will be taxed either as a PET when made, or, under (i) or (ii), (but not both), whichever gives the higher total tax.

Tutorial note

Pescara would be advised to stop using the property (or to start paying a market rent) if she wishes the gift to be advantageous from the point of view of inheritance tax.

20 Mirtoon (ATAX 12/11)

Text references. Chargeable gains in outline are covered in Chapter 11 and Chapter 14 deals with principal private residence relief. Entrepreneurs' relief and gift relief are covered in Chapter 13. Trading losses are dealt with in Chapter 8, the basis period in Chapter 6, and the basic income tax computation in Chapter 1. VAT deregistration is covered in Chapter 28. Overseas aspects of income tax and capital gains are dealt with in Chapters 10 and 14 respectively. Associated operations and gifts with reservation of benefit will be found in Chapter 18.

Top tips. In scenario questions such as this, it is important to identify all the relevant information for each requirement which may appear in different parts of the question. For example, in this question, the overlap profits could have been overlooked as they were contained in the background information, whereas the remainder of the information about trading losses was in the extract from the email from Mirtoon.

Easy marks. The computations in this question were relatively uncomplicated. In part (b), the basic rules concerning gifts with reservation with benefit should have produced easy marks provided that your explanation was clear and succinct.

Examiner's comments. Part (a) concerned Mirtoon's financial position in view of his plans to sell his house, cease his business and leave the UK. It required a calculation of the total proceeds generated by the proposed transactions.

The sale of the house was handled well with almost all candidates identifying the availability of principal private residence relief and the need to restrict the relief to 80% of the gain arising. The crystallisation of the heldover gain in respect of the agricultural land (due to Mirtoon becoming non-resident), on the other hand, was spotted by only a small minority of candidates. However, this was an easy point to miss and it was possible to obtain a perfectly good mark without any reference to it.

The treatment of the losses arising on the cessation of the business was not handled well due to a lack of knowledge of the closing year rules. This meant that many candidates struggled to determine the assessment for the final years of trading. There were also a considerable number of candidates who erroneously treated the overlap profits brought forward as taxable profits in the final tax year as opposed to being part of the allowable loss. The unincorporated trader is examined with great regularity and candidates are likely to benefit from knowing, in particular, the opening and closing years rules.

A minority of candidates demonstrated a lack of precision when considering the tax due in respect of the sale of the house and the tax saving in respect of the offset of the trading losses. This lack of precision included a failure to take account of the capital losses brought forward and/or the annual exempt amount and the omission of the personal allowance from the income tax computations. It was important to consider the personal allowance as Mirtoon's income exceeded £100,000 such that the personal allowance was restricted.

Part (b) was in three parts and produced a wide variety of answers.

Part (i) concerned the VAT implications of Mirtoon ceasing to trade. This part was done reasonably well, although, perhaps not as well as expected. Some candidates made it hard for themselves by writing generally rather than addressing the facts of the question. In particular, many candidates wrote at length about the sale of a business as a going concern. However the question made it clear that the business was to cease with the assets then being sold. The vast majority of candidates identified the need to deregister. However, a considerably smaller number pointed out the possible need to account for output tax on business assets owned as at cessation.

Part (ii) concerned Mirtoon's liability to income tax and capital gains tax whilst living overseas. There were some good answers to this part but also two particular areas of confusion.

The first area of confusion related to the taxation of income where an individual is not resident in the UK. It needs to be recognised that where an individual is not resident in the UK, any foreign income will not be subject to UK income tax. Where many candidates went wrong was to imagine that the remittance basis was relevant here. This led candidates to write at length about the remittance basis thus wasting time.

The second area of confusion concerned the temporary non-resident rules. These rules relate to capital gains tax and cause gains that would otherwise not be taxable in the UK to be so taxable if the individual is non-UK resident for less than five years. However, a minority of candidates incorrectly treated these rules as an extension of the residency rules as they relate to income tax.

Part (iii) concerned two areas of inheritance tax; associated operations and gifts with reservation. The good news was that the vast majority of candidates knew all about gifts with reservation and answered this part of the question well. Knowledge of associated operations was less common but this was to be expected. The bad news, however, was that many candidates did not restrict their answers to the above two areas but wrote at length about inheritance tax generally. Candidates must take care in identifying what has been asked and try to avoid addressing other areas.

Marking scheme

				Marks
(a)	Sale of house			
		Capital gain	½	
		Principal private residence relief	1	
		Capital gains tax	1½	
	Agricultural land		2½	
	Trading losses			
		Loss available for relief	2	
		Tax relief	4	
	Total proceeds net of tax adjustments		2	
	Explanatory notes (1 mark each – maximum 4 marks)		4	
		Max		17
(b)	(i)	Requirement to deregister	1½	
		Output tax	2	
		Max		3
	(ii)	Status	2½	
		Income tax	1½	
		Capital gains tax	5	
		Max		7
	(iii)	Associated operations	2½	
		Gift with reservation	5	
		Max		6
Approach to problem solving			1	
Appropriate style and presentation			1	
Effectiveness of communication			1	
				3
				36

(a) **Mirtoon's financial position**

	£
Proceeds from sale of home	850,000
Capital gains tax in respect of sale of home (W1)	(6,200)
Capital gains tax in respect of agricultural land (W2)	(16,184)
Proceeds from sale of business assets	14,000
Income tax relief in respect of trading losses £(41,691 – 19,851)	21,840
Total after tax proceeds	863,456

Workings

1   *Capital gains tax in respect of the sale of the house*

	£
Sale proceeds	850,000
Less: cost	(540,000)
Gain	310,000

	£
Capital gain in respect of business use £310,000 × 20% (N1)	62,000

Capital gains tax £62,000 × 10% (N2)	6,200

Notes

1   The capital gain on the disposal of an individual's principal private residence is exempt from tax. However, where part of the house has been used exclusively for business purposes an equal proportion of the gain is subject to tax.

2   The gain in respect of the business use of the house will qualify for entrepreneurs' relief. The relief is available because the house will be in use for the purposes of the business at the time at which the business ceases, the business has been owned for at least one year and the disposal will be within three years of the date of cessation. Accordingly, the rate of tax is 10%.

2   *Capital gains tax in respect of agricultural land*

	£
Chargeable gain held over subject to tax in 2015/16 (N1)	72,800
Less: capital losses brought forward (N2)	(4,000)
annual exempt amount (N2)	(11,000)
Gain	57,800

Capital gains tax £57,800 × 28% (N3)	16,184

Notes

1   Where an individual becomes non-resident within six years of receiving a gift in respect of which gift relief was claimed, the capital gain held over will become subject to capital gains tax immediately prior to his/her departure from the UK. Accordingly, the held over gain on the agricultural land will become chargeable in January 2016 and will be taxed in the year 2015/16.

2   The capital losses and the annual exempt amount can be deducted from Mirtoon's capital gains in the most tax-efficient manner. Accordingly, they will be deducted from gains that would otherwise be taxed at 28%.

3   The taxable interest income in 2015/16 together with the capital gains qualifying for entrepreneurs' relief will clearly exceed the basic rate band such that all other capital gains will be taxed at 28%.

3   *Income tax relief in respect of trading losses*

	£
Loss in the year ended 30 June 2015	20,000
Loss in the six months ending 31 December 2015	17,000
Overlap relief	7,600
Loss for the tax year 2015/16 (N1)	44,600

Income tax liability for 2014/15

	Original £	Loss relief £
Trading income	90,000	90,000
Interest income £24,128 × 100/80	30,160	30,160
Total income	120,160	120,160
Less: loss relief against general income	–	(44,600)
Net income	120,160	75,560
Less: personal allowance (N2)	–	(10,000)
Taxable income	120,160	65,560

Tax

	Original £	Loss relief £
Taxable income – no loss relief		
£31,865 × 20%	6,373	
£(120,160 – 31,865) = £88,295 × 40%	35,318	
Taxable income – after loss relief		
£31,865 × 20%		6,373
£(65,560 – 31,865) = £33,695 × 40%		13,478
Income tax liability	41,691	19,851

Notes

1   The basis period for 2015/16 runs from the end of the basis period for the previous tax year until the date of cessation, ie from 1 July 2014 until 31 December 2015. The loss will be increased by the unrelieved overlap profits.

2   An individual's personal allowance is reduced by £1 for every £2 by which adjusted net income exceeds £100,000. Accordingly, with adjusted net income of over £120,000, Mirtoon will have no personal allowance.

Tutorial note

The interest income does not fall within the starting rate limit. Accordingly, there is no need to distinguish between the trading income and the interest income when computing the income tax liability as the rates of income tax will be the same.

(b)

Firm's address

Mirtoon's address

9 December 2015

Dear Mirtoon

Departure from the UK

I set out below our advice in respect of the value added tax (VAT) consequences of your cessation of business and the tax implications of your departure from the UK.

(i) **VAT on the cessation of your business**

You must notify HM Revenue and Customs of the cessation of your business within 30 days of your ceasing to make taxable supplies, ie by 30 January 2016. You may be charged a penalty if you fail to do so.

You should charge VAT on any machinery and inventory that you sell whilst still registered for VAT. When you deregister you will need to account for output tax on all business assets that you still own in respect of which you have previously recovered input tax. There is no need to account for this output tax if it is less than £1,000.

(ii) **Liability to UK income tax and capital gains tax whilst living in Koro**

In 2015/16 you will be UK resident. This is because you do not meet any of the automatic overseas tests to be non-resident and you do meet one of the automatic UK tests of residence (being in the UK that year for 183 days or more). However, because you are leaving the UK to work full-time overseas, you are able to treat the year of departure as split into two parts, a UK part and an overseas part. You are treated as though you are non-UK resident during the overseas part (ie from 15 January to 5 April 2016). You will then be non-UK resident in the following tax years while you remain overseas.

Income tax

Generally, UK source income is subject to income tax regardless of the residence status of the individual. However, where you are non-UK resident in a tax year, your liability on your bank interest will be limited to the tax deducted at source. Further, by declaring your non-UK resident tax status to the bank you will be able to receive future interest gross, without deduction of tax such that you will not suffer any UK tax on your bank interest.

Whilst you are non-UK resident you will not be subject to UK income tax on any of your overseas income.

Capital gains tax

Generally, individuals who are not resident in the UK are not subject to UK capital gains tax. However, temporary non-residents who realise capital gains whilst non-UK resident, in respect of assets acquired when they were still UK resident, are subject to capital gains tax in the tax year when they become UK resident again.

You will be regarded as a temporary non-resident if you are not UK resident for less than five years. This is because you have been resident in the UK for at least four of the seven tax years prior to the tax year of departure from the UK.

Accordingly, if you become UK resident again before 15 January 2021, any gains you make whilst you were non-UK resident in respect of assets you owned when you ceased to be UK resident, for example your agricultural land, will be subject to UK tax on your return to the UK. If you did become UK resident in 2020/21, it may be possible to split that tax year into an overseas part and a UK part, as in the year of departure.

(iii) **Inheritance tax planning**

I summarise below the inheritance tax anti-avoidance rules you will need to be aware of when we discuss your inheritance tax planning ideas.

Associated operations

A scheme involving a series of transactions that seeks to reduce the value of a gift may be caught by the rules relating to associated operations. The definition of associated operations is quite broad but may be summarised as:

- Two or more operations which affect the same property; or

- Where one operation is carried out by reference to a second operation or in order to enable the second operation to be carried out

Where the rules apply, the series of transactions will be regarded as a single gift at the time of the final transaction in the series such that the total value transferred will be subject to tax.

Gifts with reservation

A donor of a gift who retains some interest in the asset transferred may be caught by the rules concerning gifts with reservation. A gift with reservation occurs where:

- Possession and enjoyment of the property is not genuinely obtained by the donee; or
- The property given is not enjoyed virtually to the entire exclusion of the donor.

A gift will not be treated as a gift with reservation where:

- The donor gives full consideration for the benefit retained; or
- In respect of a gift of land, the donor is an elderly or infirm relative of the donee and, due to an unforeseeable change in circumstances, there is a need for a benefit to be provided to the donor in the form of reasonable care and maintenance.

Where the rules apply:

- If the reservation is removed in the seven years prior to the death of the donor, the asset will be treated as having been gifted at the time the reservation is removed.
- If the reservation is not removed prior to the donor's death, the asset will be included in the donor's death estate at its value as at the time of death.

Provisions exist to ensure that the gift of the asset is not taxed twice, for example, at the time of the original gift and again at the time of death.

Please do not hesitate to contact me if you require any further information.

Yours sincerely

Tax manager

21 Sakura (ATAX 12/10)

Text references. Capital gains tax and compensation is dealt with in Chapter 14. Inheritance tax transfers are covered in Chapter 16. Penalties for errors in tax returns are covered in Chapter 15.

Top tips. Make sure that read the whole of the question – there was a very useful note at the end of part (a) which stated that you needed to identify the tax years of the disposals and the due date of payment of any minimised capital gains tax liability.

Easy marks. The treatment of compensation proceeds in part (a) was also covered in F6 and so should have yielded easy marks for P6.

Examiner's comments. Part (a) required candidates to consider both the capital gains tax and inheritance tax implications of the destruction of an asset and the exchange of one asset for another. This required some clear thinking as to who was disposing of what together with the ability not to confuse the two capital taxes. This part of the question was answered reasonably well by many candidates. However, some candidates would have benefited from addressing each of the taxes separately under clear headings as this would have helped them to organise their thoughts and prevent confusion.

The calculations of the capital gains were done well as were the implications of the potentially exempt transfer. However, the deferral of the gain on the asset destroyed was usually dealt with, incorrectly, by reference to business asset rollover relief.

The reliefs available in respect of capital gains involve a fairly tricky bunch of rules and definitions. Candidates would be well advised to learn the conditions that must be satisfied in order for each of the reliefs to be available.

Part (b) was very small but still required thought; it involved the disposal of a boat. For one of the two available marks candidates simply had to state that a boat is an exempt asset for the purposes of capital gains tax. However, the vast majority did not pause for thought and instead talked about the capital loss that would occur on disposal.

The final part of the question tested candidates' knowledge of the penalties that may be charged in respect of an error in a tax return. A minority of candidates were not aware of the rules.

Marks

(a)	Capital gains tax		
	Insurance proceeds	2	
	Painting	2	
	Inheritance tax		
	Figurine	1	
	Painting	2	
	Minimisation of liability		
	Availability of relief and conditions	2½	
	Quantification of relief	1½	
	Use of annual exempt amounts	1½	
	Liability and due date	1	
	Max		11
(b)	Capital gains tax	1	
	Inheritance tax	1	
			2
(c)	The penalty	2	
	Reasonable care	½	
	Maximum percentage	½	
	Disclosure	2	
	Max		4
			17

(a) **Capital gains tax and inheritance tax implications for Sakura**

Capital gains tax

The receipt of the insurance proceeds in respect of the destruction of the figurine represents a disposal for the purposes of capital gains tax. The capital gain will be £39,000 (£67,000 – £28,000). The disposal is deemed to have taken place on 1 June 2015, the date on which the insurance proceeds were received, and therefore relates to the tax year 2015/16 and not 2014/15.

Sakura intends to sell the painting for consideration worth £25,000. However, because he and Cashel are connected persons, he will be deemed to have received proceeds equal to the market value of the painting. This will result in a capital gain of £26,000 (£48,000 – £22,000).

Inheritance tax

The insurance proceeds received by Sakura are less than the value of the antique figurine such that there has been a fall in the value of his estate. However, there are no inheritance tax implications as there was no gratuitous intent on the part of Sakura.

Sakura is exchanging an asset worth £48,000 for one worth £25,000. Accordingly, there will be a fall in the value of his estate of £23,000. This will result in a potentially exempt transfer of £17,000 after deducting the annual exemptions for 2015/16 and 2014/15. If Sakura were to die within seven years of the exchange the transfer would become chargeable but would be covered by his nil rate band such that no inheritance tax would be due.

Minimisation of Sakura's capital gains tax liability

Where insurance proceeds are received on the destruction of an asset a form of rollover relief is available. In order to obtain the relief, Sakura will need to acquire a replacement asset by 31 May 2016 (ie within 12 months of receiving the insurance proceeds) and submit a claim to HM Revenue and Customs. It will need to be considered whether or not HM Revenue and Customs will accept that a 'modern glass figurine' can be a replacement for an 'antique china figurine' for the purposes of this relief.

Because the new figurine will cost less than the insurance proceeds, there will be a capital gain equal to the amount of the proceeds not spent. Accordingly, the capital gain after relief will be £10,000 (£67,000 − £57,000). This is on the assumption that the glass figurine is accepted as a suitable replacement and that it is purchased prior to 1 June 2016. The balance of the gain will not be charged but will be deducted from the base cost of the glass figurine.

Sakura has an annual exempt amount of £11,000 to deduct from his capital gains in each tax year. He can minimise his capital gains tax liability by delaying the exchange of the painting for the boat until the tax year 2016/17 such that the gain on the insurance proceeds will be covered by his 2015/16 annual exempt amount and the whole of the 2016/17 annual exempt amount will be available to deduct from the gain on the painting.

This strategy will result in a capital gains tax liability for the tax year 2016/17 of £4,200 ((£26,000 − £11,000) × 28%).

The tax will be due on 31 January 2018 (31 January following the end of the tax year in which the exchange takes place).

(b) **Cashel – the disposal of the boat**

Capital gains tax

A boat is a chattel with a useful life of less than 50 years. Accordingly, it is an exempt asset for the purposes of capital gains tax.

Inheritance tax

Cashel has received an asset worth £48,000 as consideration for the disposal of a boat that was worth only £25,000.

Accordingly, there has been no fall in the value of his estate and therefore there will be no inheritance tax implications.

(c) **The calculation of the penalty due in respect of an honest error in a tax return**

A penalty may be payable where there is an error in Sakura's tax return or any other document submitted to HM Revenue and Customs. The penalty will be a percentage of the potential lost revenue. The potential lost revenue is the additional tax and national insurance contributions due following the correction of the error. The percentage payable depends on the circumstances.

No penalty will be charged if Sakura has taken reasonable care when preparing his tax return. Reasonable care is demonstrated by, for example, keeping accurate records and checking the correct position where something is not understood.

Where an error is careless but honest, as opposed to deliberate, the maximum penalty is 30% of the potential lost revenue. This percentage will be reduced if Sakura discloses the error to HM Revenue and Customs, provides them with assistance in quantifying the error, and allows them access to his records.

Where the disclosure is unprompted, ie Sakura discloses the error whilst he has no reason to believe that HM Revenue and Customs has discovered or is about to discover the error, the percentage may be reduced to 0%. Otherwise, the minimum penalty following disclosure is 15% of the potential lost revenue.

22 Claudia

Text references. Chapter 5 covers employee shareholder shares. The seed enterprise investment scheme (SEIS) is dealt with in Chapter 2 and SEIS reinvestment relief is covered in Chapter 13.

Top tips. In part (a)(ii) the relevance of the shares being listed on the London Stock Exchange means that they are 'readily convertible assets'. You need to think what the significance of this is for tax purposes. In part (b)(ii), it is important to state that SEIS reinvestment relief exempts part of a gain rather than being a deferral relief (compare EIS deferral relief).

Marking scheme

					Marks
(a)	(i)	Employee shareholder definition		1½	
		Conditions – ½ each		3	
			Max		4
	(ii)	Income tax		1½	
		National insurance		1	
			Max		2
	(iii)	Sale to unconnected buyer		2	
		Sale to spouse		1	
		Takeover		1	
					4
(b)	(i)	Tax reducer			1
	(ii)	Matching gain with SEIS expenditure		1	
		50% of gain exempt		1	
					2
	(iii)	Gift to daughter		1½	
		Sale to unconnected buyer		2	
			Max		3
					16

(a)   (i)   An employee shareholder is an individual who works under an employee shareholder employment contract which provides for certain employment rights, such as unfair dismissal compensation and statutory redundancy pay, to be given up in exchange for shares in the employer company.

The following conditions must be met for Claudia to be an employee shareholder:

- Noble plc and Claudia must both agree that Claudia will be an employee shareholder.

- Noble plc must give Claudia a written statement of the particulars of her status as an employee shareholder.

- Noble plc must give Claudia fully paid up shares in that company, which must be worth at least £2,000.

- Claudia must not pay for the shares in any way other than giving up the employment rights.

- Claudia must obtain advice from a relevant independent adviser whose costs must be paid by Noble plc.

- Claudia must wait for seven days from the day after receiving the advice before accepting or rejecting employee shareholder status.

(ii)   On the issue of the employee shareholder shares, Claudia is treated as receiving specific employment income which is equal to the value of the shares (£5,000) less a deemed payment of £2,000, giving a taxable amount of £3,000.

As the shares are listed on the London Stock Exchange, they are 'readily convertible assets' and so the taxable amount of £3,000 will also be subject to Class 1 National Insurance as earnings.

Tutorial note

The deemed payment applies because Claudia did not have a material interest (>25% of voting rights) in Noble plc at any time in the 12 months before the acquisition of the employee shareholder shares.

(iii)   1   Since, when the employee shareholder shares were acquired, their total value was £50,000 or less, any gain on their disposal by Claudia is exempt from capital gains tax. If a loss arises on the disposal of the employee shareholder shares, the loss will not be allowable.

2   If Claudia transfers the employee shareholder shares to her husband Nigel, the usual no gain, no loss rules will not apply and so the capital gains tax consequences will be the same as in 1 above.

3   If Nobel plc is taken over by Token plc, the usual paper for paper rules will not apply so there will be a disposal of the employee shareholder shares by Claudia and so the capital gains tax consequences will be the same as in 1 above.

Tutorial note

The normal share pooling and matching rules do not apply to employee shareholder shares. If Claudia had a mixture of employee shareholder shares and other shares in Noble plc, on a disposal of Noble plc shares, she could decide which of the shares disposed of are to be treated as employee shareholder shares.

(b)   (i)   Claudia can claim SEIS income tax relief of £60,000 × 50% = £30,000 in 2014/15 against her income tax liability.

(ii)   The gain of £42,000 made on the plot of land can be matched with that amount of SEIS expenditure since they are made the same tax year (2014/15). The maximum SEIS reinvestment relief is 50% of the amount of the gain matched with the SEIS expenditure (ie £21,000). This amount of the gain is then exempted from capital gains tax.

(iii)   1   If Claudia gives her shares in Petite Ltd to Joanne in 2016, all of the SEIS income tax relief of £30,000 will be withdrawn as this is a disposal not at arm's length within three years of issue.

All of the capital gains tax SEIS reinvestment relief in respect of those shares will also be withdrawn by a chargeable gain of £21,000 being treated as arising in 2014/15.

2   If Claudia sells her shares in Petite Ltd to an unconnected buyer in 2016, £45,000 × 50% = £22,500 of the SEIS income tax relief will be withdrawn as this is a disposal at arm's length within three years of issue. This is 22,500/30,000 × 100% = 75% of the SEIS income tax relief.

The capital gains tax SEIS reinvestment relief in respect of those shares will also be reduced by a chargeable gain of £21,000 × 75% = £15,750 being treated as arising in 2014/15.

23 Hail Ltd (ATAX 12/11)

Text references. Computing corporation tax payable is covered in Chapter 22. Losses are dealt with in Chapter 24 and groups in Chapter 26. The value added tax cash accounting scheme is covered in Chapter 29. Ethics are part of Chapter 30.

Top tips. You should set out your answer to part (a) using headings and sub-headings which will give your answer a good structure. This should ensure that you cover all relevant points in a logical manner.

Easy marks. There were some easy marks for the calculation of corporation tax and the payment dates in part (a)(i). The cash accounting scheme in part (a)(iii) should also have been straightforward.

Examiner's comments. Part (a)(i) required candidates to address the acquisition of a company (Rain Ltd) by either an individual (Drench) or by a company (Hail Ltd) owned by Drench. Depending on the circumstances, Rain Ltd would be either profitable or loss making such that there were four possibilities to consider.

The question asked for the tax implications to be compared such that numbers should have been produced for each of the four possible situations. The question also stated that Drench was aware of the general implications of forming a group and that the comparison should focus on certain specific issues. It was important for candidates to be clear as to what they had been asked to do and also what they had been asked **not** to do. The answers to this question were not as good as expected.

The following general mistakes were made by many candidates:

– Many candidates did not structure their answers to this part particularly well such that it was not always clear which of the four possible situations was being addressed.

– Despite the question instructing candidates to focus on specific issues, many candidates wasted time by addressing general issues. Accordingly, a considerable amount of unnecessary information was provided in connection with groups generally and the extraction of profits from companies.

– A minority of candidates reached an initial conclusion that Rain Ltd should be acquired by Hail Ltd such that numbers were only prepared for that eventuality.

– When addressing the purchase of Rain Ltd by Drench, a minority of candidates erroneously relieved the company's losses against the income of Drench.

In addition to the general mistakes set out above, many candidates stated that the losses of Rain Ltd would have to be carried forward if the company were purchased by Drench due to the unavailability of group relief. This omitted the possibility of a current year offset against the chargeable gains in Rain Ltd. The other specific common error related to the effect of the acquisition on the accounting periods of Rain Ltd with many candidates confusing the need to time apportion losses for the purposes of group relief with the need to prepare tax computations for separate accounting periods.

Matters done well included the identification of the degrouping charge, the corporation tax payment dates and the calculations of the maximum possible group relief.

Part (a)(iii) concerned a loan from Hail Ltd to Drench and the VAT cash accounting scheme. This part was done reasonably well with many candidates demonstrating a good knowledge of the technical areas.

The question asked for the tax implications **for Hail Ltd** of the loan. Almost all candidates recognised that Hail Ltd was a close company such that a 25% charge would be payable to H M Revenue and Customs. However, very few candidates identified that Hail Ltd would have to pay class 1A national insurance contributions in respect of the benefit relating to the loan. This is not an obscure point and would have been known to almost all candidates. It may be candidates need to think about the requirement and identify all of the possible issues before commencing writing in order to identify as many relevant points as possible.

The majority of candidates were able to identify the advantages of using the VAT cash accounting scheme and to link the facts in the question to the scheme's limit in respect of annual taxable supplies; this part of the question was answered well.

The final part of the question concerned the ethical considerations relating to confidentiality and was done well by the majority of candidates.

			Marks
(a)	(i)	**Rain Ltd acquired by Drench personally**	
		Rain Ltd makes tax adjusted loss	
		Upper and lower limits	1½
		Use of losses	2½
		Rain Ltd makes tax adjusted profit	
		Corporation tax liability	1½
		Corporation tax payment date	2
		Rain Ltd acquired by Hail Ltd	
		Rain Ltd makes tax adjusted loss	5
		Rain Ltd makes tax adjusted profit	½
		Max	12
	(ii)	Degrouping charge	
		Why charge arises	½
		Calculation of gain	1½
		Added to sale proceeds for Flake Ltd's computation	½
		Substantial shareholding exemption	1
		Max	3
	(iii)	Loan to Drench	
		Close company loan to participator	1
		Payment to HMRC	2
		Employment income benefit	2½
		Cash accounting scheme	
		Advantages	2
		Conditions	2
		Max	8
Appropriate style and presentation			1
Effectiveness of communication			1
			2
(b)	Confidentiality, 1 mark per relevant point		5
			30

(a) To: The files
    From: Tax senior
    Date: 9 December 2015
    Subject: Acquisition of Rain Ltd and other corporate matters

(i) **Acquisition of Rain Ltd**

A comparison of the tax implications for Rain Ltd and Hail Ltd depending on whether Rain Ltd is acquired by Drench personally or by Hail Ltd is set out below.

Rain Ltd acquired by Drench personally

Assuming Rain Ltd does not obtain the new contracts and realises a loss

Before taking account of any loss relief, Rain Ltd will have taxable total profits of £50,750, representing the chargeable gain on the disposal of quoted shares.

Offsetting the current period loss against these taxable total profits would save corporation tax of £10,150 (£50,750 × 20%(N)).

The remaining loss of £24,250 would then be carried forward for offset against Rain Ltd's future profits of the same trade.

Note

Rain Ltd's upper and lower limits for the purposes of calculating the rate of corporation tax payable in the nine months ending 30 June 2016 will be divided by four because Rain Ltd will be associated with Hail Ltd (because they will both be controlled by Drench) and Flake Ltd and Mist Ltd (the two remaining companies in the Flake Ltd group) at some time during this accounting period. The limits will then be multiplied by 9/12 as it will be a nine-month accounting period. Accordingly, the limits will be:

Upper limit £281,250 (£1,500,000 × ¼ × 9/12)

Lower limit £56,250 (£300,000 × ¼ × 9/12)

Assuming Rain Ltd does obtain the new contracts and is profitable

The corporation tax liability of Rain Ltd

	£
Trading profit	285,000
Chargeable gain on disposal of quoted shares	50,750
Taxable total profits	335,750
Corporation tax at 21% (taxable total profits exceed the upper limit)	70,507

Corporation tax payment date

Rain Ltd will pay corporation tax at the main rate if the new contracts are obtained. However, it will not need to pay its corporation tax liability in instalments as it did not pay tax at the main rate in the previous accounting period (it had no income or chargeable gains). Accordingly, its liability will be due by 1 April 2017 (within nine months and one day of the end of the accounting period).

Rain Ltd acquired by Hail Ltd

Assuming Rain Ltd does not obtain the new contracts and realises a loss

The loss reliefs available where Rain Ltd is acquired by Drench, as set out above, would also be available in this situation.

In addition, there would be the possibility of surrendering some of the current period loss to Hail Ltd in the form of group relief. The maximum surrender would be £50,000 (6/9 × £75,000) in respect of the period from 1 January 2016 to 30 June 2016. This is less than Hail Ltd's taxable total profits for the corresponding six-month period of £120,000 (£240,000 × 6/12).

Hail Ltd has budgeted taxable total profits of £240,000. It will have one associated company (Rain Ltd) in the accounting period such that its upper and lower limits will be £750,000 and £150,000 respectively. The limits for Rain Ltd will be £281,250 and £56,250, as set out in the note above.

Accordingly, the surrender of losses to Hail Ltd will save corporation tax at the marginal rate. The tax saved will be £10,625 (£50,000 × 21.25%).

The remainder of the loss can then be offset against the taxable total profits of Rain Ltd. This will save further corporation tax of £5,000 (£25,000 × 20%).

Any amount paid or received in respect of the surrender of group relief losses is ignored for the purposes of corporation tax.

Assuming Rain Ltd does obtain the new contracts and is profitable

If Rain Ltd obtains the new contracts and is profitable, it will make no difference whether it is acquired by Drench personally or by Hail Ltd. Accordingly, the corporation tax liability of Rain Ltd and the date on which the corporation tax is payable will be £70,507 and 1 April 2017 respectively, as set out above.

(ii) **Degrouping charge**

The degrouping charge arises because Rain Ltd is leaving the Flake Ltd group when it owns an asset transferred to it on a no gain/ no loss basis by another group member (Mist Ltd) within the previous six years.

A gain will be calculated as if Rain Ltd had, at the time of its acquisition of the asset, sold and immediately re-acquired it at its then market value. The gain arising is as follows.

	£
Market value at the time of no gain/no loss transfer on 1 July 2012	260,000
Less: cost to Mist Ltd	(170,000)
Indexation allowance £170,000 × 0.357 $\left(\dfrac{242.1-178.4}{178.4}\right)$	(60,690)
Degrouping charge	29,310

The degrouping charge is added to the consideration received by Flake Ltd when calculating the gain on the disposal of shares of Rain Ltd, thus increasing the gain on the disposal.

The substantial shareholding exemption may apply to exempt this gain (including the degrouping charge element).

(iii) **Loan to Drench and value added tax (VAT) cash accounting scheme**

The tax implications for Hail Ltd of the proposed loan from Hail Ltd to Drench

This will be a loan from a close company (Hail Ltd is controlled by Drench) to a participator, or shareholder, in that company. Accordingly, Hail Ltd will be required to pay HM Revenue and Customs £4,500 (25% × £18,000) on 1 April 2017. HM Revenue and Customs will repay the £4,500 to the company nine months after the end of the accounting period in which the loan is repaid.

The loan will also give rise to an annual employment income benefit for Drench of £585 (£18,000 × 3.25%). Hail Ltd will be required to pay class 1A national insurance contributions of £81 (£585 × 13.8%) in respect of the loan benefit. The national insurance contributions will be allowable when computing the company's taxable trading profits.

VAT cash accounting scheme

The advantages of the scheme are:

- Cash flow is likely to be improved because output tax in respect of credit sales is not paid to HM Revenue and Customs until the customer has paid the invoice.

- Where a customer fails to pay an invoice, the related output tax is never paid to HM Revenue and Customs. This amounts to an automatic relief for impairment losses (bad debts).

The cash accounting scheme is only available to businesses with annual VAT-able supplies (exclusive of VAT) of no more than £1,350,000. Accordingly, if Rain Ltd acquires the new contracts, such that its sales revenue will be £1,425,000 in a nine-month period, it will not be able to join the scheme.

It should also be noted that a business cannot operate the scheme unless its VAT returns and payments are up to date and it has not been convicted of a VAT offence or found guilty of evasion of VAT.

(b) **Briefing note – Confidentiality**

- Confidentiality is one of the fundamental principles of ethics on which we should base our professional behaviour, as set out in ACCA's *Code of Ethics and Conduct*.

- We are obliged to refrain from using confidential information, acquired as a result of our professional and business relationships, to our own advantage or to the advantage of third parties.

- This principle of confidentiality continues to apply even where we have ceased to act for a client.

- Accordingly:
  - We should not use any confidential documentation relating to our ex-client to assist Rain Ltd.
  - We are permitted to use the experience and expertise gained from advising our ex-client.

24 Janus plc group (ATAX 06/12)

Text references. Losses are covered in Chapter 24 and groups and consortia in Chapter 26. Intangible fixed assets are dealt with in Chapter 20. Overseas aspects of VAT are covered in Chapter 29. Chargeable gains for companies is the subject of Chapter 21. Corporation tax administration is dealt with in Chapter 22.

Top tips. There was a very clear hint in the question that you needed to consider consortium relief in relation to Duet Ltd.

Easy marks. There were some easy marks for identifying the group structures in parts (a) and (b). Part (c)(ii) was a relatively straightforward short point about the substantial shareholding exemption.

Examiner's comments. In part (a), the majority of candidates identified most of the relevant information in the question and knew how to relieve the loss in order to maximise the tax saving. Only a minority of candidates identified that there were only four associated companies in the period prior to the loss. Some candidates spent too long on this question and provided very detailed explanations of group relief and consortium relief; the amount of detail provided must relate to the number of marks on offer.

Also, there was a tendency to repeat things, for example stating that Janus plc is in a loss group with Seb Ltd and Viola Ltd followed by a statement that it was not in a loss group with Castor Ltd. Candidates should identify the points they intend to make and then make them as concisely as possible. They will find this more efficient than making it up as they go along.

Part (b)(i) demanded a clear understanding of the conditions necessary for a chargeable gains group to exist. Unfortunately many candidates thought that Janus plc and Pollux Ltd were members of a chargeable gains group; this was not the case because Janus plc does not own at least 75% of Castor Ltd. Other candidates failed to notice that Castor Ltd and Pollux Ltd **were** members of such a group. The other technical problem that candidates had with this question was that many thought it included a degrouping charge. However, a degrouping charge can only occur when a company leaves a chargeable gains group, ie there needs to be a sale of shares, and this question involved the sale of a building. Accordingly, time spent writing about degrouping charges was wasted.

Part (b)(ii) was done well by those candidates who both knew what to do and had practised applying the rules prior to the exam. Weaker candidates had a vague, confused knowledge of the rules or simply tried to describe them as opposed to apply them to the specific circumstances of the question. Very few candidates knew how to handle the adjustment following the sale of the building.

Part (b)(iii) was done reasonably well by the majority of candidates.

Part (c)(i) was not answered particularly well; very few candidates had a clear understanding of the VAT treatment of the transaction. Part (c)(ii) was answered well. It required candidates to recognise that the substantial shareholding exemption might apply to the sale provided the conditions were satisfied. This question illustrated the need for candidates to be methodical as, if maximum marks were to be obtained, candidates needed to consider four situations; sale at a profit and sale at a loss with the substantial shareholding exemption either applying or not applying in each case.

In part (d), only a minority of candidates knew the rules, but those who did answered the question well.

				Marks
(a)	(i)	Alternative reliefs		
		Against total profits of Janus plc	1½	
		Group relief		
		Identification of group	1½	
		Amount of loss	1	
		Consortium relief	2	
	(ii)	Strategy		
		Relieve the profits at the marginal rate	1	
		Limits	2	
		Advice and summary	3½	
		Max		11
(b)	(i)	Administrative premises		
		There will be gain on the disposal	1½	
		Indexed base cost	4½	
		Information required	½	
		Max		5
	(ii)	Warehouse		4
	(iii)	Patent rights		
		Calculation	1½	
		Explanation	1½	
				3
(c)	(i)	VAT on consultancy services	Max	2
	(ii)	Sale of shares		4
(d)		Responsibility of senior accounting officer	Max	4
				33

(a) **Use of the trading loss of Janus plc**

(i) **Alternative reliefs available**

Janus plc can relieve the trading loss against its chargeable gain of £44,500 in the year ended 31 March 2015. Once this current period claim has been made, the loss can then be relieved against the company's total profits of the previous accounting period of £95,000.

Janus plc can surrender trading losses to its 75% subsidiaries. For a company to be a 75% subsidiary, Janus plc must have an effective 75% interest in the company's ordinary share capital, its distributable income and its net assets were it to be wound up. Accordingly, Janus plc is in a group relief group with Seb Ltd and Viola Ltd only.

Any amount of losses can be surrendered up to the level of the group member's taxable total profits for the corresponding accounting period. Seb Ltd and Viola Ltd did not become members of the group until 1 December 2014. Accordingly, only 4/12 of each of these companies' taxable total profits can be relieved via group relief.

Duet Ltd is a consortium company as at least 75% of its share capital is owned by companies, each of which own at least 5%. Accordingly, £110,000 (£200,000 × 55%) of its taxable total profits can be relieved via consortium relief.

Castor Ltd is not a consortium company as the minority interest shareholding is owned by an individual rather than a company.

(ii) **Strategy in order to maximise the corporation tax saved**

The maximum tax saving will be achieved where losses are relieved in the companies paying corporation tax at the marginal rate. The marginal rate is charged on taxable total profits lying between the limits.

The limits are divided by six as all five subsidiaries are controlled by, and therefore associated with, Janus plc. Accordingly, for the year ended 31 March 2015 the upper limit is £250,000 and the lower limit is £50,000. In the previous year (prior to the acquisition of Seb Ltd), there are only four associated companies such that the upper limit is £375,000 and the lower limit is £75,000.

In the year ended 31 March 2015:

- Viola Ltd has marginal profits of £(86,000 – 50,000) = £36,000
- Duet Ltd has marginal profits of £(200,000 – 50,000) = £150,000
- Janus plc and Seb Ltd are both paying tax at the small profits rate

In the year ended 31 March 2014:

- Janus plc has marginal profits of £(95,000 – 75,000) = £20,000

In order to achieve the maximum tax saving, the trading loss of Janus plc should be relieved as follows:

	Loss	Rate of tax
	£	%
Viola Ltd (maximum 4/12 × £86,000)	28,667	21.25
Duet Ltd (maximum)	110,000	21.25
Janus plc: Current year	44,500	20
Preceding year	20,000	23.75
Preceding year (remainder of loss)	833	20
Total available trading loss	204,000	

The group relief and consortium relief claims will need to be made the day before the claims to offset the loss against the total profits of Janus plc in order to avoid relieving the whole of the profits for the year ended 31 March 2014.

(b) **Assets to be sold**

(i) **P HQ**

Pollux Ltd and Janus plc are not in a capital gains group as Castor Ltd is not a 75% subsidiary of Janus plc. The sale of the building will result in a chargeable gain equal to the excess of the proceeds, £285,000, over the building's base cost.

Pollux Ltd acquired the building from Castor Ltd. The two companies are in a capital gains group as Pollux Ltd is a 75% subsidiary of Castor Ltd. Accordingly, the building would have been transferred at no gain, no loss. The base cost of the building to Pollux Ltd is the original cost when it was acquired by Castor Ltd (assuming Castor Ltd did not acquire it via a no gain, no loss transfer), together with indexation allowance from the date the building was acquired by Castor Ltd until the date it was sold to Pollux Ltd. Further indexation allowance will then be available from the date of the no gain, no loss transfer until the date of sale by Pollux Ltd. The indexation allowance reflects the movement in the retail prices index for the relevant period (rounded to three decimal places) multiplied by the relevant cost of the building.

Information required – the date the building was acquired by Castor Ltd and the price paid.

(ii)   **Warehouse**

Year ended 31 March 2014 – recoverable input tax after annual adjustment
£64,000 × 70%   £44,800
Year ended 31 March 2015
£64,000 × 15% (70% – 55%) × 1/10   £960 repayable to HMRC
Year ended 31 March 2016
£64,000 × 20% (70% – 50%) × 1/10   £1,280 repayable to HMRC
£64,000 × 30% (100% – 70%) × 7/10   £13,440 recoverable from HMRC

(iii)   **Patent rights**

The patent rights are an intangible fixed asset. On a disposal of the rights, the sales proceeds will be compared with the amortised cost.

	£	£
Proceeds		41,000
Cost	45,000	
Less amortisation £45,000 × 10% × 4	(18,000)	
		(27,000)
Profit on sale		14,000

The profit on sale will be included as part of Castor Ltd's trading income because the patent rights were purchased for the purposes of the trade.

(c)   **Investment in Kupple Inc**

(i)   **Value added tax (VAT) on consultancy services**

When services are provided to a business, the place of supply is the place where the customer's business is established. Accordingly, the consultancy services provided by Kupple Inc to Janus plc will be treated as being made in the UK. Janus plc will be required to account for output tax in respect of the supply under the reverse charge procedure. It will then be able to recover the output tax as input tax in the normal way.

(ii)   **Sale of the shares**

The tax treatment of the profit or loss on the sale of the shares will depend on when the sale occurs.

If the shares are sold during the first 12 months of ownership, the sale will result in a chargeable gain (proceeds less cost less indexation allowance) or an allowable loss (proceeds less cost). An allowable loss could be offset against the chargeable gains of Janus plc or of the other companies in its chargeable gains group (Seb Ltd and Viola Ltd).

However, as Janus plc will hold at least 10% of Kupple Inc's shares, once the shares have been held for 12 months, the substantial shareholding exemption will apply. As a result of this exemption, any profit would not be taxable and any loss would not be allowable.

(d)   **Janus plc group senior accounting officer**

The senior accounting officer of Janus plc is the director or officer with overall responsibility for the company's financial accounting arrangements. In relation to the Janus plc group of companies, this is likely to be Mrs Pairz, as she is the Group Finance Director.

The rules will only impose responsibilities if the Janus plc group of companies has a turnover of more than £200 million and/or a balance sheet total of more than £2 billion.

Where the rules apply, the senior accounting officer is required to:

- Establish and monitor accounting systems that are adequate for the purposes of accurate tax reporting

- Certify to HM Revenue and Customs that such accounting systems exist for each financial year; or notify HM Revenue and Customs of any inadequacies in the accounting systems

Penalties apply for non-compliance with the rules.

BPP
LEARNING MEDIA

25 Sperry Ltd group (ATAX 12/11)

Text references. Capital gains groups are covered in Chapter 26. Deficits on non-trading loan relationships are dealt with in Chapter 24. Value added tax group registration is contained in Chapter 28.

Top tips. Before choosing this question, you must be sure that you can answer all three parts adequately.

Easy marks. The test for members of a capital gains group should have been well-known and it was fairly obvious what advice should be given for the transfer of the gain.

Examiner's comments. Part (a) required candidates to identify the companies in a group to which a chargeable gain could be transferred and the most advantageous strategy. This was done well by the vast majority of candidates who attempted this question. A small minority of candidates incorrectly included Wahl Ltd, a 60% subsidiary, in the capital gains group. This appeared to be due to confusion over the relevance of the 50% element of the definition of a gains group. A gains group consists of a principal company together with its 75% subsidiaries and their 75% subsidiaries and so on. There is then an additional rule that requires the principal company to have an effective interest of more than 50% in all of the companies in the group. Other candidates failed to exclude Teton Inc from their strategy or failed to explain why it was not included. The question required candidates to 'explain in detail'; the majority of candidates followed this instruction.

Part (b) concerned loan relationships and was not answered as well as part (a). A minority of candidates did not give themselves time to think such that they did not identify the fundamental issues involved and simply stated, incorrectly, that the interest payable would be deducted from the rental income. A minority of those who realised that the appropriate technical area was loan relationships, did not think to address the possible reliefs available in respect of the non-trading loan relationship deficit that would arise due to the circumstances in the question. A minority of candidates produced short, precise answers that scored full marks.

Part (c) required an explanation of the effects of registering two of the companies as a group for the purposes of VAT. Candidates clearly had plenty of knowledge of VAT groups but many did not take sufficient care to address the specifics of the requirement and simply wrote down everything they knew.

The question asked for two specific areas to be addressed; the total input tax recovered by the group and the monthly management charge, but very few candidates addressed these points directly. Instead, many candidates wasted time explaining whether or not the two companies could be registered as a group and discussing the various advantages and disadvantages of so doing. Finally, a minority of candidates confused the treatment of exempt supplies with zero rated supplies in that they described Byrd Ltd as being in a repayment situation as opposed to being unable to register and, therefore, unable to recover any input tax.

Marking scheme

			Marks
(a)	Potential group members	2	
	Associates and tax rates	1	
	Position of each company	2½	
	Advice	1	
	Date of election	1	
	Max		7
(b)	Treatment of interest	2	
	Use of deficit	3	
	Max		4
(c)	No group registration in place	2	
	Group registration in place		
	Single entity	2	
	Recovery of input tax	2½	
	Max		6
			17

(a) **Minimisation of the corporation tax charge in respect of the chargeable gain of Byrd Ltd**

In order to minimise the corporation tax payable in respect of the chargeable gain, the gain should be transferred to a company such that it will be taxed at a lower rate of corporation tax.

The whole or part of the gain can be transferred to any company/companies in the Sperry Ltd capital gains group consisting of Sperry Ltd and its 75% subsidiaries. Wahl Ltd is not in the capital gains group as it is not a 75% subsidiary of Sperry Ltd.

Also, no part of the chargeable gain can be surrendered to Teton Inc as the company is neither UK resident nor carrying on a trade in the UK through a permanent establishment.

The rate of corporation tax payable by a company depends on the number of companies that are associated with it and its level of augmented profits (taxable total profits plus franked investment income).

Sperry Ltd controls the other four companies in the group. Accordingly, all five companies are associates for the purposes of calculating the upper and lower limits used to determine the rate of corporation tax payable; therefore, the upper limit for each associated company is £300,000 (£1,500,000/5) and the lower limit is £60,000 (£300,000/5).

The taxable trading profit of Byrd Ltd falls between the limits. If the chargeable gain remains with Byrd Ltd, the whole of the gain will also fall between the limits and will be taxed at the marginal rate of 21.25%.

The taxable trading profit of Sperry Ltd exceeds the upper limit, such that any amount of the chargeable gain that is transferred to that company will be taxed at the main rate of 21%.

The taxable trading profit of Neny Ltd of £35,000 is £25,000 below the lower limit. Accordingly, the first £25,000 of the gain transferred to Neny Ltd will be taxed at 20%. Any further amount transferred will be taxed at 21.25%.

Advice

The corporation tax charged in respect of the gain will be minimised if £25,000 of the chargeable gain is transferred to Neny Ltd and the remaining £25,000 is transferred to Sperry Ltd.

The elections must be submitted by 31 March 2018 (within two years of the end of the accounting period of Byrd Ltd in which the gain arose).

(b) **Borrowings**

Sperry Ltd will be entering into a non-trading loan relationship as the funds borrowed are to be used for a non-trading purpose.

Interest payable and other debits relating to a non-trading loan relationship are netted off against non-trading loan relationship credits, for example, interest income. However, because Sperry Ltd has no interest income, it will have a non-trading loan relationship deficit.

The deficit can be:

- Offset against any other profit (income and/or gains) of Sperry Ltd of the same accounting period

- Offset against non-trading loan relationship income of Sperry Ltd of the previous 12 months

- Surrendered as group relief to companies within the same group relief group

- Carried forward by Sperry Ltd and offset against future non-trading profits (income and/or gains) for succeeding accounting periods

Sperry Ltd can choose how much of the deficit to relieve in each of the above ways; they are not all or nothing claims. It also does not have to claim current period relief first, before carrying back a deficit (unlike trading loss relief).

(c)   **Value added tax (VAT)**

No group registration in place

With no group registration in place, Sperry Ltd is able to recover all of its input tax. It will charge VAT in respect of the management charge levied on Byrd Ltd.

Byrd Ltd is unable to register for VAT as it does not make taxable supplies. Accordingly, Byrd Ltd is unable to recover any of its input tax including that relating to the management charge.

Group registration in place

A group registration would treat the two companies as a single group entity for the purposes of VAT. Accordingly, Sperry Ltd would no longer charge VAT in respect of the management charge. In addition, because this single group entity would be making both taxable and exempt supplies, it would be partially exempt.

The single group entity would be able to recover the input tax directly attributable to its standard rated supplies together with 70% (the proportion of its total sales revenue represented by taxable supplies) of the input tax relating to its overheads. The remaining input tax would be irrecoverable, unless it fell within the *de minimis* limits in which case all of the group's input tax would be recoverable.

26 Sank Ltd and Kurt Ltd (ATAX 06/12)

Text references. Payment of corporation tax and administration are covered in Chapter 22. Capital allowances in general are dealt with in Chapter 7. The division of the annual investment allowance is covered in Chapter 26 and research and development expenditure in Chapter 20.

Top tips. Before choosing to do a two-part question such as this, you must be confident about being able to produce a reasonable answer to both parts.

Easy marks. In part (a), the computation of corporation tax should have been easy marks as you were told in the question that Sank Ltd had paid corporation tax at the main rate for many years and so this should have guided you about the current rate of tax. In part (b), the availability of the annual investment allowance and the writing down allowance were straightforward, even if you did not know the detail about the restriction for related companies.

Examiner's comments. In part (a)(i), the payment of corporation tax appeared to be fairly straightforward but care was needed if sufficient marks were to be earned. It was not enough to state that the company would pay corporation tax quarterly because it was paying tax at the main rate. Candidates needed to explain how they knew the rate of tax the company was paying (ie by reference to its profits and the number of associates). There was also a need to point out that the company paid tax at the main rate in the previous accounting period. Weaker candidates calculated the company's tax liability whilst ignoring the associated companies thus wasting a lot of time and confused quarterly accounting with the payments of income tax by individuals and thought that the payments were paid on account by reference to the liability for the previous year.

Part (a) (ii) required candidates to explain the validity of the compliance check enquiry 'in relation to the date on which (it)...... was raised'. Many candidates simply wrote about compliance check enquiries generally such that this part of the question was not answered well.

Most candidates produced reasonable answers to part (b), but many would have done better if they had simply read the question more carefully and identified the relevance of all of the information and slowed down. In particular, many candidates wrote about the basic rules at some length rather than thinking about the particular situation of the question.

The owner of the company concerned owned three other companies. This information was intended to elicit a discussion of the need to split the annual investment allowance between the companies. However, many candidates wrote instead about the unavailability of group relief. The question also pointed out that the relevant accounting period was only eight months. This meant that the annual investment allowance and the writing down allowance needed to be multiplied by 8/12. However, this point was missed by many candidates.

A significant number of candidates were of the opinion that, because the company was loss-making, it should not claim all of its capital allowances. It should be remembered that, where the annual investment allowance is concerned, failing to claim allowances in full will considerably slow down the time it takes for a tax deduction to be obtained for the cost incurred as, in the future, there will only be a 18% writing down allowance on a reducing balance basis. Accordingly, there needs to be a strong reason not to claim allowances in full. Such a reason might include the situation where there are insufficient profits in the group to relieve a company's losses in the current year and any losses carried forward are likely to be locked inside the company for a considerable period of time. In such a situation it may be worthwhile claiming reduced capital allowances in the current year in order to have increased capital allowances in future years that can then be group relieved.

The tax treatment of the expenditure on scientific research was explained well by the majority of candidates, many of whom were aware that there was a possibility of claiming a 14.5% repayment. However, very few candidates attempted to evaluate whether or not the repayment should be claimed.

			Marks
(a)	(i)	Rate of tax	1½
		Payments required	3
		Payment already made	1½
		Interest	1
		Future payments	½
		Max	7
	(ii)	Deadlines	2½
		Conclusion	1
		Max	3
(b)		Equipment	
		Annual investment allowance	3
		Writing down allowance	1
		Scientific research	
		Tax deduction	1
		Repayment	1
		Evaluation	2
			8
			18

(a) (i) **Sank Ltd – increase in the budgeted corporation tax liability for the 11 months ended 30 September 2015**

Sank Ltd will pay corporation tax at the main rate (its augmented profits for the period will exceed the upper limit as it has a large number of associated companies). Accordingly, its corporation tax liability for the period is expected to be £750,000 × 21% = £157,500.

It is required to pay its corporation tax liability for the period in instalments because it also paid corporation tax at the main rate in the previous accounting period.

The payments required are as follows.

14 May 2015	3/11 of the final liability for the period
14 August 2015	3/11 of the final liability for the period
14 November 2015	3/11 of the final liability for the period
14 January 2016	2/11 of the final liability for the period (balance)

A payment should have been made on 14 May 2015 of £640,000 × 21% × 3/11 = £36,655, based on the budget prepared on 31 March 2015. However, if the new figure of taxable total profits is correct, the payment required on that day was £750,000 × 21% × 3/11 = £42,955.

Interest will be charged from 14 May 2015 until the additional £(42,955 – 36,655) = £6,300 is paid. The total interest due will be calculated by HM Revenue and Customs, once the corporation tax return has been submitted.

Future payments, ie from 14 August 2015 onwards, should be based on the latest budgeted figures in order to minimise interest charges.

(ii) **Sank Ltd – circumstances necessary for the notice of the compliance check to be regarded as valid**

The deadline for raising a notice of the compliance check depends on when the corporation tax return was filed.

Where the return was filed on time (ie by 31 October 2013), the compliance check must be notified, at the latest, by 31 October 2014. Where the return was submitted late, the compliance check must be notified by the 31 January, 30 April, 31 July or 31 October next following the first anniversary of the actual date of delivery of the return. Accordingly, a notice of a compliance check dated 31 May 2015 will only be valid if the corporation tax return was submitted after 30 April 2014.

(b) **Kurt Ltd**

Machinery

A 100% annual investment allowance is available for expenditure on machinery up to a maximum of £500,000 for a 12-month period. The maximum amount available to Kurt Ltd for the period ended 31 March 2015 is therefore £500,000 × 8/12 = £333,333.

However, only one annual investment allowance is available to companies that are related to each other. The other companies controlled by Mr Quinn will be regarded as related to Kurt Ltd if they share premises or carry on similar activities. Mr Quinn can choose to allocate the allowance available to related companies in the most tax efficient manner.

The excess of the expenditure over the available annual investment allowance will be eligible for a writing down allowance of 18% × 8/12 = 12% in the period to 31 March 2015.

Scientific research

Kurt Ltd is a small enterprise for the purposes of research and development. Accordingly, the expenditure of £28,000 will result in tax deductions of £28,000 × 225% = £63,000.

Kurt Ltd can choose to claim a tax credit of 14.5% of the lower of its trading loss and £63,000. This relief is an alternative to carrying the loss forward against future profits of the same trade.

Kurt Ltd should consider claiming the 14.5% tax credit if cash flow is its main priority. Alternatively, if the company wishes to maximise the tax saved in respect of the expenditure, it should carry the loss forward; it will then save tax at a minimum rate of 20% (provided it succeeds in becoming profitable).

27 Opus Ltd group (ATAX 06/14)

Text references. Groups and consortia are the subject of Chapter 26. Chargeable gains for companies are covered in Chapter 21. Ethics are dealt with in Chapter 30.

Top tips. It is a good idea to ascertain the membership of the 75% group relief group and the 75% capital gains group before you start to work out how profits can be moved around each group.

Easy marks. There were easy marks in part (b) if you applied the test for the substantial shareholding exemption. The ethics in part (c) should have been well known.

Examiner's comments. Part (a) concerned relief for trading losses within the group. As is often the case, some thought was required before starting because the question did not have as its objective the relief of losses in order to maximise the tax saved. Instead, the question stated that all of the companies were paying tax at the main rate and therefore the objective was simply to relieve the losses as soon as possible. However, many candidates ignored this point and focussed on tax rates and tax computations. This was not necessarily that costly in terms of marks but, as the question did not require tax computations to be prepared, was potentially costly in terms of time. The question was all about identifying various individual points in respect of each of the companies. That's why the email from the manager suggested 'you should think carefully about the tax position of each company'. Akia Ltd, the loss-making company, had realised a chargeable gain against which the loss could be offset. There was also the possibility of carrying the loss back 12 months, although very few candidates identified this point. Once the position of Akia Ltd, the loss-making company, had been considered it was then necessary to consider the group and consortium position. The group position was handled well but many candidates failed to spot that because Venere Ltd was a 75% subsidiary of Jarrah Ltd, it could not be a consortium company. Ribe Ltd had trading losses brought forward. These could not be group relieved (because only current period losses can be group relieved) and therefore could only be used against that company's trading profits. However, a minority of candidates simply added the losses of Ribe Ltd to those of Akia Ltd and then addressed the total losses together. Finally, Binni Ltd was not a member of the group for the whole of the period so it was necessary to determine the maximum loss that could be surrendered to it by Akia Ltd. This is a straightforward point but it was missed by many candidates.

There were plenty of relatively straightforward marks to be earned in this part of the question but candidates needed to slow down slightly, think and, in particular, make a real effort to answer the question set as opposed to the question that they might have been expecting.

The second part of the question concerned the sale of shares by one of the group companies and the availability of the substantial shareholding exemption (SSE). This was not done well for two main reasons. First, many candidates failed to consider the SSE despite it being an important exemption at P6. There were follow through marks available for those who found themselves in this predicament but only if they answered the question set. Unfortunately, many candidates failed to do so. Two lessons may be learned from what happened here. Firstly, it is always worth thinking about how to do a calculation in an efficient manner rather than to just immediately start it. Those candidates who thought it was necessary to calculate a chargeable gain on each of the possible disposal dates should have realised that the only difference was an increase in sales proceeds of £20,000. This would, of course, increase the gain by £20,000; there was no need to repeat the whole calculation to determine this. The second lesson is that you must answer the question set. Candidates were asked to consider on which of the two dates it would be more financially advantageous to sell the shares. This required candidates to consider the post-tax proceeds on each of the potential disposal dates, but the majority of candidates simply focussed on the amount of the chargeable gain.

The final part of the question concerned an error in a corporation tax return and the matters that needed to be considered in relation to the disclosure of the error to HM Revenue and Customs. This was a standard question and an opportunity for all candidates to earn some straightforward marks. Unfortunately, a minority of candidates decided to address the penalties aspect of the question in great detail without thinking about the other relevant issues. Stronger candidates recognised the need to consider the importance of disclosing the error from the point of view of tax evasion, money laundering and the acceptability of continuing to act for the company. These stronger candidates were able to score well on this part of the question.

Marking scheme

		Marks
(a)	Loss of Akia Ltd	
	Offset against total profits of Akia Ltd	
	Against own total profits	2
	Against gain from Lido Ltd	2
	Group relief	
	Members of group and consortium	2
	Opus Ltd	2½
	Binni Ltd	1½
	Ribe Ltd	1
	Loss carried forward	2
	Loss of Ribe Ltd	1
	Capital allowances	2
	Max	14
(b)	Sale on 30 June 2015	1½
	Sale on 30 April 2016	3
	Comparison	1
	Max	5
(c)	Interest on underpaid tax	2
	Action required	
	Necessary to disclose	2
	Implications of failure to disclose	3½
	Max	6
		25

(a) **Trading losses of Akia Ltd and Ribe Ltd**

	Notes	£	£
Akia Ltd			
Trading loss for the year ended 31 March 2015			93,000
Offset of losses in Akia Ltd:			
Year ended 31 March 2015	1		(27,000)
Year ended 31 March 2014	2		Unknown
Group relief:	3		
Opus Ltd			
Trading profit		10,000	
Property business income		8,000	
Gain on shares in Venere Ltd	4	0	
			(18,000)
Binni Ltd	5		(31,000)
Ribe Ltd	6		0
Amount unrelieved	7		17,000
Ribe Ltd			
Trading loss b/f at 1 April 2014			68,000
Offset against trading profit y/e 31.3.15	6		(41,000)
Trading loss c/f at 31 March 2015			27,000

Notes

1 Lido Ltd is in a chargeable gains group with Akia Ltd. This is because Opus Ltd has a direct interest of at least 75% in Akia Ltd and has direct interest of at least 75% in Ribe Ltd which, in turn, has a direct interest of at least 75% in Lido Ltd and Opus Ltd has an effective interest in Lido Ltd of more than 50% (80% × 85% = 68%). The chargeable gain of £21,000 can therefore be transferred to Akia Ltd and added to its own gain of £6,000 to give total chargeable gains of £27,000.

2 Akia Ltd can offset its trading losses against its total profits (income and chargeable gains) of the loss making period and those of the previous 12 months. We therefore need to know the company's total profits for the year ended 31 March 2014.

3 Akia Ltd is in a 75% group relief group with Opus Ltd, Ribe Ltd and Binni Ltd. Lido Ltd is not in the group as the effective interest of Opus Ltd is less than 75%.

Venere Ltd is not a consortium company because it is a 75% subsidiary of Jarrah Ltd.

4 The chargeable gain on the sale of shares in Venere Ltd is exempt under the substantial shareholding exemption. This is because Opus Ltd and Venere Ltd are trading companies and Opus Ltd owned at least 10% of the shares in Venere Ltd for a continuous period of at least 12 months in the two years prior to the disposal.

5 Binni Ltd joined the Opus Ltd group on 1 December 2014, such that it is in a group relief group with Akia Ltd for the four months from 1 December 2014 to 31 March 2015.

The maximum loss which can be surrendered by Akia Ltd to Binni Ltd is the lower of:

Loss of Akia Ltd for the overlapping period £93,000 × 4/12   £31,000

Total profits of Binni Ltd for the overlapping period £78,000 × 4/10   £31,200

6 The trading losses brought forward in Ribe Ltd must be offset against the first available trading profits of the same trade. Therefore, the company has no profits which can be relieved through group relief.

Ribe Ltd and Lido Ltd form a 75% group relief group. However, the remaining losses cannot be surrendered as group relief to Lido Ltd as only current period losses can be group relieved.

7   The use of losses carried forward in Akia Ltd will be delayed because the company is not expected to be profitable for some time. Akia Ltd can turn what would otherwise be trading losses *carried forward* into future *current period* trading losses (available for immediate relief via group relief) by not claiming capital allowances equal to its unrelieved current period trading loss.

Reducing the capital allowances would increase the tax written down value of the main pool and consequently the capital allowances and trading loss in future periods. The increased trading loss could then be group relieved.

Reducing the capital allowances would reduce the trading loss of Akia Ltd for the year ended 31 March 2015. This in turn would reduce the maximum loss which could be surrendered to Binni Ltd.

Tutorial note

The chargeable gain of Lido Ltd could alternatively be transferred to Opus Ltd or Ribe Ltd, rather than Akia Ltd, and be relieved with Akia Ltd's loss via group relief. It would not be beneficial to transfer the gain to Binni Ltd because of the restriction on the surrender of losses to that company.

(b) **Sale of shares in Venere Ltd**

If the shares are sold on 30 June 2015, the chargeable gain arising will be exempt under the substantial shareholding exemption. This is because Opus Ltd would have owned at least 10% of the shares in Venere Ltd for a continuous period of at least 12 months (from 1 July 2013 to 30 September 2014) during the two years prior to the sale. Accordingly, the post-tax proceeds will be equal to the gross proceeds of £80,000.

If the shares are sold on 30 April 2016, there will not be a continuous 12 month period in the previous two years where Opus Ltd has owned at least 10% of the shares in Venere Ltd. Therefore, on the assumption that the shares are sold for £100,000, there will be a chargeable gain of £73,235 (W). This gain will be subject to corporation tax of £(73,235 × 21%) = £15,379. The post-tax proceeds will be £(100,000 – 15,379) = £84,621.

Therefore, while there may be a marginal increase in the post-tax proceeds from delaying the sale until after the results for the year ending 31 March 2016 are known, there is no guarantee that a higher level of sales proceeds will be achieved and there will be a significant delay in obtaining the sales proceeds. Also, these figures assume that any costs of sale will be the same at both dates, which may not be the case.

Working

	£
Proceeds	100,000
Less: cost £65,000 × 50,000/170,000	(19,118)
indexation allowance £19,118 × 0.400 (assumed)	(7,647)
Chargeable gain	73,235

(c) **Error in the corporation tax return of Binni Ltd**

Interest on underpaid tax

Binni Ltd will be regarded as having underpaid corporation tax on each of the four payment dates for the year ended 31 May 2013. Accordingly, interest may be charged from 14 December 2012, 14 March 2013, 14 June 2013 and 14 September 2013 on any amounts of underpaid corporation tax.

Disclosure of the error

The directors of Binni Ltd must be advised to make full disclosure of the error or authorise our firm to make such disclosure, without delay. If they refuse, we can no longer act for the company. The directors should be advised of this, and also that we must inform HMRC that we have ceased to act for the client. We should not, however, advise HMRC of the error unless the directors consented to such disclosure.

Even if we cease to act for Binni Ltd, we are is still under a professional duty to ensure that the directors understand the seriousness of offences against HMRC, including the possibility of criminal prosecution.

Tax evasion may also constitute money laundering and we are also bound by legislation to report suspicions to the appropriate authority. Again, this may lead to criminal prosecution.

28 Forti Ltd group (ATAX 12/13)

Text references. Computing taxable total profits is the subject of Chapter 20. Chargeable gains for companies are covered in Chapter 21. Computing corporation tax payable is dealt with in Chapter 22. Close companies are covered in Chapter 25. Groups and consortia are the subject of Chapter 26.

Top tips. If you are asked to correct a computation, don't assume that **all** the figures are incorrect. You were specifically told that some were correct, but there was an adjustment which was correct as well.

Easy marks. There were some easy marks in part (a) for computing taxable total profits and the corporation tax liability, even if you were not sure why some of the corrections to the original schedule needed to be made. The adjustment for transfer pricing should have been well known in part (b)(ii). The annual accounting scheme in part (c) was brought forward knowledge from F6.

Examiner's comments. Part (a) was well done by many candidates. In relation to the tax adjusted trading income, many candidates thought, incorrectly, that the cost of entertaining overseas customers was allowable. In addition, there was a general, correct, view that the management bonus should be disallowed but very candidates knew that it was because it had not been paid within nine months of the end of the accounting period. The majority of candidates picked up the point in relation to group relief and arrangements in force in respect of Marussia Ltd. However, candidates did not do so well in relation to the position of Eagle Ltd, which could not be a consortium company as it was a 75% subsidiary of Ligier Ltd. The majority of candidates handled the degrouping charge and the annual exempt amount correctly. When calculating the corporation tax liability, most candidates recognised that Eagle Ltd was not an associated company but very few identified the fact that Brawn Ltd was not a close investment holding company, such that the main rate of corporation tax did not apply automatically.

Part (b)(i) required candidates to set out the matters that need to be considered in order to determine whether or not a company is a close company. This was intended to be a relatively straightforward requirement, which then required some thought if a very good mark were to be obtained. However, the majority of candidates simply did not know the rules, such that the performance in this part of the question was poor. On the whole, candidates focussed on the owners of the company and knew the rules had something to do with five shareholders and any number of directors. However, the key to the rules is who controls the company as opposed to who owns it. Some candidates tried to make up for their lack of knowledge by writing about the implications of a company being close. As always, regardless of its technical accuracy, such irrelevant information did not score any marks.

Part (b)(ii) concerned transfer pricing. Many candidates were able to score two out of the three marks but very few addressed the availability or otherwise of the exemption for small and medium-sized enterprises.

Part (c) of the question required candidates to state the conditions and operation of the VAT annual accounting scheme. Candidates' performance in this part of the question was very good. A small minority of candidates confused the annual accounting scheme with group registration, perhaps because there was a group in the question, but the majority produced brief succinct answers that scored well.

			Marks
(a)	Notes		
	Tax adjusted trading income	3	
	Chargeable gains	2	
	Losses transferred from Marussia Ltd	1	
	Losses transferred from Eagle Ltd	1½	
	Rate of corporation tax	2	
	Calculation		
	Taxable total profits	3	
	Corporation tax liability	1½	
	Max		12

			Marks
(b)	(i)	Definition of close company	2½
		Associates	1½
		Application	2
		Max	5
	(ii)	Reasons why transfer pricing rules apply	2½
		Adjustment required	1
		Max	3
(c)		Conditions	3
		Operation of the scheme	3
		Max	5
			25

(a) **Brawn Ltd – Corporation tax computation for the year ended 31 March 2015**

	Notes	
		£
Tax adjusted trading income per original schedule		250,500
Less: costs relating to company share option plan	1	(6,000)
Add: accrued management bonuses	2	7,000
Tax adjusted trading income		251,500
Add: sale of Marussia Ltd:		
chargeable gain £(83,000 + 21,600 + 11,000)	3, 4	115,600
Total taxable profits before loss relief		367,100
Less: losses transferred from:		
Marussia Ltd £60,000 × 3/12	5	(15,000)
Eagle Ltd	6	(0)
Taxable total profits		352,100
Corporation tax @ 21%		73,941
Less: marginal relief		
£([1,500,000/4] – 352,100) × 1/400	7, 8	(57)
Corporation tax payable		73,884

Notes

1   The costs of setting up a company share option plan incurred by a company are deductible in the accounting period in which they are incurred.

2   The management bonuses are not an allowable cost as they have not been paid within nine months of the end of the accounting period.

3   The degrouping charge must be added to the sales proceeds on the sale of Marussia Ltd so it increases the chargeable gain arising.

4   The capital gains tax annual exempt amount of £11,000 is not available to companies.

5   For the purposes of group relief, Marussia Ltd is regarded as having left the group once there were arrangements in force for it to leave the group. The signing of the contract on 1 November 2014 amounts to such arrangements. This means that Marussia Ltd is only a member of the group relief group for the three months from 1 August 2014 until 31 October 2014 and the loss must therefore be apportioned on a time basis.

6   Consortium relief is not available as Eagle Ltd is a 75% subsidiary of Ligier Ltd. Accordingly, it is not possible for any of Eagle Ltd's trading losses to be transferred to Brawn Ltd.

7   The main rate of corporation tax applies automatically to close investment holding companies. However, Brawn Ltd is a trading company and not a close investment holding company.

8   There are four associated companies. Eagle Ltd is not an associated company as it is not controlled by Brawn Ltd.

Tutorial notes

1 The costs of entertaining customers (whether UK or overseas) are disallowable in computing the trading profit. The distinction between UK and overseas customers is only relevant for value added tax purposes.

2 Marussia Ltd is associated with Brawn Ltd because it was controlled by Brawn Ltd for part of the accounting period.

(b) **Other corporate matters**

(i) *Close companies*

Forti Ltd will be a close company if it is controlled by:

- Five or fewer shareholders, or
- Any number of its shareholder directors

A company is controlled by those shareholders who own more than half of the company's share capital.

When determining whether or not a company is close within this definition, each shareholder is regarded as owning any shares owned by their associates as well as the shares owned personally. A person's associates include their direct relatives, business partners and the trustees of certain trusts set up by the shareholder or their direct relatives.

Control of Forti Ltd can be exercised by a minimum of seven shareholders as these hold $(10,000/120,000 \times 7 \times 100) = 58.3\%$ of the shares.

Accordingly, unless Forti Ltd is controlled by shareholder directors, it will only be close if some of its shareholders are associated with each other.

Tutorial note

There are further complexities when determining whether or not a company is close but the points set out above were sufficient to score full marks.

(ii) *Transfer pricing (note 6 to the schedule)*

The transfer pricing rules will apply to the sale of components by Brawn Ltd to Gordini Co because these two companies are both controlled by Forti Ltd. The exemption for small and medium-sized enterprises is unlikely to be available, regardless of the size of the Forti Ltd group, as there is no double tax treaty between the UK and the country of Arrowsia.

Under the transfer pricing rules, if Brawn Ltd has sold components to Gordini Co for less than an arm's length price, it is required to increase its taxable profits by the excess of the arm's length price over the price charged.

(c) **Value added tax (VAT) annual accounting scheme**

Conditions

- The company's VAT reporting and payments must be up to date.

- The company's VAT exclusive taxable turnover must not be expected to exceed £1,350,000 over the following 12 months.

- If the expected value of the company's taxable supplies exceeds £1,600,000 notice must be given to HM Revenue and Customs and it may then be required to leave the scheme. If the £1,600,000 limit is actually exceeded, the company must leave the scheme.

- The scheme is not available where registration is in the name of a group or a division.

Tutorial note

Companies which are normally in a repayment situation can account for VAT annually if they wish, but this would not be advisable from a cash flow point of view as they would only receive one repayment for the whole year.

- The company must make nine equal monthly payments on account in total equal to 90% of its previous year's VAT liability, with the first payment due at the end of the fourth month of the year.

- Alternatively, a company can choose to make three larger interim payments.

- The company must submit a single VAT return within two months of the end of the year together with any final balancing payment.

29 Epon Ltd group (ATAX 06/13)

Text references. Loss relief for companies is covered in Chapter 24 and groups in Chapter 26. Overseas aspects of VAT are dealt with in Chapter 29. Purchase of own shares is in Chapter 23. Ethics are covered in Chapter 30.

Top tips. Remember that capital losses can only be set against chargeable gains, not against income.

Easy marks. The treatment of imports for VAT in part (b) should have been well known.

Examiner's comments. Part (a) was done well by the majority of candidates. Most candidates were comfortable with the group relief and the matching of the capital losses with the chargeable gains. In addition, it was particularly pleasing that the majority of candidates provided an appropriate level of relevant narrative rather than writing about all aspects of groups and corporation tax. Having said that, some candidates need to take care that they do not take their knowledge for granted. The question required explanations of the use of the losses, such that notes setting out the reason for the manner in which the losses were to be relieved needed to be provided in addition to the calculations; some candidates who clearly knew what they were doing failed to do this. Common mistakes by some candidates included offsetting the brought forward trading losses against the profits of a different trade or group relieving them and, somewhat surprisingly, offsetting capital losses against trading profits.

Part (b) was for two marks and concerned the VAT implications of importing goods from a country that is not a member of the European Union. This was simply something candidates either knew or didn't know: fortunately, most did.

Part (c)(i) required candidates to review each of the conditions for capital gains tax treatment of the transaction. This was done well by a majority of candidates. Those who did not do as well as they perhaps could have done wrote too much about each condition rather than ensuring that they addressed as many of the conditions as possible. It would perhaps have helped if they had made a brief note of all of the conditions and then wrote briefly about each of them. In addition, a minority of candidates listed the conditions but did not earn all of the available marks as they failed to relate the conditions to the specific facts of the question. Some candidates missed the point of the question, and addressed capital gains tax and entrepreneurs' relief generally, or did not have sufficient knowledge of the conditions. Part (c)(ii) required calculations of the increase in the shareholder's tax cost of the transaction being subject to income tax as opposed to capital gains tax. As always, when it comes to calculations, great care is necessary if marks are to be maximised. Accordingly, although this part was done well by many candidates, the following mistakes were common:

- Treating the amount received as the distribution rather than the excess of this amount over the amount originally subscribed

- Failing to gross up the distribution

- Failing to consider the effect of the distribution on the level of taxable income and hence on the personal allowance

- Omitting the tax credit in respect of the distribution

Part (d) concerned the acceptability or otherwise of being appointed tax advisers to both the companies and their directors. Candidates were expected to identify the potential problems associated with such an appointment together with appropriate safeguards. This was done well by the majority of candidates. However, as always, a minority of candidates wrote at length about one or two matters rather than thinking about all of the possible issues and writing briefly about each of them.

Marks were available for professional skills in this question. In order to earn these marks candidates had to use the information provided in the question correctly and then provide clear calculations that were easy to understand together with appropriate relevant explanations in an appropriately formatted memorandum. On the whole, the performance of candidates in this area was satisfactory with the majority of candidates producing a memorandum in a style that was easy to follow.

Marks

(a)	Explanation			
		Yoko Ltd trading loss brought forward	1	
		Use of capital losses	2	
		Group relief	3	
	Calculations – purchase by NewCo Ltd			
		Taxable total profits	3	
		Tax liabilities	2	
	Calculations – purchase by Yoko Ltd			
		Taxable total profits	2½	
		Tax liabilities	2	
		Max		13
(b)	Account for VAT on importation		1	
	Recover as input tax		1	
				2
(c)	(i)	Conditions		
		Period of ownership	1½	
		Resident status of Kari	1	
		Benefit of trade	1½	
		Reduction in level of shareholding	1½	
		Avoidance of tax	1	
		Max		5
	(ii)	Calculations		
		Capital receipt	1½	
		Income receipt		
		Taxable income	1½	
		Tax liability	2½	
		Increase in tax cost due to income tax treatment	½	
				6
(d)	Objectivity and conflict of interest		2	
	Notify and obtain consent		2	
	Safeguards		2	
		Max		5
	Approach in problem solving		1	
	Clarity of calculations		1	
	Effectiveness with which the information is communicated		1	
	Overall presentation of the memorandum		1	
				4
				35

To   The files
From   Tax senior
Date   7 June 2015
Subject The purchase of the Aquapower business and other matters

(a)   **The purchase of the Aquapower business – corporation tax liabilities**

NewCo Ltd purchases the business

	Epon Ltd	Wahzah Ltd	Yoko Ltd	NewCo Ltd
	£	£	£	£
Trading profit	740,000	90,000	Nil	60,000
Chargeable gain	18,000		12,000	
Wahzah Ltd capital loss (£20,000)	(18,000)		(2,000)	
	740,000	90,000	10,000	
Yoko Ltd group relief (£80,000)	(65,000)	(15,000)		
Taxable total profits	675,000	75,000	10,000	60,000
Corporation tax				
At 21%/20%/20%/20%	141,750	15,000	2,000	12,000

There are four companies in the group (Newco Ltd will no longer be a dormant company), such that the limits will be divided by four; the upper limit will be £375,000 and the lower limit will be £75,000.

The capital loss of Wahzah Ltd will be transferred to Epon Ltd in priority to Yoko Ltd because this will save corporation tax at the main rate rather than the small profits rate.

The first £15,000 of the trading loss of Yoko Ltd will be surrendered to Wahzah Ltd in order to relieve the profits that would otherwise be taxed at the marginal rate. The remaining loss will be surrendered to Epon Ltd because this will save corporation tax at the main rate rather than the small profits rate.

Yoko Ltd purchases the business

	Epon Ltd	Wahzah Ltd	Yoko Ltd	NewCo Ltd
	£	£	£	£
Trading profit	740,000	90,000	Nil	
Aquapower trading profit			60,000	
Chargeable gain	18,000		12,000	
Wahzah Ltd capital loss (£20,000)	(18,000)		(2,000)	
	740,000	90,000	70,000	
Yoko Ltd group relief (£80,000)	(80,000)			
Taxable total profits	660,000	90,000	70,000	Nil
Corporation tax				
At 21%/20%/20%	138,600	18,000	14,000	Nil

There are three companies in the group (NewCo Ltd will still be a dormant company, so will be ignored) such that the limits will be divided by three; the upper limit will be £500,000 and the lower limit will be £100,000.

The trading losses brought forward in Yoko Ltd are not available for offset against the profits of the Aquapower business as they can only be used against the future profits of the same trade.

The capital loss of Wahzah Ltd will be transferred to Epon Ltd in priority to Yoko Ltd because this will save corporation tax at the main rate rather than the small profits rate.

The trading loss of Yoko Ltd will be surrendered to Epon Ltd because this will save corporation tax at the main rate rather than the small profits rate.

(b)   **The purchase of equipment from the country of Candara**

Wahzah Ltd will be required to account for value added tax (VAT) at the point of entry into the UK.

The VAT paid can be recovered as input tax in the normal way on the company's next VAT return.

(c) **The purchase of Kari's shares**

(i) *The conditions which need to be satisfied in order to obtain capital gains tax treatment*

- Kari must have owned the shares for five years. This condition is not satisfied.

- Kari must be UK resident in 2015/16, the tax year of disposal.

- The purchase of the shares must be carried out for the benefit of Epon Ltd's trade. This condition is likely to be satisfied as the shares are being purchased in order to buy out a dissenting shareholder.

- Kari's shareholding in Epon Ltd must be substantially reduced, such that her interest in the company is no more than 75% of what it was prior to the sale of the shares. In addition, Kari must not control more than 30% of the share capital of Epon Ltd after the sale of the shares has taken place. Both of these conditions will be satisfied as Kari is selling all of her shares.

- Capital gains tax treatment will not be available if the main objective of the purchase of the shares is the avoidance of tax.

(ii) *Increase in Kari's tax cost*

Capital receipt

	£
Proceeds	90,000
Less: cost	(10,000)
	80,000
Less: annual exempt amount	(11,000)
	69,000
Capital gains tax @10% (entrepreneurs' relief will apply)	6,900

Income receipt

	£
Amount received	90,000
Less: original subscription price	(10,000)
Distribution	80,000
Annual taxable income	72,000
Taxable dividend income £80,000 × 100/90	88,889
Taxable income	160,889
Income tax in respect of sale of shares	
£(150,000 − 72,000) = £78,000 × 32.5%	25,350
£(160,889 − 150,000) = £10,889 × 37.5%	4,083
Loss of personal allowance £10,000 × 40%	4,000
Income tax liability	33,433
Less: tax credit £88,889 × 10%	(8,889)
Income tax payable	24,544

The increase in Kari's tax cost as a result of the sale of the shares being subject to income tax as opposed to capital gains tax is £(24,544 − 6,900) = £17,644.

Tutorial note

If the receipt is treated as income, Kari's adjusted net income will exceed £120,000, such that no personal allowance will be available.

(d)   **Appointment as tax advisers**

It is a fundamental principle of the ACCA *Code of Ethics and Conduct* that advice to clients should be objective. Our ability to be objective may be threatened where there is a conflict of interest between two clients. For example, the best advice for the group of companies may not be the most advantageous for one or more of the directors.

Generally speaking, this need not be a problem, provided we point out the potential conflict to all of the relevant parties. We should then obtain their consent to act for them.

However, as far as Kari is concerned, there is already a dispute between her and the Epon Ltd group, such that it is unlikely to be appropriate for us to act for both her and the companies.

If we are to act for the other directors, as well as for the group of companies, we should consider introducing the following safeguards:

- We must have clear guidelines in relation to confidentiality.
- We should consider the need to use separate teams for each client.

30 Trifles Ltd (ATAX 12/10)

Text references. Repurchase of own shares is covered in Chapter 23 and close companies are dealt with in Chapter 25.

Top tips. If you are asked to compute tax on an extra amount of income, you should compute tax at the marginal rate on that extra income rather than produce a full income tax computation. Note the acceptable 'short cut' of computing higher rate tax on dividend income using the 25% rate.

Easy marks. The calculation of the capital receipt was relatively straightforward.

Examiner's comments. Part (a) required candidates to explain whether two of the conditions necessary to enable the amount received to be treated as capital were satisfied. Many candidates answered this part well but others, with similar knowledge levels, did not perform well because they failed to answer the question. Rather than addressing the two particular conditions set out in the question, this latter group attempted to address all of the conditions despite the majority of them being irrelevant.

Candidates had a good knowledge of the five-year rule and the 30% rule but were much less comfortable with the condition relating to the shareholder's interest in the company following the purchase. The rules require the shareholder's interest to be no more than 75% of the interest prior to the purchase – this is not the same as the shareholder selling 25% of his shares because the shares sold are cancelled thus reducing the number of issued shares.

Only a minority of candidates were aware that the ownership period of the husband could be added to that of the wife. Even fewer knew that the usual five-year ownership period is reduced to three where the shares are inherited.

Part (b) required calculations of the after tax proceeds depending on the tax treatment of the sum received. This part was answered well by the vast majority of candidates. The only point that many candidates missed was the availability of entrepreneurs' relief. It was particularly pleasing to see the majority of candidates correctly identify the after tax proceeds as the amount received less the tax liability (as opposed to the taxable amount less the tax liability).

The final part of the question was more difficult and, unsurprisingly, caused more problems. The question concerned the loan of a motorcycle to a shareholder in a close company who was not an employee. Candidates had no problem recognising that the company was a close company but many then decided that this was a loan to a participator as opposed to the loan of an asset.

Another relatively common error was to state, correctly, that the benefit would be treated as a distribution but to then give an incorrect tax rate of 40%. Candidates would benefit from slowing down and ensuring that they apply their basic tax knowledge correctly in the exam.

			Marks
(a)	Victoria		
	Period of ownership	2½	
	Reduction in level of shareholding	½	
	Melba		
	Period of ownership	1	
	Reduction in level of shareholding	2½	
	Max		6
(b)	Capital receipt	4	
	Income receipt	2½	
	Max		6
(c)	Close company	1½	
	Melba		
	Recognition of distribution	1½	
	Supporting calculations	1½	
	Trifles Ltd	1	
	Max		5
			17

(a) **Purchase of own shares – conditions relating to period of ownership and reduction in level of shareholding**

Victoria

Victoria inherited the shares from her husband, Brownie. Accordingly, the required period of ownership in order for the capital treatment to apply is three years rather than the usual five years. Victoria is permitted to extend her period of ownership to include that of Brownie. Accordingly, her qualifying period is from 1 February 2012 until 28 February 2016 such that she satisfies the condition. Victoria is selling all of her shares and will therefore satisfy the condition relating to the reduction in the level of her shareholding.

Melba

Melba acquired the shares on 1 February 2008. Accordingly, she has owned them for more than five years such that she satisfies the condition for capital treatment.

After the purchase of Victoria's shares, Melba's 1,700 shares will represent 20% (1,700/(10,000 – 1,500)) of Trifles Ltd issued share capital. In order to satisfy the condition for capital treatment, her interest in the company after the purchase of her shares must be no more than 15% (20% × 75%). However, after the purchase of her shares she will own 1,250 shares (1,700 – 450) out of a total issued share capital of 8,050 shares (10,000 – 1,500 (Victoria) – 450 (Melba)) representing a 15.53% holding such that the condition is not satisfied.

(b) **Victoria – after tax proceeds from the purchase of own shares**

Capital receipt

	£
Proceeds (1,500 × £30)	45,000
Less: cost (probate value)	(16,000)
	29,000
Less: capital loss brought forward	(3,400)
	25,600
Less: annual exempt amount	(11,000)
Taxable gain	14,600
Capital gains tax @ 10% (entrepreneurs' relief rate)	1,460

		£
After tax proceeds £(45,000 − 1,460)		43,540

Income receipt

		£
Amount received (1,500 × £30)		45,000
Less: original subscription price (1,500 × £2)		(3,000)
Distribution		42,000
Income tax @ 25% (N)		10,500
After tax proceeds £(45,000 − 10,500)		34,500

Note

This is the effective rate of income tax suffered by a higher rate taxpayer on a distribution, ie 100/90 × (32.5% − 10%).

Tutorial note

If the amount received is treated as income, Victoria will also realise a capital loss of £13,000. This is the excess of her cost (£16,000) over the original subscription price of the shares (£3,000).

(c) **Tax implications of the loan of the motorcycle**

Trifles Ltd is a close company as it is controlled by five or fewer shareholders.

Melba

The loan of the motorcycle cannot give rise to an employment income benefit because Melba will not be a director or employee of Trifles Ltd. However, the provision of a benefit by a close company to a shareholder who is not a director or an employee is treated as a distribution. Melba will be treated as having received a distribution equal to the amount that would have been taxable as employment income had she been an employee, ie £1,440 (£9,000 × 20% − (12 × £30)). Income tax will be charged at 25% (N) on the £1,440, resulting in income tax payable of £360.

Note

This is the effective rate of income tax suffered by a higher rate taxpayer on a distribution, ie 100/90 × (32.5% − 10%).

Trifles Ltd

Trifles Ltd will not be able to claim capital allowances in respect of the motorcycle or a tax deduction in respect of its running costs.

31 Bamburg Ltd (ATAX 06/14)

> **Text references.** The flat rate scheme for VAT is covered in Chapter 29. Capital allowances are covered in Chapter 7 and replacement of business assets relief in Chapter 13. The computation of income tax is dealt with in Chapter 1 and national insurance contributions on employment income in Chapter 4. Close companies are covered in Chapter 25.
>
> **Top tips.** In part (c), don't forget to consider the national insurance implications of a loan benefit.
>
> **Easy marks.** There were some marks each for describing the flat rate scheme in part (a). The rules on close companies in part (c) are frequently examined.

Marking scheme

				Marks
(a)	Eligibility		1½	
	VAT due normally		1	
	VAT due under flat rate scheme		2½	
	Conclusion		1	
		Max		5
(b)	One mark for each relevant point			5
(c)	(i)	Payment of bonus	3½	
		Payment of dividend	2	
		Max		5
	(ii)	Charlotte	1½	
		Bamburg Ltd		
		Close company loan to participator	2½	
		Class 1A national insurance contribution	1	
		Exemption not applicable	1	
		Max		5
				20

(a) **Value added tax (VAT) flat rate scheme**

Bamburg Ltd will be permitted to join the flat rate scheme provided its taxable supplies for the next year are not expected to exceed £150,000. On the basis that its budgeted taxable supplies for the year ending 31 March 2016 are expected to be £114,000 (£120,000 – £6,000), it is likely that this condition will be satisfied.

Bamburg Ltd currently pays VAT to HM Revenue and Customs (HMRC) equal to the output tax on its standard rated sales less its recoverable input tax.

Under the flat rate scheme, the company would pay HMRC a fixed percentage of the total of its VAT inclusive sales. Exempt supplies are included in sales for this purpose. The percentage will depend on the particular business sector in which Bamburg Ltd operates.

Whether or not it is financially beneficial for Bamburg Ltd to join the flat rate scheme will depend on the percentage which it is required to use. However, the scheme is primarily intended to reduce administration and any financial benefit is unlikely to be significant.

(b) **Implications of selling the 'Cara' machine**

The balance on the main pool of Bamburg Ltd is nil. This means that the sale of the machine will result in a balancing charge equal to the sales proceeds received of £80,000 which will increase the taxable trade profit of Bamburg Ltd.

The 'Cara' machine is a depreciating asset for the purposes of replacement of business assets. Therefore the chargeable gain of £13,000 which was deferred in respect of the purchase of the 'Cara' machine will become chargeable when the machine is sold. This will increase the taxable total profit of Bamburg Ltd in the year of sale.

No allowable capital loss will arise on the sale of the machine because it qualified for capital allowances.

In summary, Bamburg Ltd will receive proceeds of £80,000 but will have to pay additional corporation tax of £(80,000 + 13,000) × 20% = £18,600.

Once the machine has been sold, Bamburg Ltd will have to pay rent in respect of the replacement machine. This represents an outflow of cash for the company, although it will be an allowable deduction when computing the company's taxable trading profit.

(c) (i) **Bamburg Ltd to make an additional payment to Charlotte of £14,000**

Payment of bonus

	£
Bonus required £(14,000/(100 − 42)%)	24,138
Employer's national insurance £24,138 × 13.8%	3,331
	27,469
Less: reduction in corporation tax £27,469 × 20%	(5,494)
Total cost to Bamburg Ltd	21,975

Payment of dividend

Cash dividend £(14,000/(100 − 25)%)	£18,667

Tutorial notes

1 Charlotte's salary of £46,000 will mean that the bonus will be subject to income tax at 40% and national insurance contributions at 2%.

2 The effective rate of income tax suffered by a higher rate taxpayer on dividend income is 25% (100/90 × (32.5% − 10%)).

(ii) **Tax implications of Bamburg Ltd making a loan of £14,000 to Charlotte**

Charlotte

The interest-free loan will result in an annual employment income benefit for Charlotte because she is an employee of Bamburg Ltd. The benefit will be £455 (£14,000 × 3.25%) on which Charlotte will have to pay income tax at 40%.

Bamburg Ltd

Bamburg Ltd is a close company as it is wholly owned and controlled by Charlotte. When a close company makes a loan to a participator (eg a shareholder), it must pay HMRC an amount equal to 25% of the loan, in this case £3,500. This will be payable at the same time as Bamburg Ltd's corporation tax liability by 1 January 2017.

Bamburg Ltd will also have to pay class 1A national insurance contributions of £(455 × 13.8%) = £63 in respect of the loan benefit. These contributions will be allowable when computing the company's taxable trading profits.

The payment to HMRC will be required even though the loan will be for less than £15,000. This is because Charlotte owns more than 5% of the company.

32 Liza (ATAX 06/13)

Text references. Chargeable gains for companies are covered in Chapter 21 with chargeable gains groups dealt with in Chapter 26. Capital allowances are the subject of Chapter 7. VAT groups are covered in Chapter 28.

Top tips. If you choose to answer this type of multiple topic question in the exam, it is important that you are confident that you can achieve reasonable marks on all parts.

Easy marks. The computation of the chargeable gain in part (a) should have yielded easy marks. Group registration for VAT (part (c)) is a standard exam topic.

Examiner's comments. Part (a)(i) required a calculation of the chargeable gain on the sale of a building and the correct treatment of the various expenses incurred in acquiring, enhancing and maintaining the property. This was a gentle introduction to the question and was done well. Part (a) (ii) concerned rollover relief and groups for the purposes of chargeable gains. It was done well by those candidates who knew the rules and who expressed themselves carefully. This part required candidates to know three things: that rollover relief can be claimed where one company in a gains group sells a qualifying business asset and another company in the group buys one, the definition of a gains group, and the time period in which a replacement asset needs to be purchased in order for rollover relief to be available. The majority of candidates knew the first and third points although a small minority failed to address the third point despite, probably, knowing the rule. The difficulty came in dealing with the second point and the definition of a gains group where a minority of candidates revealed a level of confusion. This stemmed from a problem in distinguishing the 75% aspect of the rule from the 51% aspect and led to some candidates concluding erroneously that Vault Ltd and Bar Ltd were in a gains group. For there to be a chargeable gains group, the direct holding between each company in the chain must be at least 75%; if it isn't, the two companies cannot be in a group regardless of the level of the indirect holding. Part (a)(ii) concerned the amount that needed to be invested in order for the maximum amount of gain to be rolled over. This was the hardest part of the question and was not done particularly well. It required candidates to know the basic rule whereby the whole of the relevant proceeds has to be spent on replacement assets in order for the maximum gain to be rolled over, whilst recognising the relevance of the non-business use of both the asset sold and the asset acquired. Almost all candidates knew the basic rule but the majority struggled to apply it in these particular circumstances.

Part (b) concerned the availability of capital allowances in respect of electrical, water and heating systems acquired as part of a building and was done well.

Part (c) concerned VAT groups. The idea here was to test another aspect of groups in order to ensure that candidates appreciated the difference between a group for the purposes of VAT and one for the purposes of chargeable gains as tested in part (a). Candidates were also required to identify the advantages and disadvantages of registering as a group for the purposes of VAT. The majority of candidates made a reasonable job of discussing the advantages and disadvantages of registering as a VAT group and made a series of concise points. However, the definition of a group for the purposes of VAT was not handled particularly well. In particular, a sizable minority of candidates thought that the required holding was 75% as opposed to control. In addition, many candidates did not appreciate that control could be exercised by an individual, ie Liza, as well as by a company, such that all of the companies in the question were able to register as a single group. As always, a minority of candidates wrote in general terms, for example, about partial exemption, rather than addressing the specifics of the question, such that they wasted time.

				Marks
(a)	(i)	Chargeable gain	Max	3
	(ii)	Chargeable gains group	2	
		Identification of relevant companies	1½	
		Qualifying period	1	
			Max	4
	(iii)	Amount relievable via rollover relief	2	
		Total acquisitions necessary	1	
		Further acquisitions necessary	1½	
			Max	4
(b)		Plant and machinery as integral feature	1	
		Special rate pool	½	
		Use of AIA	1	
			Max	2
(c)		Ability to register as a group	2	
		Discussion	6	
			Max	7
				20

(a) (i) The chargeable gain on the sale of Building 1

	£	£
Net sale proceeds		860,000
Less: purchase price	315,000	
legal fees	9,000	
work on roof to make fit for use	38,000	
		(362,000)
		498,000

Less: indexation allowance

$$\frac{263.7 - 213.4}{213.4} = 0.236 \times £362,000$$

		(85,432)
Chargeable gain		412,568

Tutorial note

A deduction is available for the legal fees incurred in acquiring the building and the costs incurred shortly afterwards in order to make the building fit for use (see *Law Shipping Co Ltd v CIR 1923*). The cost of repainting the building would have been an allowable deduction in calculating the company's trading profits and would not be allowable when computing the chargeable gain.

(ii) Acquisition of qualifying assets for the purposes of rollover relief

The assets can be purchased by companies within the Bar Ltd chargeable gains group. A chargeable gains group consists of a principal company, Bar Ltd, its 75% subsidiaries, the 75% subsidiaries of those subsidiaries and so on.

Bar Ltd must have an effective interest of more than 50% in all of the companies in the group. Accordingly, the only companies able to purchase qualifying replacement assets are Bar Ltd and Pommel Ltd. Ring Ltd is not a 75% subsidiary of Bar Ltd, such that it and Vault Ltd cannot be members of the Bar Ltd chargeable gains group. The Hoop Ltd group is a separate group.

The qualifying replacement assets must be purchased in the period from 1 June 2014 to 31 May 2018.

(iii) **The additional amount that would need to be spent on qualifying assets**

Bar Ltd owned the building from 1 June 2009 to 31 May 2015, a period of 72 months. The building was not used for trading purposes from 1 January 2011 to 30 June 2012, a period of 18 months. Accordingly, the building was used for the purposes of the trade for a period of 54 (72 – 18) months, such that only 54/72 of the gain can be relieved via rollover relief.

Therefore, qualifying business assets costing £645,000 (£860,000 × 54/72) will need to be acquired in order to relieve the whole of the gain qualifying for rollover relief.

Only two-thirds of the new building is to be used for trading purposes, such that only £480,000 (£720,000 × 2/3) of its cost will be a qualifying acquisition for the purposes of rollover relief. Accordingly, the additional amount that would need to be spent on qualifying acquisitions in order to relieve the whole of the gain that qualifies for rollover relief would be £165,000 (£645,000 – £480,000).

(b) **Capital allowances available in respect of the new building**

Electrical, water and heating systems qualify for plant and machinery capital allowances.

They are classified as integral features, such that they are included in the special rate pool where the writing down allowance is only 8%.

The annual investment allowance available to the Bar Ltd group should be set against these additions in priority to those assets which qualify for the 18% writing down allowance.

(c) **Group registration for the purposes of value added tax (VAT)**

The companies able to register as a group

Two or more companies may register as a group provided they are established in the UK, or have a fixed establishment in the UK, and they are controlled by the same person. The person can be an individual, a company, or a partnership. Accordingly, all of the companies in the Bar Ltd and Hoop Ltd groups can register as a single group for the purposes of VAT.

The potential advantages and disadvantages of registering as a group

The advantage of a group registration would be that there would be no need to charge VAT on the transactions between the group companies. This would reduce administration and improve the group's cash flow.

The group would have to appoint a representative member which would account for the group's VAT liability as if the group were a single entity. Consequently, there would be a need to collate information from all of the members of the group and to present it in a single VAT return. This may not be straightforward, depending on the accounting systems and procedures used by the various companies within the two separate groups.

Vault Ltd makes zero rated supplies and will therefore be in a repayment position, such that it can improve its cash flow by accounting for VAT on a monthly basis. However, if it were registered as part of a VAT group, it would not be able to do this as the group, as a single entity, is very unlikely to be in a regular repayment position. Accordingly, if a group registration is to be entered into, consideration should be given to excluding Vault Ltd from that registration.

Finally, it should be recognised that all of the companies within the group registration would have joint and several liability for the VAT due from the representative member. Liza, and the minority shareholders, should give careful consideration to the possible dangers of linking the two groups in such a manner.

33 Swan plc, Gosling plc and Mallard Ltd

> **Text references.** The patent box election is covered in Chapter 20. Research and development relief is covered in Chapter 20. Disincorporation relief is dealt with in Chapter 21.
>
> **Top tips.** In part (a), you can check the corporation tax liability with the patent box election by working out how much of the taxable total profits are taxable at the main rate and how much at the reduced 10% rate. In part (b), don't forget to deduct the R&D expenditure as well as dealing with the additional elements which give extra relief.
>
> **Easy marks.** In part (a), you were given the formula for the patent box and so there were easy marks for inserting the relevant figures and computing the actual deduction. In part (c), you should learn the conditions for disincorporation relief for easy marks.

Marking scheme

			Marks	
(a)		Tax without patent box election	1	
		Tax with patent box election		
		Non patent profit	½	
		Patent box deduction	1½	
		Tax	½	
		Tax saving	½	
				4
(b)	(i)	Deduction relief		
		Deduct R&D expenditure	½	
		Additional deduction	1	
		Corporation tax	½	
				2
	(ii)	ATL relief		
		Add tax credit	1	
		Deduct R&D expenditure	½	
		Corporation tax	½	
		Deduct tax credit	1	
				3
(c)	(i)	Going concern transfer to shareholder	1	
		All assets except cash	½	
		MV does not exceed £100,000 – information needed	1	
		Individuals and shares held at least 12 months	1	
		Dates	½	
				4
	(ii)	Election by company and shareholder	1	
		Date for election	1	
				2
	(iii)	Shop	1½	
		Goodwill	2	
			Max	3
	(iv)	Motor car	1	
		Inventory	1	
				2
				20

(a) **Swan plc – Tax saving for the year to 31 March 2015 with patent box election**

	£	£	£
Tax without patent box election			
£2,000,000 × 21%			420,000
Tax with patent box election			
Non-patent profit £(2,000,000 – 500,000)		1,500,000	
Net patent profit	500,000		
Less: deduction			
£500,000 × 70% × $\dfrac{(21\% - 10\%)}{21\%}$	(183,333)		
		316,667	
		1,816,667	
£1,816,667 × 21%			(381,500)
Tax saving with patent box election			38,500

Tutorial note

The corporation liability with the patent box election can be analysed as follows.

	£
Net patent profit @ 10% £(500,000 × 70%) = £350,000 × 10%	35,000
Balance of taxable total profits £(2,000,000 – 350,000) = £1,650,000 × 21%	346,500
Corporation tax liability	381,500

(b) **Gosling plc – R&D reliefs**

(i) *Deduction relief*

	£
Taxable total profit before R&D expenditure	4,500,000
Less R&D expenditure	(500,000)
R&D additional deduction £500,000 × 30%	(150,000)
Taxable total profit	3,850,000
Corporation tax payable £3,850,000 × 21%	808,500

(ii) *ATL tax credit*

	£
Taxable total profit before R&D expenditure	4,500,000
Add ATL credit £500,000 × 10%	50,000
Less R&D expenditure	(500,000)
Taxable total profit	4,050,000
Corporation tax £4,050,000 × 21%	850,500
Less ATL credit £500,000 × 10%	(50,000)
Corporation tax payable	800,500

(c) **Mallard Ltd – Disincorporation relief**

(i) An election for disincorporation relief may be made where:

1   The company is transferring its business as a going concern to an individual who is a shareholder.

2   All of the assets of the business (except cash) are being transferred.

3   Market value of the goodwill and land and buildings does not exceed £100,000 – further information is required to confirm whether this condition is met.

4   The transfer is to individuals who have held shares in the company for at least 12 months prior to the transfer.

5   The transfer will occur after 1 April 2013 but before 31 March 2018.

(ii) Mallard Ltd and Nathan must make a joint election for disincorporation relief.

The election must be made within two years of the transfer to Nathan.

(iii) The freehold shop is deemed to have been disposed of by Mallard Ltd at the lower of market value and cost. Therefore no chargeable gain will arise. Nathan will acquire the shop at the deemed disposal value.

The goodwill is deemed to have been disposed of at the lower of market value and tax written down value. Since the goodwill has been built up since incorporation (rather than being purchased), the tax written down value is nil and so the deemed proceeds are therefore nil. Therefore no profit will arise on disposal. Nathan will acquire the goodwill at nil value.

(iv) Motor car – since Mallard Ltd and Nathan are connected persons, an election can be made to transfer the motor car at its tax written down value.

Inventory – since Mallard Ltd and Nathan are connected persons, an election can be made to transfer the inventory at the greater of original cost and transfer price.

34 Jerome (ATAX 06/12)

Text references. Value added tax on the incorporation of a business is covered in Chapter 30. Taxable benefits and expenses for employees are deal with in Chapter 4. Allowable expenses for business are covered in Chapter 6. Corporation tax payable is the subject of Chapter 22.

Top tips. It is important to state that the transfer of assets on incorporation will be a supply for VAT unless the conditions for transfer of the business as a going concern are satisfied.

Easy marks. The conditions for VAT TOGC in part (a) should have been well known. In part (b), the calculation of car and fuel benefits and the mileage allowance were straightforward.

Examiner's comments. In part (a), candidates first needed to recognise that the sale was a transfer of a business as a going concern such that VAT should not be charged. This was done well with the majority of candidates listing the conditions that needed to be satisfied. Candidates were then expected to realise that the building being sold was a commercial building that was less than three years old. Accordingly, VAT would need to be charged in respect of the building unless the purchaser made an election to tax the building at the time of purchase. Very few candidates identified this point.

Part (b) required calculations of the total tax cost for Tricycle Ltd and Jerome in relation to the lease of car. The car would be leased by Jerome, an employee of the company, or by Tricycle Ltd. This was a practical problem that was not particularly technically difficult but required care and thought in order to score well. It was not done as well as it should have been.

The point here was that Jerome owned Tricycle Ltd such that he was interested in the total tax cost to himself and the company in respect of each of the two options. Candidates needed to recognise that there were tax implications for both the employer, Tricycle Ltd, and the employee, Jerome, in each situation. For example, if Jerome leased the car, the payment of 50 pence per business mile was tax deductible for the company but resulted in taxable income for Jerome. There was also the need to consider national insurance contributions as well as income tax and corporation tax.

The main problem for candidates was a lack of exam technique. In particular, weaker candidates did not spend sufficient time thinking about the different tax implications for both parties in each situation but focussed on Jerome when he leased the car and on Tricycle Ltd when it leased the car.

				Marks
(a)	Administration – one mark for relevant point		1	
	Charge VAT unless transfer of a going concern		1	
	Conditions (one mark each, maximum three marks)		3	
	Land and buildings		2½	
		Max		6
(b)	(i) Motor car leased by Tricycle Ltd			
	Income tax payable by Jerome		2½	
	Net taxes saved by Tricycle Ltd		3	
	Net tax cost		½	
	(ii) Motor car leased by Jerome			
	Total tax payable by Jerome		3	
	Net taxes saved by Tricycle Ltd		1½	
	Net tax saved		½	
		Max		10
(c)	Conditions – one mark each			2
				18

(a) **Value added tax (VAT) on the sale of the business**

HM Revenue and Customs should be notified of the sale of the business within 30 days.

Jerome's VAT registration will need to be cancelled unless it is to be taken over by Tricycle Ltd.

VAT must be charged on the sale of the business assets unless it qualifies as a transfer of a going concern. For the sale of the business to be regarded as a transfer of a going concern, the following conditions must be satisfied:

- The business must be a going concern.
- Tricycle Ltd must use the assets to carry on the same kind of business as that carried on by Jerome.
- Tricycle Ltd must be VAT registered or be required to be VAT registered as a result of the purchase (based on the turnover of the purchased business in the previous 12 months).
- There should be no significant break in trading before or after the purchase of the business.

Even if the transfer satisfies the above conditions, Jerome will need to charge VAT on the sale of the building as it is a commercial building that is less than three years old. The only exception to this is if Tricycle Ltd makes an election to tax the building at the time of purchase.

(b) **Tax costs incurred in respect of the motor car**

(i) **Motor car is leased by Tricycle Ltd**

Jerome

	£
Taxable benefit in respect of the private use of the motor car	
155 (rounded down) – 95 = 60 ÷ 5 =	
12% + 12% + 3% (diesel) = 27%	
27% × £31,000	8,370
Taxable benefit in respect of the private fuel	
27% × £21,700	5,859
	14,229
Income tax at 40% payable by Jerome	5,692

Tricycle Ltd

	Allowable expenses £	Tax £
Lease payments		
£4,400 × 85% (100% – 15%)	3,740	
Running costs	5,000	
Class 1A NICs £14,229 × 13.8%	1,964	1,964
	10,704	
Reduction in corporation tax £10,704 × 20%		(2,141)
Net taxes saved by Tricycle Ltd		(177)
Total tax cost £(5,692 – 177)		5,515

Tutorial notes

1 Jerome's salary of £48,000 per year exceeds the personal allowance plus the basic rate band, such that he will be a higher rate taxpayer.

2 15% of the lease payments will be disallowed because the CO_2 emissions of the car are above 130 g/km.

3 Tricycle Ltd will pay corporation tax at the small profits rate as the profits of the business (£75,000 less the allowable costs of employing Jerome) are less than the lower limit.

(ii) **Motor car is leased by Jerome**

Jerome

	£
Taxable mileage allowance	
10,000 × (50 – 45)p	500
(14,000 – 10,000) × (50 – 25)p	1,000
	1,500
Income tax at 40% payable by Jerome	600
Class 1 NICs payable by Jerome	
14,000 × (50 – 45)p × 2%	14
Total tax payable by Jerome	614

Tricycle Ltd

	Allowable expenses £	Tax £
Mileage allowance paid 14,000 × 50p	7,000	
Class 1A NICs payable by Tricycle Ltd		
14,000 × (50 – 45)p × 13.8%	97	97
	7,097	
Reduction in corporation tax £7,097 × 20%		(1,419)
Net taxes saved by Tricycle Ltd		(1,322)
Net taxes saved £(1,322 – 614)		708

Tutorial notes

1 The calculations reflect the tax implications of the two alternatives. Jerome controls the company such that the non-tax costs incurred (lease payments, running costs and mileage allowances) are going to be incurred regardless of who leases the car and are therefore only relevant to the extent that they increase or reduce a tax liability. However, Jerome may need to

extract funds from the company in order to pay the costs relating to the motor car. This would give rise to further tax liabilities that would need to be considered.

2   Class 1 national insurance contributions are payable in respect of mileage allowances on the excess of the rate paid over the HMRC rate for up to 10,000 miles. Jerome's salary of £48,000 exceeds the upper earnings limit of £41,865 so the rate of Jerome's national insurance contributions will be 2%.

(c) **Conditions for deduction of travel costs**

- The employee must be absent from the UK for a continuous period of at least 60 days for the purposes of performing the duties of his employment.

- The journey must be from the UK to the place where the employee is carrying out the duties of his employment.

Tutorial note

A deduction is only available for two outward and two return journeys by the same person(s) in the same tax year.

35 Spetz Ltd group (ATAX 12/13)

Text references. Value added tax partial exemption is dealt with in Chapter 29. Company residence is covered in Chapter 20 and double taxation relief and the exemption for overseas branches in Chapter 27.

Top tips. Remember to round up the percentage recovery for partial exemption to the nearest whole number.

Easy marks. The computation of corporation tax and double tax relief in part (b)(ii) was not particularly complicated. You might have guessed that travel for a private holiday in part (c) was not relevant for tax purposes.

Examiner's comments. Part (a) was done reasonably well by those candidates who had a working knowledge of the *de minimis* rules. A minority of candidates had very little awareness of the rules, such that their performance was poor. Candidates who did not have a precise knowledge of the rules were able to score reasonably well provided they satisfied the requirement and attempted to address all three *de minimis* tests.

Part (b)(i) required an explanation of how to determine whether or not the company was resident in the UK. This simply required a statement of the rules regarding country of incorporation and place of management and control but the majority of candidates were unable to state these fundamental rules.

Part (b)(ii) required an explanation of the company's corporation tax liability together with the advantages and disadvantages of making an election to exempt the profits of an overseas permanent establishment from UK tax. This was done well. The majority of candidates prepared a short accurate calculation and were able to state the particular disadvantages of making such an election.

Part (c) concerned the travel and subsistence costs of an employee seconded to work overseas. This was relatively tricky but was done reasonably well by those candidates who were methodical in their approach. In particular, candidates who did not necessarily know all of the detailed rules were still able to score an acceptable mark if they applied basic principles to all three elements of the question. Very few candidates identified that the overseas workplace would be a temporary workplace. In addition, a minority of candidates discussed the tax implications for the company rather than for the employee. Candidates must read the requirement for each question carefully and ensure that their answer is always focussed on satisfying that requirement.

Marking scheme

		Marks
(a)	Test 1	1
	Test 2	1½
	Input tax attributed to taxable supplies and unattributed input tax	1½
	Test 3	1½
	Adjustment and date	1½
		7

(b) (i) Not incorporated in UK   1
          Central management and control   <u>2</u>

                                                                        3

     (ii) Calculation of liability   1½
          Taxation of worldwide profits   1
          Discussion of election
               Advantage   1½
               Disadvantage   <u>2</u>
                                                             Max   5

(c) Flights at start and end of contract   3
     Return flight in February   1½
     Laundry and telephone calls   <u>2</u>
                                                             Max   <u>5</u>
                                                                         <u>20</u>

(a) **Novak Ltd – Value added tax (VAT) partial exemption annual adjustment**

     Test 1 is not satisfied, as the total input tax exceeds an average of £625 per month (£625 × 12 = £7,500).

     Test 2 is not satisfied, as the total input tax less that directly attributed to taxable supplies exceeds an average of £625 per month (£12,200 + £4,900 + £16,100 – £12,200 = £21,000, £21,000/12 = £1,750).

	£
Input tax attributable to taxable supplies	12,200
Unattributed input tax £16,100 × 74% (W1)	11,914
Recoverable input tax (W2)	24,114
Less: input tax recovered on quarterly returns	(23,200)
Annual adjustment – additional input tax recoverable	(914)

     The annual adjustment must be made on the final VAT return of the year, which is the return for the period ended 30 September 2015, or the first VAT return after the end of the year at the option of the company.

     Workings

     1   *Recoverable unattributed input tax*

         $$\frac{£1,190,000}{£1,190,000 + £430,000} \times 100 = 73.4\%, \text{ rounded up to } 74\%.$$

     2   *Recoverable input tax*

         Exempt input tax of (£4,900 + £[16,100 – 11,914]) = £9,086 exceeds the Test 3 limit of £625 per month and is therefore irrecoverable.

(b) (i) **Residence status of Kraus Co**

          A company is regarded as resident in the UK if it is incorporated in the UK or if its central management and control is exercised in the UK. Kraus Co was incorporated in the country of Mersano.

          Accordingly, Kraus Co will only be resident in the UK if its central management and control is exercised in the UK. The central management and control of a company is usually regarded as being exercised in the place where the meetings of the board of directors are held.

     (ii) **Kraus Co**

          UK resident companies are subject to corporation tax on their worldwide income.

	£
Corporation tax: main rate £520,000 × 21%	109,200
Less: unilateral double taxation relief £520,000 × 18%	(93,600)
UK corporation tax liability	15,600

Tutorial note

The profits will be subject to tax because no election has been made to exempt the profits and losses of the overseas permanent establishment from UK corporation tax.

Election to exempt the overseas profits from UK tax

The advantage of making such an election would be that the profits made in Mersano would not be subject to UK corporation tax. Based on the current rates of corporation tax in the two countries, this would save corporation tax at the rate of (21% − 18%) = 3%.

When considering this election, it should be recognised that it is irrevocable and would apply to all future overseas permanent establishments of Kraus Co. Accordingly, there would be no relief in the UK for any losses incurred in the trade in Mersano in the future or for any other losses incurred in any additional overseas trades operated by Kraus Co.

(c) **Meyer's secondment to Kraus Co**

The reimbursement of expenses by an employer represents taxable income for an employee. Accordingly, the cost of the flights at the start and end of the contract represents taxable income for Meyer. However, a deduction of an equal amount will be available because:

- It is necessary for Meyer to travel to Mersano in order to perform the duties of his employment; and

- The workplace in Mersano is a temporary workplace (the secondment is for less than 24 months), so the travelling does not constitute ordinary commuting.

The cost of the return journey to the UK in February 2016 has no UK tax implications. Meyer will not be able to claim a tax deduction for the costs incurred because the journey is for a private purpose and he, rather than Spetz Ltd, will bear the cost.

The reimbursement of the cost of laundry and telephone calls home will be exempt from tax if less than £10 per night. If this limit is exceeded, the whole of the amount reimbursed will be subject to UK income tax.

Tutorial note

Credit was also available to candidates who focused their answers on the special rules relating to travel cost where duties are performed abroad.

36 Desiree (ATAX 06/10)

Text references. Basis of assessment for unincorporated businesses is covered in Chapter 6 and losses in Chapter 8. The basis of assessment for companies is covered in Chapter 20 and losses in Chapter 24. Registration for VAT is covered in Chapter 28.

Top tips. The trading loss for a tax year is usually simply the trading loss in the basis period for that tax year. However, if basis periods overlap, as in this question, then a loss in the overlap period is a trading loss for the earlier tax year only.

Easy marks. The basis of assessment for companies and sole traders should have produced easy marks.

Examiner's comments. The majority of candidates scored high marks in part (a)(i) although some had difficulty calculating the figure for the second tax year of an unincorporated business based on the first 12 months of trading. Those who did not do so well simply did not know the basic mechanical rules and either missed out this part of the question or tried to make it up. The opening and closing year's rules for unincorporated traders are examined regularly and candidates preparing for future sittings are likely to benefit from being able to handle them.

Part (a) (ii) was done well by almost all of the candidates who attempted it. In order to maximise marks here it was necessary to be precise in terms of language used. For example, it was not sufficient to state that losses can be carried forward against future profits. Instead, candidates needed to state that losses could be carried forward for offset against future profits of **the same trade**.

There was also a requirement to state which business structure would best satisfy the client's objectives. The mark available for this was missed by those candidates who had stopped thinking and were simply writing down everything they knew about loss relief.

The other difficulty which candidates had with this part of the question was a failure to recognise that not all possible loss reliefs were available due to the particular facts of the question. Candidates should ensure that they do not write at length about matters which are irrelevant.

Marking scheme

				Marks
(a)	(i)	Business is unincorporated		
		Application of opening year rules	2½	
		Losses counted once only	1	
		Business operated as a company	1	
		Max		4
	(ii)	Business is operated via a company	2½	
		Business is unincorporated		
		Reliefs available	2½	
		Application to Desiree's position	3	
		Conclusion	1	
		Max		8
(b)		Advantages		
		Recovery of input tax	1½	
		Pre-registration input tax	1½	
		Disadvantages	1½	
		Max		4
				16

(a) (i) **Taxable profit/allowable loss for each of the first three taxable periods**

Business is unincorporated

	Taxable profit £	Allowable loss £
2015/16		
1 September 2015 to 5 April 2016 (actual)		
Taxable profit	0	
Allowable loss £(46,000) × 7/10		32,200

	Taxable profit £	Allowable loss £
2016/17		
1 September 2015 to 31 August 2016 (first 12 months)		
Taxable profit	0	
Loss of period ending 30 June 2016		46,000
Less: loss allocated to 2015/16		(32,200)
Loss allocated to 2016/17		13,800
Profit of period 1 July 2016 to 31 August 2016		
£22,000 × 2/12		(3,667)
Loss 2016/17		10,133

	Taxable profit £	Allowable loss £
2017/18		
1 July 2016 to 30 June 2017 (current year basis)		
Taxable profit	22,000	
Allowable loss		0

Business operated via a company

	Taxable profit £	Allowable loss £
10 month period ending 30 June 2016	0	46,000
Year ending 30 June 2017	22,000	0
Year ending 30 June 2018	64,000	0

(ii) **Advice on whether or not the business should be incorporated**

Business is operated via a company

If the business is operated via a company, the loss of the period ending 30 June 2016 will be carried forward for offset against future trading profits of the same trade.

The earliest that any of the company's losses will be relieved is the year ending 30 June 2017 thus reducing the corporation tax payable on 1 April 2018. However, the tax savings will only arise if the budgeted profits are achieved. If the business does not achieve profitability the losses will be wasted.

Business is unincorporated

If the business is unincorporated, the loss in each of the two tax years can be offset against:

- The general income of the year of loss and/or the previous year

- The general income of the three years prior to the year of loss starting with the earliest of the three years

This enables Desiree to obtain immediate relief for the losses.

Desiree has employment income in 2015/16 of only £12,000 (£72,000 × 2/12) together with bank interest of less than £1,000. Most of this income will be covered by her personal allowance. Her general income in earlier years is her salary of £72,000 and the bank interest. Accordingly, she should offset the losses against the income of 2014/15 and earlier years rather than the income of 2015/16.

The loss of 2015/16 could be offset against the general income of 2014/15 (the previous year) or 2012/13 (the first of the three years prior to 2015/16) under early years loss relief.
The loss of 2016/17 could be offset against the general income of 2013/14 (the first of the three years prior to 2016/17) under early years loss relief.

This will obtain full relief for the losses mostly at the higher rate of tax.

Conclusion

Desiree's primary objective is the most beneficial use of the loss. She should run the business as an unincorporated sole trader in order to obtain relief for the losses as soon as possible.

(b) **Financial advantages and disadvantages of Desiree registering voluntarily for VAT**

Advantages

Registering for VAT will enable the business to recover input tax, where possible, on expenses and capital expenditure. This will reduce the costs incurred by the business thus reducing its losses and its capital allowances.

The VAT incurred on the fees paid to the market research consultants in March 2015 can be recovered as pre-registration input tax. The payment in November 2014 is more than six months prior to registration and therefore the input tax in relation to it cannot be recovered.

Disadvantages

The business will have to charge its customers VAT at 20%. This will represent an increase in the prices charged to those customers who are unable to recover VAT, ie domestic customers and non-VAT registered business customers. Desiree may need to consider reducing prices in order to reduce the impact of the additional VAT on these customers.

37 Poblano (ATAX 06/10)

Text references. Employment income is covered in Chapter 4. The personal accountability of senior accounting officer of large company is described in Chapter 22. Inheritance tax on lifetime gifts is dealt with in Chapter 16 and on the death estate in Chapter 17. Trusts are described in Chapter 18 and trust income is covered in Chapter 3.

Top tips. You must attempt all the parts of a question if you are to be successful in the P6 examination.

Easy marks. The calculation of inheritance tax liabilities in part (iii) was reasonably straightforward.

Examiner's comments. Part (i) concerned the implications of a change to an employee's location of work. On the whole this part of the question was done reasonably well. However, in order to score a high mark for this part it was necessary to focus on the client's financial position and calculate how much better or worse off he was going to be as a result of the change. This required candidates to think in terms of income and costs (with tax as a cost) and to recognise that costs that are not tax deductible are still costs and are therefore still relevant. This aspect of the question was not handled particularly well.

The calculation of the benefit in respect of the flat provided by the company was done well. However, the majority of candidates failed to recognise that the mileage allowance related to travel to and from work and was therefore taxable in full.

It was pleasing to note that fewer candidates than in the past provided lengthy explanations of what they were going to do before getting on and doing it. However, the question asked for an explanation of the tax treatment of two particular points; the receipt of the mileage allowance and the receipt of the rent. Many candidates failed to provide these explanations. Candidates must identify and carry out all of the tasks in the question in order to maximise their marks.

Part (ii) concerned the rules in relation to senior accounting officers. The majority of candidates were not aware of them and, consequently, found it difficult to score well on this part of the question. Having said that, there were also marks available for pointing out that the client's error needed to be communicated to HMRC and for identifying the action necessary if the client was unwilling to make such disclosure. Accordingly, it was possible to score reasonably well in this part of the question without any knowledge of the senior accounting officer rules.

Part (iii) of the question concerned inheritance tax and the advantages of lifetime giving. At first sight it was a daunting question requiring the consideration of three possible property values, two dates of death and a lifetime gift or gift via will; a total of 12 possible situations. However, there was guidance from the 'manager' as to where to start together with the reassurance that 'you should find that the calculations do not take too long'.

It was very pleasing to find that the majority of candidates had no problem with this part of the question and that their knowledge of the basic mechanics of inheritance tax was sound. Candidates benefited from thinking rather than writing such that they were then able to realise that, for example, with a lifetime gift, the only difference between the two possible dates of death was the availability of taper relief. The best answers were admirably short and to the point.

The one area where candidates could have done better was in identifying the possible gift with reservation. The failure by many candidates to do this indicates, yet again, that some candidates do not take enough care in identifying all that has been asked of them.

The final part of the question concerned the tax treatment of income received from a trust. This was a test of knowledge, as opposed to application of knowledge, and candidates should have scored well. However, the marks for this part were not as high as expected because candidates were not sufficiently careful in their approach. As always, the advice here is to stop and think. The question made it clear that the nature of the trust was not known and therefore candidates were expected to consider the income tax position of receipts from both an interest in possession trust and a discretionary trust. There was also the need to be specific and precise, as regards grossing up fractions and tax rates, rather than superficial and general in order to maximise the marks obtained.

			Marks
(a)	Salary less tax, national insurance contributions and motoring expenses	2	
	Living in the company flat		
	Tax on the benefit	2	
	Contribution	½	
	Additional salary required	1	
	Further information required	2	
	Staying with aunt in Manchester		
	Calculations	1½	
	Mileage allowance	1½	
	Rent paid to aunt	1½	
		Max	10
(b)	Senior accounting officer	3½	
	The need to disclose the errors	2½	
	The implications of non-disclosure	2	
		Max	7
(c)	Inheritance tax liabilities		
	Nil band	1	
	Lifetime gift		
	Value at time of gift and tax rate	1	
	Fall in value post gift	1	
	Taper relief	1	
	Gift via will	1½	
	Full set of outcomes	2	
	Conclusions (1 mark each, maximum 2 marks)	2	
	Gift with reservation	2½	
	Capital gains tax	1½	
		Max	12
(d)	Nature of the trust	2	
	Tax treatment – 2 × 2 marks	4	
			6
	Appropriate style and presentation	1	
	Effectiveness of communication	1	
			2
			37

Meeting notes

Date: 7 June 2015

Re: Poblano

(a)   **Working in Manchester – Poblano's financial position**

Living in the company flat

The calculations set out below are based on the information currently available.

	£
Additional salary	15,000
Less tax £15,000 × 40% (N1)	(6,000)
national insurance contributions £15,000 × 2%	(300)
petrol and depreciation £(1,400 + 1,500) (N2)	(2,900)
Additional salary after tax, NICs and motoring expenses	5,800
Less tax on benefit in respect of use of the flat (W) £17,100 × 40% (N1)	(6,840)
contributions by Poblano £200 × 12	(2,400)
Poblano would be worse off by	(3,440)
Additional salary required for Poblano not to be out of pocket	
£3,440/58%	5,931

Not living in the company flat

	£
Additional salary after tax, NICs and motoring expenses	5,800
Mileage allowance 9,200 × 50p	4,600
Tax and NICs on mileage allowance £4,600 × 42% (N3)	(1,932)
Rent £325 × 12 (N4)	(3,900)
Poblano would be better off by	4,568

Notes

1   The marginal tax rate would be 40% as Poblano's adjusted net income would remain below £100,000 and so there would be no reduction in his personal allowance. This assumes any benefits eg furniture provided at the flat (see below) do not cause this limit to be exceeded.

2   The depreciation is not an immediate cost but will increase the funds needed by Poblano to purchase his next car. Poblano will not be able to claim a tax deduction for the petrol costs as they relate to travelling to and from work and not to the performance of his duties.

3   The mileage allowance would be subject to tax and national insurance contributions as Poblano would be travelling to and from work and not in the performance of his duties. Manchester will not be a temporary workplace for Poblano because he expects to work there for more than two years.

4   Poblano's aunt will not be subject to income tax on the rent. This is because it will be in respect of a (presumably) furnished room in her house and the rent does not exceed £4,250 per year.

Further information required

The cost of the furniture provided in the flat – there will be an annual taxable benefit equal to 20% of the cost.

Any running costs (utilities and maintenance etc) in respect of the flat borne by Capsicum Ltd – there will be a taxable benefit equal to the costs incurred.

Any capital improvements made to the property before the start of the tax year for which the benefit is being calculated.

Working

Taxable benefit in respect of use of the flat

	£
Annual value	8,450
Additional benefit £(415,000 − 75,000) = £340,000 × 3.25%	11,050
Contribution to be made by Poblano	(2,400)
Taxable benefit	17,100

Note

The cost of £415,000 will be increased by any capital improvements made to the property before the start of the tax year for which the benefit is being calculated.

(b) **Financial accounting problems in Manchester**

Responsibilities of a senior accounting officer

The senior accounting officer of a qualifying company or group of companies are required to:

- Ensure that a company's accounting systems are adequate for the purposes of calculating the company's tax liabilities.

- Certify to HM Revenue and Customs that such accounting systems exist for each financial year.

- Notify HM Revenue and Customs of any inadequacies in the accounting systems.

These rules apply to a company, or a group of companies, with turnover (revenue) of more than £200 million and/or a balance sheet total of more than £2 billion. Penalties apply for non-compliance with the rules.

The senior accounting officer of Capsicum Ltd is the director or officer with overall responsibility for the company's financial accounting arrangements. This could be Poblano or another director within the group.

Errors in the corporation tax computation

We have submitted the corporation tax return of the subsidiary of Scoville plc. We cannot allow HM Revenue and Customs to continue to rely on it now that we know it contains errors.

The company must disclose the errors to HM Revenue and Customs or authorise us to do so. This can be done via an amendment to the corporation tax return as we are within 12 months of the filing date. Disclosure of the errors is likely to increase the company's tax liability. However, we cannot continue to act for the company unless this disclosure is made.

If the company refuses to disclose the errors we will advise HM Revenue and Customs that we no longer act for the company. We would not, however, provide any details of the errors in the financial statements.

Non-disclosure of the errors would also represent tax evasion by the company, which could result in criminal proceedings under both the tax and money laundering legislation.

(c) **Property in Chilaca**

Inheritance tax liabilities

Lifetime gift on 1 August 2015

Value at death (assumed) £	Death on 31 December 2017	£	Death on 31 December 2019 (N3)	£
450,000 (N1)	£(450,000 − 35,000) (N2) × 40%	166,000	£166,000 × 60%	99,600
600,000	£(600,000 − 35,000) × 40%	226,000	£226,000 × 60%	135,600
900,000	£(600,000 − 35,000) × 40%	226,000	£226,000 × 60%	135,600

Gift via will on 31 December 2017 or 31 December 2019 (N4)

Value at death (assumed) £		£
450,000	£(450,000 – 35,000) (N2) × 40%	166,000
600,000	£(600,000 – 35,000) × 40%	226,000
900,000	£(900,000 – 35,000) × 40%	346,000

Notes

1   When made the gift will be a potentially exempt transfer, thus, if the value of the property at the time of death is less than it was at the time of the gift, the inheritance tax payable will reflect the fall in value.

2   The nil band remaining following the gift into trust on 1 June 2014 will be £35,000 (£325,000 – £290,000).

3   31 December 2019 would be between four and five years after the gift such that 40% taper relief would be available. Accordingly, the liability will be 60% of the liability calculated in respect of death occurring on 31 December 2017.

4   The date of death will not affect the amount of inheritance tax due if the property is left in the will.

Inheritance tax liabilities – conclusions

If the property is gifted on 1 August 2015, the inheritance tax due on death will never be more than that due if the property is transferred via Paprikash's will, even if the value of the property falls prior to death.

Making a lifetime gift would turn out to be particularly beneficial if:

• The value of the property increases, as the tax would be based on the value as at 1 August 2015 rather than the value at the time of death.

• Paprikash survives the gift by more than three years such that taper relief would be available.

Gift with reservation

Once the property has been given to Poblano, the occasional use of it by Paprikash may result in the gift being treated as a gift with reservation. In these circumstances, the transactions would be subject to IHT in one of two ways. The first way would be for the gift to be ignored for inheritance tax purposes and the property included in Paprikash's death estate at its value at the time of death. The second way would be for the gift to be charged to IHT and the property not included in Paprikash's death estate. The treatment which gives the greater IHT liability will apply.

In order to ensure that the gift is effective for inheritance tax purposes Paprikash should have only minimal use of the property unless he pays Poblano a market rent.

Capital gains tax

If Paprikash is resident in the UK in the year in which he gives the property to Poblano, it will be necessary to calculate a capital gain on the gift of the property.

The gain would be the market value of the property less its cost. The gain, less any available annual exempt amount, would be taxed at 28%.

There would be no capital gains tax if the property were given to Poblano via Paprikash's will.

(d)   **Tax treatment of trust income received by Poblano's daughter**

The trust will be either an interest in possession trust or a discretionary trust. It will be an interest in possession trust if Piri has an absolute right to the income generated by the trust assets. It will be a discretionary trust if the trustees have the right to accumulate the income and pay it to Piri when they choose.

It is understood that the only income received by the trustees of the trust is dividend income.

Interest in possession trust

The income to which Piri is entitled must be grossed up at 100/90. Where the income falls into Piri's basic rate band (after calculating the tax on her salary) it will be taxed at 10%. The balance of the income will be taxed at 32.5%. There will be a 10% tax credit.

Discretionary trust

The income received must be grossed up at 100/55. Where the income falls into Piri's basic rate band it will be taxed at 20%. The balance of the income will be taxed at 40%. There will be a 45% tax credit.

38 Dokham (ATAX 06/10)

Text references. Pensions are covered in Chapter 2 and the EMI scheme in Chapter 5. Lifetime transfers of value for IHT are dealt with in Chapter 16 and capital gains disposals in Chapter 11. Chargeable gains reliefs are covered in Chapter 13.

Top tips. Make sure that you make an attempt to answer all the requirements of the question. A good tip is to tick off each requirement after you have dealt with it in your answer.

Easy marks. There were some easy marks for basic points about inheritance tax and capital gains tax in part (b).

Examiner's comments. The pension scheme element of part (a) was not done particularly well. Candidates struggled in an attempt to produce detailed calculations when a few well chosen sentences would have been much more efficient. Many candidates failed to consider national insurance contributions and there was particular confusion in relation to the employer's contributions to the pension scheme with many candidates deducting the contributions from the employee's salary.

The main problem here was an inability to set down a clear explanation of the rules. Before starting to write an answer, candidates should be willing to stop and think in order to plan what they want to say. Also, as, part of their preparation for the exam, candidates should practise explaining the tax implications of transactions in writing in order to improve their ability to get to the point in a clear and precise manner.

A small minority of candidates failed to address the three additional questions raised by the client in respect of pension scheme benefits. This was a shame as there were some relatively straightforward marks available here.

The enterprise management incentive scheme element of part (a) again required candidates to address particular points as opposed to writing generally. Although many candidates were aware that there was a maximum value to the options granted under such a scheme, not all of them applied the rule to the facts of the question in terms of the restriction on the number of share options granted by the company. A significant number of candidates confused the enterprise management incentive scheme with the enterprise investment scheme.

Part (b) was done well by many candidates. Those who did not do so well were often too superficial in their explanations; the question required candidates to 'explain in detail'. Also, weaker candidates failed to consider the capital gains tax implications of the gifts and/or the possibility of the exemption in respect of normal expenditure out of income being available in relation to inheritance tax. Of those who did address capital gains tax, many thought, incorrectly, that gift relief would be available in respect of the proposed gift of quoted shares.

			Marks
(a)	Additional pension contributions		
	Income tax	2½	
	National insurance contributions	1	
	Benefits from pension scheme	2	
	Enterprise management incentive scheme		
	Maximum number of shares	1½	
	Exercise of option	1½	
	Sale of shares	2	
	Max		9

(b) One-off gift of cash

Potentially exempt transfer	1
Death within 7 years	2
Taper relief	1
Payment of tax	1
Capital gains tax	½

One-off gift of shares

Inheritance tax	½
Capital gains tax	1

Series of gifts

Exemption for normal expenditure out of income	1
Able to maintain standard of living	1
If exemption does not apply	½
Max	7
	16

(a) **The information requested by Dokham**

Additional salary instead of pension contributions

There are no tax implications for you when Criollo plc makes contributions into your personal pension scheme.

If you received additional salary instead, your taxable income would increase by £8,000 resulting in additional tax of £3,200 (£8,000 × 40%). However, you would pay the additional pension contributions net of 20% income tax (saving you £1,600) and, as a result of the pension contributions, £8,000 of your taxable income would be taxed at 20% rather than 40% (saving you a further £1,600).

Accordingly, the effective income tax implications of the two alternatives are the same.

However, you would have to pay additional national insurance contributions of £160 (£8,000 × 2%) if Criollo plc paid you additional salary of £8,000.

Benefits from the pension scheme

You cannot receive any benefits from the pension scheme until you are 55 (unless you are incapacitated by ill health). Once you are 55, you can receive up to a quarter of the value of the fund as a tax free one-off payment. The balance of the fund is usually then be used to purchase a pension (an annuity) which will be subject to income tax as and when it is received. However, an alternative to buying an annuity would be for you to drawdown income from the pension fund, although this is usually subject to an annual maximum amount. This income, again, would be taxable as pension income.

The number of shares within the enterprise management incentive (EMI) scheme

The value of shares over which you can be granted options within the EMI scheme rules is restricted to £250,000. This rule results in a maximum number of shares of 26,233 (£250,000/£9.53) at the current share price of £9.53. Accordingly, it appears that Criollo plc is intending to grant you an option in respect of the maximum possible number of shares whilst allowing for a small increase in the company's share price between now and when the option is granted to you.

Exercise of option and sale of shares

When you exercise the option and purchase shares in Criollo plc you will be liable to income tax and national insurance on the amount by which the value of the shares at the time the option is granted exceeds the price you pay for the shares, ie £13,878 (26,185 × (£9.53 – £9)). When you sell the shares, the excess of the sale proceeds over the amount paid for them plus the amount charged to income tax, ie £249,543 ((26,185 × £9) + £13,878) less your capital gains tax annual exempt amount (currently £11,000) if available, will be taxable. The rate of tax will be 10% since a claim for entrepreneurs' relief can be made, provided you wait at least a year between being granted the options and selling the shares.

Tutorial note

Entrepreneurs' relief applies to shares acquired under an EMI option if the option was granted at least one year prior to the date of disposal of the shares and the individual was an officer or an employee of the trading company throughout that one year period. There is no minimum ownership period for the shares themselves nor a minimum percentage shareholding.

(b) **The tax implications of Virginia contributing towards the children's school fees**

One-off gift to Dokham of cash of £54,000

The gift will be a potentially exempt transfer for the purposes of inheritance tax. There will be no Inheritance tax liability if Virginia survives the gift for seven years.

If Virginia were to die within seven years of the gift inheritance tax would be charged at 40% on the excess of the gift over the available nil rate band. The available nil rate band is the nil rate band (currently £325,000) as reduced by chargeable transfers in the seven years prior to the gift. Chargeable transfers include, broadly, transfers into trust in the seven years prior to the gift and transfers to individuals prior to the gift that take place within the seven years prior to death.

Any inheritance tax due in respect of the gift will be reduced by 20% if Virginia survives the gift for three years and by a further 20% for each additional year she survives.

Any tax due will be payable by Dokham within six months of the end of the month of death.

There is no liability to capital gains tax on a gift of cash.

One-off gift to Dokham of quoted shares worth £54,000

The inheritance tax implications are the same as for the one-off cash gift of £54,000.

However, Virginia will be subject to capital gains tax at 28% on the excess of the value of the shares over the price she paid for them.

Tutorial note

Gift relief would not be available on the gift of the shares as Panatella plc is a quoted company and Virginia owns less than 5% of the company.

Gift to Dokham of cash of £8,000 every year for the next seven years

Virginia should argue that this series of gifts represents normal expenditure out of her income such that each gift is an exempt transfer for the purposes of inheritance tax. For this exemption to be available, Virginia would have to show that:

*   Each gift is part of her normal expenditure.
*   The gifts are made out of income rather than capital.
*   Having made the gifts, she still has sufficient income to maintain her usual standard of living.

Virginia's taxable income of more than £120,000 per year would help to support this argument.

If the exemption in respect of normal expenditure out of income is not applicable, each gift of £8,000 would be a potentially exempt transfer and the inheritance tax implications of each gift would be the same as for the one-off cash gift of £54,000. Again, there will be no liability to capital gains tax on these cash gifts.

39 Robusto Ltd (ATAX 12/10)

Text references. Tests of employment and NICs for employers are covered in Chapter 4. Overseas aspects of VAT and partial exemption are to be found in Chapter 29.

Top tips. Since you were told in the question that irrecoverable VAT for the year will exceed the *de minimis* limits, there was no need to use the de minimis tests, merely the relevant percentage.

Easy marks. The tests for employment should have been well known but make sure that you apply them to the question and do not just put down all the tests you can remember.

Examiner's comments. Part (a) required candidates to determine the cost of buying in services from three possible suppliers. Candidates were told that the purchasing company was partially exempt for the purposes of VAT and the vast majority realised that the key to the question was the impact of irrecoverable VAT on the cost. There were minor errors in determining the percentage of input tax that could be recovered involving the need to include the zero rated supplies on the top and bottom of the fraction and also the requirement to round up the fraction to the nearest whole percentage; more care here could have earned some candidates an extra mark. A more common error was a failure to realise that the purchasing company would need to account for output tax on the purchase of the services from overseas thus increasing the cost by the amount of irrecoverable VAT. Having said that, this was a tricky point and it was very pleasing that a large number of candidates identified this issue. The calculation of the maximum salary that could be paid such that the total cost would be no more than the cheapest service provider was done well with the majority of candidates identifying the need to include employer's national insurance contributions in their calculations.

Part (b) required three examples of specific contractual arrangements that would indicate an employer/employee relationship. This was a simple test of knowledge and was done well by most candidates. Having said that, candidates were asked to give examples that related to the facts of this particular question as opposed to the first three that they thought of; the question made it clear that a fixed fee would be paid for the work so it was not appropriate to write about the payment of holiday pay or sick pay.

The final part of the question was more difficult. It required candidates to recognise that the personal service company rules would apply and to explain the implications for the various parties. Candidates' performance here was mixed. Many candidates identified that the issue related to personal service companies but got confused as to which of the companies would be regarded as making the deemed salary payment. Weaker candidates assumed that the question was still about VAT and repeated matters already covered in part (a).

Marking scheme

			Marks
(a)	Partial exemption position	2	
	Cognac Ltd	1	
	Fonseca Inc	3	
	Pisco	2	
	Maximum salary	2½	
		Max	9
(b)	One mark for each contractual arrangement		3
(c)	Implications for Robusto Ltd and Cognac Ltd		
	Tax treatment of the fee	1	
	Additional implications for Cognac Ltd		
	Personal service company rules apply	½	
	Deemed salary payment	2½	
	Robusto Ltd's preference		
	Employer's class 1 NIC	1	
	Comparison with Cognac Ltd	1	
		Max	5
			17

(a)   **Market analysis services**

Cheapest provider

Robusto Ltd is partially exempt for the purposes of value added tax (VAT) and can only recover 75% (W) of its input VAT. Accordingly, purchasing the services from Cognac Ltd would result in irrecoverable VAT that would increase the overall cost of the services.

	£
Fee excluding VAT	28,500
Irrecoverable VAT (£28,500 × 20% × 25%)	1,425
	29,925

Purchasing the services from Fonseca Inc would cause a similar problem. International services provided by one business to another are treated as supplied in the country where the customer carries on its business. Accordingly, the services would be treated as supplied in the UK. Robusto Ltd would have to apply the reverse charge procedure and account for output tax at the rate of 20%. It could then recover 75% of the VAT as input tax in the normal way. Fonseca Inc has quoted a higher fee than Cognac Ltd and therefore the total cost including irrecoverable VAT would also be higher.

Pisco is not registered for VAT and therefore the total cost would be the fee of £29,500, which would appear to be the cheapest option.

However, it should be borne in mind that Pisco will need to register for VAT if, as a result of the supply of the market analysis services to Robusto Ltd, its total supplies in a 12-month period exceed the registration limit of £81,000. If this were to occur, it would then become more expensive than Cognac Ltd.

Tutorial note

Robusto Ltd will obtain a tax deduction for the cost incurred but, since this will be the case in each situation, this will not affect the decision as to which is the cheapest supplier of the services.

Working

Proportion of recoverable input tax

	£
Standard rated supplies	850,000
Zero rated supplies	120,000
	970,000
Exempt supplies	330,000
Total supplies	1,300,000

Recoverable input tax – £970,000/£1,300,000 rounded up	75%

Maximum salary

The cost of taking on an employee to carry out the analysis will include the employer's class 1 national insurance contributions. The salary (y) that would result in a total cost of £29,500 is calculated below.

$$y + ((y - £7,956) \times 13.8\%) = £29,500$$
$$y + 0.138y - (£7,956 \times 13.8\%) = £29,500$$
$$1.138\,y - £1,098 = £29,500$$
$$1.138\,y = £29,500 + £1,098 = £30,598$$
$$y = £30,598/1.138$$
$$y = £26,888$$

Tutorial note

Proof of maximum salary (difference due to rounding)

	£
Salary	26,888
Class 1 national insurance contributions ((£26,888 - £7,956) × 13.8%)	2,613
Total cost	29,501

(b)   **Contractual arrangements that would indicate an employer/employee relationship**

Any THREE of the following:

- Any necessary equipment or tools to be provided by Robusto Ltd.
- Robusto Ltd to have control over when and how the work is to be carried out by Pisco.
- Pisco is not permitted to provide a substitute to carry out the work.
- No obligation for Pisco to correct any unsatisfactory work at his own expense.
- The right to dismiss Pisco before the contract has been completed.

Tutorial note

Other contractual arrangements that would indicate an employer/employee relationship would include rewarding Pisco by reference to time spent rather than work done or provision for payments to be made in respect of illness or holidays. However, it is clear from the question that Pisco would charge a fixed fee for the work so it would not be possible for the contract to include such terms.

(c)   **Employer/employee relationship between Robusto Ltd and the individual carrying out the services**

Tax implications for Robusto Ltd and Cognac Ltd

The fee, including the irrecoverable VAT, will be tax deductible for Robusto Ltd.

The fee, net of VAT, will be taxable trading income for Cognac Ltd.

The contract between Robusto Ltd and Cognac Ltd would be a relevant engagement for the purposes of the personal service company rules and thus:

- Cognac Ltd will be deemed to have made a salary payment to Offley on 5 April each year based on the amounts it has received in respect of all such relevant engagements less certain allowable deductions.

- Cognac Ltd will have to pay employers' class 1 national insurance contributions in respect of the payment and deduct PAYE and employees' class 1 national insurance contributions from the payment.

- The deemed salary payment, together with the employers' national insurance contributions, will be deductible when calculating Cognac Ltd's taxable trading profits.

Robusto Ltd's preference

If HM Revenue and Customs could successfully argue that the relationship between Robusto Ltd and Pisco is one of employer and employee, Robusto Ltd would be required to pay employers' class 1 national insurance contributions on behalf of Pisco. This would increase the cost of the services to Robusto Ltd.

If the services are purchased from Cognac Ltd there is no effect on Robusto Ltd because the national insurance contributions are borne by Cognac Ltd under the personal service companies rules as set out above.

Accordingly, Robusto Ltd might prefer to offer the contract to Cognac Ltd rather than to Pisco.

40 Tetra (ATAX 06/12)

Text references. Redundancy payments are covered in Chapter 5. Partnerships are dealt with in Chapter 9 and national insurance contributions for the self-employed in Chapter 6. Pensions and venture capital trusts are covered in Chapter 2 and the income tax computation in Chapter 1.

Top tips. It is very important to read the question thoroughly. The note to part (c) was vital information to enable you to answer that part correctly.

Easy marks. Part (b) required a straightforward division of partnership profits and the application of Class 4 NICs should have presented few problems.

Examiner's comments. Part (a) was a test of knowledge and was done well by the majority of candidates with many scoring full marks. The only problem that some candidates had was a tendency to write too much. There were only three marks available so only three points were required. Some candidates wrote significantly more than this and used time that they should have been using elsewhere.

Part (b) required knowledge of the opening year rules, the allocation of profits between partners and the calculation of national insurance. It was done well. Common errors included the treatment of the partner's salary as employment income rather than trading income and the failure to adjust the profit for the partners' salaries before splitting the remainder between the partners.

The final part of the question concerned the tax implications of investing in a venture capital trust and of making pension contributions; it was not done as well as expected. Candidates were required to 'compare the effect of the two alternative investments on Tetra's income tax liability'. This meant that calculations were required. However, many candidates simply treated the question as being about venture capital trusts and pension contributions and explained all the rules they could remember that related to these two areas of the syllabus. Marks are only awarded in the exam for relevant points that address the requirements and much time was wasted here that could have been spent earning marks.

There were, however, many knowledgeable answers to this part of the question. Many candidates successfully identified the effect of making pension contributions on Tetra's personal allowance situation. In addition, the majority of candidates were able to explain the effect on the basic rate band of making pension contributions and the tax relief available in respect of the investment in a venture capital trust.

Marking scheme

			Marks
(a)	Statutory redundancy	1	
	£30,000 exemption	1½	
	Restrictive covenant	1	
	Max		3
(b)	Tetra's shares of the adjusted trading profit	3½	
	Tetra's taxable trading profit	2	
	Class 4 national insurance contributions	1½	
			7
(c)	Income tax		
	Venture capital trust		
	Personal allowance	1½	
	Tax liability with VCT credit	1½	
	Pension contributions		
	Basic rate band	1	
	Tax liability with pension contributions	1	
	Tax relief at source	1	
	Risk	1½	
	Timing	1½	
	Max		8
			18

(a) **Income tax implications of the redundancy payments made by Ivy Ltd**

The statutory redundancy of £4,200 falls within the £30,000 exemption such that it is not subject to income tax.

The first £(30,000 – 4,200) = £25,800 of the non-contractual payment is also exempt from income tax, provided it relates solely to redundancy and is not simply a terminal bonus. The remainder of the payment of £(46,000 – 25,800) = £20,200 is subject to income tax in full.

The payment in consideration of Tetra agreeing not to work for any competitor of Ivy Ltd for 12 months is subject to income tax because it is a restrictive covenant.

(b)   **Class 4 national insurance contributions for 2015/16**

Tetra's share of the adjusted trading profits

Period from 1 June 2015 to 31 December 2015

	Profit £	Tetra £
Profit £300,000 × 7/12	175,000	
Salary payable to Fore £24,000 × 7/12	(14,000)	
Salary payable to Tetra £18,000 × 7/12	(10,500)	10,500
	150,500	
Tetra's profit share £150,500 × 30%		45,150
		55,650

Year ending 31 December 2016

	Profit £	Tetra £
Profit	380,000	
Salary payable to Fore	(24,000)	
Salary payable to Tetra	(18,000)	18,000
	338,000	
Tetra's profit share £338,000 × 30%		101,400
		119,400

Tetra's taxable trading profit for the tax year 2015/16

Period from 1 June 2015 to 31 December 2015

	£
1 June 2015 to 31 December 2015	55,650
1 January 2016 to 5 April 2016 £119,400 × 3/12	29,850
	85,500

Class 4 national insurance contributions

	£
£(41,865 − 7,956) = £33,909 × 9%	3,052
£(85,500 − 41,865) = £43,635 × 2%	873
	3,925

(c)   **The alternative investments**

Effect on income tax liability

In the absence of any pension contributions, Tetra's net income would exceed £120,000 (£100,000 + (2 × £10,000)) such that he would not receive any amount of personal allowance.

If Tetra subscribes for the shares in the venture capital trust, his income tax liability would be as follows.

	£
Net income	125,000
Less: personal allowance	0
Taxable income	125,000
£31,865 × 20%	6,373
£93,135 × 40%	37,254
	43,627
Less: relief for investment in VCT £28,000 × 30%	(8,400)
Income tax liability	35,227

If Tetra were to make pension contributions of £28,000, the pension fund would receive a further £7,000 (£28,000 × 20/80) from HMRC as the contributions would be deemed to be made net of basic rate tax.

Tetra's basic rate band limit would be increased by £35,000 (£28,000 × 100/80) to £(31,865 + 35,000) = £66,865. His adjusted net income for the purposes of determining his personal allowance would be reduced by the same amount to £(125,000 – 35,000) = £90,000. He would therefore receive the whole of the personal allowance as his adjusted net income would be less than £100,000. His income tax liability would be as follows.

	£
Net income	125,000
Less personal allowance	(10,000)
Taxable income	115,000
£66,865 × 20%	13,373
£48,135 × 40%	19,254
Income tax liability	32,627

By making personal pension contributions, Tetra would save income tax of £(35,227 – 32,627) = £2,600. This, together with the additional contributions into the pension fund of £7,000 from HMRC, would result in an overall financial advantage of £9,600 (£2,600 + £7,000).

Risk

A VCT is a relatively high-risk investment in that it must hold at least 70% of its investments in unquoted trading companies.

A personal pension fund is permitted to hold a very wide range of investments such that the level of risk can be varied to suit the preferences of Tetra.

Timing

A VCT is a medium-term investment; the tax relief will be withdrawn if Tetra holds the shares for less than five years.

A pension fund is a long-term investment; Tetra cannot withdraw benefits from the scheme until he is 55 years old (unless he is incapacitated due to ill health).

41 FL Partnership (ATAX 12/13)

Text references. Ethics are covered in Chapter 30. Capital allowances are dealt with in Chapter 7. Inheritance tax basic principles are covered in Chapter 16, reliefs in Chapter 17 and trusts in Chapter 18. Capital gains tax principles will be found in Chapter 11 and reliefs in Chapter 13.

Top tips. Did you remember to include a summary of your calculations and a statement of the key issues in part (b)(iii)? These were awarded four valuable marks.

Easy marks. You should have been able to obtain some easy marks in part (a) for common-sense points. In part (b) there were some easy marks for basic computations. Make sure you get the easy mark for format and presentation!

Examiner's comments. Part (a) should have been straightforward but, on the whole, it was not done particularly well. The main problem was a lack of thought before answering the question. The question asked for the information required before becoming advisers to the partners but a significant number of candidates listed the information they would need in order to be able to give advice to them once they had become clients (including personal details, information in respect of prior years and so on). Candidates will always benefit from reading the requirement carefully and thinking before they begin to write their answers. It is important to think about the specifics of the situation, for example, the fact that the partners required sophisticated and specialised tax planning work, such that the firm needed to be sure that it had staff with sufficient knowledge and competence.

Part (b)(i) was reasonably straightforward and again, on the whole, it was not done well. The answer should have explained how the balancing adjustment would be calculated and explained why the assets could not be transferred at tax written down value. However, many answers included detailed calculations of capital allowances over many years (despite the fact that the question did not include the information necessary to prepare such calculations) or tried to explain everything about capital allowances, very little of which was relevant to this particular question. A short thoughtful answer was able to score three marks whereas many answers covering more than a page only scored a single mark.

Part (b)(ii) mainly required an explanation of the calculation of an inheritance tax liability. This was done very well by most candidates. However, performance in respect of the availability of capital gains tax gift relief was not quite as strong; candidates must learn when the various capital gains tax reliefs are available. Gift relief is available where a transfer is immediately subject to inheritance tax regardless of the nature of the assets disposed of.

Part (b)(iii) was the more demanding part of this question and was not done well. It was important that candidates approached the question methodically. There was to be a sale of the business followed by a gift of shares and subsequent sales of shares in the future. The question stated that incorporation relief was available on the sale of the business. Candidates needed to calculate the tax that would be charged in respect of these transactions both with and without incorporation relief and then make some sensible comments regarding their findings. The first thing to note is that many candidates did not have a thorough attempt at this part of the question. Many answers were very short, despite the number of marks available, and some candidates omitted it altogether. Other candidates avoided producing calculations and simply wrote about the issues in general terms which was never going to be particularly successful. In addition, most candidates who attempted the question did not give it sufficient thought before starting their answers. As a result, many answers were confused and did not cover sufficient ground to score well. In particular, it was often not obvious which aspect of the question was being addressed and the summary of calculations and statement of key issues required by the question were often missing. Finally, many candidates addressed inheritance tax in this part of the question, which was not required and, therefore, could not score any marks.

In addition to the general problems regarding the approach to the question, there were two specific technical problems. Firstly, the majority of candidates tried to calculate the gain on the disposal of the business by reference to the total value of the assets sold as opposed to calculating the gain on each individual chargeable asset. There was only one chargeable asset in the question, goodwill, so all that was needed was the gain on the goodwill. Secondly, many candidates then struggled with the calculation of incorporation relief and its effect on the base cost of the shares.

The general impression was that many candidates had not practised sufficient past exam questions, such that they were unable to plan their approach to a question of this type and then to carry that plan out.

Marks were available for professional skills in this question. In order to earn these marks candidates had to provide a suitable amount of appropriate narrative, calculations that were clear and logical and sensible analysis in relation to the position of Lauda in an appropriately formatted memorandum. On the whole, the performance of candidates in this area was good with the majority of candidates producing a memorandum in a style that was easy to follow.

Marking scheme

				Marks
(a)		Information required	1	
		Contact existing tax adviser	1	
		Fundamental principles	1	
		Competence	1	
		Conflict of interest	2	
		Max		5
(b)	(i)	Allowances available	1½	
		Calculation of balancing adjustment	2	
		Consideration of transfer at tax written down value	1½	
				5
	(ii)	Inheritance tax		
		Tax may be payable at time of gift	1	
		Business property relief	1½	
		Valuation and exemptions	1½	
		Inheritance tax and due date	3	
		Capital gains tax: gift relief	1½	
		Max		7

		Marks
(iii) Capital gains tax on sale of business	1½	
With incorporation relief		
Incorporation relief	1½	
Capital gains tax and due date	1	
Capital gains tax on gift of shares	2	
Capital gains tax and due date	1	
Without incorporation relief		
Capital gains tax on sale of business	1	
Capital gains tax on gift of shares	1½	
Explanations	4	
Summary and key issues	4	
Max		14
Format and presentation	1	
Analysis	1	
Quality of explanations and calculations	2	
		4
		35

(a) **Becoming tax advisers to Farina and Lauda**

Information required in respect of Farina and Lauda

- Independent evidence of their identities (eg passport)
- Proof of their addresses

Action to be taken by the firm

- The firm should contact the existing tax advisers of Farina and Lauda. This is to ensure that there has been no action by either Farina or Lauda which would preclude the acceptance of the appointment on ethical grounds.

- The firm should consider whether becoming tax advisers to Farina and Lauda would create any threats to compliance with the fundamental principles of professional ethics. Where such threats exist, the appointment should not be accepted unless the threats can be reduced to an acceptable level via the implementation of safeguards.

- With this in mind, the firm must ensure that its engagement team possesses the necessary skills to carry out the sophisticated tax planning required by Farina and Lauda.

- In addition, it is possible that providing advice to Farina and Lauda on the sale of their business could give rise to a conflict of interest, as a course of action (for example, the timing of the sale) which is beneficial for one of them may not be beneficial for the other. The firm should obtain permission from both Farina and Lauda to act for both of them and should consider using separate engagement teams.

(b)

To:	The files
From:	Tax senior
Date:	6 December 2015
Subject:	The FL Partnership

The purpose of this memorandum is to advise Farina and Lauda, the partners in the FL Partnership, on the sale of the business to JH plc and on the proposed disposals of shares in JH plc in the future.

(i) **Capital allowances of the FL Partnership for its final trading period**

There will be no annual investment allowance, first year allowances or writing down allowances in the period in which the partnership business ceases. Instead, there will be a balancing adjustment which will either be a balancing allowance or a balancing charge.

The balancing adjustment will be calculated as follows:

	£
Tax written down value brought forward at the start of the period	X
Add: Additions in the period	X
Less: Disposals during the period at the lower of cost and sales proceeds	(X)
	X
Less: Proceeds on the sale of the equipment on 1 March 2016	(150,000)
Balancing allowance/(balancing charge)	X/(X)

It is not possible for an election to be made to transfer the equipment to JH plc at its tax written down value because Farina and Lauda will not be connected with JH plc as they will not control the company.

(ii) **Farina**

(1) *Inheritance tax*

The gift of the JH plc shares to the trustees will be a chargeable lifetime transfer, so inheritance tax may be due at the time of the gift. Business property relief will not be available as JH plc is a quoted company and Farina will not be a controlling shareholder.

The shares will be valued at £4 per share, such that the value of the gift will be 15,000 × £4 = £60,000. This will be reduced by the annual exemptions for the tax year 2016/17 and also for the tax year 2015/16 if they have not been used against any other gifts. The annual exemption is £3,000.

The transfer must be grossed up because the tax will be paid by Farina so the tax is 20/80 of the net chargeable transfer in excess of the available nil rate band. The available nil rate band will be £325,000 as reduced by any chargeable transfers made by Farina in the previous seven years.

Any inheritance tax due will be payable on 30 April 2017.

(2) *Capital gains tax gift relief*

Gift relief will be available in respect of the transfer of the shares to the trustees because, as noted above, the transfer is immediately subject to inheritance tax. For the same reason, gift relief will also be available in respect of any subsequent transfers of shares from the trustees to the beneficiaries as there will be exit charges for inheritance tax on these transfers.

(iii) **Lauda**

The sale of the business will result in a chargeable gain in respect of the goodwill. The gain, equal to the market value of the goodwill of £1,300,000, will be split equally between Farina and Lauda. Lauda's chargeable gain will therefore be £650,000. As all of the equipment qualified for capital allowances, no capital losses will arise on its disposal.

With incorporation relief

Sale of business on 1 March 2016

	£
Chargeable gain on the sale of the goodwill	650,000
Less: incorporation relief £650,000 × $\frac{£600,000}{£740,000}$ (N1)	(527,027)
Chargeable gain after incorporation relief	122,973
Capital gains tax @ 10% (N2)	12,297

The tax will be payable on 31 January 2017.

Shares in JH plc – Lauda's base cost

	£
Market value of shares received 200,000 × £3	600,000
Less: incorporation relief	(527,027)
Base cost	72,973

Gift of 40,000 shares on 1 June 2017 (N3)

	£
Deemed proceeds (market value) 40,000 × £5	200,000
Less: cost £72,973 × $\dfrac{40,000}{200,000}$	(14,595)
Chargeable gain	185,405
Capital gains tax @ 28% (N4)	51,913

The tax will be payable on 31 January 2019.

Notes

1   The relief is restricted by reference to the value of the shares divided by the value of the total consideration received. Lauda will receive a total of £740,000, consisting of cash of £140,000 and shares worth 200,000 × £3 = £600,000.

2   Capital gains tax will be charged at 10% because entrepreneurs' relief will be available. This relief is available because the business is to be sold as a going concern and has been owned for at least a year. It is assumed that Lauda has not exceeded the lifetime limit of £10,000,000 and will claim this relief.

3   Gift relief will not be available in respect of this gift because the shares are quoted and Lauda will hold 200,000/8,400,000 = 2.38% of the shares which is less than 5% of the company so it is not Lauda's personal company.

4   Capital gains tax will be charged at 28% because Lauda pays income tax at the additional rate and so has used up her basic rate band. Entrepreneurs' relief will not be available because Lauda will hold less than 5% of JH plc.

Tutorial note

In order for entrepreneurs' relief to be available in respect of the gift of the shares, Lauda would also need to be an officer or employee of JH plc.

Without incorporation relief

Sale of business on 1 March 2016

	£
Chargeable gain on the sale of the goodwill	650,000
Capital gains tax @ 10% (N2 above)	65,000

The tax will be payable on 31 January 2017.

Shares in JH plc – Lauda's base cost

	£
Market value of shares received 200,000 × £3	600,000

Gift of 40,000 shares on 1 June 2017 (N3 above)

	£
Deemed proceeds (market value) 40,000 × £5	200,000
Less: cost £600,000 × $\dfrac{40,000}{200,000}$	(120,000)
Chargeable gain	80,000
Capital gains tax @ 28% (N4 above)	22,400

The tax will be payable on 31 January 2019.

Summary

	With incorporation relief	Without incorporation relief
	£	£
Capital gains tax on sale of business	12,297	65,000
Capital gains tax on gift of shares 1 June 2017	51,913	22,400
	64,210	87,400

Effect of incorporation relief on base cost of shares

	With incorporation relief	Without incorporation relief
	£	£
Base cost	72,973	600,000
Less: used on gift of shares 1 June 2017	(14,595)	(120,000)
	58,378	480,000
Increase in gain on eventual disposal of shares if incorporation relief applies £(480,000 – 58,378)		421,622
Increase in capital gains tax £421,622 @ 28%		118,054

Key issues

If Lauda were to disclaim incorporation relief, she would have higher initial capital gains tax liabilities.

However, disclaiming incorporation relief will result in a higher base cost in the shares, such that on a sale of the shares in the future, there will be tax savings which will exceed the increased initial liability.

Tutorial notes

1   Incorporation relief reduces the capital gains tax payable on the sale of the business and the gift of the shares by £23,190 (£87,400 – £64,210). When this amount is deducted from the additional tax due because of the reduced base cost, we arrive at an overall increase in the capital gains tax liability of £94,864 (£118,054 – £23,190).

   This overall increase in the capital gains tax liability is simply the tax on the deferred gain of £527,027 at 28% in the future rather than at 10%, due to the availability of entrepreneurs' relief, now: £527,027 × 18% (28% – 10%) = £94,865 (and a rounding difference of £1).

2   Capital gains tax gift relief in respect of gifts of business assets will not be available on the sale of the business to JH plc, because Farina and Lauda are not gifting the business to the company. They are selling the business for market value, which is received in the form of cash and shares.

Mock exams

ACCA Professional Paper P6 – Options Module

Advanced Taxation (UK)

Mock Examination 1

Question Paper	
Time allowed	*Reading and planning: 15 minutes* *Writing: 3 hours*
This paper is divided into two sections	
Section A	*BOTH questions are compulsory questions and MUST be attempted*
Section B	*TWO questions ONLY to be attempted*

During reading and planning time only the question paper may be annotated

DO NOT OPEN THIS PAPER UNTIL YOU ARE READY TO START UNDER EXAMINATION CONDITIONS

ACCA Professional Paper P6

Options Module

Advanced Taxation (UK)

Mock Examination 1

During reading and planning time only the question paper may be annotated.

DO NOT OPEN THIS PAPER UNTIL YOU ARE READY TO START UNDER EXAMINATION CONDITIONS

BPP
LEARNING MEDIA

SECTION A: BOTH questions are compulsory and MUST be attempted

1 Calisia (ATAX 06/11)   63 mins

Your manager has sent you an email with two attachments in respect of a new client called Calisia. The first attachment is an extract from a letter from Calisia, in which she has asked the firm to consider how she can increase the income of her daughter, Farfisa, and to review her own inheritance tax position.

The second attachment is a schedule setting out what your manager wants you to do in order to prepare for a meeting with Calisia.

Attachment 1 – Extract from letter from Calisia

(a)   **Farfisa – Additional income**

My daughter, Farfisa, who was born in 1993, will leave home and start her first job on 1 October 2015 in London. She will be working for Jelmini Ltd and will be paid a salary of £28,000 (gross) per year. Jelmini Ltd will also provide Farfisa with an interest free loan of £2,700 in order for her to purchase suitable business clothing. The loan is to be repaid on 30 September 2017.

We have estimated that Farfisa's expenses will be £2,500 per month (of which £550 will be rent) so her salary after tax will be insufficient. At present Farfisa has no other income so I have identified three possible transfers of capital that I could make to her in order to generate the income she requires.

(i)   **Gift of shares quoted on UK stock exchange**

I would give Farfisa sufficient quoted shares to generate the additional income she requires. On average the quoted shares would generate dividends equal to 4% of their current market value. It can be assumed that, on average, the capital gain arising on the quoted shares will equal a quarter of their market value. I do not hold more than 1% of the share capital of any quoted company.

(ii)   **Sale of investment property followed by gift of proceeds**

I own a two-bedroom investment property situated in London. I bought it in 2003 for £90,000 and it is now worth £270,000. I have always rented it out to tourists such that it qualifies as commercially let furnished holiday accommodation.

I would give Farfisa the net proceeds of the sale after paying any tax and other costs. Farfisa would place the cash on bank deposit; I estimate that the deposit would earn interest at 3% (gross). Farfisa would only spend the interest, not the capital, so I would then give Farfisa quoted shares to generate the remainder of the additional income she requires as in (i) above.

(iii) **Gift of investment property**

Under this option, instead of selling the property, I would give it to Farfisa who would then receive the annual rental income, after all allowable expenses, of £5,100. Again, I would then give Farfisa quoted shares to generate the remainder of the additional income she requires as in (i) above.

(b)   **Calisia – Inheritance tax**

I would like to discuss my inheritance tax position with you so that I can understand the amount of tax that would be payable if I were to die now. I set out below the assets I own together with their current market values. I have not included my home as I assume that it is not subject to inheritance tax. I have never made any lifetime gifts and neither did my husband before he died. I intend to leave £150,000 to the Fairness for All political party when I die and the rest of my estate to Farfisa.

	£
Investment property in London	260,000
Investment property in Sakura	380,000
Share (25%) in the 'Therson Partnership'	700,000
Building used by the 'Therson Partnership'	440,000
Shares quoted on the UK stock exchange	1,300,000
Art and antiques	200,000
Motor cars	100,000
Cash and other possessions	320,000

Attachment 2 – Schedule from your manager

(a) **Farfisa – Additional income**

During the meeting I only want to focus on any immediate tax liabilities as opposed to liabilities that may or may not arise in the future.

Prepare notes, with supporting calculations, showing Calisia's capital gains tax liability in respect of:

– Each of the three possibilities identified by her; and

– A fourth possibility (which I expect to be more tax efficient) whereby Calisia gifts the property to Farfisa who then lives in it. Any shortfall in income could then be satisfied by renting out the second bedroom. You should include a calculation of the minimum monthly rent that would need to be charged in order to provide sufficient income for Farfisa.

Start by calculating the excess of Farfisa's budgeted expenditure over her salary after all taxes for a 12-month period. This will enable you to determine the value of shares she will need to be given under each of the possibilities in order to provide her with the income she needs. Remember to take into account any income tax due on the income received by Farfisa when calculating the income she will retain in respect of the assets transferred.

Conclude with a summary, showing the capital gains tax payable in respect of each of the four alternatives.

Please include a note of the stamp duty or stamp duty land tax implications of each proposal.

You should assume the following:

– A sale or gift of the investment property will result in legal fees of £6,000.
– There will be no disposal costs in relation to any gift of shares.
– All claims and elections necessary to reduce immediate tax liabilities will be made.

Further information

Calisia and Farfisa are resident in the UK.

Calisia is a higher rate taxpayer who makes sufficient capital gains every year to utilise her annual exempt amount.

Calisia has not made a claim for entrepreneurs' relief in the past.

(b) **Calisia – Inheritance tax**

Calisia is domiciled in the UK and has not made any lifetime gifts. I want you to prepare a comprehensive explanation of how Calisia's inheritance tax liability would be calculated if she were to die today. Please try to identify all of the issues that are relevant to Calisia's situation together with any matters that need to be confirmed with her in order for reliefs and/or exemptions to be available. I do not want you to perform any calculations as we do not have sufficient information at present.

Further information

Calisia's husband died in 2005. He had not made any lifetime gifts and he left the whole of his estate, consisting principally of quoted shares and UK property, to Calisia.

Required

(a) **Farfisa – Additional income**

Prepare the notes and supporting calculations as set out in the schedule from your manager.   **(21 marks)**

(b) **Calisia – Inheritance tax**

Prepare the explanation as set out in the schedule from your manager.   **(10 marks)**

Professional marks will be awarded in this question for the effectiveness with which the information is communicated and the extent to which the calculations are approached in a logical manner.   **(4 marks)**

(Total = 35 marks)

You should assume that the tax rates and allowances of the tax year 2014/15 will continue to apply for the foreseeable future.

2 Petzold (ATAX 06/11)

45 mins

Your manager has sent you an email concerning a client, Petzold. An extract from the email together with two schedules of information from Petzold are set out below.

Email from your manager

Petzold has owned 100% of the ordinary share capital of Glenz Ltd for many years. Glenz Ltd is a profitable trading company that provides Petzold with the majority of his income. However, the company is currently suffering from a short-term cash flow problem.

Petzold also owns 100% of the ordinary share capital of Clementi Ltd. Clementi Ltd has three wholly owned trading subsidiaries but all of the companies in the group are very small. Petzold purchased Clementi Ltd in December 2014.

I want you to draft a letter to Petzold from me that deals with the following issues.

(a)   **Glenz Ltd – Payments to the tax authorities**

(i)   Calculations of the payments that will be made by Glenz Ltd to the tax authorities in respect of the three months ended 30 June 2015 and the equivalent figure for the three months ended 30 September 2015 based on the company's budgeted figures as set out in Schedule 1 from Petzold.

Petzold is only interested in those payments which affect the company's cash flow position. Accordingly, as the annual salaries shown represent the gross salaries earned there is no need to calculate the income tax or employees' national insurance contributions payable in respect of them.

Glenz Ltd is partially exempt for the purposes of value added tax (VAT) and was unable to recover all of its input tax in the year ending 31 March 2015.

Please provide explanations of the amount of input tax recoverable by Glenz Ltd but do not include any other narrative.

(ii)   Confirmation, or otherwise, of the accuracy of Petzold's calculation of the company's corporation tax liability for the year ending 31 March 2015 (see Schedule 1) including an explanation of any difference and a reminder of when the tax is payable.

(b)   **Glenz Ltd – cash flow**

(i)   The implications of the following suggestions from Petzold to improve the company's cash flow position.

        –   Paying Glenz Ltd's VAT liabilities in respect of the quarters ending 30 June 2015 and 30 September 2015 late. Glenz Ltd's previous four VAT returns have been submitted on time with the exception of the return for the three months ended 30 June 2014.

        –   The retention by Glenz Ltd of a refund of corporation tax of £21,000 that it received from HM Revenue and Customs in May 2015. Petzold has not been able to identify any reason for this refund.

(ii)   I have suggested to Petzold that Glenz Ltd could improve its cash flow position by selling its warehouse and then renting it back. I have agreed to provide him with a summary of the corporation tax implications of this proposal together with supporting calculations.

The summary should include a detailed explanation of how the chargeable gain arising on the sale of the warehouse could be relieved via rollover relief into a new warehouse.

You should assume that any sale of the warehouse will take place on 1 July 2015 and that rent will be paid from that date. Base your calculations on the figures provided by Petzold in Schedule 2.

I do not want you to address the VAT or the stamp duty land tax implications of this proposal.

Tax manager

Schedules provided by Petzold

Schedule 1

Glenz Ltd – Budgeted figures

	Three months ending 30 June 2015	Three months ending 30 Sept. 2015
	£	£
Sales revenue – Standard rated (excluding VAT)	360,000	365,000
Sales revenue – Exempt	24,500	23,400
Input tax:		
Attributable to taxable supplies	40,000	42,000
Attributable to exempt supplies	950	2,200
Non-attributable	800	1,500
Total	41,750	45,700

Total annual salaries for the company's eight full-time employees – £332,000

Corporation tax liability for the year ended 31 March 2015 £83,500 × 20% = £16,700

Schedule 2

The warehouse

Cost (1 February 2005)	£180,000
Current market value	£330,000
Estimated commercial annual rent payable to the new owner	£22,000

Required

Prepare the letter to Petzold requested in the email from your manager. The following marks are available.

(a)	Glenz Ltd – Payments to the tax authorities	**(11 marks)**
(b)	Glenz Ltd – Cash flow	**(14 marks)**

Note. The following figures from the Retail Prices Index should be used.

February 2005   189.6

July 2015   263.4 (assumed)

You should assume that the tax rates and allowances of the tax year 2014/15 and the Financial Year 2014 will continue to apply for the foreseeable future.

(Total = 25 marks)

SECTION B: TWO questions ONLY to be attempted

3 Faure (ATAX 06/11)   36 mins

Faure expects her new business to make a loss in its first trading period. She requires advice on the choice of year end, on the difference between employing her husband in the business, and running the business as a partnership.

The following information has been obtained from discussions with Faure.

Faure:

- Was born in 1970 and is married to Ravel
- Has not had an income tax liability since the tax year 2006/07
- Intends to start a new business on 1 July 2015 under the trading name 'Bah-Tock'
- 'Bah-Tock' will be Faure's only source of income

The 'Bah-Tock' business:

- Is expected to make a loss throughout the first 12 months of trading
- Is expected to be profitable from 1 July 2016 onwards

Structure of the 'Bah-Tock' business:

- The business will be unincorporated.

- Faure and Ravel will both work full-time on the affairs of the business.

- Faure will either employ Ravel, and pay him a commercial salary, or the two of them will run the business as a partnership.

Ravel:

- Was born in 1967
- Inherited a significant portfolio of quoted shares on the death of his mother in February 2006
- Has annual taxable income, after deduction of the personal allowance, of £31,865
- This income consists of bank interest and dividends only

Required

(a)   Explain why a year end of 30 June, as opposed to 31 March, is likely to delay the first tax year in which the 'Bah-Tock' business makes a taxable profit rather than an allowable loss.   **(5 marks)**

(b)   On the assumption that the 'Bah-Tock' business will have a 30 June year end, analyse the issues that Faure and Ravel should be aware of from a tax point of view if:

(i)   Faure employs Ravel
(ii)   Faure and Ravel are partners in the business and summarise your findings

Notes in relation to part (b)

1   Your analysis should be based on the information provided and should be restricted to the situation where the business is loss-making.

2   You should address the effect of the choice of business structure on:

- The size of the loss made by the business

- The reliefs available to Faure and Ravel in respect of the initial losses

- The income tax and national insurance contributions liabilities of Faure and Ravel for the tax years 2015/16 and 2016/17   **(15 marks)**

You should assume that the tax rates and allowances of the tax year 2014/15 will continue to apply for the foreseeable future.

                                                                                        (Total = 20 marks)

4 Capstan (ATAX 06/11)   36 mins

Capstan requires advice on the transfer of a property to a trust, the sale of shares in respect of which relief has been received under the Enterprise Investment Scheme (EIS), and the sale of shares and qualifying corporate bonds following a takeover.

The following information was obtained from a meeting with Capstan.

Capstan:

- Expects to have taxable income in the tax year 2015/16 of £80,000
- Transferred a UK property to a discretionary trust on 1 May 2015
- Plans to sell ordinary shares in Agraffe Ltd and loan stock and ordinary shares in Pinblock plc
- Will make all available claims to reduce the tax due in respect of his planned disposals
- Entrepreneurs' relief is not available in respect of any of these disposals

Transfer of a UK property to a discretionary trust:

- Capstan acquired the property in May 2007 for £285,000.
- The market value of the property on 1 May 2015 was £425,000.
- Capstan had used the property as a second home throughout his period of ownership.
- Capstan will pay any inheritance tax due on the gift of the property to the trust.

Sale of ordinary shares in Agraffe Ltd:

- Capstan subscribed for 18,000 shares in Agraffe Ltd for £32,000 on 1 February 2013.
- He obtained EIS relief of £9,600 against his income tax liability.
- Capstan intends to sell all of the shares for £20,000 on 1 July 2015.
- Capstan will relieve the loss arising on the shares in the most tax efficient manner.

Sale of loan stock and ordinary shares in Pinblock plc:

- Capstan will sell £8,000 7% Pinblock plc non-convertible loan stock for £10,600.
- Capstan will also sell 12,000 shares in Pinblock plc for £69,000.
- The sales will take place on 1 August 2015.

Capstan's acquisition of loan stock and ordinary shares in Pinblock plc:

- Capstan purchased 15,000 shares in Wippen plc for £26,000 on 1 May 2008.

- Pinblock plc acquired 100% of the ordinary share capital of Wippen plc on 1 October 2011.

- The takeover was for *bona fide* commercial reasons and was not for the avoidance of tax.

- Capstan received £8,000 Pinblock plc non-convertible loan stock (a qualifying corporate bond) and 20,000 ordinary shares in Pinblock plc in exchange for his shares in Wippen plc.

- The loan stock and the shares were worth £9,000 and £40,000 respectively as at 1 October 2011.

Required

(a) Set out, together with supporting calculations, the inheritance tax and capital gains tax implications of the transfer of the UK property to the trust and the date(s) on which any tax due will be payable. **(7 marks)**

(b) Explain, with supporting calculations, in connection with the sale of shares in Agraffe Ltd

- The tax implications of selling them on 1 July 2015
- Any advantages and disadvantages to Capstan of delaying the sale **(8 marks)**

(c) Calculate Capstan's taxable capital gains for the tax year 2015/16. **(5 marks)**

Note. In parts (a) and (b) you should clearly state any assumptions you have made together with any additional information that you would need to confirm with Capstan before finalising your calculations.

You should assume that the tax rates and allowances of the tax year 2014/15 will continue to apply for the foreseeable future.

(Total = 20 marks)

5 Loriod plc group (ATAX 06/11)   36 mins

The Loriod plc group intends to acquire an overseas business. It requires advice on the relief available in respect of any initial losses made by the business, the use of foreign tax credits, and transfer pricing. The following information has been obtained from the management of the Loriod plc group.

Loriod plc group:

- Loriod plc is a UK resident trading company.
- Loriod plc has a large number of wholly-owned UK resident trading subsidiary companies.
- It should be assumed that all group companies pay corporation tax at the main rate of 21%.
- Elivar Ltd, one of the Loriod plc group subsidiaries, is to acquire the 'Frager' business.
- The purchase of the 'Frager' business will follow either Strategy A or Strategy B.

Elivar Ltd:

- Makes qualifying charitable donations of £2,000 each year
- Has taxable total profits of approximately £90,000 per year

The 'Frager' business:

- Is carried on in the country of Kuwata and is owned by Syme Inc, a company resident in Kuwata
- Manufactures components used by Elivar Ltd and other Loriod plc group companies
- Carries on the same trade as Elivar Ltd
- Is expected to make a loss in the year following its acquisition by Elivar Ltd
- Is expected to have taxable profits of £120,000 per year following the year of acquisition

Strategy A:

- Elivar Ltd will purchase the trade and all of the assets of Syme Inc such that Elivar Ltd will be carrying on the 'Frager' business through a permanent establishment in Kuwata.
- The permanent establishment will be controlled from the UK.

Strategy B:

- Elivar Ltd will purchase the whole of the share capital of Syme Inc such that Syme Inc will be a subsidiary of Elivar Ltd resident in Kuwata.
- It has been determined that no charge would arise within the controlled foreign company (CFC) regime in respect of Syme Inc.

The tax system in the country of Kuwata:

- Is broadly the same as that in the UK with a corporation tax rate of 18%
- Trading losses may only be utilised by companies resident in Kuwata.
- Kuwata is not a member of the European Union and there is no double tax treaty between the UK and Kuwata.

Required

(a)   Provide a detailed explanation of the relief available in respect of the expected loss to be made by the 'Frager' business depending on whether the purchase follows Strategy A or Strategy B.   **(8 marks)**

(b)   For this part of the question it should be assumed that the purchase has followed Strategy A, the 'Frager' business is now profitable and that no election has been made in respect of the profits of the business.

   Explain, with supporting calculations, how to determine the maximum loss that can be surrendered to Elivar Ltd by the Loriod plc group companies if relief in respect of the tax suffered in Kuwata is not to be wasted.
   (6 marks)

(c)   For this part of the question it should be assumed that the purchase has followed Strategy B.

   Explain the effect of the prices charged by the subsidiary in Kuwata to other companies in the Loriod plc group on the total tax paid by the group and the implications of the transfer pricing legislation.   **(6 marks)**

You should assume that the tax rates and allowances of the Financial Year 2014 will continue to apply for the foreseeable future.

(Total = 20 marks)

Answers

DO NOT TURN THIS PAGE UNTIL YOU HAVE
COMPLETED THE MOCK EXAM

A plan of attack

What's the worst thing you could be doing right now if this was the actual exam paper? Wondering how to celebrate the end of the exam in about three hours time? Panicking, flapping and generally getting in a right old state?

Well, they're all pretty bad, so turn back to the paper and let's sort out a **plan of attack**!

First things first

You have 15 minutes of reading time. Make sure you spend it wisely, looking through the paper in detail working out which optional questions to do and the order in which to attack the questions. You've got **two options**. Option 1 is the option recommended by BPP.

Option 1 (if you're thinking 'Help!')

If you're a bit worried about the paper, do the questions in the order of how well you think you can answer them. If you find the questions in Section B less daunting than the compulsory questions in Section A start with Section B. Remember you only need to do two of the three questions in Section B; you may find it easier if you start by deciding which question you will not do and put a line through it.

- **Question 3** is about an unincorporated business making a loss and also choice of business medium.
- **Question 4** requires a knowledge of capital gains tax and inheritance tax.
- **Question 5** is a corporate tax question about groups and overseas aspects.

Do not spend longer than the allocated time on Section B. When you've spent the allocated time on **two** of the three questions in Section B turn to the longer questions in Section A. Read these questions through thoroughly before you launch into them. Once you start make sure you allocate your time to the parts within the questions according to the marks available and that, where possible, you attempt the easy marks first.

Lastly, what you mustn't forget is that you have to **answer both questions in Section A and TWO in Section B**.

Option 2 (if you're thinking 'It's a doddle')

It never pays to be overconfident but if you're not quaking in your shoes about the exam then **turn straight to the compulsory questions** in Section A.

Once you've done these questions, move to Section B. The question you attempt first really depends on what you are most confident at. You then have to select one of the two remaining questions. If you are undecided look at the requirements. It maybe easier to obtain more marks if these are broken down into several smaller parts.

No matter how many times we remind you....

Always, always **allocate your time** according to the marks for the question in total and then according to the parts of the question. And **always, always follow the requirements** exactly. Question 1 part (a), for example, asks you to conclude with a summary showing the capital gains tax payable in respect of four alternatives.

You've got spare time at the end of the exam.....?

If you have allocated your time properly then you **shouldn't have time on your hands** at the end of the exam. But if you find yourself with five or ten minutes to spare, check over your work to make sure that you have answered all the requirements of the questions and all parts of all requirements.

Forget about it!

And don't worry if you found the paper difficult. More than likely other candidates will too. If this were the real thing you would need to **forget** the exam the minute you leave the exam hall and **think about the next one**. Or, if it's the last one, **celebrate**!

1 Calisia (ATAX 06/11)

Text references. Principles of income tax are covered in Chapter 1. Property income is dealt with in Chapter 3. Employment income is dealt with in Chapter 4. Chargeable gains are covered in Chapter 11. Reliefs are in Chapter 13. Stamp duty and stamp duty land tax will be found in Chapter 19. Inheritance tax is covered in Chapters 16 to 18.

Top tips. It was very important in part (a) to deal with each of the situations in turn and then to compare the capital gains tax payable at the end. There was a big hint that the fourth scenario should have given the least capital gains tax payable!

Easy marks. The inheritance tax aspects of this question were relatively straightforward and should have yielded easy marks. As usual, easy marks could also be obtained for professional skills such as using appropriate language and style.

Examiner's comments. Part (a) was for 21 marks. With a question part of this size it was important for candidates to be clear as to what they had been asked to do and how they were going to do it. It was very pleasing to see the majority of candidates taking a well-structured approach to this question and addressing all of the alternatives in a consistent manner. There were some very good answers to this question with some candidates scoring full marks.

The question centred on capital gains business reliefs and the taxation of various sources of income. The income tax elements were done well but candidates' knowledge of business reliefs was often not as good as it could have been. However, there was a clear indication that candidates were taking the right approach to capital gains tax in that they were considering the availability of reliefs every time a gain arose. This was very good to see and it now remains for candidates to improve their knowledge of the conditions that must be satisfied for the reliefs to be available.

The first task was to calculate the amount of additional income required by the client's daughter, Farfisa. This was a relatively simple task and many candidates scored full marks. Other candidates failed to identify that the proposed loan was for less than £10,000 such that it was an exempt benefit or were not careful enough in distinguishing taxable income (income less personal allowance) from post-tax income (income less tax).

Under the first alternative the income was to be provided via a transfer of quoted shares. The majority of candidates were happy calculating the number of shares to be transferred but many failed to consider how the dividends would be taxed in the hands of Farfisa. Those who did address this point often considered the rate of tax but not the credit. The point that needed to be identified was that there would be no tax to pay on the dividend income because, as Farfisa would be a basic rate taxpayer, the tax liability would be covered by the tax credit.

Under the first alternative candidates then had to calculate the capital gain on the proposed gift of the shares. This is where some candidates began to have problems as they thought that gift relief would be available. However, the relief was not available because the shares were quoted and Calisia did not own at least 5% of the voting rights.

Under the second alternative candidates had to calculate the capital gains on the proposed sale of a building that was rented out as qualifying furnished holiday accommodation. Calculating the gain was simple; but again there was the need to consider the availability of business reliefs. Many candidates failed to realise that entrepreneurs' relief would be available such that tax would only be taxed at 10%. A minority of candidates also had the problem here of distinguishing a taxable gain (proceeds less cost) from post-tax proceeds (proceeds less tax).

Under the third and fourth alternatives the rental property was to be gifted rather than sold. Candidates had to identify that gift relief would be available under both alternatives. It was then necessary to consider how the rental income received by Farfisa in respect of the property would be taxed. Under the third alternative the income would be simply be taxed at 20%. But under the fourth alternative rent a room relief would be available. These points were identified by the vast majority of candidates.

Candidates were also asked to consider stamp duty and stamp duty land tax and to prepare a summary of the capital gains tax liabilities under each of the alternatives. A minority of candidates did not carry out one or both of these tasks thus sacrificing some fairly easy marks.

Part (b) required candidates to prepare a comprehensive explanation of how Calisia's inheritance tax liability would be calculated; this was done well by many candidates.

This question was fairly unstructured such that candidates had to think and impose their own structure in order to maximise their marks. Candidates who failed to do this often repeated themselves, did not cover sufficient aspects of the question and included material in their answers which was irrelevant. In particular, some candidates wasted time by writing about inheritance tax in general terms, including giving general advice on inheritance tax planning, or by preparing computations when they were told not to.

Candidates' knowledge of inheritance tax was often very good. The link between domicile and the taxation of overseas assets, the transfer of the husband's nil rate band, the treatment of the donation to the political party and the taxation of the client's home were identified and understood by the majority of candidates.

Business property relief was often explained well although, as always, there was a small minority of candidates who confused reliefs available in respect of capital gains tax with those available in respect of inheritance tax. It was important to provide some detail here (the requirement was for a comprehensive explanation) so a statement that 'business property relief would be available' was, despite being true, insufficient to score. Candidates needed to address the assets that would qualify for the relief, the qualifying ownership period and the rate of relief; many candidates did not address as much as they could have.

In respect of the property situated overseas, the marks available for explaining the relief in respect of tax suffered overseas were missed by many candidates. Other marks that were often missed included the deduction available for the costs of administering the property situated overseas, the treatment of Calisia's home, the deduction available in respect of funeral costs and the need for the political party to qualify in order for the donation to be exempt.

Marking scheme

			Marks
(a)	Calculation of additional income required	3½	
	Gift of shares		
	Tax on dividends	1½	
	Capital gains tax	3½	
	Sale of investment property followed by gift of proceeds		
	Capital gains on investment property	2½	
	Farfisa's income position	3½	
	Capital gains tax on transfer of shares	1½	
	Gift of investment property – rented out by Farfisa		
	Gift relief available	1	
	Farfisa's income position	2	
	Capital gains tax on transfer of shares	1	
	Gift of investment property – to be lived in by Farfisa	2½	
	Summary of capital gains tax payable	1	
	Stamp duty and stamp duty land tax	2	
		Max	21
(b)	Relevance of domicile	1	
	Calisia's home subject to tax	½	
	Business property relief	4	
	Cost of administering the property in Sakura	1	
	Political party	1½	
	Funeral costs	½	
	Nil rate bands	1½	
	Tax and double tax relief	2	
		Max	10
Appropriate style and presentation		1	
Effectiveness of communication		2	
Approach to problem solving		1	
			4
			35

Prepared by A. N. Taxadviser

Date 6 June 2015

Subject Farfisa – Additional income

Calisia – Inheritance tax

(a) **Farfisa – Additional income**

Additional income required

	£
Salary	28,000
Less: Income tax £(£28,000 – 10,000) × 20%	(3,600)
Class 1 national insurance contributions £(£28,000 – 7,956) × 12%	(2,405)
Income receivable from Jelmini Ltd	21,995
Less: Estimated expenditure £2,500 × 12	(30,000)
Additional income required	(8,005)

The interest free loan will not result in a tax liability because it is for less than £10,000.

(i) **Gift of shares quoted on UK stock exchange**

If Farfisa were to be given shares resulting in dividend income of £8,005, her taxable income would remain below the higher rate threshold of £31,865 as set out below. There would be no income tax to pay on the dividend income as the tax liability will be covered by the 10% tax credit.

	£
Salary	28,000
Dividend income £8,005 × 100/90	8,894
Less: personal allowance	(10,000)
Taxable income	26,894

Accordingly, with a yield of 4%, Farfisa would need to own shares valued at £200,125 (£8,005/4%).

The gift would give rise to a capital gain calculated by reference to market value. Holdings in quoted companies do not qualify for gift relief, except in the case of an individual's personal trading company in which they own at least 5% of the voting rights.

Calisia has estimated that the gain on the shares will be one quarter of their market value, ie £50,031 (£200,125 × ¼).

Calisia is a higher rate taxpayer who uses her annual exempt amount every year. Accordingly, her capital gains tax liability would be £14,009 (£50,031 × 28%).

Stamp duty is charged on the amount of consideration paid. Accordingly, there would be no stamp duty on a gift of quoted shares.

(ii) **Sale of investment property followed by gift of proceeds**

	£
Proceeds	270,000
Less: disposal costs	(6,000)
cost	(90,000)
Chargeable gain	174,000

Entrepreneurs' relief is available in respect of capital gains on furnished holiday accommodation. Accordingly, capital gains tax of £17,400 (£174,000 × 10%) would be due.

The gift of cash to Farfisa would be £246,600 (£270,000 – £6,000 – £17,400). This would give rise to gross interest of £7,398 (£246,600 × 3%).

Farfisa's taxable income would remain below the higher rate threshold of £31,865 as set out below. Accordingly, the interest income would be taxed at 20% and Farfisa's after-tax income would be £5,918 (£7,398 × 80%).

	£
Salary	28,000
Interest income	7,398
Less: personal allowance	(10,000)
Taxable income	25,398

In addition to the interest income, Farfisa would require after-tax dividend income of £2,087 (£8,005 – £5,918) in order to meet her budgeted expenditure. There would be no income tax to pay on this dividend income as her taxable income will clearly still remain below the higher rate threshold (£31,865 – £25,398 = £6,467) such that the tax liability will be covered by the 10% tax credit.

Calisia's capital gains tax liability on the gift of the shares would be £3,652 (£2,087/4% × ¼ × 28%).

Calisia will not be liable to stamp duty land tax on the sale of the property as this would be payable by the purchaser of the property.

There would be no stamp duty on the gift of the shares.

(iii) **Gift of investment property – rented out by Farfisa**

The property qualifies as commercially let furnished holiday accommodation. Accordingly, gift relief would be available in respect of the capital gain and no capital gains tax would be payable. Farfisa would pay tax on the rental income at 20%. Accordingly, her rental income, after tax, would be £4,080 (£5,100 × 80%).

In addition to the rental income, Farfisa would require after-tax dividend income of £3,925 (£8,005 – £4,080) in order to meet her budgeted expenditure. There would be no income tax to pay on this dividend income as her taxable income will clearly still remain below the higher rate threshold such that the tax liability will be covered by the 10% tax credit.

Calisia's capital gains tax liability on the gift of the shares will be £6,869 (£3,925/4% × ¼ × 28%).

Stamp duty and stamp duty land tax is charged on the amount of consideration paid. Accordingly, there would be no duty on either of the gifts.

(iv) **Gift of investment property – lived in by Farfisa**

If Farfisa were to live in the investment property she would not have to pay the rent of £550 per month. Also, she could rent out the spare room to generate additional income. Provided the room is furnished and the rent does not exceed £4,250, the rental income would not be subject to income tax.

As above in (iii), gift relief would be available in respect of the gain on the property.

	£
Additional income required	8,005
Less: Rental expenditure no longer incurred £(550 × 12)	(6,600)
	1,405
Minimum monthly rent required in respect of spare room £(1,405/12)	117

There would be no stamp duty land tax on the gift of the property.

Summary

Capital gains tax payable by Calisia under each alternative:

(i) £14,009
(ii) £21,052 (£17,400 + £3,652)
(iii) £6,869
(iv) Nil

(b) **Calisia – Inheritance tax**

Explanation of inheritance tax liability on death

The amount subject to inheritance tax on Calisia's death (her taxable estate) will be the value of all of the assets she owns when she dies, including her home and any assets situated overseas (because she is domiciled in the UK) less certain deductions.

The following amounts will be deducted from the value of her assets in arriving at her taxable estate.

– The interest in the 'Therson Partnership' will be 100% relieved by business property relief provided the partnership carries on a qualifying business; this excludes dealing in securities and shares or land and buildings and the making or holding of investments. Calisia's share of the value of the partnership assets not used wholly or mainly for business purposes (ie investments) will not qualify for this relief.

– The building used by the 'Therson Partnership' will be 50% relieved by business property relief provided it is used wholly or mainly for the purposes of a qualifying business carried on by the partnership.

– Calisia will need to satisfy the minimum qualifying ownership period of two years in respect of her interest in the partnership and the building used by the partnership in order for business property relief to be available.

– The cost of administering or realising the property in the country of Sakura up to a maximum of 5% of the property's value will be deducted from the property's value.

– The legacy to the Fairness for All political party will be deducted only if it is a qualifying political party. A qualifying political party is one which has two elected members in the House of Commons or one member and at least 150,000 votes at the last general election.

– Liabilities due at the time of death, reasonable funeral costs including the cost of a tombstone are also deductible.

Because Calisia has made no lifetime gifts, there will be no tax on the first £325,000 (the nil rate band) of her estate. An additional deduction of £325,000 will also be available in respect of her husband's nil rate band as it was not used on his death.

Tax will be charged at 40% on the taxable estate.

Any inheritance tax suffered in the country of Sakura will be deducted from the UK inheritance tax liability up to a maximum of the UK inheritance tax on the Sakuran property. The UK inheritance tax on the Sakuran property will be calculated by determining the percentage, by reference to the market values, of Calisia's assets represented by the Sakuran property and applying that percentage to the total inheritance tax due.

Confirmations required

For business property relief, as set out above, to be available the following matters need to be confirmed:

– The partnership carries on a qualifying business.
– Calisia satisfies the minimum qualifying ownership period.

2 Petzold (ATAX 06/11)

Text references. VAT is covered in Chapters 28 and 29. Employer's national insurance is dealt with in Chapter 4. Calculation of corporation tax is covered in Chapter 22. Ethical issues are in Chapter 30. Chargeable gains for companies are covered in Chapter 21.

Top tips. Don't neglect ethical aspects of taxation practice in your preparation for the P6 exam – this topic is often examined.

Easy marks. There were some easy marks for basic computations related to national insurance computations, corporation tax and chargeable gains.

Examiner's comments. Part (a) concerned value added tax (VAT), corporation tax and national insurance. Candidates' performance was pretty mixed with some very good scripts, some very poor ones and a range in between.

The VAT element required calculations and explanations of the company's VAT liabilities for two quarters. This was done well by those candidates who knew how to do it but, unfortunately, many candidates had little more than an awareness of the rules and did not know how to apply them to the facts. There are always a reasonable number of marks in the exam relating to VAT and changes introduced by the latest Finance Act are often examined so it should not have been surprising to see partial exemption being tested. (**BPP note.** This comment relates to the situation when this question was originally set in June 2011 but has been retained as an important point for students to note about the examination of the most recent Finance Act.)

The corporation tax element required calculations and explanations of the company's corporation tax liability. This was done well by the majority of candidates. The question required an *explanation* of the number of associated companies (ie by reference to Petzold's control of Glenz Ltd and Clementi Ltd) and the consequent rate of tax payable by reference to the limits. Many candidates took these points for granted such that they did not score as well as they could have.

The information in the question relating to the two three-month periods resulted in a small minority of candidates preparing meaningless calculations of tax for each of the periods. This is something they would never have done in their preparation for the exam or ever seen in a textbook. A small minority of candidates recognised that the company was marginal and proceeded to calculate the tax on the whole of the taxable profits at the marginal rate. This is not the way the marginal rate works; the marginal rate is only relevant in relation to the profits between the limits.

The national insurance element was straightforward and done well by those who attempted it. The problem was that many candidates did not identify the need to carry out the calculations despite the clues in the question.

Part (b) concerned the company's cash flow position in relation to VAT, the treatment of a refund of corporation tax and the sale and leaseback of a warehouse.

The VAT element concerned the default surcharge penalty. Just as with the VAT element of part (a), it was done very well by those who knew the rules and (inevitably) considerably less well by those who did not. As noted above, candidates would do well to recognise that VAT features in every exam.

The client was proposing to retain a recently received tax refund despite not knowing what it was for. Candidates were expected to recognise that this was not acceptable behaviour and the vast majority were able to do so. However, a minority of candidates did not do much more than that such that they failed to explain the implications of not returning the money in relation to both the client and its advisers.

The implications of the sale and leaseback were covered well by many candidates. Candidates had to slow down and think in order to provide sufficient information. The question asked for a 'detailed explanation' of relief of the gain via rollover relief. This required candidates to consider the period in which the replacement assets needed to be acquired, the implications of reinvesting some, rather than all, of the proceeds and the manner in which the relief would be given. Very few candidates addressed all of these matters but it is likely that the vast majority of candidates knew something about all of them. When asked to write in detail, candidates must plan their answers such that they cover all of the relevant issues.

			Marks
(a)	**VAT**		
	Three months ending 30 June 2015	3	
	Three months ending 30 September 2015	3½	
	Employer's national insurance contributions	3	
	Corporation tax		
	Calculations	1½	
	Explanations	2½	
	Max		11
(b)	Late payment of VAT		
	Explanation	3½	
	Calculations	1½	
	Retention of the tax refund	4	
	Sale of the warehouse		
	Chargeable gain	1½	
	Rollover relief and time period	1½	
	Proceeds not reinvested	1½	
	Manner of relief	1	
	Treatment of rent	1	
	Max		14
			25

Firm's address

Petzold's address

6 June 2015

Dear Petzold

Glenz Ltd

I set out below the information you require to assist you in dealing with the company's cash flow problems.

(a) **Glenz Ltd – Payments to the tax authorities**

The payments that will be made by Glenz Ltd to the tax authorities in respect of the two, three-month periods ending 30 June 2015 and 30 September 2015 are calculated at appendix 1. The calculations are based on the budgeted figures provided by the company. In summary, the following payments will be due:

	Three months ending 30 June 2015 £	Three months ending 30 September 2015 £
Value added tax (VAT)	30,250	29,590
Employer's national insurance contributions	7,258	9,258

Glenz Ltd's corporation tax liability for the year ended 31 March 2015 is £16,994 (see appendix 1). The limits used to determine the rate of tax paid by Glenz Ltd must be divided by five because you controlled five companies (Glenz Ltd and the four companies in the Clementi group) during the year. This reduces the lower limit to £60,000 (£300,000/5) such that Glenz Ltd is a marginal company paying tax at the main 21% rate less marginal relief.

The corporation tax is due on 1 January 2016.

(b) **Glenz Ltd – Cash flow**

(i) *Your proposals to improve the company's cash flow position*

Late payment of VAT

When the company submitted its return late for the three months ended 30 June 2014 it would have received a surcharge liability notice.

A late payment of VAT in respect of one of the subsequent four quarters will result in a penalty of 2% of the VAT payable and an extension of the 12-month surcharge period. Accordingly, if Glenz Ltd's payment for the three months ending 30 June 2015 is made late, there will be a penalty of £605 (£30,250 × 2%).

The penalty for a second late payment within the surcharge period is 5% of the VAT payable. Accordingly, there will be a further penalty of £1,479 (£29,590 × 5%) if the payment for the three months ending 30 September 2015 is also late and the surcharge period will be extended again to include the following four quarters, ie to 30 September 2016.

The surcharge liability period will only end when four consecutive quarterly returns have been submitted on time and any VAT due has been paid on time. The penalties for a third and subsequent defaults are 10% and 15% respectively of the VAT payable.

Retention of the tax refund

I suggest that we carry out a review of the company's tax affairs in order to identify the reason for the tax refund. If, as you suspect, it is an error it should be repaid immediately. You may well be committing a civil and/or a criminal offence if you fail to return the money in these circumstances. Immediate voluntary disclosure is advisable in order to minimise any interest and penalties that may otherwise become payable.

In addition, unless you return the money, we would have to consider ceasing to act as your advisers. In these circumstances we are required to notify the tax authorities that we no longer act for you, although we would not provide them with any reason for our action.

(ii) *Sale of warehouse*

Chargeable gain

The chargeable gain on the sale of the warehouse would be £79,980 (appendix 2). This would be subject to corporation tax in the year ending 31 March 2016 unless it is relieved via rollover relief.

Rollover relief would be available if a new warehouse was purchased for use in the business within the period beginning one year prior to the sale and ending three years after the sale.

In order for the whole of the gain to be relieved you would need to reinvest the whole of the sale proceeds the new warehouse. Otherwise, there would be a chargeable gain equal to the amount of proceeds not reinvested subject to a maximum of £79,980.

The gain relieved is deducted from the cost of the new warehouse. This will increase the gain on a future disposal of the new warehouse.

Rent paid

The rent paid following the sale of the warehouse would be a tax-deductible expense when calculating the company's corporation tax liability. Accordingly, there would be a tax deduction in the year ending 31 March 2016 of £16,500 (£22,000 × 9/12).

Please contact me if you require any further information.

Yours sincerely

Tax Manager

Appendix 1

Glenz Ltd – Payment to the tax authorities

Value added tax (VAT)

Glenz Ltd does not satisfy the partial exemption annual test as it was unable to recover all of its input tax in the year ended 31 March 2015. However, it can still provisionally recover all of its input tax in any quarter of the current year in which it passes the *de minimis* test.

	Three months ending 30 June 2015 £
Output tax £360,000 × 20%	72,000
Recoverable input tax £(40,000 + 950 + 800) (N2)	(41,750)
Amount payable to HMRC	30,250

	Three months ending 30 September 2015 £
Output tax £365,000 × 20%	73,000
Recoverable input tax	
Attributable to taxable supplies	(42,000)
Non-attributable £1,500 × 94% (N3,4,5)	(1,410)
Amount payable to HMRC	29,590

Notes

1   Partial exemption simplified test 1 is clearly not satisfied in either quarter, as total input tax incurred exceeds £625 per month on average.

2   Partial exemption simplified test 2 will be satisfied in the quarter ending 30 June 2015 because:

Total input tax less that directly attributable to taxable supplies does not exceed £625 per month on average ((£41,750 – £40,000)/3 = £583); and

The value of exempt supplies does not exceed 50% of the value of all supplies (£24,500/(£360,000 + £24,500) = 6.4%).

Accordingly, Glenz Ltd can provisionally recover all of its input tax.

3   Partial exemption simplified test 2 will not be satisfied in the quarter ending 30 September 2015 because:

Total input tax less that directly attributable to taxable supplies exceeds £625 per month on average ((£45,700 – £42,000)/3 = £1,233).

4   Exempt input tax of £2,290 (£2,200 + (£1,500 – (£1,500 × 94% (N5)))) exceeds £625 per month (main test) and is therefore not *de minimis*.

5   Glenz Ltd's taxable supplies represent 93.97% (£365,000/(£365,000 + £23,400)) of its total supplies. This figure is rounded up to 94% for the purpose of calculating recoverable input tax.

Employer's Class 1 national insurance contributions

	£
Average annual liability per employee £((332,000/8) – 7,956) × 13.8%	4,629
Quarterly liability for eight employees £4,629 × 3/12 × 8	9,258

The employment allowance of £2,000 will be set against the liability for the quarter ended 30 June 2015 so the liability for this quarter will be £7,258.

Corporation tax liability for the year ended 31 March 2015 – due on 1 January 2016

Upper limit £1,500,000/5 = £300,000

	£
Corporation tax at main rate £83,500 × 21%	17,535
Less: marginal relief £(300,000 – 83,500) × 1/400	(541)
Corporation tax payable	16,994

Appendix 2

Chargeable gain on sale of warehouse

	£
Proceeds	330,000
Less: cost	(180,000)
indexation allowance £180,000 × 0.389 ((263.4 – 189.6)/189.6)	(70,020)
Chargeable gain	79,980

3 Faure (ATAX 06/11)

Text references. The basis of assessment and national insurance for the self-employed are both dealt with in Chapter 6. Losses are covered in Chapter 8. Partnerships are covered in Chapter 9.

Top tips. The notes at the end of the question contain vital information about how this question should be approached. Make sure you follow them!

Easy marks. There were a lot of marks for basic knowledge from F6 level such as the basis of assessment and national insurance contributions.

Examiner's comments. Part (a) concerned the choice of year end for the new business; it was answered poorly by a majority of candidates but very well by the remainder.

The question was slightly unusual in that it required candidates to explain why something was true; namely that one year end rather than another would be likely to delay the first tax year in which the business makes a taxable profit. This required candidates to apply their technical knowledge to the facts of the question.

In order to answer this question, candidates needed to know the opening year rules for an unincorporated business. However, they also had to reach the conclusion set out in the question. The problem here was that many candidates did not pause and think about what they had been asked to do. Instead, they simply wrote about opening years in relation to overlap profits, utilisation of losses or tax payment dates.

Candidates who did well either thought before they began writing, such that they submitted very concise answers that neatly summarised the position, or explored the opening year rules for each of the year ends and reached the required conclusion.

Part (b) required a comparison of employing someone with going into partnership with them. There were lots of marks available, many of which were straightforward and, on the whole, this part was answered reasonably well. However, many candidates could have done considerably better if they had recognised all of the help that was provided to them in the question and had taken the time to consider whether or not they had addressed all of the relevant points.

Candidates' first impression on reading this question may have been favourable in that the technical area was one they were likely to be comfortable with (although the lack of numbers may have worried some). However, in order to maximise their marks candidates needed to follow the instructions given in the notes to the question. Note 1 required candidates' answers to be restricted to losses; this was ignored by many candidates. Note 2 provided a structure to what was otherwise an awkward open ended question; unfortunately, this suggested structure was also ignored by many candidates.

Those candidates who ignored the notes lost marks for two reasons; they wasted time writing about matters that did not score (principally the taxation of profits) and they failed to address all of the relevant issues (as listed in note 2). For example, candidates wrote about how Class 4 national insurance contributions would be calculated when they should have written that no such contributions would be due until the business was profitable.

				Marks
(a)	30 June year end		2	
	31 March year end		2	
	Comparison		1	
				5
(b)	(i)	Faure employs Ravel		
		Effect on results of business	1	
		Class 1 national insurance contributions	1½	
		Faure – income tax	2	
		Ravel – income tax	2½	
	(ii)	Faure and Ravel are partners in the business		
		Allocation of loss and no taxable income	1½	
		Faure – use of loss	½	
		Ravel – use of loss		
		Alternatives available	2½	
		Tax relief and timing	2½	
	Class 2 national insurance contributions		1	
	Conclusion		1	
		Max		15
				20

(a) **The advantages of a 30 June year end**

The business is expected to make a loss in the 12-month trading period ending on 30 June 2016. Where the business adopts a 30 June year end this 12-month period will be the basis period for the first two tax years: 2015/16 (1 July 2015 to 5 April 2016) and 2016/17 (the first 12 months). Accordingly, there will be no taxable profits for the first two tax years.

If the business were to adopt a 31 March year end there would be a loss in the nine months ending 31 March 2016 resulting in no taxable profits in 2015/16. However, the year ended 31 March 2017 may produce a profit as it will consist of three months of loss and nine months of profit. This would result in a taxable profit in 2016/17.

Accordingly, the adoption of a 30 June year end is likely to delay the first tax year in which the business makes a taxable profit rather than an allowable loss.

(b) **Tax issues relating to the structure of the 'Bah-Tock' business**

(i) **Faure employs Ravel**

The cost of employing Ravel will increase the loss made by the business. This cost will consist of Ravel's salary and the related employer's Class 1 national insurance contributions of (salary – £7,956) × 13.8% (reduced by up to £2,000 employment allowance).

Faure

Faure will have a trading loss for 2015/16 and 2016/17 and will therefore have no income tax or Class 4 national insurance liability in respect of the business for those two years.

Faure will have to carry forward the whole of the tax-adjusted loss for relief against future profits of the same trade as she has no other sources of income against which to relieve it.

Faure will not have to pay Class 2 national insurance contributions until the accounting profit of the business exceeds the small earnings limit of £5,885.

Ravel

Ravel is currently a basic rate taxpayer such that the whole of his income tax liability is satisfied by the tax credits relating to his income. His salary from the business will be taxed in priority to his investment income and will displace the investment income from the starting rate and basic rate bands. The displaced investment income will become taxable at the higher rates of 40% for interest income and 32.5% for dividend income and will then be reduced by the related tax credits.

Ravel will also pay Class 1 national insurance contributions in respect of his salary of (salary − £7,956) × 12%.

(ii) **Faure and Ravel are partners in the business**

The tax adjusted loss will be split between the two partners in accordance with the profit sharing arrangements of the partnership.

The two partners will each have a trading loss for 2015/16 and 2016/17 and will therefore have no income tax or Class 4 national insurance liability in respect of the business for those two years.

Faure and Ravel will not have to pay Class 2 national insurance contributions so long as each of the them has income from the business below the small earnings limit of £5,885.

Faure

Faure will carry forward her share of the loss as set out above.

Ravel

Ravel can choose to offset his share of the loss against his total income:

- For the year of the loss and/or the previous year; or
- For the three tax years preceding the year of the loss on a first in-first out basis

Where the loss is relieved against interest income Ravel will be able to recover the tax he has paid in respect of that income.

Where the loss is relieved against dividend income there will be no repayment as the 10% tax credit on dividends is not repayable.

Alternatively, Ravel could choose to carry forward the loss for offset against future profits of the same trade. Once the business is profitable Ravel is likely to be paying tax at the higher rates in the same way as he would if Faure were to employ him (see above). Accordingly, Ravel could increase the amount of tax saved by carrying the loss forward but this would delay obtaining relief for the loss.

Summary

If Faure employs Ravel the couple's total tax liability in 2015/16 and 2016/17 will increase even though the business will have made a loss.

If Faure and Ravel run the business as a partnership part of the loss will be available for relief against the income of Ravel.

Ravel is able to claim loss relief either earlier or at a higher rate than Faure.

4 Capstan (ATAX 06/11)

Text references. Lifetime transfers for IHT are covered in Chapter 16. The enterprise investment scheme is dealt with in Chapter 2. The CGT aspects of shares and securities are covered in Chapter 12.

Top tips. The P6 exam is not just about technical tax knowledge. When thinking about advantages and disadvantages which might arise on delaying the sale of the shares in Agraffe Ltd, don't forget about practical and commercial aspects that might be important to the client.

Easy marks. The inheritance tax calculation was very straightforward. The sale of the loan stock after a takeover should also have given easy marks.

Examiner's comments. Part (a) required candidates to consider both the capital gains tax and inheritance tax implications of the transfer of a property to a discretionary trust. The inheritance tax implications were addressed very well by all but a tiny minority of candidates. The only common error was a failure to set out any assumptions made as required by the note to the question.

The capital gains tax element of this part was not answered well. The problem here was that most candidates did not think; instead they simply deducted the cost from the proceeds and addressed rates of tax. Some candidates then realised that gift relief was available and that, per the question, all available claims would be made. As a result, although they had wasted some time, they were still able to score full marks. Other candidates, however, did not address the gift relief point and consequently did not score any marks for the capital gains tax element of the question.

Part (b) concerned the sale of shares in respect of which EIS relief had been claimed. Almost all candidates identified the claw back of the relief if the shares were sold within three years of the acquisition. However, many stated that the whole of the relief obtained would be withdrawn as opposed to a proportion of it.

The implications of delaying the sale were not identified particularly well. Many candidates simply stated the opposite of what they had already written, ie that the relief obtained would not be withdrawn if the shares were held for three years. More thoughtful candidates considered other matters and recognised that delaying the sale delayed the receipt of the sales proceeds and that the value of the shares might change (for the better or the worse).

The final part of the question concerned the sale of shares and qualifying corporate bonds that had been acquired following a paper for paper exchange. This part was done well by those candidates who knew how to handle this type of transaction.

The first task was to recognise that the cost of the original shares needed to be apportioned between the new shares and the corporate bonds. Many candidates knew what they were doing here and were on the way to doing well in this part of the question.

However, there was often confusion as to the treatment of the sale of the corporate bonds. Many candidates who knew that corporate bonds are exempt from capital gains tax went on to calculate a gain on the sale and include it in the taxable capital gains for the year. Also, many candidates were not able to identify the gain on the original shares that was frozen at the time of the paper for paper exchange and then charged when the corporate bonds were sold.

Marking scheme

			Marks
(a)	Inheritance tax		
	Explanations and assumptions	3½	
	Calculations	2	
	Capital gains tax	1½	
			7
(b)	Withdrawal of EIS relief	2	
	Loss on sale	1½	
	Offset of loss	1	
	Advantage of delay	2	
	Disadvantages of delay	2	
	Max		8
(c)	Sale of loan stock	3½	
	Gain on sale of shares	1	
	Annual exempt amount	½	
			5
			20

(a) **Transfer of a UK property to a discretionary trust**

Inheritance tax

A lifetime transfer to any form of trust is immediately chargeable to inheritance tax.

	£
Market value of property	425,000
Less: AE 2015/16	(3,000)
AE 2014/15 b/f	(3,000)
Net transfer of value (Capstan pays IHT)	419,000

				£
IHT	£325,000	× 0% =		Nil
	£ 94,000	× 20/80 =		23,500
	£419,000			23,500

The gross transfer of value for accumulation is £(419,000 + 23,500) = £442,500.

Check

				£
IHT	£325,000	× 0% =		Nil
	£117,500	× 20% =		23,500
	£442,500			23,500

It has been assumed that:

- Capstan has made no other transfers of value in 2014/15 or in 2015/16 prior to 1 May 2015 such that there are two annual exemptions available.

- Capstan has made no chargeable lifetime transfers in the seven years prior to 1 May 2015 such that the whole of the nil rate band is available.

Since the transfer took place between 6 April and 30 September 2015, the tax will be due on 30 April 2016. Inheritance tax on land and buildings can be paid by instalments but not where the tax is being paid by the donor.

Capital gains tax

Gift relief will be available on the transfer because the gift is immediately chargeable to inheritance tax. Accordingly, there will be no capital gains tax liability in respect of the transfer.

(b) **Agraffe Ltd**

A sale on 1 July 2015 will result in a withdrawal of the EIS income tax relief as the shares will have been held for less than three years. On the assumption that the sale is a bargain at arm's length the withdrawal of relief will be £(20,000/32,000) × £9,600 = £6,000.

There will also be a loss on the sale of the shares. However, when calculating the loss, the allowable cost of the shares will be reduced by the EIS relief obtained.

	£
Proceeds	20,000
Less: cost £(32,000 − (9,600 − 6,000))	(28,400)
Allowable loss	(8,400)

Capstan can offset the loss against his general income of 2015/16 and/or 2014/15 because the shares qualified for EIS relief.

This is advantageous as Capstan will save income tax at 40% (he is a higher rate taxpayer) rather than capital gains tax at 28%.

There would be no withdrawal of EIS relief if Capstan were to sell the shares after 1 February 2016 as he would then have held them for three years. However, this would reduce the allowable loss on the sale by £6,000 (because the allowable cost would be £6,000 less) such that the tax saved via the offset of the loss would be reduced by £2,400 (40% × £6,000). The overall saving to Capstan would be £3,600 (£6,000 − £2,400).

The disadvantages of delaying the sale are that the receipt of the sales proceeds will be delayed and that the value of the shares could continue to fall such that Capstan's financial loss would increase.

(c)   **Capstan's taxable capital gains for the tax year 2015/16**

	£
Gain arising on sale of Pinblock plc loan stock (W1)	4,224
Gain arising on sale of the shares in Pinblock plc (W2)	56,265
	60,489
Less: annual exempt amount	(11,000)
Taxable gains	49,489

Tutorial note

Candidates who assumed in their answer to part (b) above that the loss arising on the sale of the shares in Agraffe Ltd would be set off against Capstan's capital gains were given full credit in this part of the question.

Workings

1   *Capital gain arising on sale of loan stock*

The profit on the sale of the 7% Pinblock plc non-convertible loan stock will not be subject to capital gains tax because qualifying corporate bonds are exempt assets.

However, a gain will have arisen when the shares in Wippen plc were exchanged for the loan stock. This gain will become chargeable on the sale of the loan stock.

	£
Market value of loan stock on 1 October 2011	9,000
Less: cost £(26,000 × (9,000/(9,000 + 40,000)))	(4,776)
Chargeable gain	4,224

2   *Capital gain arising on the sale of shares in Pinblock plc*

	£
Proceeds	69,000
Less: cost 12,000/20,000 × £(26,000 × (40,000/(9,000 + 40,000)))	(12,735)
Chargeable gain	56,265

5 Loriod plc group (ATAX 06/11)

Text references. Overseas aspects of corporation tax are covered in Chapter 27. Transfer pricing is dealt with in Chapter 20.

Top tips. Read the question carefully. For example, in part (c), you are told to consider the position for transfer pricing if Strategy B is adopted. (You might like to think why the question directs you to do this.)

Easy marks. There were some easy marks in this question for basic comparisons between permanent establishments and subsidiaries, and transfer pricing.

Examiner's comments. Part (a) required candidates to explain the relief available in respect of the expected loss to be made by the business depending on whether it was established as a branch or a subsidiary of the UK company. This was an area where candidates had a certain amount of knowledge but, on the whole, did not score as well as they could have done because they wrote generally about branch versus subsidiary as opposed to addressing the particular facts and requirements of this question.

In particular, despite being asked to address loss relief, many candidates wrote about the taxation of profits. Many of those who did address losses did not address them as precisely as they could have done in the context of the question such that they did not consider the relevance of the tax rates provided.

Part (b) concerned group relief and the preservation of double tax relief. It required technical knowledge that almost all candidates had regarding double tax relief being the lower of the UK tax and the overseas tax on the overseas income. However, it also required candidates to be able to work out how to ensure that sufficient overseas profits remained within the charge to tax such that relief in respect of the overseas tax was not wasted. This task was carried out elegantly by a minority of candidates but the majority struggled with the problem. Credit was available for approaching the question by reference to double tax relief but many candidates simply stated that group relief was restricted to the lower of the losses available and the profits subject to tax.

The final part of the question concerned transfer pricing and was done reasonably well by many candidates who had a good knowledge of the transfer pricing rules. However, only a small minority made reference to the relevance of the size of the companies in determining whether or not the rules would apply or to the possibility of reaching an agreement with HM Revenue and Customs.

The question also required candidates to explain how the prices charged between the group companies would affect the total tax paid by the group. In order to do this, candidates had to focus on the difference between the tax rate in the UK and that in Kuwata and the possibility of group profits being taxed at the lower rate. It was important here to address the situation from a group perspective rather than that of a particular company. However, the majority of candidates did not address this element of the question.

Marking scheme

			Marks
(a)	Use of permanent establishment	4	
	Use of subsidiary	3	
	Comparison	1	
			8
(b)	Explanations		
	Double taxation relief	2	
	UK tax on overseas profits	2	
	Calculations	2	
			6
(c)	Impact of prices on total tax paid by the group	2	
	Transfer pricing		
	Why the rules apply	2	
	Application of the rules	1½	
	HMRC confirmation of pricing arrangements	1	
	Max		6
			20

(a) The relief available in respect of the expected loss

Strategy A – Elivar Ltd purchases the trade and all of the assets of Syme Inc

The business in Kuwata would be an overseas permanent establishment of Elivar Ltd. The permanent establishment would be an extension of Elivar Ltd. Accordingly, because the overseas operations are to be controlled from the UK, the loss made in the year following the acquisition will be offset in calculating Elivar Ltd's trading income. If Elivar Ltd makes a trading loss, the overseas losses can be included in a group relief surrender to other group companies. Any unrelieved losses will be carried forward for relief against future profits of the same trade. The relief of the overseas losses will save UK corporation tax at 21%.

Strategy B – Elivar Ltd purchases the share capital of Syme Inc

Syme Inc would be a subsidiary of Elivar Ltd resident in Kuwata. It would be a separate legal entity and its losses would be subject to the tax regime of Kuwata. This will save tax in Kuwata at only 18% as opposed to the 21% relief available under strategy A. However, it may be possible for the loss generated by the 'Frager' business to be carried back for relief in earlier years in Kuwata if strategy B is adopted.

(b) Strategy A – 'Frager' business operated via a permanent establishment

Maximum loss to be surrendered to Elivar Ltd

The tax suffered in Kuwata of £21,600 (£120,000 × 18%) can be offset against the corporation tax liability of Elivar Ltd up to a maximum of the UK tax on the overseas income. Accordingly, in order not to waste double tax relief, the UK tax on the overseas profits must be at least £21,600.

In determining the UK tax on the profits of Elivar Ltd, the company can choose to offset the qualifying charitable donations and the group relief in the most tax efficient manner. Accordingly, the qualifying charitable donations and the group relief will be deducted first from the UK profits, reducing them to zero. It should then be used to reduce the overseas profits to the amount that results in the UK corporation tax being equal to the tax suffered in Kuwata.

The overseas profits in respect of the permanent establishment should not be reduced below £102,857 (£21,600/21%).

The maximum loss that should be surrendered to Elivar Ltd is set out below.

	£
In respect of:	
UK profits less qualifying charitable donations £(90,000 – 2,000)	88,000
Overseas profits £(120,000 – 102,857)	17,143
Maximum loss to be surrendered to Elivar Ltd	105,143

(c) **Strategy B – 'Frager' business operated via a subsidiary**

Transfer pricing

The rate of corporation tax in Kuwata is lower than that in the UK. Accordingly, the total tax paid by the group will be reduced if more of the group's profits are generated in Kuwata. This could be achieved by increasing the prices charged by the subsidiary in Kuwata.

The transfer pricing rules will apply to transactions between Elivar Ltd and its subsidiary in Kuwata because Elivar Ltd controls the subsidiary. The exemption for small and medium sized enterprises is unlikely to be available, regardless of the size of the Loriod plc group, as there is no double tax treaty between the UK and Kuwata.

Any reduction in Elivar Ltd's profits caused by paying inflated prices to the subsidiary in Kuwata would be regarded as a potential tax advantage. The transfer pricing rules would counteract such an advantage by requiring Elivar Ltd to calculate its taxable profits as if it had been charged arm's length prices by its overseas subsidiary.

Elivar Ltd could approach HMRC for confirmation that its pricing arrangements with its overseas subsidiary are acceptable in order to remove uncertainty in this area.

ACCA Professional Paper P6 – Options Module
Advanced Taxation (UK)

Mock Examination 2

Question Paper	
Time allowed	*Reading and planning: 15 minutes* *Writing: 3 hours*
This paper is divided into two sections	
Section A	*BOTH questions are compulsory questions and MUST be attempted*
Section B	*TWO questions ONLY to be attempted*

During reading and planning time only the question paper may be annotated

DO NOT OPEN THIS PAPER UNTIL YOU ARE READY TO START UNDER EXAMINATION CONDITIONS

SECTION A: BOTH questions are compulsory and MUST be attempted

1 Flame plc group (ATAX 12/12)   63 mins

Your manager has had a meeting with Gordon, the Group Finance Director of the Flame plc group of companies. Flame plc is quoted on the UK Stock Exchange. An extract from the memorandum prepared by your manager after the meeting, together with an email from him detailing the tasks for you to perform, is set out below.

Extract from the memorandum prepared by your manager

Background

Flame plc is a UK resident company, which has annual taxable profits of more than £200,000. It owns the whole of the ordinary share capital of Inferno Ltd, Bon Ltd and six other companies. All of the companies in the Flame plc group are UK resident companies with a 31 March year end.

Flame plc – sale of Inferno Ltd

Flame plc purchased the whole of the ordinary share capital of Inferno Ltd on 1 March 2011 for £600,000. The value of Inferno Ltd has increased and Gordon has decided to sell the company. For the purposes of our work, we are to assume that the sale will take place on 1 January 2016. The budgeted taxable profits of Inferno Ltd for the nine months ending 31 December 2015 are £160,000.

The sale will be carried out in one of two ways:

(i)   A sale by Flame plc of the whole of the ordinary share capital of Inferno Ltd for £1 million; or

(ii)   A sale by Inferno Ltd of its trade and assets for their market value

Gordon needs to know the tax cost for the Flame plc group of each of these options to help him in his negotiations.

Inferno Ltd owns the following assets.

	Note	Cost	Current market value
		£	£
Equipment	1,3	100,000	60,000
Milling machine	2,3	95,000	80,000
Goodwill	4	Nil	530,000
Building – business premises	5	300,000	490,000

Notes

1   No item of equipment will be sold for more than cost.

2   The milling machine is an item of fixed plant and machinery that was purchased on 1 June 2012. Inferno Ltd claimed rollover relief in respect of the purchase of this machine to defer a chargeable gain of £8,500 made on 1 May 2011.

3   Capital allowances have been claimed in respect of the equipment and the milling machine. The tax written down value of the main pool of Inferno Ltd as at 1 April 2015 was zero. There have been no additions or disposals since that date.

4   The goodwill has been generated internally by Inferno Ltd since it began trading on 1 May 2006.

5   Inferno Ltd purchased the building from Flame plc on 15 March 2011 for its market value at that time of £300,000. Flame plc had purchased the building on 1 January 2007 for £240,000.

Flame plc – employee share scheme

Gordon is planning to introduce a share option scheme in order to reward the senior managers of Flame plc.

> **Bon Ltd – the grant of a lease**
>
> Part of the trading premises of Bon Ltd, a subsidiary of Flame plc, is surplus to requirements. Bon Ltd intends to grant a lease to an independent third-party company in respect of that part of its premises.
>
> **Bon Ltd – refund of corporation tax**
>
> Bon Ltd received a refund of corporation tax from HM Revenue and Customs on 1 June 2015. The company has not been able to identify any reason for this refund.

Email from your manager

> (a)   I want you to draft a report to the Group Finance Director that addresses the following:
>
> (i)   **Flame plc – sale of Inferno Ltd**
>
>   The tax cost of each of the two possible ways of carrying out the sale. Please note that I have already considered the availability of the substantial shareholding exemption and concluded that it will not be available in respect of the sale of Inferno Ltd because the Flame plc group is not a trading group.
>
>   The report should include concise explanations of matters where the calculations are not self-explanatory.
>
> (ii)   **Flame plc – employee share scheme**
>
>   - The tax advantages for the employees of introducing a Schedule 4 company share option plan (CSOP) as opposed to a non-tax advantaged share option scheme.
>
>   - Why a CSOP would be a suitable tax advantaged scheme for Gordon to choose.
>
>   - The restrictions within the CSOP rules in respect of the following:
>
>   – The number of share options that can be granted to each employee
>   – The price at which the shares can be sold to the employees
>
> (iii) **Bon Ltd – the grant of a lease**
>
>   The value added tax (VAT) implications for the lessee if Bon Ltd were to opt to tax the building prior to granting the lease.
>
> (b)   **Bon Ltd – refund of corporation tax**
>
> Prepare a summary of the actions that we should take and any matters of which Bon Ltd should be aware in respect of the refund of corporation tax.
>
> Tax manager

Required

(a)   Draft the report to the Group Finance Director requested in the email from your manager. The following marks are available.

    (i)   Flame plc – sale of Inferno Ltd

       Notes for part (a)(i)

       1   For guidance, approximately equal marks are available for calculations and explanations.

       2   The following indexation factors should be used, where necessary.

January 2007 to March 2011	0.153
January 2007 to January 2016	0.321 (assumed)
March 2011 to January 2016	0.146 (assumed)

                                                                                                    (15 marks)

    (ii)   Flame plc – employee share scheme   **(8 marks)**

    (iii) Bon Ltd – the grant of a lease   **(3 marks)**

Professional marks will be awarded in part (a) for the overall presentation of the report, the provision of relevant advice and the effectiveness with which the information is communicated. **(4 marks)**

(b)   Prepare the summary requested in the email from your manager. **(5 marks)**

                                                                (Total = 35 marks)

2 Dana (ATAX 12/12)

45 mins

Your manager has received a letter from Dana, a new client of your firm. Extracts from the letter and from an email from your manager are set out below.

Extract from the letter from Dana

Relief available in respect of a trading loss

I resigned from my job on 31 December 2012, having earned an annual salary of £40,000 for the previous three years. I spent the whole of 2013 planning my new business and began trading on 1 January 2014. The business was profitable initially but I made a loss in the year ended 30 September 2015.

The results of the business have been:

Period ended 30 September 2014 – a profit of £14,900.
Year ended 30 September 2015 – a loss of £30,000.

I own a number of rental properties that are let on long-term tenancies. On 1 February 2015, I sold one of these properties for £310,000. I paid £250,000 for this property on 1 December 2013.

My taxable property business profits in recent tax years have been:

	£
2011/12	13,000
2012/13	14,565
2013/14	26,890
2014/15	32,865
2015/16 (estimated)	43,465

Please let me know how much tax I can save by relieving my trading loss for the year ended 30 September 2015.

Transfer of a rental property to a trust on 1 September 2015

On 1 September 2015, I transferred a rental property worth £270,000 to a trust for the benefit of my brother's children. I assume that there will be no tax liabilities for me or the trustees in respect of this gift. I also transferred a rental property to a trust in December 2010 and I am sure that no tax was paid in respect of that gift. I have never made any other gifts apart from gifts of cash to members of my family; none of these gifts exceeded £2,000.

Email from your manager

Dana is unmarried and has no children. She was born in 1977 and is resident and domiciled in the UK.

I have just spoken to Dana and she has provided me with the following additional information.

- Dana received a bonus of £2,000 from her employer when she left her job in December 2012. The bonus was to thank her for all of the work she had done over the years.

- The results Dana has provided in respect of her unincorporated business have been adjusted for tax purposes but do not take account of expenditure she incurred during 2013. During that year, Dana spent £1,400 on petrol as she travelled around the UK visiting potential customers.

Dana had no income or capital gains in the tax years concerned other than those referred to in her letter and in the additional information set out above.

Work required:

Please prepare the following for me for my next meeting with Dana.

(a)   **Relief available in respect of the trading loss**

A reasoned explanation, with supporting calculations, of the most tax efficient manner in which Dana's trading loss can be relieved, together with a calculation of the total tax relief obtained by following the most tax efficient strategy. I want you to consider all of the ways in which Dana could relieve the loss with the exception of carry forward for relief in the future. You should assume that gift relief will be claimed in respect of the transfer of the rental property to the trust on 1 September 2015 when carrying out this work.

Your explanation should include:

- A brief summary of the other reliefs available for relieving the loss, together with your reasons for rejecting them
- The implications of the additional information provided by Dana

(b) **Transfer of the rental property to the trust on 1 September 2015**

    (i)   *Capital gains tax*

    An explanation as to whether or not gift relief is available in respect of the transfer of the rental property on 1 September 2015 and, on the assumption that it is available, the action required in order to submit a valid claim.

    (ii)   *Inheritance tax*

    In relation to Dana's gifts prior to 1 September 2015:

- A list of the precise information we need to request from Dana in order to enable us to determine whether the gifts to her family members were exempt and to calculate the inheritance tax due on the transfer to the trust on 1 September 2015
- An explanation of why the information is required

Tax manager

Required

Carry out the work required as requested in the email from your manager. The following marks are available.

(a) Relief available in respect of the trading loss.

In respect of part (a) of this question you should:

1   Ignore national insurance contributions.
2   Assume that the tax rates and allowances for the tax year 2014/15 apply to all years.   **(18 marks)**

(b) Transfer of the rental property to the trust on 1 September 2015.

    (i)   Capital gains tax   **(2 marks)**
    (ii)   Inheritance tax   **(5 marks)**

(Total = 25 marks)

SECTION B: TWO questions ONLY to be attempted

3 Banger Ltd and Candle Ltd (ATAX 12/12)   36 mins

Banger Ltd and Candle Ltd are two unrelated companies.

The management of Banger Ltd requires advice on the implications for one of the company's shareholders of the use of a motor car owned by the company and the proposed liquidation of the company.

The management of Candle Ltd has asked for a calculation of the company's corporation tax liability. Candle Ltd is a close investment-holding company.

(a) **Banger Ltd:**

- Banger Ltd is a UK resident trading company.
- Sixty-five per cent of the company's share capital is owned by its managing director, Katherine.
- The remaining shares are owned by a number of individuals who do not work for the company.
- None of the shares has been acquired under the Enterprise Management Investment scheme.

Motor car provided to minority shareholder throughout the year ended 31 March 2015:

- Banger Ltd paid £17,400 for the motor car, which had a list price when new of £22,900.
- The car has a petrol engine and has CO_2 emissions of 127 grams per kilometre.

Liquidation of Banger Ltd:

- It is intended that a liquidator will be appointed on 31 January 2016 to wind up the company.

Distributions of company assets to shareholders being considered by Banger Ltd:

- A total distribution of £280,000 in cash to the shareholders prior to 31 January 2016
- The distribution of a building with a market value of £720,000 to Katherine after 31 January 2016

Required

(i) Explain, with supporting calculations, the amount of the minority shareholder's taxable income in respect of the use of the motor car.   **(3 marks)**

(ii) Explain in detail the tax implications for Banger Ltd, the minority shareholders and Katherine of the distributions that the company is considering.   **(7 marks)**

(b) **Candle Ltd:**

- Is a UK resident close investment-holding company with no associated companies

The results of Candle Ltd for the year ended 31 March 2015:

	£
Interest receivable	41,100
Chargeable gains realised in the country of Sisaria, net of 19% Sisarian tax	15,390
Chargeable gains realised in the UK, excluding the sale of shares in Rockette plc	83,700
Fees charged by a financial institution in respect of an issue of loan stock	14,000
Interest payable on loan stock	52,900
General expenses of management	38,300

Sale of shares in Rockette plc on 1 January 2015:

- Candle Ltd purchased a 2.2% holding of the shares in Rockette plc for £31,400 in 2001.
- Piro plc acquired 100% of the ordinary share capital of Rockette plc on 1 January 2015.
- Candle Ltd received shares in Piro plc worth £147,100 and cash of £7,200 in exchange for its shares in Rockette plc.
- Piro plc's acquisition of Rockette plc was a commercial transaction and was not part of a scheme to avoid tax.
- The relevant indexation factor is 0.510.

Required

Calculate the corporation tax liability of Candle Ltd for the year ended 31 March 2015, giving explanations of your treatment of the disposal of the shares in Rockette plc and the rate of corporation tax payable. You should assume that Candle Ltd will claim all reliefs available to reduce its tax liability and you should state any further assumptions you consider necessary.

(10 marks)

(Total = 20 marks)

4 Ash (ATAX 12/12)   36 mins

Ash requires a calculation of his capital gains tax liability for the tax year 2014/15, together with advice in connection with entrepreneurs' relief, registration for the purposes of value added tax (VAT) and the payment of income tax.

Ash:

- Is resident in the UK

- Had taxable income of £29,000 in the tax year 2014/15

- Was the owner and managing director of Lava Ltd until 1 May 2014, when he resigned and sold the company

- Is a partner in the Vulcan Partnership

Ash – disposals of capital assets in the tax year 2014/15:

- The sale of the shares in Lava Ltd resulted in a capital gain of £235,000, which qualified for entrepreneurs' relief.

- Ash assigned a 37-year lease on a property for £110,000 on 1 May 2014.

- Ash sold two acres of land on 1 October 2014 for £30,000.

- Ash sold quoted shares and made a capital loss of £17,400 on 1 November 2014.

The lease:

- The lease was previously assigned to Ash for £31,800 when it had 46 years remaining.
- The property has always been used by Lava Ltd for trading purposes.
- Lava Ltd paid Ash rent, equivalent to 40% of the market rate, in respect of the use of the property.

The sale of the two acres of land:

- Ash purchased eight acres of land for £27,400 on 1 June 2006.
- Ash sold six acres of the land for £42,000 on 1 August 2009.
- The remaining two acres of land were worth £18,000 on 1 August 2009.

Vulcan Partnership (Vulcan):

- Has a 31 March year end.
- Has monthly turnover of:

Standard-rated supplies	£400
Exempt supplies	£200
Zero-rated supplies	£5,600

- Its turnover is expected to increase slightly in 2016.

- None of its customers is registered for the purposes of VAT.

- Ash expects to receive less profit from Vulcan for the tax year 2015/16 than he did in 2014/15.

Required

(a) (i) State the conditions that must be satisfied for Ash's assignment of the lease to be an associated disposal for the purposes of entrepreneurs' relief. **(3 marks)**

(ii) Calculate Ash's capital gains tax liability for the tax year 2014/15 on the assumption that the assignment of the lease does qualify as an associated disposal and that entrepreneurs' relief will be claimed where possible.

Note. The following lease percentages should be used, where necessary.

37 years 93.497
46 years 98.490 **(7 marks)**

(b) Discuss in detail whether the Vulcan Partnership may be required to register for value added tax (VAT) and the advantages and disadvantages for the business of registration. **(7 marks)**

(c) Set out the matters that Ash should consider when deciding whether or not to make a claim to reduce the payment on account of income tax due on 31 January 2016. **(3 marks)**

(Total = 20 marks)

5 Cuthbert (ATAX 12/12) **36 mins**

Cuthbert requires advice on the tax implications of the payment of capital gains tax by instalments and an error he has made in an income tax return. He has also requested calculations in respect of the inheritance tax payable on the death of his uncle, Pugh.

Cuthbert:

- Is resident and domiciled in the UK
- Intends to give a building to his brother on 1 March 2016
- Made an error in his income tax return for the tax year 2013/14

Cuthbert – proposed gift of a building to his brother on 1 March 2016:

- The building is currently let to long-term tenants and has a market value of £460,000.

Cuthbert – error in his income tax return for the tax year 2013/14:

- HM Revenue and Customs have written to Cuthbert in respect of his income tax return.
- HM Revenue and Customs are claiming that Cuthbert has under-declared his UK property income.

Pugh – valuation of assets owned at death on 1 February 2015:

	£
Home in the UK	720,000
Vintage motor cars located in the country of Camberia	490,000
Quoted shares (holdings of less than 1%) registered in Camberia	330,000
Cash held in bank accounts in the UK	45,000

Pugh – UK inheritance tax liability:

- Was calculated on the basis that Pugh was domiciled in the country of Camberia and that he had made no lifetime gifts
- Was paid on time

Pugh – information discovered after the payment of the UK inheritance tax:

- Pugh had been domiciled in the UK since 1 January 2005.
- Pugh had made a gift of UK quoted shares (all holdings of less than 1%) to a trust on 10 June 2008.
- The quoted shares were worth £322,400 and Pugh paid the UK inheritance tax due.

The system of inheritance tax in the country of Camberia:

- There is no nil rate band and the rate of inheritance tax is 25%.
- Inheritance tax is only charged on the value of land and buildings and quoted shares owned at the time of death and located in Camberia.
- There is no double tax treaty between the UK and Camberia.

Required

(a)   Explain whether or not the capital gains tax due on the proposed gift of the building could be paid by instalments and the matters that Cuthbert would need to be aware of in respect of this method of payment.

(6 marks)

(b)   Explain how any penalty would be calculated if it is determined that Cuthbert made a careless error when completing his 2013/14 tax return. **(4 marks)**

(c)   Calculate the UK inheritance tax liability in respect of Pugh's estate following the discovery of the additional information, together with the interest on overdue tax that will be payable if the inheritance tax is paid on 1 January 2016. **(10 marks)**

(Total = 20 marks)

Answers

DO NOT TURN THIS PAGE UNTIL YOU HAVE
COMPLETED THE MOCK EXAM

A plan of attack

What's the worst thing you could be doing right now if this was the actual exam paper? Wondering how to celebrate the end of the exam in about three hours time? Panicking, flapping and generally getting in a right old state?

Well, they're all pretty bad, so turn back to the paper and let's sort out a **plan of attack**!

First things first

You have 15 minutes of reading time. Make sure you spend it wisely, looking through the paper in detail working out which optional questions to do and the order in which to attack the questions. You've got **two options**. Option 1 is the option recommended by BPP.

Option 1 (if you're thinking 'Help!')

If you're a bit worried about the paper, do the questions in the order of how well you think you can answer them. If you find the questions in Section B less daunting than the compulsory questions in Section A start with Section B. Remember you only need to do two of the three questions in Section B; you may find it easier if you start by deciding which question you will not do and put a line through it.

- **Question 3** deals with close companies, liquidations and overseas aspects of corporation tax.
- **Question 4** is about entrepreneurs' relief, leases and part disposals for CGT, VAT registration and income tax payments on account.
- **Question 5** concerns payment of CGT, income tax errors and inheritance tax.

Do not spend longer than the allocated time on Section B. When you've spent the allocated time on **two** of the three questions in Section B turn to the longer questions in Section A. Read these questions through thoroughly before you launch into them. Once you start make sure you allocate your time to the parts within the questions according to the marks available and that, where possible, you attempt the easy marks first.

Lastly, what you mustn't forget is that you have to **answer both questions in Section A and TWO in Section B**.

Option 2 (if you're thinking 'It's a doddle')

It never pays to be overconfident but if you're not quaking in your shoes about the exam then **turn straight to the compulsory questions** in Section A.

Once you've done these questions, move to Section B.

- The question you attempt first really depends on what you are most confident at.
- You then have to select one of the two remaining questions. If you are undecided look at the requirements. It maybe easier to obtain more marks if these are broken down into several smaller parts.

No matter how many times we remind you....

Always, always **allocate your time** according to the marks for the question in total and then according to the parts of the question. And **always, always follow the requirements** exactly.

You've got spare time at the end of the exam.....?

If you have allocated your time properly then you **shouldn't have time on your hands** at the end of the exam. But if you find yourself with five or ten minutes to spare, check over your work to make sure that you have answered all the requirements of the questions and all parts of all requirements.

Forget about it!

And don't worry if you found the paper difficult. More than likely other candidates will too. If this were the real thing you would need to **forget** the exam the minute you leave the exam hall and **think about the next one**. Or, if it's the last one, **celebrate**!

1 Flame plc group (ATAX 12/12)

Text references. Chargeable gains for companies are covered in Chapter 21 and the degrouping charge in Chapter 26. Capital allowances are dealt with in Chapter 7 and the calculation of taxable total profits in Chapter 20. Corporation tax liability is in Chapter 22. Company share option plans are covered in Chapter 5. VAT on land and buildings will be found in Chapter 29. Ethics is covered in Chapter 30, which also has a section on approaching questions on the impact of taxes.

Top tips. There was a key piece of information in the email from the manager concerning the substantial shareholding exemption. This emphasises the need to read the whole question before starting your answer – don't expect all the information you need to be in one place in the question.

Easy marks. The capital allowances and gains calculations in section (a) were straightforward. The ethical matters in section (b) should have been well-known.

Examiner's comments. Answers to part (a)(i) varied in quality quite considerably. There were many candidates who clearly understood the two alternatives and the related tax implications whilst weaker candidates were unsure of the precise nature of the transactions and the related tax implications, such that they produced confused answers. A small minority of candidates treated the companies as individuals.

The sale of Inferno Ltd had two main implications; a chargeable gain on the sale of the shares and a degrouping charge. The chargeable gain was worth one mark. However, it took some candidates half a page or more to calculate and write about this gain in order to score that mark. This was most likely because it was the first thing they did in the exam and there were still almost three hours to go, such that the pressure was not yet on. Candidates must approach every mark in the exam in the same way and get on with it. There is no time to dither when there is so much to do.

Frustratingly, it was not uncommon for some candidates to only score half a mark for this gain because they based the indexation allowance on the unindexed gain rather than the cost. This may have been a lack of concentration rather than a lack of knowledge but the half mark was still lost.

It was stated in the question that the substantial shareholding exemption was not available. Many candidates simply included a statement to that effect in their report and earned a mark. However, a small minority of candidates wasted time writing at length about the exemption rather than getting on with the question.

The degrouping charge was done well on the whole. Those candidates who did not do so well were divided into two groups. The first group missed the degrouping charge altogether. This was perhaps due to a lack of knowledge but, in view of the fact that degrouping charges are examined regularly, was more likely due to a lack of thought. Candidates must give themselves time in the exam to think about issues before they start writing; it is difficult to successfully think of one issue whilst writing about a different one.

The second group of candidates knew that there would be a degrouping charge somewhere in the answer and earned most of the marks available for saying why and for calculating it. However, they did not know which of the two possible transactions would give rise to the charge and either put it into the wrong section of the report or put it into both sections. This was not particularly costly, but would have been in a different question which was only concerned with one of these two transactions. Candidates must know their stuff; degrouping charges only occur on the sale of a company, ie on the sale of shares, and not on the sale of assets.

The sale by Inferno Ltd of its trade and assets was not done particularly well. A small minority of candidates treated the disposal as the disposal of a single asset by adding up all of the proceeds and then deducting the total cost. Even those candidates who knew that each asset had to be handled separately failed to apply basic rules concerning capital allowances and chargeable gains.

Capital allowances were handled particularly poorly with very few candidates identifying that where the tax written down value is zero, any sale of machinery must result in a balancing charge. In addition, most candidates calculated capital losses on the sale of the machinery, thus failing to recognise that, due to the claiming of capital allowances, no capital losses would be available. Finally, only a minority of candidates identified that the deferred gain of £8,500 would crystallise on the sale of the milling machine; most candidates thought, incorrectly, that the gain would be deducted from the asset's base cost. A final thought on part (a) (i) relates to the narrative provided by candidates in their reports. The question required candidates to include concise explanations of matters where the calculations were not self-explanatory. On the whole this was done well. Most candidates kept their answers brief and very few fell into trap of writing down everything they knew about the broad technical areas relating to the question.

Part (a) (ii) concerned a Schedule 4 company share option plan. This was a straightforward question that tested candidates' knowledge of a particular share scheme. In order to do well, candidates needed to slow down for a moment and make sure that they were about to write about the correct scheme. They then needed to ensure that they addressed all of the issues set out in the question. The majority of candidates did both of these things and therefore scored well.

In part (b), candidates needed to realise that this refund had been received some time ago and that, if it had been paid in error, it had to be returned to HM Revenue and Customs. Most candidates recognised this situation and were able to list the actions that the firm needed to take and the matters that needed to be drawn to the attention of Bon Ltd.

Marking scheme

				Marks
(a)	(i)	*Sale of share capital*		
		Calculations		
		Degrouping charge	2	
		Other matters	1½	
		Narrative – one mark for each relevant point	6	
		Sale of trade and assets		
		Calculations		
		Equipment and milling machine	2	
		Goodwill	½	
		Premises	1½	
		Liability	½	
		Narrative – one mark for each relevant point	4	
		Max		15
	(ii)	*Advantages*		
		Timing	2½	
		Taxes	3½	
		Suitability of CSOP	1	
		Restrictions	2	
		Max		8
	(iii)	Nature of supply	1	
		Recoverable input tax	2	
				3
		Format and presentation	1	
		Analysis	2	
		Quality of calculations and explanations	1	
				4
(b)		The need to repay the tax	3	
		Ceasing to act	3	
		Max		5
				35

(a)   (i)   **Flame plc – sale of Inferno Ltd**

Sale by Flame plc of the whole of the ordinary share capital of Inferno Ltd for £1 million

A sale of the share capital will result in a liability to corporation tax calculated as follows:

	£	£
Proceeds on sale of shares		1,000,000
Degrouping charge – deemed sale proceeds		
Market value of the premises at 15 March 2011	300,000	
Less: cost of premises 1 January 2007	(240,000)	
indexation allowance £240,000 × 0.153	(36,720)	
		23,280
Total sale proceeds		1,023,280
Less: cost of shares in Inferno Ltd 1 March 2011		(600,000)
indexation allowance £600,000 × 0.146		(87,600)
Chargeable gain		335,680
Corporation tax £335,680 @ 21%		70,493

Due to the unavailability of the substantial shareholding exemption, the sale of Inferno Ltd will result in a gain chargeable to corporation tax.

A degrouping charge will arise in respect of the building because it was transferred at no gain, no loss (Flame plc and Inferno Ltd are members of a capital gains group) within the six years prior to the sale of Inferno Ltd. Inferno Ltd will be regarded as having sold the building at the time of the no gain, no loss transfer for its market value at that time. Inferno Ltd's base cost in the building, resulting from the no gain, no loss transfer, is the original cost to Flame plc plus indexation allowance up to 15 March 2011, the date Inferno Ltd purchased the building. The degrouping charge will increase the sales proceeds on the disposal of Inferno Ltd.

The corporation tax limits of Flame plc for the year ending 31 March 2016 will be divided by nine (Flame plc and eight subsidiaries), so the upper limit will be (£1,500,000 ÷ 9) = £166,667. Accordingly, because the annual taxable profits of Flame plc exceed £200,000, the chargeable gain will be taxed at the main rate of corporation tax.

Sale by Inferno Ltd of its trade and assets for their market value

A sale of the trade and assets will result in a liability to corporation tax calculated as follows:

	£	£
Balancing charge on sale of equipment and		
milling machine £([60,000 + 80,000] – 0)		140,000
Profit on sale of goodwill £(530,000 – 0)		530,000
Additional trading profits		670,000
Crystallisation of gain deferred on milling machine		8,500
Chargeable gain on sale of premises		

	£	£	
Proceeds		490,000	
Cost	240,000		
Indexation allowance to March 2011			
£240,000 × 0.153	36,720		
Indexed cost: no gain/no loss transfer		(276,720)	
Indexation allowance to January 2016			
£276,720 × 0.146		(40,401)	
			172,879
Taxable profits			851,379
Corporation tax £851,379 @ 21%			178,790

The excess of the sales proceeds (market value) of the equipment and the milling machine over the balance on the main pool will result in a taxable balancing charge.

BPP
LEARNING MEDIA

The goodwill is a trading asset so the profit on its sale will be additional trading income.

When a rollover relief claim has been made in respect of the purchase of a depreciating asset, as in the case of the milling machine, the deferred gain crystallises on the sale of that replacement asset.

The equipment and the milling machine are to be sold for less than cost. However, no capital loss will arise because capital allowances have been claimed.

As noted above, Inferno Ltd's base cost in the building is the original price paid by Flame plc plus indexation allowance up to March 2011.

Inferno Ltd will cease trading when it sells its business on 1 January 2016. This will bring about the end of an accounting period. The corporation tax limits will be divided by nine (in respect of the number of associates) and multiplied by 9/12 in respect of the nine-month accounting period, so the upper limit will be £(1,500,000 ÷ 9 × 9/12) = £125,000. Accordingly, because the taxable profits of Inferno Ltd for the nine-month period are expected to be £160,000, the trading income and chargeable gains arising on the sale of the business will be taxed at the main rate of corporation tax.

(ii) **Flame plc – employee share scheme**

The tax advantages of a Schedule 4 company share option plan (CSOP) over a non-tax advantaged scheme

- With a CSOP, there would be no income tax or national insurance contributions liability on the grant or exercise of the option, provided it is exercised between three and ten years after it is granted. Under a non-tax advantaged scheme, there would be a liability when the option is exercised.

- With a CSOP, the whole of the employee's profit on the shares will be subject to capital gains tax when the shares are sold. Under a non-tax advantaged scheme, the excess of the market value of the shares at the time the option is exercised over the amount paid by the employee for the shares will be taxable as specific employment income and so subject to income tax and national insurance contributions in the year the option is exercised; any subsequent increase in the value of the shares will be subject to capital gains tax when the shares are sold.

    The advantages of a charge to capital gains tax over charges to income tax and national insurance contributions are the availability of the annual exempt amount and the lower tax rates.

Suitability of a CSOP

Gordon wants to use the scheme to reward the company's senior managers as opposed to all of the company's staff. Accordingly, he needs to use a scheme that allows him to choose which employees are able to join. The two tax advantaged schemes that allow this are the CSOP and the enterprise management incentive scheme.

Restrictions

- The value of shares in respect of which an employee holds options cannot exceed £30,000.

- The exercise price of the shares must not be less than the value of the shares at the time of the grant of the option.

(iii) **Bon Ltd – the grant of a lease**

If Bon Ltd were to opt to tax the building, the proposed granting of the lease would be a standard rated supply rather than an exempt supply, so Bon Ltd would have to charge value added tax (VAT) on the rent. A lessee that was registered for VAT and making wholly taxable supplies would be able to recover all of the VAT charged. However, some or all of the VAT would be a cost for a lessee that was not registered or one that was partially exempt and not within the *de minimis* limits.

(b) **Refund of corporation tax**

We should review the tax affairs of Bon Ltd in order to identify the reason for the tax refund.

If, as would appear likely, it is an error on the part of HM Revenue and Customs (HMRC), we should inform Bon Ltd that it should be repaid immediately. Failure to return the money in these circumstances may be a civil and/or criminal offence.

We should advise Bon Ltd to disclose the matter to HMRC immediately in order to minimise any interest and penalties that might otherwise become payable.

In addition, unless the money is returned, we would have to consider ceasing to act as advisers to Bon Ltd. In these circumstances, we are required to notify the tax authorities that we no longer act for the company, although we would not provide them with any reason for our action. We should also consider whether or not we are required to make a report under the money laundering rules.

2 Dana (ATAX 12/12)

Text references. Trading losses for individuals are covered in Chapter 8 and the income tax computation in Chapter 1. Employment income generally is covered in Chapter 4 and terminal bonuses are dealt with in Chapter 5. Pre-trading expenditure and the basis of assessment for trading profits are covered in Chapter 6. Gift relief for capital gains tax is one of the topics in Chapter 13. Inheritance tax on lifetime transfers will be found in Chapter 16.

Top tips. When thinking about the use of trade loss relief, the three key aspects are the rate of relief, the timing of the relief and the loss of personal allowances.

Easy marks. Nearly all of the marks in this question were for knowledge from F6. You should have been able to gain easy marks for working out the trading profit for the period to 30 September 2014 and the opening years assessments in part (a). The technical information in part (b) was not difficult but you needed to keep your answer succinct and to the points required.

Examiner's comments. In part (a), the first task was to determine the trading profit/loss for each of the tax years. This required candidates to deduct the pre-trading expenditure from the profit of the first trading period and then to apply the opening years rules. They also needed to know that losses are only recognised once in the opening years. The treatment of the pre-trading expenditure was done well by only a minority of candidates. Other candidates either missed it out altogether or deducted it from the taxable profit for the tax year 2013/14 rather than the profit of the first trading period. The opening year rules and the treatment of the loss within those rules were done well by the majority of candidates. This was a significant improvement over the performance in recent exams.

Once the profits and losses had been determined, candidates needed to consider the reliefs available in respect of the loss. There were two aspects to this. First, candidates needed to know all of the available reliefs for the losses. This was done very well by the vast majority of candidates.

Secondly, candidates needed to compare the different reliefs and then calculate the total tax relief obtained by the most efficient strategy. Performance of this second task was mixed with some candidates calmly and efficiently calculating the tax due before and after claiming relief in order to determine the tax saving, whilst others wrote about how to do it in general terms without actually doing it. This is perhaps a confidence issue; candidates should ensure that they have practised as many questions as possible prior to sitting the exam and, once in the exam, should have the self-belief to address the figures and come up with specific advice.

Part (b)(i) concerned the availability of gift relief on the transfer of a rental property to a trust and was not done particularly well. The issue here was that gift relief would be available because the transfer was immediately subject to inheritance tax. This is true regardless of the nature of the asset, such that those candidates who focussed on whether or not the property was a business asset had missed the point. This was not too great a problem as there were only two marks available. However, a minority of candidates made things worse by ignoring the fact that this question part needed to be answered in approximately 3.5 minutes and wrote about gift relief at length, thus wasting time.

Part (b)(ii) concerned Dana's inheritance tax position. Those candidates who made a genuine attempt to answer the question here did well. The technical issues in this question were:

- The transfer of the rental property in December 2010 was a chargeable lifetime transfer, such that we needed a value for the property in order to determine the nil band available for the transfer in September 2015.

- The gifts of cash to family members were potentially exempt transfers, such that they would not affect the nil band whilst Dana is alive.

- The cash gifts may be exempt depending on the amount given, the date of the gift and the reason for the gift. Exempt gifts would not use Dana's annual exemptions, such that they may be available for relief against the transfer to the trust.

This question was different from past inheritance tax questions and required some thought before it could be answered. It was not technically difficult but required candidates to address the specific question; the minority of candidates who wrote about inheritance tax in general terms and ignored the specifics of the question did poorly, as did those who tried to calculate inheritance tax liabilities. Some candidates let themselves down by writing that they needed 'the details of the gifts' without specifying what those details were and why they needed them.

Marking scheme

					Marks
(a)	Identification of years in which relief available		4		
	Employment income		1		
	Trading income		4		
	Income taxable at the higher rate		4		
	Capital gains taxable at the higher rate		1½		
	Tax savings		5		
	Notes in respect of additional information		2		
		Max			18
(b)	(i) Capital gains tax				2
	(ii) *Inheritance tax*				
	Gift in December 2010		1½		
	Gifts to family members				
	Information required		1½		
	Relevance of information		3		
		Max			5
					25

(a) Relief available in respect of trading loss

A trading loss for tax purposes of £22,500 (W2) has arisen in the tax year 2015/16.

It can be relieved against Dana's total general income of 2015/16, the year of the loss, and/or 2014/15.

Alternatively, because the loss has arisen in one of the first four tax years of trading, it can be relieved against Dana's total general income of the three years prior to the year of the loss starting with the earliest year, ie 2012/13.

The income taxable at the higher rate in each of the tax years is set out below.

	2012/13	2013/14	2014/15	2015/16
	£	£	£	£
Employment income (W1)	32,000	0	0	0
Trading income (W2)	0	4,500	6,000	0
Property business income	14,565	26,890	32,865	43,465
Less: personal allowance	(10,000)	(10,000)	(10,000)	(10,000)
Taxable income	36,565	21,390	28,865	33,465
Less: basic rate band	(31,865)	(31,865)	(31,865)	(31,865)
Income taxable at higher rate/(basic rate band remaining)	4,700	(10,475)	(3,000)	1,600

Taxable gain: £([310,000 – 250,000] – 11,000)	49,000
Gains taxable at the higher rate	46,000

The claims against general income are 'all or nothing' claims. This means that the trading loss will be offset in full in one of 2012/13 or 2014/15 or 2015/16, depending on which relief is claimed. Because an early years trading loss relief claim would relieve the loss in full in 2012/13, it is not possible to relieve the loss in 2013/14.

The year with the most income taxable at the higher rate is 2012/13. Relieving the loss of £22,500 in that year would save income tax as follows:

	£
£4,700 × 40%	1,880
£(22,500 – 4,700) = £17,800 × 20%	3,560
Tax saving	5,440

Relieving the loss in 2015/16 would clearly save less tax, as there is less income taxable at the higher rate in that year than there is in 2012/13.

There is no income taxable at the higher rate in 2014/15 but there is a capital gain. Relieving the loss against the general income in the basic rate band would allow an equivalent amount of the capital gain to be taxed in the basic rate band rather than the higher rate band.

Accordingly, relieving the loss in 2014/15 would save tax as follows:

	£
Income tax	
£22,500 × 20%	4,500
Capital gains tax	
£22,500 × (28% – 18%)	2,250
Tax saving	6,750

The most beneficial claim is to relieve the loss in 2014/15 in order to save tax of £6,750.

Notes in respect of the additional information provided by Dana

- The bonus is in respect of work carried out by Dana for her employer. Accordingly, it is taxable in full in the year of receipt.

- The cost of travelling around the UK in 2013 would have been allowable had it been incurred after Dana began to trade. Accordingly, because it was incurred in the seven years prior to commencing to trade, it is treated as if it had been incurred on the first day of trading.

Workings

1   *Employment income in 2012/13*

	£
Salary for nine months £40,000 × 9/12	30,000
Bonus	2,000
	32,000

2   *Trading income*

	£
2013/14 (1 January 2014 to 5 April 2014)	
£13,500 (W3) × 3/9	4,500
2014/15 (1 January 2014 to 31 December 2014)	
£13,500 – 7,500 (£30,000 × 3/12)	6,000
2015/16 (Year ended 30 September 2015)	
Loss £(30,000 – 7,500)	(22,500)

The trading loss of £7,500 deducted in arriving at the taxable profit for the tax year 2014/15 is excluded from the loss available for relief in respect of the tax year 2015/16.

3   *Trading profit for the nine months ended 30 September 2014*

	£
Original figure	14,900
Less: pre-trading expenditure	(1,400)
	13,500

(b)   **Transfer of the rental property to the trust on 1 September 2015**

(i)   *Capital gains tax*

Dana can claim gift relief in respect of the transfer of the property to the trustees because a lifetime transfer to any trust is a chargeable lifetime transfer for inheritance tax. The election must be signed by Dana and submitted by 5 April 2020 (ie four years after the end of the tax year in which the gift was made).

(ii)   *Inheritance tax*

Information required in respect of the transfer to the trust in December 2010

- The value of the property at the time of the gift: the gift in December 2010 is within the seven-year period prior to the gift on 1 September 2015, and so will reduce the nil rate band available for the latter gift.

Information required in respect of the gifts to family members

- Date, value, recipient and occasion of each gift: this information is required in order to determine whether the gifts to family members are exempt or not. This will affect the annual exemptions available in respect of each of the gifts to the trusts

In addition to the annual exemption, the following lifetime gifts are exempt:

- Gifts of less than £250 in total to any individual in a tax year
- Gifts of no more than £1,000, made on the occasion of a marriage or civil partnership
- Normal (regular) gifts made out of income that do not affect Dana's standard of living

3 Banger Ltd and Candle Ltd (ATAX 12/12)

Text references. Close companies and close investment-holding companies are covered in Chapter 25. Liquidations are dealt with in Chapter 23. Chargeable gains for companies is the topic of Chapter 21 and overseas aspects are covered in Chapter 27.

Top tips. In part (a)(ii), it was important that you dealt with the tax implications for the company and then for the shareholders (which include Katherine who will receive both cash and the building).

Easy marks. The treatment of close companies is often examined and there should have been easy marks on the use of the motor car in part (a)(i). The double taxation relief in part (b) was straightforward.

Examiner's comments. Part (a)(i) required candidates to explain the taxable income arising out of the use by a minority shareholder of a car owned by the company. Almost all candidates were able to calculate the benefit in respect of the use of the car but not all of them realised that this would be taxed as a distribution rather than employment income. Many of those who knew this point still failed to earn full marks because they did not state the reasons for this treatment; those reasons being that the company is a close company and that the individual is not an employee.

Part (a)(ii) concerned the treatment of company distributions before and after the appointment of a liquidator. Performance in this part of the question was mixed. Those candidates who did not do well either did not know the rules or were not careful enough in addressing the requirements. A lack of knowledge of the rules was unfortunate and not something that could easily be rectified in the exam room. Failure to address the requirements carefully was a greater shame as potentially easy marks were lost. The requirement asked for the tax implications for 'Banger Ltd, the minority shareholders and Katherine'. Most candidates dealt with the minority shareholders and Katherine but many omitted the implications for Banger Ltd. Candidates should always read the requirement carefully and identify all of the tasks. It would have been helpful then to use sub-headings for each of the three aspects of the requirement to ensure that all of the aspects of the requirement were addressed.

Part (b) required candidates to calculate the corporation tax liability of Candle Ltd. On the whole, this part was done quite well by many candidates.

The two more difficult areas of this part of the question concerned loan relationships and a share for share disposal. The loan relationships issue was not done well. The vast majority of candidates failed to apply the basic rules such that they did not offset the amounts in order to arrive at a deficit on non-trading loan relationships. This was not a difficult or obscure matter; it simply felt as though candidates were not giving themselves the time to think before answering the question.

The share for share disposal was identified by the vast majority of candidates who went on to point out that no chargeable gain would arise in respect of the shares. There was then a further mark for recognising that there would also be no gain in respect of the cash received as it amounted to less than 5% of the total consideration received. This point was picked up by only a small number of candidates.

Marking scheme

				Marks
(a)	(i)	Explanation	2	
		Calculations	1½	
		Max		3
	(ii)	*Banger Ltd*	2½	
		Shareholders	1½	
		Katherine		
		Capital gain	1½	
		Taxation	2½	
		Max		7

(b) *Taxable total profits*

Loan relationships	3½
Chargeable gains	1½
Sale of shares in Rockette plc	½
Management expenses	½
Corporation tax liability	
Corporation tax	½
Double taxation relief	1
Explanations	4
Max	10
	20

(a) **Banger Ltd**

(i) **Minority shareholder's taxable income in respect of the use of the motor car**

The minority shareholder is not employed by Banger Ltd. Accordingly, because Banger Ltd is a close company (it is controlled by Katherine), the use of the motor car will be treated as a distribution. The distribution will equal the amount that would have been taxable as employment income in respect of the motor car:

Amount by which CO_2 emissions exceed base level: (125 (rounded down) − 95) = 30 ÷ 5 = 6

Add to 12% = 18%.

The car benefit is therefore £22,900 (list price) × 18% = £4,122.

The taxable income will be the distribution multiplied by 100/90, ie £4,122 × 100/90 = £4,580.

(ii) **The tax implications of the distributions being considered**

Banger Ltd

The distribution of cash will be a normal dividend with no tax implications for Banger Ltd.

The distribution of the building is a dividend in specie and therefore a deemed disposal of the building by Banger Ltd at market value. This will result in a chargeable gain or allowable loss equal to the market value of the building less its cost. Indexation allowance will be deducted from any chargeable gain arising.

The shareholders

- The distribution of cash to all the shareholders

  The distribution of cash is to be made prior to the appointment of the liquidator and will therefore be taxed as a normal dividend. It will be grossed up at 100/90 and subject to income tax at 10%, 32.5% and 37.5%, depending on the income tax position of the individual shareholders. A 10% tax credit will be available.

- The distribution of the building to Katherine

  The distribution is to be made after the appointment of the liquidator and will therefore be taxed as a capital receipt in relation to Katherine's shares. The market value of the building will be treated as the sales proceeds of Katherine's shares in Banger Ltd from which the base cost (or part of the base cost if there are to be further distributions to Katherine) will be deducted in order to calculate the capital gain.

  The gain will be taxable at 18% and/or 28% depending on Katherine's tax position or, alternatively, at 10% where entrepreneurs' relief is available. Banger Ltd is a trading company. Accordingly, entrepreneurs' relief will be available, provided that Katherine has owned at least 5% of the ordinary share capital and can exercise at least 5% of the voting rights in the company by virtue of that holding of shares, and has been an officer or employee of Banger Ltd. Both these conditions must have been satisfied throughout the period of one year ending with the date of disposal (ie the date of the distribution).

(b) **Candle Ltd – Corporation tax liability for the year ended 31 March 2015**

	Total £	UK £	Non-UK £
Chargeable gain realised in Sisaria			
£15,390 × 100/81	19,000		19,000
Chargeable gains realised in the UK	83,700	83,700	
Sale of shares in Rockette plc (N1)	0	0	
	102,700	83,700	19,000
Less deficit on non-trading loan			
relationship (W1)	(25,800)	(25,800)	
general expenses of			
management	(38,300)	(38,300)	
Taxable total profits	38,600	19,600	19,000
Corporation tax @ 21% (N2)	8,106	4,116	3,990
Less double taxation relief (W2)	(3,610)		(3,610)
	4,496	4,116	380

Notes

1   *Disposal of shares in Rockette plc*

The acquisition of the shares in Rockette plc by Piro plc was a qualifying 'paper for paper' takeover because Piro plc acquired more than 25% of Rockette plc and the acquisition was a commercial transaction that did not have the avoidance of tax as one of its main purposes. Accordingly, no gain arose in respect of the shares in Piro plc received by Candle Ltd.

In addition, no gain arose in respect of the cash received because the cash represented less than 5% of the value of the total consideration received:

	£
Value of shares received in Piro plc	147,100
Cash received	7,200
Total value received	154,300

The cash received is $\dfrac{7,200}{154,300} \times 100 = 4.67\%$ of the total consideration.

2   *Rate of corporation tax*

Candle Ltd is a close investment-holding company and so pays corporation tax at the main rate of 21%.

Workings

1   *Deficit on non-trading loan relationship*

	£
Interest receivable	41,100
Less: interest payable	(52,900)
fees charged by financial institution	(14,000)
Net deficit	(25,800)

It has been assumed that the company has chosen to offset the deficit against its current period profits.

2   *Double taxation relief*

Lower of:

UK tax	£3,990
Overseas tax £(19,000 – 15,390)	£3,610
ie £3,610	

4 Ash (ATAX 12/12)

Text references. Entrepreneurs' relief is covered in Chapter 13. Leases are dealt with in Chapter 14 and part disposals in Chapter 11. VAT registration is covered in Chapter 28. Payments on account are covered in Chapter 15.

Top tips. Although P6 is not primarily a computational exam, it is important to set out the computations you do produce in a way that is easy for marking. Look at the layout of the division of gains between those on which entrepreneurs' relief can be claimed and those on which it could not be claimed.

Easy marks. There were some easy marks in part (a) for basic capital gains computations. Even if you did not know the detail of the rules about leases, you could have guessed how to deal with the cost from the lease percentages given in the question. There were also some easy marks for explaining VAT registration – remember that the limits are in the Tax Tables.

Examiner's comments. Part (a)(i) required a statement of the conditions necessary for the disposal of an asset to be an associated disposal for the purposes of entrepreneurs' relief and was not done well. This is not an area of the syllabus that one would expect to see examined regularly and many candidates will have known immediately on reading the requirement that they did not know the answer. However, the sensible approach would then have been to write a very brief answer with some sensible comments on entrepreneurs' relief. It was pretty likely that this would then score one of the three marks available.

Part (a) (ii) was more straightforward and required candidates to calculate a capital gains tax liability. In order to do so, candidates had to know how to calculate a gain on the assignment of a lease and on the disposal of a remaining piece of land following an earlier part disposal. Entrepreneurs' relief was available in respect of some of the gains and there was also a capital loss and the annual exempt amount that needed to be offset correctly.

In general this question was done well by many candidates. There was no problem in deciding what needed to be done, so those candidates who did poorly simply did not have sufficient knowledge of the rules.

Part (b) concerned registration for the purposes of VAT. The majority of the question was done very well including, in particular, the advantages and disadvantages of registering for VAT. However, some candidates' answers lacked precision when it came to the circumstances where compulsory registration is required in that taxable supplies were not clearly defined and/or the 12-month period was not clearly stated. Other candidates wasted time by writing far too much on the recovery of input tax. The one area where performance was not good was the exceptions to the need to register, which were only referred to by a very small number of candidates.

The final part of the question concerned the matters to consider when making a claim to reduce a payment on account of income tax. This was an area that candidates would have been familiar with but it approached it from a slightly unusual angle: it was not done well. Candidates needed to use their common sense as much as anything else here and to recognise that the claim would need to be made before the end of the tax year. This in turn meant that the tax liability would need to be estimated and that interest would be payable if the final liability turned out to be more than the estimated liability. Making these two points would have scored two of the three marks available for this part of the question.

Marking scheme

				Marks
(a)	(i)	Conditions – 1 mark each		3
	(ii)	*Taxable gains*		
		Assignment of lease	2½	
		Sale of land	2	
		Other matters	1½	
		Capital gains tax	1½	
			Max	7

			Marks
(b)	Requirement to register	1½	
	Exceptions	2	
	Advantages	2	
	Disadvantages	2	
		Max	7
(c)	Context	1½	
	Circumstances in which a claim can be made	2	
	Interest and penalties	1½	
		Max	3
			20

(a) (i) **The availability of entrepreneurs' relief in respect of the assignment of the lease**

The following conditions must be satisfied in order for the assignment of the lease to qualify as an associated disposal so entrepreneurs' relief will be available.

- Ash's disposal of the shares in Lava Ltd (the main disposal) must qualify for entrepreneurs' relief.

- The lease of the building must have been owned by Ash and the building used for the purposes of the business of Lava Ltd for at least one year.

- Ash must have sold the shares in Lava Ltd and the lease as part of a single process of withdrawing from participating in the business of Lava Ltd.

(ii) **Ash – capital gains tax (CGT) liability for the tax year 2014/15**

	Entrepreneurs' relief available £	Entrepreneurs' relief not available £
Gain on sale of shares	235,000	
Gain on assignment of lease £79,812 (W1) × 60:40	47,887	31,925
Gain on sale of land (W2)		21,780
Loss on sale of quoted shares (best use)		(17,400)
		36,305
Annual exempt amount		(11,000)
	282,887	25,305
CGT @ 10%/28%	28,289	7,085
Total CGT liability £(28,289 + 7,085)		35,374

Workings

1 *Gain on the assignment of the lease*

	£
Proceeds	110,000
Less: cost £31,800 × $\dfrac{93.497}{98.490}$	(30,188)
Gain	79,812

2 *Gain on the sale of the land*

	£
Proceeds	30,000
Less: cost £27,400 – £(27,400 × $\dfrac{42,000}{42,000 + 18,000}$)	(8,220)
Gain	21,780

Tutorial notes

1   Entrepreneurs' relief in respect of the lease will be restricted to 60% (100% – 40%) of the gain, due to the rent charged by Ash to Lava Ltd.

2   Ash's taxable income is less than his basic rate limit. However, the gains qualifying for entrepreneurs' relief use up the remainder of the basic rate band so all of the non-qualifying gains are taxed at 28%.

(b)   **Vulcan Partnership (Vulcan) – Value added tax (VAT) registration**

Whether or not Vulcan may be required to register

Subject to the exceptions noted below, Vulcan will be required to register for VAT once its cumulative taxable supplies (those that are standard rated or zero rated) in a 12-month period exceed £81,000.

However, Vulcan will not be required to register if HM Revenue and Customs are satisfied that its total supplies for the following 12 months will be less than £79,000.

Vulcan could request to be exempt from registration because only a small proportion of its supplies are standard rated. This exemption will be available provided it would normally be in a repayment position if registered.

Advantages of registration

Vulcan will be able to recover all of its input tax if the amount relating to exempt supplies is de minimis under the partial exemption rules. Where Vulcan does not satisfy one of the de minimis tests, it will still be able to recover the majority of its input tax.

Registration may give the impression of Vulcan being a substantial business.

Disadvantages of registration

Registration will add to the amount of work required to administer the business. In addition, Vulcan may be subject to financial penalties if it fails to comply with the obligations imposed by the VAT regime.

The partnership's customers would be unable to recover any output tax charged by the partnership as they are not registered for VAT. Accordingly, the prices charged to the small proportion of customers purchasing standard rated items would increase unless Vulcan decides to reduce its profit in respect of these sales.

(c)   **Payment on account on 31 January 2016**

The payment on account due on 31 January 2016 is the first payment in respect of Ash's income tax payable (income tax liability as reduced by tax deducted at source) for 2015/16. The payment due is half of the income tax payable for 2014/15 unless Ash makes a claim to reduce the payment.

Ash can make a claim to reduce the payment if he expects the amount payable for 2015/16 to be less than that for 2014/15. The income tax payable for 2015/16 is likely to be less than that for 2014/15 due, principally, to Ash receiving less profit from Vulcan.

Ash will need to estimate his income tax payable for 2015/16 in order to decide whether or not to reduce the payment on account. Ash will be charged interest if the payment on account is reduced to an amount that is less than half of the final agreed amount payable for 2015/16. In addition, a penalty may be charged if Ash is fraudulent or negligent when he makes the claim to reduce the payment.

5 Cuthbert (ATAX 12/12)

Text references. Payment of CGT and income tax errors are covered in Chapter 15. Inheritance tax on lifetime transfers is dealt with in Chapter 16, the death estate in Chapter 17 and overseas aspects in Chapter 18.

Top tips. Make sure you read the question thoroughly and use all the information you are given to formulate your answer. For example, in part (c) you were told that the original computation of inheritance tax was based on the donor being non-UK domiciled and having made no lifetime gifts. This made a significant difference to the death estate tax computation.

Easy marks. The computation of inheritance tax in part (c), even with the overseas aspects, was straightforward.

Examiner's comments. Part (a) required detailed knowledge of the payment of capital gains tax by instalments. It was the most difficult part of the question and was not done well. The fundamental problem here was that candidates simply did not know the rules, such that they had very little to say. The smart candidates kept their answers brief and moved on to the easier marks in part (b) and, particularly, part (c).

Part (b) concerned the penalty for making a careless error in a tax return. The question stated that the error was careless but many candidates described the full range of penalties available for all error types thus wasting time. Having said that, candidates' performance in this part of the question was good with the exception of the meaning of potentially lost revenue (PLR), the figure on which the penalty would be based. PLR is the additional tax due following the correction of the error and not the amount of the undeclared income.

Part (c) required calculations of inheritance tax and was done well. Almost all candidates understood the relevance of the tax payer being UK domiciled rather than non-UK domiciled and most candidates handled the chargeable lifetime transfer correctly.

There were two common areas where marks were lost. First, many candidates omitted to calculate the original inheritance tax liability that would have been paid before the additional information was discovered. This calculation was necessary in order to calculate the tax underpaid. Secondly, many candidates were not sure of the due date for inheritance tax or, if they knew the six-month rule, they did not know how to apply the rule to the facts.

A minority of candidates did not know the mechanics of inheritance tax particularly well. As a result, they did not deal with the nil rate band correctly or they included the chargeable lifetime transfer in the death estate. Other errors involved applying capital gains tax exemptions to inheritance tax and failing to calculate an estate rate in order to justify the double tax relief available.

Marking scheme

			Marks
(a)	*Payment of capital gains tax by instalments*		
	Availability of payment by instalments	1½	
	Availability of gift relief	1½	
	Matters that Cuthbert would need to be aware of		
	Need for election	1½	
	Payment and interest	2	
	Subsequent sale of asset	1	
		Max	6
(b)	Maximum penalty	1½	
	Disclosure	1½	
	Minimum penalty	1½	
		Max	4

		Marks
(c)	Gift in seven years prior to death	2½
	Death estate – if UK domiciled	
	Assets in UK	1
	Assets in Camberia	1½
	Nil rate band	1
	Inheritance tax and double tax relief	2½
	Death estate - if non-UK domiciled	1
	Interest on underpayment	1½
	Max	10
		20

(a) Payment of capital gains tax (CGT) by instalments

Availability

Payment of CGT by instalments is available in respect of gifts of certain assets, including land (this term includes buildings), where gift relief is not available. Gift relief will not be available in respect of the gift of the building as the building is not used in a business and is let to a long-term tenant so it cannot be a furnished holiday letting.

Matters that Cuthbert would need to be aware of

It is necessary to make an election to pay by instalments before the date that the CGT is normally due (ie 31 January 2017). There will be ten annual instalments beginning on 31 January 2017. Interest will be charged on the outstanding balance of the tax liability.

Cuthbert will be required to pay all of the remaining instalments immediately if the property is sold because Cuthbert and his brother are connected persons for the purposes of CGT.

(b) The penalty due in respect of a careless error in Cuthbert's tax return

The maximum penalty for a careless error is 30% of the potential lost revenue. The potential lost revenue in this case is the additional tax due following the correction of the error.

The penalty may be reduced depending on the level of disclosure Cuthbert provides to HM Revenue and Customs (HMRC) in terms of telling them about the error, providing them with assistance in quantifying it and allowing them access to his records.

Any disclosure provided by Cuthbert will be regarded as prompted, rather than unprompted, because Cuthbert is aware that HMRC suspect that an error has been made. The minimum penalty in these circumstances is 15% of the potential lost revenue.

(c) Pugh – UK inheritance tax (IHT) liability

Gift in the seven years prior to death

There would be no further tax due in respect of the gift on 10 June 2008 as the gross transfer of £317,500 (W1) is covered by the nil rate band of £325,000. However, the tax already paid will not be repaid.

Death estate

Pugh was UK domiciled and will therefore be subject to IHT on his Camberian assets as well as his UK assets.

	£	£
Home in the UK		720,000
Cash held in bank accounts in the UK		45,000
Vintage motor cars located in Camberia		490,000
Quoted shares registered in Camberia		330,000
		1,585,000
Nil rate band available		
Nil rate band at death	325,000	
Less: transfer in previous seven years (W1)	(317,500)	
		(7,500)
Amount chargeable to inheritance tax @ 40%		1,577,500
Inheritance tax @ 40%		631,000
Less: double taxation relief (W2)		(82,500)
Inheritance tax payable		548,500

The additional IHT due is £(548,500 – 176,000 (W3)) = £372,500.

Interest of £(372,500 × 3% × 4/12) = £3,725 will be charged in respect of the period from 31 August 2015 (six months after the end of the month of death) until the tax is paid on 1 January 2016.

Workings

1   *Gift in the seven years prior to death*

	£
Value transferred	322,400
Less: annual exemptions 2008/09 and 2007/08 b/f	(6,000)
Net chargeable transfer of value	316,400
Less: nil rate band in 2008/09	(312,000)
Amount chargeable to inheritance tax	4,400
Inheritance tax × 20/80	1,100
Gross chargeable transfer tax £(316,400 + 1,100)	317,500

2   *Double taxation relief*

Average rate of inheritance tax is $\dfrac{631,000}{1,585,000} \times 100 = 39.811\%$

This is clearly more than the Camberian inheritance tax rate of 25% and so double taxation relief is limited to the Camberian tax paid which was £330,000 × 25% = £82,500.

3   *Original calculation of IHT liability*

	£
Home in the UK	720,000
Cash held in bank accounts in the UK	45,000
	765,000
Nil rate band at death	(325,000)
Amount chargeable to inheritance tax @ 40%	440,000
Inheritance tax @ 40%	176,000

Tutorial note

Business property relief is not available in respect of quoted shares unless the donor controls the company.

ACCA Professional Paper P6 – Options Module

Advanced Taxation (UK)

Mock Examination 3 (December 2014 paper)

Question Paper	
Time allowed	*Reading and planning: 15 minutes* *Writing: 3 hours*
This paper is divided into two sections	
Section A	*BOTH questions are compulsory questions and MUST be attempted*
Section B	*TWO questions ONLY to be attempted*

During reading and planning time only the question paper may be annotated

DO NOT OPEN THIS PAPER UNTIL YOU ARE READY TO START UNDER EXAMINATION CONDITIONS

SECTION A: BOTH questions are compulsory and MUST be attempted

1 Kantar (ATAX 12/14)   63 mins

Your manager has had a meeting with Kantar. Kantar recently appointed your firm to be his tax advisers. Extracts from the memorandum recording the matters discussed at the meeting and from an email from your manager are set out below.

Extract from the memorandum

Kantar was born on 1 May 1963. He is resident and domiciled in the UK.

Kantar has owned and operated his unincorporated business since 2002. In February 2015 Kantar disposed of some land. He used the proceeds to purchase equipment and vans on 1 May 2015 in order to expand his business.

Kantar's only other income consists of UK property business income of £5,000 per year.

Capital transactions

1 November 2013	Kantar inherited eight acres of land from his uncle. Kantar's uncle had purchased the land for £70,000 in 1997. At the time of the uncle's death, the land was worth £200,000.
5 November 2013	Kantar gave £400 to each of his three nephews.
1 February 2015	On this date, when the eight acres of land were worth £290,000, Kantar gave two acres, valued by an independent expert at £100,000, to his son. Capital gains tax gift relief was not available in respect of this gift.
2 February 2015	Kantar sold the remaining six acres of land at auction for £170,000.

Kantar has not made any disposals for the purposes of capital gains tax other than those set out above.

Kantar has not made any transfers of value for the purposes of inheritance tax other than those set out above.

Kantar's business

Kantar's business provides delivery services. The majority of its customers are members of the public. Kantar is not registered for the purposes of value added tax (VAT).

The recent actual and budgeted results of the business are set out below.

	Year ended 31 March		
	Actual 2014 £	Actual 2015 £	Budgeted 2016 £
Sales	48,000	65,000	96,000
Expenses	(6,000)	(8,000)	(13,000)
Profit per the accounts	42,000	57,000	83,000
Adjustment for tax purposes	2,000	1,000	4,000
Capital allowances	(1,000)	(1,000)	(155,000)
Tax adjusted profit/(loss)	43,000	57,000	(68,000)
Income tax liability for the tax year	9,022	14,427	Nil

In the year ending 31 March 2017, no capital allowances will be available to Kantar. With the exception of capital allowances, the results for the year ending 31 March 2017 are expected to be the same as those for the year ended 31 March 2016.

Extract from an email from your manager

Additional information

- The income tax liabilities in the memorandum take account of Kantar's UK property business income as well as his trading income and are correct.

- Kantar pays all of his tax liabilities on or before the due dates.

Please prepare notes for use in a meeting with Kantar. The notes should address the following issues:

(a) **Capital transactions**

    (i) **Inheritance tax**

        - The availability of the small gifts exemption in respect of Kantar's gifts to his nephews.

        - A calculation of the potentially exempt transfer on 1 February 2015 after deduction of any available exemptions.

    (ii) A calculation of Kantar's chargeable gains and capital gains tax liability for the tax year 2014/15.

(b) **Budgeted trading loss for the year ending 31 March 2016**

    (i) Calculations, with **brief** supporting explanations where necessary, of the tax which would be saved in respect of the offset of the trading loss for the tax year 2015/16 if:

        (1) The loss is relieved as soon as possible;
        (2) The loss is carried forward for relief in the future.

    A brief evaluation of your findings and the relevance to Kantar of the £50,000 restriction on the offset of trading losses.

    (ii) On the assumptions that the trading loss is carried forward and that Kantar wishes to maximise his cash flow position, prepare a schedule of the dates and amounts of the payments on account and balancing payments Kantar would expect to make, post 1 January 2016, in respect of his tax liabilities for 2014/15, 2015/16 and 2016/17. Include brief explanations of the payments on account amounts.

(c) **Reporting of chargeable gains**

    Kantar does not intend to report his chargeable gains on his income tax return as he believes that the tax authorities should be able to obtain this information from other sources. Explain the implications for Kantar, and our firm, of Kantar failing to report the chargeable gains to HM Revenue and Customs.

(d) **Value added tax (VAT)**

    Explain, without performing any calculations, Kantar's obligation to compulsorily register for VAT; and state Kantar's ability, following registration, to recover the input tax incurred prior to registering.

Tax manager

Required

Prepare the meeting notes requested in the email from your manager. The following marks are available:

(a)   Capital transactions.

    (i)   Inheritance tax   **(4 marks)**

    (ii)   Capital gains tax   **(4 marks)**

(b)   Budgeted trading loss for the year ending 31 March 2016.

    (i)   Offset of the trading loss   **(10 marks)**

    (ii)   Further tax payments if the loss is carried forward

        Note. Ignore national insurance contributions and value added tax (VAT).   **(5 marks)**

(c)   Reporting of chargeable gains   **(4 marks)**

(d)   Value added tax (VAT)   **(4 marks)**

Professional marks will be awarded for the clarity of the calculations, analysis of the situation, the effectiveness with which the information is communicated, and the quality of the overall presentation. **(4 marks)**

(Total = 35 marks)

2 Bond Ltd group (ATAX 12/14) 45 mins

You have received an email with an attachment from your manager relating to a new client of your firm.

The attachment is a memorandum prepared by the client, Mr Stone, who owns the whole of the ordinary share capital of Bond Ltd. The email from your manager contains further information in relation to the Bond Ltd group of companies and sets out the work you are to perform. The attachment and the email are set out below.

Attachment – Memorandum from Mr Stone

Bond Ltd group of companies

Formation of the group

The Bond Ltd group consists of Bond Ltd, Ungar Ltd and Madison Ltd.

1 April 2013	I purchased the whole of the ordinary share capital of Bond Ltd.
1 December 2013	Bond Ltd purchased the whole of the ordinary share capital of Ungar Ltd.
1 October 2015	Madison Ltd was incorporated on 1 October 2015. Bond Ltd acquired 65% of the ordinary share capital of Madison Ltd on that date.

Bond Ltd – Results for the six months ended 30 September 2015

	£	Notes
Trading losses brought forward	(20,000)	1
Tax adjusted trading income for the period	470,000	2, 3
Chargeable gain	180,000	4

Notes

1. On 31 March 2013, Bond Ltd had trading losses to carry forward of £170,000. The company's total taxable trading income for the two years ended 31 March 2015 was only £150,000, such that on 31 March 2015 it had trading losses to carry forward of £20,000.

2. Bond Ltd's trade consists of baking and selling bread and other baked products. Up to 31 March 2015, its main product had always been low-cost bread which was sold to schools, hospitals and prisons. In April 2015, Bond Ltd introduced a new range of high quality breads and cakes. This new range is sold to supermarkets and independent retailers and, for the six months ended 30 September 2015 represents 65% of the company's turnover and 90% of its profits.

3. In order to produce the new product range, Bond Ltd invested £285,000 in plant and machinery in April 2015. The tax adjusted trading income is after deducting capital allowances of £285,000, ie 100% of the cost of the plant and machinery.

   The tax written down value brought forward on the company's main pool as at 1 April 2015 was zero and there were no other additions or disposals of plant and machinery in the period.

4. The chargeable gain arose on the sale of a plot of land on 1 May 2015 for proceeds of £350,000. The land had always been used in the company's business but was no longer required.

Ungar Ltd

The trade of Ungar Ltd consists of baking high quality cakes. Ungar Ltd trades from premises purchased on 1 July 2014 for £310,000.

Ungar Ltd also develops new baking processes and techniques which it has patented. It uses these processes and techniques itself and licenses the patents to other manufacturers.

Madison Ltd

Madison Ltd purchased a building for £400,000 (plus 20% value added tax (VAT)) and machinery for £300,000 (plus 20% VAT) and began to trade on 1 October 2015.

Madison Ltd is partially exempt for the purposes of VAT. In the year ending 30 September 2016, its VAT recovery percentage is expected to be 80%. However, I expect this percentage to fall slightly in future years.

Email from your manager

Additional information

*   Bond Ltd, Ungar Ltd and Madison Ltd are all resident in the UK.

*   Bond Ltd and Ungar Ltd had always prepared accounts to 31 March. However, in 2015 it was decided to change the group's year end to 30 September and accounts have been prepared for the six months ended 30 September 2015.

*   The original cost of the land sold by Bond Ltd on 1 May 2015 was £150,000. The chargeable gain of £180,000 is after the deduction of indexation allowance and is correct.

Please carry out the following work:

(a)   Corporation tax liability of Bond Ltd

Calculate the corporation tax liability of Bond Ltd for the six months ended 30 September 2015 based on the information provided by Mr Stone. You should review Mr Stone's capital allowances figure of £285,000 and assume the company will claim the maximum possible rollover relief.

Include notes on the following matters.

(i)   The capital allowances available.

(ii)   The use of Bond Ltd's trading losses brought forward bearing in mind that Mr Stone only recently acquired the company.

(iii) The availability of rollover relief in respect of the chargeable gain on the land.

You should **ignore VAT** when carrying out this work.

We will need to do further work in order to finalise this computation. In the meantime, make a note of any assumptions you have made in order to complete the computation as far as possible for now.

(b)   Ungar Ltd – Patent box regime

State, giving reasons, whether or not the patent box regime is available to Ungar Ltd and briefly describe the operation of the regime.

(c)   Madison Ltd – Recovery of input tax

Explain how much of the input tax in respect of the purchase of the building and machinery can be recovered by Madison Ltd in the year ending 30 September 2016 and how this may be adjusted in future years. Include an example of a possible adjustment in the year ending 30 September 2017.

Tax manager

Required

Carry out the work required as requested in the email from your manager. The following marks are available:

(a)　Corporation tax liability of Bond Ltd

　　　Note. For guidance, approximately two-thirds of the available marks relate to the written notes.　**(17 marks)**

(b)　Ungar Ltd – Patent box regime　**(4 marks)**

(c)　Madison Ltd – Recovery of input tax　**(4 marks)**

(Total = 25 marks)

SECTION B: TWO questions ONLY to be attempted

3 Cada (ATAX 12/14)   36 mins

Your firm has been asked to provide advice in connection with inheritance tax and capital gains tax following the death of Cada. The advice relates to the implications of making lifetime gifts, making gifts to charity, varying the terms of a will and other aspects of capital gains tax planning.

Cada and her family:

*   Cada, who was UK domiciled, died on 20 November 2015.
*   Cada is survived by two daughters: Raymer and Yang.
*   Raymer has an adult son.
*   Yang has no children.

Cada – Lifetime gifts and available nil rate band:

*   Cada had not made any lifetime gifts since 30 November 2011.
*   Cada's nil rate band available at the date of her death was £220,000.

Cada's death estate and the details of her will:

*   Cada owned assets valued at £1,000,000 at the time of her death.
*   Cada left her house, valued at £500,000, to Raymer.
*   Cada left cash of £60,000 to a UK national charity.
*   Cada left her remaining assets (including a portfolio of shares) valued at £440,000, to Yang.
*   None of the remaining assets qualified for any inheritance tax reliefs.

Raymer:

*   Is not an accountant, but has some knowledge of the UK tax system
*   Has made four observations regarding her mother's estate and her inheritance

Raymer's four observations:

*   'My mother should have made additional gifts in her lifetime.'

*   'The tax rate on the chargeable estate should be less than 40% due to the gift to charity.'

*   'I do not intend to live in the house but will give it to my son on 1 July 2016.'

*   'My mother paid capital gains tax every year. However, when she died, some of her shareholdings had a value of less than cost.'

Cada's shareholdings at the time of her death:

*   Quoted shares in JW plc valued at more than cost
*   Quoted shares in FR plc valued at less than cost
*   Unquoted shares in KZ Ltd valued at £nil

Required

(a)   Explain the inheritance tax advantages, other than lifetime exemptions, which could have been obtained if Cada had made additional lifetime gifts of quoted shares between 1 December 2011 and her death.

(4 marks)

(b)   Calculate the increase in the legacy to the charity which would be necessary in order for the reduced rate of inheritance tax to apply and quantify the reduction in the inheritance tax liability which would result.

(5 marks)

(c)   Explain the capital gains tax and inheritance tax advantages which could be obtained by varying the terms of Cada's will and set out the procedures required in order to achieve a tax-effective variation.   (6 marks)

(d)   In relation to capital gains tax, explain what beneficial actions Cada could have carried out in the tax year of her death in respect of her shareholdings.   (5 marks)

(Total = 20 marks)

4 Piquet and Buraco (ATAX 12/14)

36 mins

Your firm has been asked to provide advice to two unrelated clients, Piquet and Buraco. Piquet, an unincorporated sole trader, requires advice on a proposed change to the date to which he prepares his accounts. Buraco requires advice on his residence status and the remittance basis.

(a)   **Piquet:**

- Began trading as an unincorporated sole trader on 1 January 2008
- Has always prepared accounts to 31 October
- Has overlap profits of £15,000 for a five-month overlap period
- Is planning to change his accounting date to 28 February 2016

Actual and budgeted tax adjusted trading profit of Piquet's business:

	Profit per month	Profit for the period
	£	£
Year ended 31 October 2014	4,500	54,000
16 months ending 28 February 2016	5,875	94,000
Year ending 28 February 2017	7,333	88,000
Year ending 28 February 2018	9,000	108,000

Alternative choice of accounting date:

- Piquet is also considering a year end of 30 April.

- To achieve this, Piquet would prepare accounts for the 18 months ending 30 April 2016 and annually thereafter.

Required

(i)   On the assumption that Piquet changes his accounting date to 28 February, state the date by which he should notify HM Revenue and Customs of the change, and calculate the taxable trading profit for each tax years 2015/16 and 2016/17. **(3 marks)**

(ii)   On the assumption that Piquet changes his accounting date to 30 April, state the basis periods for the tax years 2015/16 and 2016/17 and the effect of this change on Piquet's overlap profits.   **(3 marks)**

(iii) Identify and explain TWO advantages for Piquet of using a year end of 30 April rather than 28 February. **(4 marks)**

Note

Ignore 29 February in the calendar year 2016.

(b)   **Buraco's links with the country of Canasta:**

- Buraco is domiciled in Canasta.
- Buraco owns a home in the country of Canasta.
- Buraco's only income is in respect of investment properties in Canasta.
- Buraco frequently buys and sells properties in Canasta.

Buraco's links with the UK:

- Buraco's ex-wife and their 12-year-old daughter moved to the UK on 1 May 2014.
- Buraco first visited the UK in the tax year 2014/15 but was not UK resident in that year.
- Buraco did not own a house in the UK until he purchased one on 6 April 2015.
- Buraco expects to live in the UK house for between 100 and 150 days in the tax year 2015/16.

Required

(i)   Explain why Buraco will not satisfy any of the automatic overseas residence tests for the tax year 2015/16, and, on the assumption that he does not satisfy any of the automatic UK residence tests, explain how his residence status will be determined for that tax year. **(7 marks)**

(ii)   On the assumption that Buraco is resident in the UK in the tax year 2015/16, state the tax implications for him of claiming the remittance basis for that year and explain whether or not there would be a remittance basis charge. **(3 marks)**

(Total = 20 marks)

5 Klubb plc (ATAX 12/14)   36 mins

Klubb plc, a client of your firm, requires advice on the penalty in respect of the late filing of a corporation tax return, the establishment of a tax-advantaged share scheme, and its shareholding in an overseas-resident company.

Klubb plc

- Is a UK resident trading company
- Has been charged a penalty in respect of the late filing of corporation tax return
- Intends to establish a tax-advantaged share plan
- Purchased 30% of the ordinary share capital of Hartz Co from Mr Deck on 1 April 2015

Late filing of corporation tax returns:

- Klubb plc prepared accounts for the 16-month period ended 31 March 2014.
- The corporation tax returns for this period were filed on 31 May 2015.

Tax-advantaged share plan:

- The plan will be either a Schedule 2 share incentive plan (SIP) or a Schedule 4 company share option plan (CSOP).

- If a SIP, the shares would be held within the plan for five years.

- If a SIP, members will not be permitted to reinvest dividends in order to purchase further shares.

- If a CSOP, the options would be exercised within five years of being granted.

- In both cases it can be assumed that the plan members would sell the shares immediately after acquiring them.

Klubb plc wants the share plan to be flexible in terms of:

- The employees who can be included in the plan.
- The number or value of shares which can be acquired by each plan member.

Hartz Co:

- Is resident in the country of Suta
- Mr Deck continues to own 25% of the company's ordinary share capital.
- Kort Co, a company resident in the country of Suta, owns the remaining 45%.

Budgeted results of Hartz Co for the year ending 31 March 2016:

- Trading profits of £330,000
- Chargeable gains of £70,000
- All of Hartz Co's profits have been artificially diverted from the UK.
- Hartz Co will pay corporation tax at the rate of 11% in the country of Suta.
- Hartz Co will not pay a dividend for the year ending 31 March 2016.

Required

(a)   State the corporation tax returns required from Klubb plc in respect of the 16-month period ended 31 March 2014 and the due dates for filing them. Explain the penalties which may be charged in respect of the late filing of these returns. **(4 marks)**

(b)   Compare and contrast a Schedule 2 share incentive plan with a Schedule 4 company share option plan in relation to:

- The flexibility desired by Klubb plc regarding the employees included in the plan and the number or value of shares which can be acquired by each plan member; and

- The income tax and capital gains tax implications of acquiring and selling the shares under each plan.

(9 marks)

(c)   (i)   Explain whether or not Hartz Co will be regarded as a controlled foreign company (CFC) for the year ending 31 March 2016 and the availability or otherwise of the low profits exemption.   **(4 marks)**

(ii)   On the assumption that Hartz Co is a CFC, and that no CFC exemptions are available, calculate the budgeted CFC charge for Klubb plc based on the budgeted results of Hartz Co for the year ending 31 March 2016.   **(3 marks)**

(Total = 20 marks)

Answers

**DO NOT TURN THIS PAGE UNTIL YOU HAVE
COMPLETED THE MOCK EXAM**

A plan of attack

What's the worst thing you could be doing right now if this was the actual exam paper? Wondering how to celebrate the end of the exam in about three hours time? Panicking, flapping and generally getting in a right old state?

Well, they're all pretty bad, so turn back to the paper and let's sort out a **plan of attack**!

First things first

You have 15 minutes of reading time. Make sure you spend it wisely, looking through the paper in detail working out which optional questions to do and the order in which to attack the questions. You've got **two options**. Option 1 is the option recommended by BPP.

Option 1 (if you're thinking 'Help!')

If you're a bit worried about the paper, do the questions in the order of how well you think you can answer them. If you find the questions in Section B less daunting than the compulsory questions in Section A start with Section B. Remember you only need to do two of the three questions in Section B; you may find it easier if you start by deciding which question you will not do and put a line through it.

- **Question 3** deals with inheritance tax and capital gains tax on a death estate, including a gift to charity, variation of the will and use of losses.
- **Question 4** is in two parts. The first covers change of accounting date and the second the residence status of an individual.
- **Question 5** has three parts covering corporation tax administration, tax advantaged share schemes and controlled foreign companies.

Do not spend longer than the allocated time on Section B. When you've spent the allocated time on **two** of the three questions in Section B turn to the longer questions in Section A. Read these questions through thoroughly before you launch into them. Once you start make sure you allocate your time to the parts within the questions according to the marks available and that, where possible, you attempt the easy marks first.

Lastly, what you mustn't forget is that you have to **answer both questions in Section A and TWO in Section B**. Do not miss out more than one question in Section B and do not waste time answering three questions in Section B or you will seriously affect your chance of passing the exam.

Option 2 (if you're thinking 'It's a doddle')

It never pays to be overconfident but if you're not quaking in your shoes about the exam then **turn straight to the compulsory questions** in Section A.

Once you've done these questions, move to Section B.

- The question you attempt first really depends on what you are most confident at.
- You then have to select one of the two remaining questions. If you are undecided look at the requirements. It maybe easier to obtain more marks if these are broken down into several smaller parts.

No matter how many times we remind you....

Always, always **allocate your time** according to the marks for the question in total and then according to the parts of the question. And **always, always follow the requirements** exactly. For example, in Question 1 you were required to produce calculations of the tax saving for trading loss relief with **brief** supporting explanations. You would have gained no extra marks by providing long, detailed explanations.

The examiner has commented that **some candidates write about general issues that relate to the facts of the question but have not been asked for**. This occurs particularly in the Section A questions. It can sometimes look to be a way of avoiding having to get to grips with the requirements or perhaps it is a form of 'warming up' but, either way, **it creates unnecessary time pressure**.

You've got spare time at the end of the exam.....?

If you have allocated your time properly then you **shouldn't have time on your hands** at the end of the exam. But if you find yourself with five or ten minutes to spare, check over your work to make sure you've answered all the requirements.

Forget about it!

And don't worry if you found the paper difficult. More than likely other candidates will too. If this were the real thing you would need to **forget** the exam the minute you leave the exam hall and **think about the next one**. Or, if it's the last one, **celebrate**!

1 Kantar (ATAX 12/14)

> **Text references.** Inheritance tax exemptions and lifetime transfers are covered in Chapter 16. The basics of capital gains tax are dealt with in Chapter 11. Trading losses are the subject of Chapter 8. Self assessment for individuals is covered in Chapter 15. Ethics will be found in Chapter 30. Value added tax registration is dealt with in Chapter 28.
>
> **Top tips.** In part (b)(i) there are a lot of figures involved so it was important to lay out your computations in an orderly manner so that the tax savings could be picked out easily when making the evaluation of which loss relief would be more beneficial.
>
> **Easy marks.** There were some easy marks in part (a)(i) for describing the small gifts exemption. The ethical points in part (c) should have been well known. The registration requirements in part (d) were basic knowledge from F6.

Marking scheme

				Marks
(a)	(i)	Small gifts exemption	1½	
		Potentially exempt transfer	2½	
				4
	(ii)	Chargeable gain: gift 1 February 2015	2	
		Chargeable gain: sale 2 February 2015	1	
		Capital gains tax liability	1	
				4
(b)	(i)	Loss relieved as soon as possible		
		Income tax	1	
		Capital gains tax	3	
		Loss carried forward		
		Taxable incomes	2½	
		Tax liabilities and saving	2	
		£50,000 restriction	1	
		Evaluation	1	
		Explanatory notes	1½	
		Max		10
	(ii)	Payments required if loss carried forward		
		2014/15	2½	
		2015/16	1½	
		2016/17	2	
		Max		5
(c)		Implications for Kantar	2	
		Fundamental principles	1	
		Cease to act	2½	
		Max		4
(d)		When registration required	2	
		VAT incurred prior to registrar	2	
				4
		Format and presentation	1	
		Analysis	1	
		Quality of explanations	1	
		Quality of calculations	1	
				4
				35

Notes for meeting

(a)   (i)   **Inheritance tax**

Small gifts exemption

Outright gifts to individuals totalling £250 or less per donee in any one tax year are exempt. If gifts total more than £250 the whole amount is chargeable. Therefore the small gifts exemption does not apply to the gifts of £400 each to Kantar's nephews.

Potentially exempt transfer on 1 February 2015

	£
Value of the land prior to gift	290,000
Less: value of land after gift	(170,000)
Diminution in value (transfer of value)	120,000
Less: annual exemption 2014/15	(3,000)
unused annual exemption 2013/14 b/f £[3,000 – (3 × £400)]	(1,800)
Potentially exempt transfer	115,200

   (ii)   **Capital gains tax liability for tax year 2014/15**

	£	£
1 February 2015 gift		
Proceeds (market value)	100,000	
Less: cost		
$£200,000 \times \dfrac{100,000}{100,000 + 170,000}$	(74,074)	
Gain		25,926
2 February 2015 sale		
Proceeds	170,000	
Less: cost £(200,000 – 74,074)	(125,926)	
Gain		44,074
Chargeable gains		70,000
Less: annual exempt amount		(11,000)
Taxable gains		59,000
Capital gains tax £59,000 × 28% (higher rate taxpayer)		16,520

Tutorial note

Rollover relief will not be available in respect of the chargeable gain on the sale of the land, as it is not a business asset.

(b)   (i)   **Budgeted trading loss for the year ended 31 March 2016**

1   *Loss relieved as soon as possible*

The trading loss can be relieved against general income in the tax year of the loss (2015/16) and the previous tax year (2014/15).

Kantar should not make a claim to relieve the loss in 2015/16 as his only income for this tax year is £5,000 property business income which will be covered by the personal allowance.

If Kantar makes a claim to relieve the loss in 2014/15, he cannot choose the amount of loss to relieve so the loss must be set against income which would be covered by the personal allowance. He would therefore set off £(57,000 + 5,000) = £62,000 of the loss against general income and the tax saving would be the whole tax liability for the tax year 2014/15 of £14,427.

The £50,000 relief cap does not apply to trading income of the same trade and is therefore not relevant to the claim for the tax year 2014/15.

Kantar may include a further claim to set the remaining loss of £(68,000 – 62,000) = £6,000 against his chargeable gains for the tax year 2014/15. Since Kantar has no taxable income following loss relief against general income, his basic rate band is now available to be set against the taxable gains. This would result in a capital gains tax saving of £4,866 as shown below.

	£
Chargeable gains (part (a)(ii))	70,000
Less: loss relief	(6,000)
	64,000
Less: annual exempt amount	(11,000)
Taxable gains	53,000
Capital gains tax	
£31,865 × 18%	5,736
£(53,000 – 31,865) = £21,135 × 28%	5,918
	11,654
Capital gains tax saving £(16,520 (part (a)(ii)) – 11,654)	4,866

The total tax saving would therefore be £(14,427 + 4,866) = <u>£19,293</u>

2   *Loss carried forward for future relief*

The loss would be set against Kantar's trading income for the tax year 2016/17. The tax saving would be <u>£23,627</u> as shown below.

	Without loss relief £	*With loss relief* £
Trading income 2016/17		
£(83,000 + 4,000)	87,000	87,000
Less: trading loss brought forward		(68,000)
		19,000
Property business income	5,000	5,000
Net income	92,000	24,000
Less: personal allowance	(10,000)	(10,000)
Taxable income	82,000	14,000
Income tax		
£31,865/£14,000 × 20%	6,373	2,800
£(82,000 – 31,865) = £50,135 × 40%	20,054	
	26,427	2,800
Income tax saving £(26,427 – 2,800)		23,627

Carrying forward the loss would therefore increase the tax saving. However, Kantar cannot be certain that he will make the budgeted profit in the year to 31 March 2017. The tax saving will also be delayed.

(ii) **Future tax payments if loss carried forward**

	Notes	£
2014/15		
Balancing payment 31 January 2016		
Income tax £(14,427 – 9,022)	1	5,405
Capital gains tax (part (a)(ii))		16,520
		21,925

	Notes	£
2015/16		
Payments on account	2	0
Balancing payment		0
2016/17		
Payments on account	3	0
Balancing payment 31 January 2018 (part (b)(i)(2)		2,800

Notes

1   Kantar will have made payments on account equal to his tax liability for the previous tax year (2013/14).

2   Kantar should make a claim to reduce his payments on account to nil as he does not expect to have any tax liability for 2015/16.

3   Kantar will not have to make any payments on account for the tax year 2016/17 as he will not have a tax liability for the tax year 2015/16.

(c)   **Reporting of chargeable gains**

Kantar may be liable to interest and penalties (based on potential lost revenue) if he does not report his chargeable gains to HM Revenue and Customs (HMRC).

The evasion or attempted evasion of tax by Kantar may also be the subject of criminal charges under both tax law and money laundering legislation. We may need to submit a report under the money laundering rules.

Our firm must not be associated with a client who has deliberately evaded tax as this is against the ACCA fundamental principles of integrity and professional behaviour.

We should not continue to act for Kantar if he does not agree to disclose the chargeable gains to HMRC. If he does not agree to disclosure, we are still under a professional duty to ensure that he understands the seriousness of offences against HMRC.

If we do cease to act for Kantar, we must inform HMRC of this cessation but not the reasons for it. We should advise Kantar that the notification that we are no longer acting for him may alert HMRC that tax irregularities have taken place and urge on Kantar the desirability of making a full disclosure.

(d)   **Value added tax (VAT)**

Kantar will be liable to register for VAT if the value of his cumulative taxable supplies (excluding VAT) exceeds £81,000 in any 12 month period. At the end of every month he must therefore calculate his cumulative turnover of taxable supplies to date. Kantar is required to notify HMRC within 30 days of the end of the month in which the £81,000 limit is exceeded.

VAT incurred before registration can be treated as input tax and recovered from HMRC subject to certain conditions. For input tax on goods purchased prior to registration the following conditions apply:

- Acquired for the purposes of business carried on by Kantar at the time of supply
- Not supplied onwards or consumed before the date of registration
- Input tax incurred in the four years prior to the date of registration

For input tax on the supply of services prior to registration the following conditions apply.

- Supplied for the purposes of business carried on by Kantar at the time of supply
- Input tax incurred in the six months prior to the date of registration

Tutorial note

The recovery of input tax will reduce the expenses incurred by the business. It will also reduce the cost of the equipment purchased in the year ending 31 March 2016 for the purposes of capital allowances.

2 Bond Ltd group (ATAX 12/14)

> **Text references.** Computation of taxable total profits and the patent box election are dealt with in Chapter 20. Losses are covered in Chapter 24. Capital allowances are the subject of Chapter 7 and the allocation of the annual investment allowance is dealt with in Chapter 26. Rollover relief for companies is covered in Chapter 21. Partial exemption and the capital goods scheme are dealt with in Chapter 29.
>
> **Top tips.** In part (a), 11 or 12 marks were available for the written notes on the calculation of the corporation tax liability of Bond Ltd so it was important that you dealt with the matters raised in detail.
>
> **Easy marks.** There were some easy marks in part (a) for explaining basic principles such as capital allowances in a short period of account, losses brought forward, rollover relief and the rate of corporation tax.

Marking scheme

			Marks
(a)	Corporation tax computation		
	Taxable total profits	2	
	Corporation tax liability	½	
	Capital allowances		
	Maximum AIA for short accounting period	1	
	Group aspect	1	
	Calculation of adjustment to capital allowances	1½	
	Losses brought forward		
	Set against future profits of same trade	2	
	Major change in the nature or conduct of trade	3	
	Replacement of business assets relief	5	
	Rate of corporation tax	1	
			17
(b)	Identification of each relevant point – one mark		
	Possible points include:		
	Availability of scheme		
	Election for treatment		
	Meaning of patent profits		
	10% rate		
	Phasing in of scheme		
		Max	4
(c)	Building		
	Original recovery	1	
	Capital goods scheme	1	
	Example	2	
	Machinery	1	
		Max	4
			25

(a) **Bond Ltd – Corporation tax computation for the six months ended 30 September 2015**

	Notes	£
Tax adjusted trading income as previously calculated		470,000
Add: reduction in capital allowances		
£(285,000 – 253,150)	1	31,850
Less: trading losses brought forward	2	(0)
Revised tax adjusted trading income		501,850
Chargeable gain	3	40,000
Taxable total profits		541,850
Corporation tax @ 21%	4	113,788

Notes

1 *Capital allowances*

The maximum annual investment allowance (AIA) for the six month period to 30 September 2015 is £500,000 × 6/12 = £250,000. Bond Ltd and Ungar Ltd are in a group and therefore are entitled to a single AIA between the group companies. Bond Ltd and Ungar Ltd can decide how to allocate the AIA between them and they should do so in the most beneficial way, taking into account the nature of the expenditure by each company (eg main pool, special rate pool) and the rate of corporation tax payable by each company.

Assuming that the AIA is wholly allocated to Bond Ltd, the capital allowances for the period are:

	AIA	Main pool	Allowances
	£	£	£
Additions qualifying for AIA	285,000		
AIA	(250,000)		250,000
Transfer to pool	35,000	35,000	
WDA @ 18% × 6/12		(3,150)	3,150
TWDV c/f		31,850	
Maximum capital allowances			253,150

2 *Trading losses brought forward*

Trading losses can be carried forward and deducted from income of the same trade in future accounting periods. Bond Ltd is carrying on the same trade before and after 1 April 2013 (baking and selling bread and other baked profits).

However, trading losses may be restricted where there is a change in ownership of a company and, for example, there has been a major change in the nature or conduct of the trade within three years after the change of ownership. This restriction will probably apply in the case of Bond Ltd as it previously only sold low cost products to schools, hospital and prisons but now 65% of its turnover and 90% of its profits relate to high quality products sold to supermarkets and independent retailers.

If the restriction applies, losses incurred before the change in ownership on 1 April 2013 cannot be carried forward against post acquisition profits. Therefore, the trading losses which arose up to 31 March 2013 cannot be set against the profits for the period ended 30 September 2015.

Tutorial note

If the restriction is relevant, it also applies to the two previous accounting periods ended 31 March 2014 and 31 March 2015. This means that it will be necessary to recalculate Bond Ltd's corporation tax liability for those periods.

3   *Rollover relief*

A gain on a qualifying business asset may be relieved where the proceeds on the disposal of that asset are matched with expenditure on another qualifying business asset under replacement of business assets (rollover) relief. The members of a chargeable gains group are treated as a single unit for the purpose of claiming such relief. Bond Ltd and Ungar Ltd are in a chargeable gains group because Bond Ltd owns at least 75% of Ungar Ltd. Madison Ltd is not in the chargeable gains group because Bond Ltd only owns 65% of that company.

Bond Ltd can therefore match its gain with acquisitions made by itself or by Ungar Ltd within the period starting 1 May 2014 and ending 30 April 2018. Full relief will be available if the expenditure is at least £350,000. Otherwise, there will be a chargeable gain equal to the amount of proceeds not reinvested, up to a maximum equal to the gain of £180,000.

The only qualifying acquisition about which there is information is the building acquired by Ungar Ltd on 1 July 2014 for £310,000. Rollover relief of £140,000 (£180,000 - £40,000) would be available on this acquisition as £(350,000 − 310,000) = £40,000 of the gain is left in charge.

Further relief may be available if there are more acquisitions of qualifying assets, for example items of fixed plant purchased by Bond Ltd.

4   *Rate of corporation tax*

The upper limit is divided by two as Bond Ltd has one associated company (Ungar Ltd) in the accounting period ended 30 September 2015. It is also pro-rated for the short accounting period. Therefore the upper limit is £1,500,000/2 × 6/12 = £375,000 and so Bond Ltd is a main rate company for this period.

(b)   **Ungar Ltd – Patent box election**

The patent box scheme could apply to Ungar Ltd as it has patent profits attributable to qualifying patents because it has carried on qualifying development in relation to the patents for new baking processes and techniques.

Ungar Ltd would need to make an election to HM Revenue and Customs for the patent box scheme to apply.

Patent profits within the patent box would include royalty income received directly from qualifying patents and a proportion of Ungar Ltd's profits in respect of the sale of products incorporating the use of those patents.

A reduced rate of corporation tax applies to profits within the patent box by deducting an amount from the company's taxable profits so that, when the corporation tax rate is applied to the reduced figure, the effective rate is 10% on the patent box profits.

In FY 2014, only 70% of the profits within the patent box are taxed at the effective 10% rate. In future years, this percentage will increase until all the profits within the patent box are taxed at an effective 10% rate.

(c)   **Recovery of Value added tax (VAT) on assets acquired by Madison Ltd**

Building

The capital goods scheme will apply to the building because it cost £250,000 or more.

Madison Ltd will be able to recover (£400,000 × 20% = £80,000) × 80% = £64,000 on the building in the year ended 30 September 2016.

For each subsequent VAT year, during the recovery period of 10 years, an adjustment will be made to the VAT recovery. The adjustment is equal to the difference in percentage use between the first VAT year and the VAT year under review × 1/10 × the original input tax. For example, if the percentage in the year to 30 September 2017 is 75%, Madison Ltd would need to repay to HM Revenue and Customs:

((80% − 75%) = 5%) × 1/10 × £80,000 = £400.

Machinery

The capital goods scheme does not apply to machinery. Madison Ltd will be able to recover £300,000 × 20% × 80% = £48,000 on the machinery in the year ended 30 September 2016 and there will be no adjustment in later years.

3 Cada (ATAX 12/14)

Text references. The implication so lifetime transfers for inheritance are dealt with in Chapter 16. The death estate is covered in Chapter 17. The inheritance tax implications of altering dispositions made on death is dealt with in Chapter 18 and the capital gains aspects in Chapter 13. Capital losses are covered in Chapter 11 and negligible value claims in Chapter 14.

Top tips. In part (b) you can save some time by working out the original inheritance tax liability (based on the original gift to charity) and the reduced inheritance tax liability (based on the increased gift to charity) side by side.

Easy marks. There were some easy marks in part (a) for explaining taper relief. In part (d) the explanation of losses should have been straightforward.

Marking scheme

				Marks
(a)	Value of lifetime transfer		1	
	Relief for fall in value		1	
	Taper relief availability		1	
	Taper relief: effect		1½	
		Max		4
(b)	Original liability		2½	
	Revised gift to charity		2½	
	Net saving		1	
		Max		5
(c)	Additional gift to charity		1	
	House		3½	
	Procedure for variation		2	
		Max		6
(d)	No relief for losses accrued at death		1	
	Realisation of losses on FR plc shares		1	
	Negligible value claim on KZ Ltd shares		2	
	Use of losses		2	
		Max		5
				20

(a) **Inheritance tax advantages of additional lifetime gifts**

If Cada had made additional lifetime gifts of quoted shares between 1 December 2011 and her death, the transfers of value would have been based on the value of the quoted shares at the date of the gifts, rather than their value at the date of Cada's death. Therefore, although the transfers of value would be chargeable to inheritance tax because Cada died within seven years of making them, if the shares had increased in value between the lifetime transfers and her death that increase would not be subject to inheritance tax.

In addition, if the shares had fallen in value between the date the lifetime transfers and her death, fall in value relief could be claimed in computing the lifetime transfers of value chargeable at death.

Taper relief of 20% would also apply to the death tax on the additional gifts if they were made between 1 December 2011 and 20 November 2012 (three to four years before Cada's death) and to the extent that they exceeded the nil rate band available, taking into account transfers in the seven years before the additional gift.

(b) **Additional gift to charity**

	Original gift to charity £	Increased gift to charity £
Assets owned at death	1,000,000	1,000,000
Less: original gift to charity	(60,000)	
increased gift to charity		
£(1,000,000 – 220,000) × 10%		(78,000)
Chargeable estate	940,000	922,000
Inheritance tax		
£220,000 × 0%	0	0
£(940,000 – 220,000) = £720,000 × 40%	288,000	
£(922,000 – 220,000) = £702,000 × 36%		252,720
	288,000	252,720
Additional gift to charity £(78,000 – 60,000)		18,000
Reduction in inheritance tax £(288,000 – 252,720)		35,280

Tutorial note

There is a reduced rate of inheritance tax (36%, rather than 40%) available on the chargeable death estate if Cada gifts at least 10% of her net estate to charity. For the purpose of determining whether the 10% condition is met, the net estate is calculated as the assets owned at death as reduced by liabilities, exemptions, reliefs and the available nil rate band, but before the charitable legacy itself is deducted.

(c) **Variation of Cada's will**

Gift to charity: potential tax advantages

If Cada's will were varied to gift £78,000 to charity instead of £60,000, the inheritance tax liability on the estate would be reduced by £35,280 as shown above.

Gift of house by Raymer: potential tax advantages

Cada's will could be varied to give the house directly to Raymer's son who would take the house at the probate value of £500,000 for capital gains tax purposes. Raymer would not be treated as making a disposal for capital gains tax purposes by making the variation.

If the will is not varied in this way, Raymer would make a disposal of house on 1 July 2016 at its market value at that time and there will be a chargeable gain if this value exceeds the probate value of £500,000. Raymer would not be able to claim principal private residence relief, as she does not intend to live in the house, and gift relief would not available as the house is not a business asset nor is the gift a chargeable lifetime transfer for inheritance tax.

For inheritance tax, the variation would mean that the house is treated as being given to Raymer's son in Cada's will so would be chargeable to inheritance tax as part of the chargeable estate in the same way as if gifted to Raymer. Raymer would not be treated as making a transfer of value for inheritance tax purposes by making the variation.

If the will is not varied in this way, Raymer would make a potentially exempt transfer of the market value of the house on 1 July 2016 and this would become a chargeable transfer if she dies within seven years (ie on or before 30 June 2023).

Procedures

A written variation must be made by 19 November 2017 (two years after Cada's death) by Raymer and Yang as they are the persons who benefit under Cada's will and whose entitlements to property under the will are reduced by the variation.

As Raymer and Yang wish the relevant terms of the will to be treated as replaced by the terms of the variation for both inheritance tax and capital gains tax purposes, this must be stated in the variation.

Tutorial note

Yang's entitlement under Cada's will is reduced by the variation because the increased gift to charity must come from the remaining assets of Cada's estate which have been given to Yang. However, the value of Yang's entitlement will actually increase due to the reduction in inheritance tax.

(d) **Capital gains tax – Beneficial actions in respect of shareholdings**

The shares in Cada's estate will pass at probate value to Yang and the accrued losses up to the date of Cada's death will therefore not be available for relief.

The FR plc shares which are valued at less than cost could have been sold in the tax year of Cada's death, thus realising the loss on those shares. This loss could have been offset against chargeable gains in that tax year and then carried back against chargeable gains of the three tax years before death on a last in, first out (LIFO) basis.

A negligible value claim could have been made in respect of the KZ Ltd shares to treat them as sold, and immediately reacquired, for no value so realising the loss on those shares. The sale and reacquisition would have been treated as taking place when the claim was made, or at a specified earlier time. The earlier time could have been any time up to two years before the start of the tax year in which the claim was made. The loss would be relieved in a similar way to the loss on the FR plc shares.

4 Piquet and Buraco (ATAX 12/14)

Text references. Change of accounting date is dealt with in Chapter 6. Overseas aspects of income tax are the subject of Chapter 10.

Top tips. In part (a)(i) it is important to identify the tax year of change of the accounting date as this will affect both the treatment of the long period of account and the date of notification to HM Revenue and Customs.

Easy marks. The accounting date change to 28 February in part (a)(i) was reasonable straightforward. The implications of claiming the remittance basis in part (b)(ii) should have been well known.

Marking scheme

				Marks
(a)	(i)	Date for notification to HMRC	1	
		Calculations of taxable trading profits	2	
				3
	(ii)	Basis periods for two tax years	1½	
		Creation of overlap profits	1½	
				3
	(iii)	Identification of issue – one mark each	2	
		Explanation of issue – one mark each	2	
				4

			Marks
(b)	(i)	Automatic overseas tests	1
		Days in UK and UK ties	2½
		Work, family and available accommodation ties	3
		90 day tie	1½
		Conclusion	1
		Max	**7**
	(ii)	UK tax on overseas income and gains	1
		Personal allowance and annual exempt amount	1
		No remittance basis charge	2
		Max	**3**
			20

(a) (i) **Accounting date changed to 28 February**

If Piquet changes his accounting date to 28 February, the year of change is 2015/16 so he must notify HMRC of the change by 31 January following the end of the tax year (ie 31 January 2017).

Taxable trading profits

	£
2015/16 (year of change)	
16 months ended 28 February 2016 (long period of account ending in year)	94,000
Less: relief for overlap profits £15,000 × 4/5	(12,000)
Taxable trading profits	82,000
2016/17	
Year ended 28 February 2017 (current year basis)	88,000

(ii) **30 April year end – Basis periods and overlap profits**

The basis period for 2015/16 is the 12 months to the new accounting date which would have fallen in that tax year which is 30 April 2015.

This will create additional overlap profits as profits for the period 1 May 2014 to 31 October 2014 have already been taxed in the tax year 2014/15. These overlap profits are £4,500 × 6 = £27,000.

The basis period for the tax year 2016/17 is the 12 months ended 30 April 2016.

Tutorial note

If accounts are prepared for the 18 month period to 30 April 2016, there will be no period of account ending in the tax year 2015/16. A basis period for 2015/16 must be manufactured by taking the actual new accounting date of 30 April 2016 and deducting one year.

(iii) **Advantages of 30 April year end**

As Piquet's profits are rising, a date early in the tax year, such as 30 April, delays the time when rising accounts profits feed through into rising taxable profits, whereas a date late in the tax year, such as 28 February, accelerates the taxation of rising profits. This is because with an accounting date of 30 April, the taxable profits for each tax year are mainly the profits earned in the previous tax year. With an accounting date of 28 February the taxable profits are almost entirely profits earned in the current year.

An accounting date of 30 April gives the maximum interval between earning profits and paying the related tax liability. For example if Piquet prepares accounts to 30 April 2017, this falls into the tax year 2017/18 with payments on account being due on 31 January 2018 and 31 July 2018, and a balancing payment due on 31 January 2019. If he prepares accounts to 28 February 2017, this falls in the tax year 2016/17 and the payments will be due one year earlier (ie on 31 January 2017, 31 July 2017 and 31 January 2018).

Knowing profits well in advance of the end of the tax year makes tax planning much easier. For example, if Piquet wants to make personal pension contributions and prepares accounts to 30 April 2017 (2017/18), he can make contributions up to 5 April 2018 based on those relevant earnings. If he prepares accounts to 28 February 2017, he will probably not know the amount of his relevant earnings until after the end of the tax year 2016/17, too late to adjust his pension contributions for that tax year.

Note

Only TWO advantages were required.

Tutorial note

Credit would also be given to students who explained the effect of a trader's year end on the basis period in the tax year of cessation (although this may be a disadvantage since, with an accounting date of 30 April, the assessment for the year of cessation could be based on up to 23 months of profits).

(b)   (i)   **Residence status for the tax year 2015/16**

Automatic overseas residence tests

Buraco does not satisfy the only relevant automatic overseas residence test for the tax year 2015/16 as he will spend less than 46 days in the UK in that tax year and was not resident in the UK for any of the previous three tax years.

Tutorial note

As Buraco does not work full-time overseas, the spending less than 91 days in the UK test is not relevant.

Residence status for tax year 2015/16

As Buraco meets none of the automatic overseas tests and (as stated in the question) none of the automatic UK tests, the 'sufficient ties' test must be considered to decide if he is UK resident for the tax year 2015/16.

As Buraco was not UK resident in any of the previous three tax years, the relevant ties are:

- UK resident close family: Buraco has a minor child who is UK resident so this is a tie.

- Substantive UK work: Buroco does not work in the UK so this is not a tie.

- Available UK accommodation: Buraco has accommodation available him for a consecutive period of 91 days or more in the tax year and in which he spends one or more nights during the tax year so this is a tie.

- 90 day tie: if Buraco spent more than 90 days spent in the UK in either or both of the previous two tax years (in this case only 2014/15 is relevant based on the information in the question) this would be a tie. More information is needed on this point.

Buraco therefore has two definite UK ties and one possible UK tie.

As Buraco was not previously resident in the UK in any of the previous three tax years, if he has two ties he will be UK resident for the tax year 2015/16 if he spends between 121 days and 150 days in the UK, but not UK resident if he spends between 100 days and 120 days in the UK.

If, however, it is found that Buraco has three UK ties, he will be UK resident for the tax year 2015/16 based on any number of his expected days in the UK since the minimum number of days for this test is 91 days.

(ii)   **Tax implications of claiming remittance basis**

If Buraco claims the remittance basis for the tax year 2015/16, he will be liable to UK tax on overseas income and gains arising in that tax year only to the extent that they are remitted to the UK.

Buraco would not be entitled to the personal allowance for income tax or the annual exempt amount for capital gains tax for the tax year 2015/16.

The remittance basis charge would not apply in the tax year 2015/16 as Buraco has not been UK resident for at least seven of the nine tax years preceding that tax year.

5 Klubb plc (ATAX 12/14)

Text references. Corporation tax administration is covered in Chapter 22. Share schemes are dealt with in Chapter 5. Controlled foreign companies are covered in Chapter 27.

Top tips. In part (c)(i), state the conditions for a controlled foreign company to exist and then apply them to the question. The key point is the residence of the individual shareholder.

Easy marks. There were easy marks in part (a) for basic corporation tax administration. The computation of the CFC charge in part (c)(ii) was also straightforward.

Marking scheme

				Marks
(a)	Two accounting periods		1	
	Filing date		1	
	Penalty		2	
				4
(b)	Employees included		2	
	Number or value of shares acquired			
	SIP		4	
	CSOP		2	
	Tax implications of acquiring and selling shares			
	SIP		2	
	CSOP		2	
		Max		9
(c)	(i)	Status of Hartz Co	2½	
		Low profits exemption	2	
		Max		4
	(ii)	Profits apportioned	1½	
		Calculation of charge	1½	
				3
				20

(a) **Late submission of corporation tax returns**

There are two accounting periods within the long period of account. These are for the 12 month period ended 30 November 2013 and the four month period ended 31 March 2014.

As the relevant period of account is not more than 18 months long, the filing date for both periods is 12 months from the end of the period of account which is 31 March 2015.

There is a £100 penalty for a failure to submit each return on time, as each return is made within three months of the filing date.

The £100 penalty is increased to £500 when a return was late (or never submitted) for each of the preceding two accounting periods.

Tutorial note

It has been assumed that HM Revenue and Customs issued notices requiring the returns to be made before 1 January 2015 so that the later three-month filing date rule does not apply.

(b)   **Comparison of share incentive plan (SIP) with company share option plan (CSOP)**

Employees

Klubb plc would need to offer all full and part-time employees the opportunity to participate in a SIP, although a minimum qualifying period of employment of up to 18 months may be specified.

All the employees and full-time directors of Klubb plc can participate in a CSOP, but the scheme need not be open to all of them. Klubb plc can therefore select the employees it wishes to include.

A CSOP is therefore more likely to achieve the flexibility that Klubb plc wants, rather than a SIP.

Number or value of shares which can be acquired by each plan member

In a SIP, employees would be given free shares in Klubb plc, which are held in the plan, up to the value of £3,600 each tax year. Employees must be awarded free shares on similar terms to all of the plan members. This means that any variation in the number of free shares must be made by reference to objective criteria, such as level of remuneration, length of service or hours worked. However, Klubb plc can also specify the award can be conditional on the meeting of performance targets (within rules prescribed in the legislation) but there can be no deliberate weighting of rewards in favour of directors and the more highly paid employees. Employees can also purchase partnership shares through deduction from pre-tax salary up to the lower of £1,800 and 10% of salary in any tax year. Klubb plc can also award matching shares free to employees who purchase partnership shares at a maximum ratio of 2:1.

In a CSOP employees can be granted options to buy shares in Klubb plc up to the value of £30,000 (at the date of grant). Subject to that maximum amount, Klubb plc can decide how many options to grant to each employee.

Again, a CSOP is therefore more likely to achieve the flexibility that Klubb plc wants, rather than a SIP.

Tax implications of acquiring and selling the shares

There are no income tax implications when shares are given to employees in a SIP. Since the shares will be held within the SIP for five years, there will be no income tax charge when the shares are taken out of the SIP. There will also be no charge to capital gains tax on shares taken out of the SIP and sold immediately because their base cost will be equal to their market value at the time they are withdrawn from the SIP.

There is no income tax on the grant of options in a CSOP, nor on the exercise of an option under a CSOP since it will be exercised between three and ten years after the grant, which is a condition for a CSOP. When the shares acquired under a CSOP are sold, any gain is subject to capital gains tax. The cost in the gain calculation is the option price paid by the employee to acquire the shares. It is a condition for a CSOP that the option price must not be less than their market value at the time of the grant of the option.

Therefore, there will be no charge to income tax on either the SIP or the CSOP, but capital gains tax may be payable on the disposal of shares acquired under a CSOP, but not on those acquired under a SIP.

Tutorial note

It was not necessary to make all of the above points in order to score full marks for this question.

(c)   (i)   **Status of Hartz Co and availability of low profits exemption**

A controlled foreign company is a company which is not resident in the UK but is controlled by persons resident in the UK.

Hartz Co is owned 30% by Klubb plc (UK resident), 45% by Kort Co (non-UK resident) and 25% by Mr Deck. Therefore, Hartz Co will be a CFC only if Mr Deck is UK resident.

The chargeable profits of Hartz Co will not be exempt from apportionment under either of the conditions for the low profits exemption. This is because its profits are more than £50,000, and although they are under £500,000, its non-trading profits (chargeable gains) exceed £50,000.

(ii) **CFC charge for Klubb plc**

	£
Chargeable profits of Hartz Co	330,000
Apportioned to Klubb plc £330,000 × 30%	99,000
Tax on apportioned profits £99,000 × 21%	20,790
Less: creditable tax £99,000 × 11%	(10,890)
CFC charge	9,900

Tutorial note

Chargeable gains are not part of chargeable profits for the purposes of the CFC charge so only the trading profits are included.

Tax tables

SUPPLEMENTARY INSTRUCTIONS

1. You should assume that the tax rates and allowances for the tax year 2014/15 and for the financial year to 31 March 2015 will continue to apply for the foreseeable future unless you are instructed otherwise.

2. Calculations and workings need only be made to the nearest £.

3. All apportionments may be made to the nearest month.

4. All workings should be shown.

TAX RATES AND ALLOWANCES

The following tax rates and allowances are to be used in answering the questions.

Income tax

		Normal rates	Dividend rates
Basic rate	£1 – £31,865	20%	10%
Higher rate	£31,866 – £150,000	40%	32.5%
Additional rate	£150,001 and over	45%	37.5%

A starting rate of 10% applies to savings income where it falls within the first £2,880 of taxable income.

Personal allowances

Personal allowance

Born on or after 6 April 1948	£10,000
Born between 6 April 1938 and 5 April 1948	£10,500
Born before 6 April 1938	£10,660

Income limit

Personal allowance	£100,000
Personal allowance (born before 6 April 1948)	£27,000

Residence status

Days in UK	Previously resident	Not previously resident
Less than 16	Automatically not resident	Automatically not resident
16 to 45	Resident if 4 UK ties (or more)	Automatically not resident
46 to 90	Resident if 3 UK ties (or more)	Resident if 4 UK ties
91 to 120	Resident if 2 UK ties (or more)	Resident if 3 UK ties (or more)
121 to 182	Resident if 1 UK tie (or more)	Resident if 2 UK ties (or more)
183 or more	Automatically resident	Automatically resident

Child benefit income tax charge

Where income is between £50,000 and £60,000, the charge is 1% of the amount of child benefit received for every £100 of income over £50,000.

Car benefit percentage

The base level of CO_2 emissions is 95 grams per kilometre.

The percentage rates applying to petrol cars with CO_2 emissions up to this level are:

75 grams per kilometre or less	5%
76 grams to 94 grams per kilometre	11%
95 grams per kilometre	12%

Car fuel benefit

The base figure for calculating the car fuel benefit is £21,700.

New individual savings accounts (NISAs)

The overall investment limit is £15,000.

Pension scheme limits

Annual allowance	– 2014/15	£40,000
	– 2011/12 to 2013/14	£50,000
Lifetime allowance		£1,250,000
The maximum contribution that can qualify for tax relief without any earnings		£3,600

Authorised mileage allowances: cars

Up to 10,000 miles	45p
Over 10,000 miles	25p

Capital allowances: rates of allowance

Plant and machinery

Main pool	18%
Special rate pool	8%

Motor cars

CO_2 emissions up to 95 grams per kilometre	100%
CO_2 emissions between 96 and 130 grams per kilometre	18%
CO_2 emissions over 130 grams per kilometre	8%

Annual investment allowance

Rate of allowance	100%
Expenditure limit	£500,000

Cap on income tax reliefs

Unless otherwise restricted, reliefs are capped at the higher of £50,000 or 25% of income.

Corporation tax

Financial year	2012	2013	2014
Small profits rate	20%	20%	20%
Main rate	24%	23%	21%
Lower limit	£300,000	£300,000	£300,000
Upper limit	£1,500,000	£1,500,000	£1,500,000
Standard fraction	1/100	3/400	1/400

Marginal relief

Standard fraction $\times$ (U – A) $\times$ N/A

Patent box – deduction from net patent profit

Net patent profit x ((main rate – 10%)/main rate)

Value Added Tax (VAT)

Standard rate	20%
Registration limit	£81,000
Deregistration limit	£79,000

Inheritance tax: nil rate bands and tax rates

	£
6 April 2014 to 5 April 2015	325,000
6 April 2013 to 5 April 2014	325,000
6 April 2012 to 5 April 2013	325,000
6 April 2011 to 5 April 2012	325,000
6 April 2010 to 5 April 2011	325,000
6 April 2009 to 5 April 2010	325,000
6 April 2008 to 5 April 2009	312,000
6 April 2007 to 5 April 2008	300,000
6 April 2006 to 5 April 2007	285,000
6 April 2005 to 5 April 2006	275,000
6 April 2004 to 5 April 2005	263,000
6 April 2003 to 5 April 2004	255,000
6 April 2002 to 5 April 2003	250,000
6 April 2001 to 5 April 2002	242,000
6 April 2000 to 5 April 2001	234,000

Excess	Death rate	40%
	Lifetime rate	20%

Inheritance tax: taper relief

Years before death	*Percentage reduction*
Over 3 but less than 4 years	20%
Over 4 but less than 5 years	40%
Over 5 but less than 6 years	60%
Over 6 but less than 7 years	80%

Capital gains tax

Rates of tax	Lower rate	18%
	Higher rate	28%

Annual exempt amount	£11,000

Entrepreneurs' relief	Lifetime limit	£10,000,000
	Rate of tax	10%

National insurance (not contracted out rates)

Class 1 employee	£1 – £7,956 per year	Nil
	£7,957 – £41,865 per year	12%
	£41,866 and above per year	2%
Class 1 employer	£1 – £7,956 per year	Nil
	£7,957 and above per year	13.8%
	Employment allowance	£2,000
Class 1A		13.8%
Class 2	£2.75 per week	
	Small earnings exception limit	£5,885
Class 4	£1 – £7,956 per year	Nil
	£7,957 – £41,865 per year	9%
	£41,866 and above per year	2%

Rates of interest (assumed)

Official rate of interest	3.25%
Rate of interest on underpaid tax	3%
Rate of interest on overpaid tax	0.5%

Stamp Duty Land Tax

£150,000 or less [1]	Nil
£150,001 to £250,000	1%
£250,001 to £500,000	3%
£500,001 to £1,000,000	4%
£1,000,001 to £2,000,000[2]	5%
£2,000,001 or above[2]	7%

[1] For residential property, the nil rate is restricted to £125,000.

[2] The 5% and 7% rates do not apply to non-residential property. The 4% rate applies to all non-residential properties where the consideration is in excess of £500,000.

Stamp duty

Shares	0.5%

Review Form – Paper P6 Advanced Taxation (UK) (01/15)

Name: _____   Address: _____

_____

_____

How have you used this Kit?
(Tick one box only)

☐ Home study (book only)

☐ On a course: college _____

☐ With 'correspondence' package

☐ Other _____

Why did you decide to purchase this Kit?
(Tick one box only)

☐ Have used the complementary Study text

☐ Have used other BPP products in the past

☐ Recommendation by friend/colleague

☐ Recommendation by a lecturer at college

☐ Saw advertising

☐ Other _____

Which BPP products have you used?

Text	☐	Passcards	☐
Kit	☑	i-Pass	☐

During the past six months do you recall seeing/receiving any of the following?
(Tick as many boxes as are relevant)

☐ Our advertisement in *Student Accountant*

☐ Our advertisement in *Pass*

☐ Our advertisement in *PQ*

☐ Our brochure with a letter through the post

☐ Our website www.bpp.com

Which (if any) aspects of our advertising do you find useful?
(Tick as many boxes as are relevant)

☐ Prices and publication dates of new editions

☐ Information on product content

☐ Facility to order books off-the-page

☐ None of the above

Your ratings, comments and suggestions would be appreciated on the following areas.

	Very useful	Useful	Not useful
Passing P6	☐	☐	☐
Planning your question practice	☐	☐	☐
Questions	☐	☐	☐
Top Tips etc in answers	☐	☐	☐
Content and structure of answers	☐	☐	☐
Mock exam answers	☐	☐	☐

Overall opinion of this Kit	Excellent ☐	Good ☐	Adequate ☐	Poor ☐

Do you intend to continue using BPP products?   Yes ☐   No ☐

The BPP author of this edition can be emailed at: AlisonPriest@bpp.com

The BPP Learning Media ACCA Range Manager of this edition can be emailed at: accaqueries@bpp.com

Please return this form to: ACCA Range Manager, BPP Learning Media Ltd, FREEPOST, London, W12 8AA

Review Form (continued)

TELL US WHAT YOU THINK

Please note any further comments and suggestions/errors below.